# British Prehistory
## A New Outline

# British Prehistory
## A New Outline

### edited by
# COLIN RENFREW

*Professor of Archaeology*
*in the University of Southampton*

Duckworth

*Second impression 1976*
*First published in 1974 by*
*Gerald Duckworth and Co. Ltd.*
*The Old Piano Factory*
*43, Gloucester Crescent*
*London NW1*

© *1974 Colin Renfrew*
*Chapter 6* © *1974 Barry Cunliffe*

ISBN 7156 0670 0 cloth
     7156 0671 9 paper

*Typeset by*
*Specialised Offset Services Limited, Liverpool,*
*printed in Great Britain by*
*Unwin Brothers Ltd., Old Woking, Surrey.*

To the three wise men of British prehistoric studies:

GRAHAME CLARK
CHRISTOPHER HAWKES
STUART PIGGOTT

# CONTENTS

# List of figures

# *Preface*

## COLIN RENFREW

Britain's past has changed in the past few years almost beyond recognition: the new datings, new discoveries and new assessments have come so fast that any survey written more than five or so years ago is inevitably out of date. Not surprisingly, many professional prehistorians, as well as those with a general interest in the past, find the present situation unsatisfactory and confused. The standard work on the neolithic period of Britain, for instance, recently reprinted, sets the beginning of that period after 2000 BC, yet recent work indicates that a date of 4000 BC may not be early enough. Or again, the view until recently widely and authoritatively held, that Stonehenge was built, or designed, or at least influenced, by Mycenaeans from the Mediterranean, is now almost universally rejected. And the well-established classification of our iron age into three phases, A, B and C, each corresponding to the arrival of new immigrants from the continent of Europe, has been discarded by many leading authorities. Many more such instances could be found.

Despite the pace and the often revolutionary nature of such changes, the broad outlines of a new picture can now be seen to be emerging. The initial effects of the radiocarbon dating method have already been agreed and assimilated. The more recently introduced calibration of radiocarbon dates, while not yet in precise or final form, is now very widely accepted in its broad outlines, so that the basic structure of the new chronology is becoming clear.

Now is the time, then, to take stock of these changes, and to examine the effect that the new radiocarbon datings will have upon the outline of British prehistory — upon the basic sequence and development of events as well as on their precise dating. This was the thought and the aim which, in

May 1972, brought together the contributors to this volume at a conference organised for the Department of Extra-Mural Studies of the University of Sheffield by Professor Maurice Bruce and the late Mr John Bestall. It is likewise the aim here, where each chapter is based upon a paper presented at the Sheffield conference, subsequently revised and extended.

Surprising as it may seem, the last comprehensive survey of the field of British prehistory, indeed the only such survey — V. Gordon Childe's *Prehistoric Communities of the British Isles* — was published as long ago as 1940. Grahame Clarke's useful introduction *Prehistoric England* was published in the same year, and the only other general survey, *Prehistoric Britain* by Jacquetta and Christopher Hawkes, in 1944. There has been no similar attempt for thirty years. A contributory reason may be that probably no one man today could cover the whole growing field, from palaeolithic to iron age, at a sufficient level of detail. The solution here has been to assign each division of British prehistory to an acknowledged expert for the period in question. Each was asked to review, in some eight to ten thousand words, the archaeological material for that period, and to set that material in a new order, in the light of developments in chronology and of recent discoveries. A short bibliography was also requested, with ample footnotes controlling the principal published excavations and discussions in the literature.

In addition to the period chapters, I have been particularly glad to include a summary by Audrey Henshall of the field so comprehensively treated in her work *The Chambered Tombs of Scotland*, itself the most impressive contribution to British prehistoric archaeology for many years.

Our emphasis has deliberately been upon chronology, upon the ordering of the materials. There are at last sufficient radiocarbon dates to sustain an outline radiocarbon chronology for each period. Each chapter is therefore followed by a list of relevant radiocarbon dates (expressed in radiocarbon years bc on the conventional 5568 half-life for radiocarbon, as recommended in the periodical *Radiocarbon*). An attempt has, however, been made throughout to use the tree-ring calibration of radiocarbon and to think out its implications, talking not simply in these purely notional radiocarbon years, but in true or calendar years BC. The date lists therefore give calibrated dates obtained by means of the Suess calibration curve (discussed in Chapter 1) as well as the radiocarbon dates themselves.

The new chronology, and the new approach to Britain's past which has accompanied it, now offer the promise of a new prehistory of Britain, where we shall much better understand the working of those processes which led to the striking changes seen in the archaeological record. Our aim here, however, has not been to champion a 'new archaeology' or to focus disproportionately upon new methods and approaches. The first task must be to examine and summarise the existing evidence.

For this reason I resolved to invite contributors to write within the general framework of the old three age system of stone age, bronze age and iron age. No one today attaches undue importance to terms such as palaeolithic, mesolithic or neolithic, and the contributors are well aware of their limitations, already fully documented by Glyn Daniel in 1943 in his *The Three Ages*. It is clear today, for instance, that many things formerly considered exclusively iron age, such as the British hillforts, had their origins in the bronze age, and that no clear boundary can be set between them. Nor, by including the 'copper age' with its beakers in the bronze age chapter, are we denying that it could go just as well in the chapter on neolithic Britain. Such terms today are nothing more than broad descriptive labels, convenient divisions for general discussion: they are no longer meaningful concepts for detailed study. It would indeed be possible to equate the iron age with the 1st millenium BC, and the bronze age with the 2nd millenium BC, but as labels such broad categories would in practice be no more convenient than the familiar, traditional terms.

We see no need for a clear break with the traditional objectives of archaeological research in Britain, many of which remain entirely valid today. On the contrary, it is pleasant, among all the recent revisions and amidst the rejection of so many traditional interpretations, to acknowledge that these earlier studies still offer the sound factual basis from which we must all start. Grahame Clark's treatment of the mesolithic age in Britain may have been modified with the years, or Stuart Piggott's neolithic chronology substantially revised, or Christopher Hawkes's iron age classification fundamentally re-modelled, yet these remain the basic and seminal treatments of their subjects.

At a time when prehistorians are emphasising continuities of development in the cultures of the past, rather than sudden shifts produced by extraneous influences, it is appropriate also to acknowledge the continuity in our own discipline. While sometimes we may write of the works of an older generation in order to modify (or in our less temperate moments to rebut), we continue to read and refer to them, often and with profit. To these three scholars – Grahame Clark, Christopher Hawkes and Stuart Piggott – who have encouraged and led the study of British prehistory over the past forty years, this book is gratefully dedicated.

Colin Renfrew
Southampton, January 1974


NOTE

Throughout this book a clear distinction is made between:

(a) *radiocarbon dates* (C14 dates), expressed in *radiocarbon years bc* (calculated using the conventional Libby value of 5568 years for the half-life of radiocarbon), and

(b) *calendar dates*, expressed in *calendar years BC*. Calendar dates for prehistoric Britain are obtained from radiocarbon dates by means of the tree-ring calibration of radiocarbon, and are in consequence very approximate (see Chapter 1).

The following abbreviations have been used:

bc   radiocarbon years before Christ
BC   calendar (solar) years before Christ
bp   radiocarbon years before present
BP   calendar years before present (calculated from AD 1950)

# 1. British prehistory: changing configurations

## COLIN RENFREW

Radiocarbon dating has fundamentally changed British pre-history, altering not merely dates, but historical reconstructions and interpretations as well. This implies, of course, that some of the earlier interpretations were wrong, and it is worth asking why and how such erroneous interpretations were made. Simply to accept the new dates and new reconstructions without such analysis would deny us the insight into the structure of prehistoric archaeology that such corrections should offer: we must learn by our mistakes.

The two objectives, of dating and of reconstructing the past, have traditionally been very closely linked, perhaps much more so than was generally realised. During the first century of serious prehistoric study, from about 1860, archaeological dating in fact always depended upon historical interpretation, while sound interpretation could not be undertaken without a chronological framework. Only with the introduction of radiocarbon dating has this dangerous interdependence, which at times became a circularity, been removed.

For the archaeologist, as for the historian, some kind of chronology, if only a relative one, has always been a basic requirement. Without some way of ordering the abundant material, in museums and in the field, of separating it into groups or periods, the record of the past remains a bewildering palimpsest where everything happens at once, the relics of the old stone age rubbing shoulders with those of Roman Britain with no hope of interpreting either.

This bewildering confusion of an undifferentiated past faced the early antiquaries in the 16th and 17th centuries. A monument such as Stonehenge could be attributed with equal ease to the Romans, the Danes or even the Druids, and no one could say with certainty how it related to the British hillforts, for instance, or to those 'thunderbolts' today termed hand-axes, which the antiquaries were beginning to collect.

The first breakthrough, the introduction of a time dimension, was made by the geologists with their principle of stratigraphic succession. The archaeologists soon adopted this as a basis for archaeological excavation, and made their own contribution with the Scandinavian three age system, first published in English in 1848. This division of the materials of Danish prehistory was logical and sound, but it was not applied to British prehistory without a fierce debate. Thomas Wright[1] described it as 'specious and attractive in appearance, but without foundation in truth'. He wrote: 'There is something, we may perhaps say, poetical, certainly imaginative, in talking of an age of stone, or an age of bronze, or an age of iron, but such divisions have no meaning in history, which cannot be treated as a physical science, and its objects arranged in genera and species.'

Of course the three age system was widely adopted, for sixty years providing the essential structure for British prehistory, and opening the way to the 'typological method' of the great Swedish scholar Oscar Montelius and to the work of his successor as Europe's leading prehistorian, Gordon Childe. But Wright's words are interesting because they readily remind us of so many subsequent reactions to new concepts and new approaches in the study of prehistory, where unfamiliar terms are categorised as 'imaginative' or worse, and as having 'no meaning in history, which cannot be treated as a physical science'.

Such old controversies remain relevant today, and will do so until it is everywhere realised that the only way we can discuss the past is by means of *constructs* — terms and concepts of our own devising, which we can apply to the solid and obstinately mute remains of the past, in very much the same manner as physical scientists do indeed treat their data. All our discussions, our period divisions, cultural groupings and type names are entirely dependent on the use of such constructs, and indeed are constructs themselves. The development of British prehistory, therefore, is not simply the story of the important excavations and discoveries over the years but of the formulation of new ways of looking at the past and talking about the past.

In order to understand the prehistory of today, and the shortcomings so recently revealed in the prehistory of yesterday, it is essential to focus on the constructs which we use, and to bring out the tacit assumptions which lie hidden in our thinking. The prehistory of today is built not just on the discoveries but on the assumptions of yesterday.

## The first phase (1860-1920): the old age of the three age system

The term 'prehistory' was first used in 1851 by Daniel Wilson, at the beginning of that decade which was to see the publication of Charles Darwin's *The Origin of Species* and the acceptance by Britain's leading geologists and archaeologists of the antiquity of man. The traditional, scholastic view, built on a very literal interpretation of the Bible, that the world was created in the year 4004 B C, was dropped and the story of man was seen to extend back over hundreds of thousands, perhaps over millions of years.

Before this time, careful field workers like Stukeley, and dedicated excavators like Colt Hoare, had amassed a substantial body of observations clearly relevant to Britain's early past. Now, with the great expanse of empty time extending back before the Roman invasions, there was a need to order this material in a systematic way. Thomsen's three age system, itself of course a relative chronology, now offered the conceptual means, and for the next sixty years it held undisputed sway.

To obtain a good picture of the achievements of the first phase of British prehistory, which we may set from 1860 to 1920, it is sufficient to look at the seventh and last edition of Lord Avebury's famous book *Prehistoric Times*, published in the year of his death in 1913. It was the first edition of this work in 1865 which proposed the fundamental division of Thomsen's stone age into a palaeolithic or old stone age period and a neolithic period.

The seventh edition reiterates this division into phases,[2] demonstrating at once how far prehistoric archaeology had come in the past 60 years and yet how simple the basic framework still remained:

From the careful study of the remains which have come

down to us, it would appear that Prehistoric Archaeology may be divided into four great epochs:

I. That of the Drift; when man shared the possession of Europe with the Mammoth, the Cave bear, the Woolly-haired rhinoceros, and other extinct animals. This I have proposed to call the 'Palaeolithic' Period.

II. The later or polished Stone Age; a period characterized by beautiful weapons and instruments made of flint and other kinds of stone; in which, however, we find no trace of the knowledge of any metal excepting gold, which seems to have been sometimes used for ornaments. For this period I have suggested the term 'Neolithic'.

III. The Bronze Age, in which bronze was used for arms and cutting instruments of all kinds.

IV. The Iron Age, in which that metal had superseded bronze for arms, axes, knives, etc.; bronze, however, still being in common use for ornaments, and frequently also for the *handles* of swords and other arms, though never for the blades.

For Avebury these were not merely classifications of convenience: they were the basic units in terms of which he thought about and described the past. It is true that, following the recently published work of Oscar Montelius, he did subdivide the bronze age into five phases or periods, but these were to him purely notional subdivisions which did not reflect any changes in population or fundamental alterations in the way of life.

Gordon Childe, writing in 1940, was critical of this stage in the development of prehistoric research:[3]

The scientific observation of prehistoric monuments and the systematic collection of relics began effectively only with the eighteenth century . . . Next came the collectors, offspring of Victorian capitalism, not unversed in the new learning called Science. For arranging their collections they borrowed methods of classification from geology and palaeontology. And by classifying they made archaeology a science as well as a diversion. The outline of the chronological framework we still employ is due to the collectors. But their interests were too often in the objects

rather than in their makers. They presented an evolution
of implements and arms, but left them dead fossils, not the
expressions of living societies.

Here Childe was not entirely fair to Avebury, and indeed
with his reference to Victorian capitalism was probably
thinking rather of Sir John Evans, whose two great works
*Ancient Stone Implements: Weapons and Ornaments of
Great Britain*, published in 1872, and *Ancient Bronze
Implements*, published in 1881, represent the first systematic
attempt in Britain to describe and order a wide range of
prehistoric artefacts. Avebury's book, on the other hand,
today looks extremely modern, with its colour frontispiece
of a bison from Altamira, drawn by the young Abbé Breuil.
Indeed, lacking as it does any detailed subdivision of his four
main 'epochs', or any precise definition of regional groupings
of cultures, which since Childe has been obligatory to all
prehistorians, it is refreshingly un-taxonomic. He drew
heavily on recent ethnographic accounts of living societies in
order to give flesh to the bare archaeological record. In the
last three chapters of his book, all entitled 'Modern Savages',
he described in turn the Australian aborigines, the Fiji
islanders, the Maori, the Tahitians, the Esquimaux, the North
American Indians, the Patagonians and the Fuegians, finding
in these societies and their customs models for the four basic
divisions of prehistoric society which he had earlier outlined.
Today we use ethnographic analogies more cautiously, if at
all. But this was a splendid achievement, speaking vividly of
prehistory within a real chronological framework.

The modern reader is soon struck, however, by the
considerable oversimplification implicit in concepts such as
'Neolithic Man' or 'Bronze Age Man', as if all men lived alike
in each of these epochs, and that what was true of a neolithic
lake village in Switzerland would also automatically be true
of the neolithic age anywhere. The archaeology of this first
phase of British prehistoric studies did give a number of
pictures of life in prehistoric times, which were indeed based
upon an understanding of the excavated evidence. What it
lacked, however, was any clear understanding as to how these
three or four modes of life came about, or of why they
should change at all.

It was indeed felt that the transition in Britain from one age to the next was brought about by the arrival of a new group or race of people from the continent, but this idea was scarcely explored in detail nor was the supposed place of origin seriously sought at that time. This was a static picture of the past, and a much simplified one, which rather unquestioningly accepted the divisions set up by the three age system.

Within the broad epochs outlined by Avebury, however, subdivision was entirely appropriate, and it was here that the classifiers and the collectors made their most valuable contribution. Indeed in retrospect we should reproach them not with overclassifying, but with not taking their own period divisions seriously enough. For at this time their sub-periods and phases were viewed merely as elaborations within the grand framework of the four basic epochs. Only later did archaeologists seriously examine the idea that each of these subdivisions might represent a different adaptation, a different way of life or a different group of people.

The basic subdivisions for the palaeolithic period were of course worked out in the Périgord region of southern France. Here excavations by Lartet in the middle of the 19th century had already produced a sequence of phases, based on the different types of flint implements found, and more especially on the bones of the different extinct animals which accompanied them. This system was modified by Gabriel de Mortillet, the first scholar to give to periods names derived from type sites, like Mousterian (after Le Moustier) or Aurignacian (after Aurignac). Already in 1872[4] Sir John Evans proposed a classification of the old stone age of Britain into five periods, based upon those of de Mortillet. These were discussed and refined by a series of scholars, including the Abbé Breuil, in the early years of the 20th century. Before this first phase of British prehistory was over, the British palaeolithic was being classified on a modified version of the French palaeolithic schema into Pre-Chellean, Chellean, Acheulean, Mousterian, Aurignacian, Solutrean and Magdalenian. The recognition in Britain of 'eoliths' — regarded as crudely worked flint tools earlier than the first hand-axes — proved a short-lived diversion. And so with one or two variations — for instance the recognition of the early

Clactonian flake industry – the British sequence was classified essentially on the basis of the French typology. This was natural enough, but it took with it the assumption that these were phases of some very wide and general validity: the notion of independent regional variation was not fashionable at this time.

Here then were laid the foundations for later work on the British palaeolithic. The problem of assigning dates to these phases was obviously an extremely difficult one, and the estimates varied very widely. Most were based upon geologists' estimates of sedimentation rates, coupled with known depths of deposits. The end of the palaeolithic, or more accurately of the last glaciation, was however fixed more precisely at c. 8000 BC by the Baron de Geer on the basis of a series of deposits in Scandinavia of varves, the sediments deposited annually by the meltwaters of glaciers.

The neolithic of Britain remained a very obscure period throughout this first phase of British prehistoric research, and no coherent attempt was made to subdivide it. The only systematic approach to its dating was on the basis of the chambered tombs of megalithic construction. Oscar Montelius made a systematic study of such tombs in western Europe, and on the assumption that their distribution was the product of cultural influences from the east Mediterranean, felt able to date their arrival in northern Europe between 4000 and 3000 BC.

The bronze age did, however, offer a great scope for classification and subdivision, on the basis of the wide range of metal types and their frequent associations in hoards. Sir John Evans in 1881 proposed a classification into three phases. But it was the great advocate of the 'typological method', Montelius, who, in a masterly paper surveying the whole field, proposed the classification which, in a number of its essentials, is still followed today. Montelius's typological method involves arranging the various types in an evolutionary sequence, so that their natural evolution can be followed. This is then, quite reasonably, seen as representing the order in which they developed – a relative chronology. Then, by comparing these developments with those already dated in the Mediterranean (ultimately on the basis of the historical chronology of Ancient Egypt), and by assuming that those in north Europe followed and were influenced by those further south, approximate calendar dates could be assigned to the phases. Montelius first set out his ideas in 1885, and in 1896 delivered a lecture to the Royal Anthropological Institute applying them to Italy.[5] In 1908, at the Society of Antiquaries, he proposed his 'Chronology of the Bronze Age in Great Britain and Ireland'.[6] This was much more than simply a chronology, although he did feel able to assign absolute dates, on the basis of his comparison with the Italian sequence. It was above all a detailed and scholarly subdivision of the bronze age, offered with a wealth of associations and illustrations, and as such was at once generally accepted. It formed the basis of all subsequent classifications for many years.[7] It is interesting today to see how many of Montelius's observations still seem entirely sound, and indeed that the absolute chronology which he proposed for Britain is more in keeping with modern ideas than some of those which succeeded it:

Period I. (more properly the Copper Age, before bronze was known), from about 2500 to 2000 B.C. Leading types: flint celts and stone axe-hammers, daggers, spearheads and arrow-heads of flint, flat 'celts' of copper imitating flint forms, daggers of copper or poor bronze, buttons with v-perforations, 'drinking cups' and 'food vessels' of pottery, burials in barrows, or tree-coffins, also after cremation in cists or urns.

Period II. (first pure Bronze Age), 2000 to 1650 B.C. Leading types: flat celts with spreading edge and flanged celts, daggers with rivets, halberd blades, gold *'lunulae'*, cinerary urns, also unburnt burials in barrows. Stonehenge and Avebury already built.

Period III. 1650 to 1400 B.C. Leading types: celts with high ridges, palstaves, daggers tanged, riveted, or socketed, bronze and gold torcs, burials probably after cremation (but rare), metal hoards.

Period IV. 1400 to 1150 B.C. Leading types: later palstaves, socketed celts, rapiers and leaf-shaped swords, long chapes, razors, socketed spearheads with loops, cylindrical ferrules, torcs and armlets, cremations in barrows or cairns, hoards of metal.

Period V. 1150 to 800 B.C. Leading types: winged celts

of Continental type, socketed celts, tanged or socketed chisels, gouges, and daggers, winged chapes, circular shields, trumpets, socketed spearheads with openings in blade, pins, bracelets, buckets of bronze, cremations in barrows or urnfields, hoards common.

I find it fascinating that the evidence first used to question the long chronology and the early dates offered by Montelius — and this was apparently the only criticism which the paper received — took the form of the little blue 'faience' beads, which today, 65 years later, are still the subject of heated controversy. It was Sir Arthur Evans himself, the discoverer and excavator of Minoan Crete, who was the first to bring up here the possibility of direct contacts between Britain and the Aegean world, a question still disputed and perhaps not finally settled today. Evans referred to the body of material subsequently termed the 'Wessex culture' by Stuart Piggott, namely:

> ... Dr Montelius's Second Period, the first of the pure Bronze Age in this country, the rough chronological limits of which he fixes between 2000 and 1650 B.C. Moreover with regard to this he seems to have left out of account the evidence afforded by the finds of certain small imported objects which serve as a direct link between prehistoric Britain and the Mediterranean world.
>
> These are the beads and quoit-like pendants of faience, or Egyptian porcelain, found chiefly in the South of England, as well as in various parts of Scotland and Ireland. Among these a particular class of beads of elongated form, consisting of a series of sub-globular beads welded together to the number of from three to nine, will be found to have a special chronological importance ... We have now to deal with the remarkable fact that the glazed compound beads answer to those of a special Egyptian fabric within approximately-fixed limits ... we may take the middle of the fourteenth century B.C. as the limit beyond which it is hardly safe to carry back the interments with which this class of bead is associated.[8]

Here Evans was radically transforming Montelius's absolute

chronology, reducing the age by several centuries. In doing so he developed a new argument which was to become a leitmotiv of the second phase of British prehistoric study, the question of continental influences:

> It must, however, be further remarked that though the 'compound' beads may have been in part at least manufactured in Egypt itself, certain varieties of these . . . do not answer to any Egyptian form. The disk-shaped pendants of the same glazed material seem also to be non-Egyptian. All this points to the conclusion that these small faience ornaments were partly at least imported from some intermediate centre of manufacture . . . Was there in the Mediterranean area any intermediate agency to which we may reasonably ascribe the origin of these derivative types?
>
> It is certain that faience beads imitated from the Egyptian were very early manufactured in Minoan Crete . . . The fact thus established that the Cretan artificers made glazed beads of this class suggests the possibility that the distribution of this and other types derived from the Egyptian may have been due to a colonial expansion of the great Minoan Empire.

These were seminal ideas, subsequently developed and elaborated by several generations of scholars. In 1908, however, they were no more than suggestions and did little to disrupt the static and placid order of the three age system and its subdivisions.

During this first phase of investigation, the problem of giving a more detailed reconstruction for the iron age, or of subdividing it, seems to have been somewhat neglected. Neither Sir John Evans nor Lord Avebury discussed the iron age in detail, although there was, of course, a steady accumulation of evidence, as in other periods, from systematic excavations such as those of General Pitt Rivers in Dorset or the work by Bulleid and Gray at the Glastonbury lake village in Somerset, published in 1911. A misleadingly precise picture was given in 1907 by Rice Holmes in his *Ancient Britain and the Invasions of Julius Caesar*. But a more important contribution was offered, again by Sir Arthur

Evans, by his publication in 1890 of the finds from the cremation cemetery at Aylesford in Kent. In the words of Glyn Daniel:

> This paper is outstanding not only for its clear analysis of the elements in La Tène art. Sir Arthur Evans identified the Aylesford people with the Belgic invaders of south-east Britain, and in doing so recognised a group of invaders within the framework of the Iron Age. It was a challenge to the idea of the three invasions of the Neolithic, Bronze and Iron Ages as constituting British prehistory, but a challenge which, for the time, passed unheeded.[9]

The challenge, indeed, was not met for more than two decades, until the work of Gordon Childe and Christopher Hawkes.

## Phase 2 (1920-1960): cultures and invasions

The fifteen years from 1925 to 1940 were decisive for the development of British prehistoric archaeology. At their beginning the general view of prehistory was, in its fundamentals, little different from that set out in the early years of the first phase, when Avebury published his *Prehistoric Times* and Sir John Evans his *Ancient Stone Implements*. By 1940 the shape and nature of British prehistory had been re-defined, with a wealth of detailed analysis, so that for the next twenty years the bulk of further work refined this structure, modifying it, elaborating it, and adding detail, but did not challenge it.

The prehistorians of the 1920s created a new archaeology. They formulated a new paradigm, a new concept of the past which was needed in order to break out of the static framework of the three ages, with its purely typological subdivisions. They looked on the past in a new way, and this led them not only to offer new interpretations but to order the data more effectively, revealing fresh patterns within it.

To do this at all required a new model, and the ingenious one then formulated — which today, in rejecting it, we would call 'invasionist' — responded very well to the needs of the time. The prehistorians of the first phase of development had been concerned primarily with chronological sequence and chronological divisions. This was their great contribution: to divide the past up into periods or epochs, workable units for discussion, which could then be subdivided further chronologically by means of the typological method.

The new archaeology of the 1920s was the first to tackle spatial variation in a systematic way. Already in 1904, Abercromby[10] had published the first distribution map of a British ceramic type, which he distinguished as 'the Drinking Cup or Beaker class of fictilia in Britain', and in his *Study of Bronze Age Pottery* he gave further distribution maps. It was, however, O.G.S. Crawford who first advocated an essentially geographical approach to British archaeology. His aim, formulated in 1912, was 'to isolate a single culture period, and to examine it from a geographical point of view'.[11] And in his *Man and His Past*, published in 1921, Crawford developed these geographical ideas. By the beginning of that decade, therefore, spatial analysis and a geographical approach were well established in Britain, as also in Ireland.

The ingenious idea which gave point and purpose to this new interest in distribution was that these types and assemblages of artefacts, found in a specified area and over a definite time range, were to be regarded as the material equipment of specific groups of people. This idea, of course, was natural at a time when scholars were preoccupied with ethnic groups and national origins, as well as with the origins of the Indo-European languages. But it was not one imposed from above: it grew from the data. What more natural, when faced with a 'beaker class of fictilia in Britain', whose distribution and associations could be plotted on a map, and which belonged to a specific time range (Montelius's Period I or copper age), to think and speak of a 'beaker folk'? It is a mode of thought which still comes easily today.

Gordon Childe was the principal exponent of this idea that the prehistoric past is best divided into 'cultures', a term which he was able to use while avoiding the pitfalls of racist thought:

We find certain types of remains — pots, implements, ornaments, burial sites, house forms — constantly recurring together. Such a complex of regularly associated traits we shall term a 'cultural group' or just a 'culture'. We assume that such a complex is the material expression of what today would be called a 'people'.[1 2]

It was this concept of culture which, utilising the insights of the new geographical approach, made it possible to break out of the restrictions of the three age system. So far, however, this is still a fairly static concept. What gave it life, and imposed a vivid sense of reality, was the realisation that the changing spatial limits of these cultures could be seen as the result of the movement of the peoples with which they were identified. As Childe put it:

> The same complex may be found with relatively negligible diminutions or additions over a wide area. In such cases of the total and bodily transferance of a complete culture from one place to another we think ourselves justified in assuming a 'movement of people'.[1 3]

Using this idea Childe was able to propose a brilliantly dynamic view of prehistory, where changes and developments were due either to movements of peoples, or at least to contacts and interactions between them, where ideas and innovations were transmitted by a process of diffusion. This became the central theme: 'Prehistoric archaeology is largely devoted to isolating such cultural groups of peoples, tracing their differentiations, wanderings and interactions'.[1 4] As he wrote again, in relation to Britain: 'Thus prehistory can recognise peoples and marshal them on the stage to take the place of the personal actors who form the historian's troupe. Their interactions are no less a part of the drama of prehistory than are their reactions to the external environment.'

Childe himself, writing in 1940, stressed the revolutionary significance of this idea in allowing the prehistorian to think now in human terms:

> It was, in fact, not till Abercromby in 1901 used the sepulchral vessel then termed a Drinking Cup to identify a group of prehistoric invaders and to trace them to their Continental homes that archaeology really became pre-

history. In England the new conceptions did not bear fruit
till after 1920. It was not till 1922, when the Cunningtons
excavated All Cannings Cross, that the first Iron Age
farmers who really created the rural economy of pre-
Roman Britain, were properly defined. The Neolithic
people, now regarded as the first food-producers in
England, were first characterised by Leeds in 1927. The
most distinctive megalithic monuments of Northern
Ireland, the horned cairns of Carlingford type, were
unrecognised before 1932![16]

The idea of continental invaders thus became the story
line, and two basic and unifying ideas in prehistory, the
migrations of peoples and the diffusion of culture, became
the central theme for much that was written for the next
forty years. Yet while today one questions the validity of
much of this theoretical structure, we should not overlook
the tremendous stimulus which it gave for detailed research
into local distributions, and for the recognition of new,
distinctive assemblages of material. The ultimate aim might
be to relate that material to a similar assemblage elsewhere,
hence documenting migration or diffusion – and of this we
are often sceptical today. But the first and laudable objective
was to study the British material *in its own right*, recognising
and describing local groupings, and the ultimate aim gave
point to such an exercise. As Grahame Clark wrote in 1933:
'The science of archaeology might well be defined as the
study of the past distribution of culture traits in space and
time, and of the factors govering their distribution.'[17]
Excavation itself gained new point, and so did the task of
reconstruction. No longer were prehistorians merely digging
up artefacts to illustrate the way of life of 'Neolithic Man' or
'Bronze Age Man'. They were reconstructing the prehistory
of Britain, conceived as a sequence of past events. Their
work, as Childe was later to write, 'aimed at distilling from
archaeological remains a preliterate substitue for the conventional politico-military history, with cultures, instead of
statesmen, as actors, and migrations in place of battles'.[18]
The new vitality of British prehistory at that time can be
experienced, even today, by reading the early volumes of
*Antiquity*, founded by O.G.S. Crawford in 1928 and edited

by him, in which the impact of his original mind can be felt. The role of Childe has already been stressed, and with the publication of his magisterial *The Dawn of European Civilisation* in 1925, British prehistorians could perceive more clearly the close relationship between their subject and European prehistory in general. The third founding father in the early 1920s was Sir Cyril Fox, whose *Archaeology of the Cambridge Region*, published in 1923, was the model for so much later work. It was the first detailed regional study in British archaeology, and in effect brought prehistory and geography together as related disciplines. His *Personality of Britain*, published in 1932, is a classic of geography as well as archaeology.

Much of the detailed work involved in following up the implications and possibilities of the new archaeology of the 1920s was undertaken by a new generation of scholars, so that in the next few years the essential structure of the new prehistory became established. Already in 1926, Dorothy Garrod, later to be the first woman professor in Cambridge, had published *The Upper Palaeolithic Age in Britain*, which gave a thorough and sustained analysis of the material in terms first of what was found, and only then of how it related to the French sequence. In 1932 Grahame Clark, in *The Mesolithic Age in Britain*, defined for the first time those cultures, formerly often designated 'epi-palaeolithic', occupying the period between the end of the last ice age around 800 BC and the arrival of the first neolithic farmers, then set at the earliest around 2500 BC. It was in 1931 that Stuart Piggott published his important paper, 'The Neolithic pottery of the British Isles',[19] where for the first time the material was studied in detail and divided into an 'A' series and a 'B' series. Most influential of all was the brilliant paper published by Christopher Hawkes in *Antiquity* in the same year, entitled 'Hillforts', in which he proposed a subdivision of the British iron age into three groups of cultures, 'A', 'B' and 'C', of which 'A' came first and 'C' last.[20] The division was made on the basis of a very close knowledge of the British and continental material, and Hawkes equated the three bodies of material with immigrant groups from the continent:

The great Celtic expansion over Europe of which these

formed part . . . reached its height in the sixth century, when those groups who crossed over to Britain became our principal Early Iron Age immigrants . . . The main block of their area remained in their undisturbed tenure till the 1st century BC, and their civilisation, though essentially of Hallstatt character, soon began to absorb influence from the La Tène culture across the Channel. Thus it really requires a name of its own: here we shall be content to call it 'Iron Age A', and the succeeding immigrant cultures 'Iron Age B' and 'C'.

Here was the clearest expression of the new archaeology of this second phase, where the simple and static picture of the three age system was superseded by the livelier and more human analysis into immigrant cultures and groups, whose movements and influences could be followed in the geographical and temporal distributions of the archaeological data.

The new and revitalised state of British archaeology was made very clear in 1932 in *Archaeology in England and Wales 1914-1931* by T.D. Kendrick and Hawkes. In it the two authors offered a fresh outline of the British bronze age, and presented the first coherent review of the field for many years. At the end of the decade British prehistory was given its first definitive survey by Gordon Childe in his *Prehistoric Communities of the British Isles.*

It is probably true to say that most archaeological work of synthesis for the next twenty years operated within the framework already codified by Childe in 1940. Stuart Piggott's monumental *Neolithic Cultures of the British Isles*, published in 1954, is a case in point. The most important contribution of its decade, undertaking for the first time a full regional and chronological survey, its admirable and detailed analysis was nonetheless conducted within this general framework established twenty-five years earlier. The same is true of Christopher Hawkes's 'The ABC of the British Iron Age', presented at a conference in 1958, which provided the ultimate elaboration of his 1931 scheme,[21] with periods and areas subdivided and the presence of 'A', 'B' or 'C' cultures indicated. Hawkes there stressed the continuity in the development of iron age studies:

This surely means — and I think we can be gratified all round — that in the dozen years since the CBA last caused a general survey to be put forward, or in the twenty years since Childe was writing in *Prehistoric Communities*, we have taken our Iron Age studies through a process of expansion and revaluation, and yet have emerged still pretty well together.

This was indeed the general position at that time: the intervening years had been a period of consolidation in British prehistory. Of course in retrospect we can see in them many of the roots of developments taking place today in the third phase of study — the geographical approach pioneered by Fox and Crawford, for instance, or the interest in bronze technology evinced by Childe in *The Bronze Age* in 1930, where he considered the bronze age not as an epoch, in the three age sense, but as a major technological stage where metallurgy was at the forefront of technological advance, and hence in Childe's eyes of social advance too. We can discern also in E.C. Curwen's work, surveyed in 1946 in his *Plough and Pasture*, the preoccupations later to be designated the 'ecological approach'. And in major excavations, such as Wheeler's dig at Maiden Castle,[22] and especially Gerhard Bersu's pioneering settlement excavations at Little Woodbury,[23] new techniques and goals were developed that continue to inspire good work thirty years later.

In general, however, the principal preoccupation throughout this period was 'the study of the past distribution of culture traits in space and time', to quote Clark's words again, and their interpretation in human terms, as the result of the movements of peoples and the diffusion of culture.

In this interpretation chronology was crucial. Throughout the second phase the framework used for dating was essentially that built by Montelius and elaborated by Childe. For the end of the palaeolithic and for the mesolithic, the development of the techniques of pollen analysis established for the first time a reliable relative chronology entirely independent of the artefacts themselves. But this useful division into climatic zones could not, of course, yield absolute dates, for which de Geer's varve chronology offered the only hope.

For the neolithic period, Childe modified and shortened Montelius's chronology. Again the megalithic tombs of western Europe offered the key. Childe, like Montelius, assumed that the practice of collective burial derived ultimately from the east Mediterranean, so that its earliest occurrence in Europe would therefore be in Spain. He derived the Spanish tombs from the round tombs of the Mesara plain in Crete, which are dateable to around 2700 BC. This then was the earliest possible date for the megalithic tombs of Europe, and in the final edition of *The Dawn* in 1957 the beginning of the British neolithic was set at about that time.

Stuart Piggott in his *Neolithic Cultures of the British Isles* in 1954 used a different argument. The end of the neolithic was determined by the beginning of the early bronze age, which he placed at 1500 or 1450 BC. He estimated the duration of the British neolithic: 'It is difficult to believe, on *a priori* grounds, that all three phases together could span more than four centuries. It should be possible in fact to contain the whole of the British Neolithic cultures described in this book within the first half of the second millennium BC.'[24] At this time, then, the beginning of the British neolithic was set after 2000 BC.

Here the responsibility for dating the end of the neolithic (and from this its beginning), as well as for fixing the bronze age chronological sequence, falls upon the early bronze age 'Wessex culture'. This was first defined by Piggott himself in 1938 in a penetrating paper.[25] At its end he listed a number of resemblances which objects from the rich graves of Wessex show with finds in the Mycenaean world of Greece. In this he was following in the footsteps of Sir Arthur Evans, who thirty years earlier had stressed the chronological importance of the faience beads, attributing to them an Aegean origin, in the words quoted above. Evans used this link to modify the date for the beginning of the early bronze age from the 2000 BC suggested by Montelius to about 1350 BC. Piggott himself proposed a date of 1800 BC for the beginnings of the Wessex culture,[26] but later work on the various Aegean 'parallels' came much closer to Evans's estimate. The most impressive British analysis of the European bronze age during this second phase of study was conducted by Childe and Hawkes,[27] and as a result of their treatment the beginning of the Wessex culture was generally set between 1500 and 1450 BC.

This conclusion has recently been called into question, as we shall see below. But for the moment we need simply observe that the date is based upon two diffusionist assumptions:

(1) Similarities are observed between finds from Britain and those in the Mediterranean, and these may be taken to indicate some form of contact between the two regions.
(2) The direction of influence may be taken as being from south to north, and from east to west.

In this way, if the Mediterranean finds are dated, which they can reliably be by reference to the calendar of ancient Egypt, then the British finds can safely be assigned a date a little later.

The date reached by this procedure is of course dependent upon an interpretation of the material in terms of the diffusion of ideas or the movement of peoples. The willingness to think and speak in these terms was the characteristic feature of this second phase of British prehistoric studies. As Grahame Clark has written:

> For much of the first half of the 20th century British archaeologists felt themselves under strong compulsion to ascribe every change, every development to overseas influences of one kind or another. The more accessible parts of the Continent, between Portugal and Norway, or more often the literature bearing on these, were searched hopefully for analogies. So sure were prehistorians that every new thing must have come from the Continent that even quite vague similarities sufficed to define and denote not merely culture contact but actual invasion. In the final stage of the neurosis, hypothetical invasions became so real that they, instead of the archaeological material itself, were actually made the basis of classification.[28]

## Absolute dating and the radiocarbon calendar

In the decade prior to 1960 several things went wrong with British prehistoric studies. Until then the task of the British archaeologist had been a clear one: by the well established methods of excavation and research to obtain further information which would fill in the outlines of the emerging picture of Britain's past. Painstaking work would yield more elements of the prehistoric jigsaw puzzle to fit into this emerging picture.

But in the first place the dates obtained by the new method of radiocarbon dating did not fit very well with the already established chronology. At the same time there was a developing dissatisfaction with the prevailing idea that the significant changes in the early past were the result of invasions from abroad. There was a growing awareness too that the kind of prehistory written in the textbooks did not really answer all of the questions which we would wish to ask of the prehistoric past.

In the succeeding years some of the older assumptions were increasingly questioned. The final blow to the traditional picture came with the tree-ring calibration of radiocarbon, which further upset the existing chronology. The basis of the calibration will first briefly be described, and then in the next section the fundamental changes in thought and in objectives to which it contributed will be reviewed.

### Radiocarbon dating

Radiocarbon dating offered to the British prehistorian, for the first time, a way of obtaining dates, absolute dates measured in years BC, which did not at the time require a whole series of basic assumptions about British prehistory. Of course radiocarbon dating itself makes a number of assumptions, but they are geophysical, not archaeological. As we have seen, prior to radiocarbon, the dating of prehistoric Britain entailed comparison with the historical chronology of early Egypt. Such comparison in turn implied assumptions both about the diffusion of culture and the direction in which it diffused. As we shall see, these assumptions were not warranted.

The method of radiocarbon dating was invented by the American chemist Willard Libby in 1949. It is based on the discovery that all living things, whether plant or animal, contain, together with the carbon of which they are in part composed, a tiny proportion of a radioactive variety of carbon, called radiocarbon or carbon 14. It is formed by the action of cosmic radiation upon the upper atmosphere, and is present in the atmosphere, in plants which obtain their carbon from the atmosphere by photosynthesis, and in animals which eat those plants, in a constant small proportion relative to the ordinary carbon, carbon 12.

Libby realised that this was so.[29] He also knew that radiocarbon, like all radioactive elements, decays in a regular way, so that after a fixed length of time, known as the half-life, half of the original sample has undergone radioactive decay, while the other half remains. After two half lives only a quarter remains, and so on. He had the brilliant insight to realise that, since we can measure today the supposedly constant ratio of radiocarbon to ordinary carbon in the atmosphere and in living things, and since we can measure the half-life, a measurement of the amount of radiocarbon in an old sample will allow us to calculate its age. Subsequent to the time of its death, the plant or animal has no longer been taking in radiocarbon with the ordinary carbon, whether by photosynthesis or by eating plants. And all the time since death the radiocarbon present in its body has been decaying at a known rate, this radioactive decay being quite unaffected by the ordinary processes of chemical decay which go on after death. We know the initial concentration, and we know the rate of decay, so by measuring the concentration of radiocarbon today we can measure how long this radioactive decay has gone on since the time of death.

There are, of course, a number of assumptions here, but Libby was able to test a good many of them. He and his colleagues measured the half-life and found it to be about 5568 years. They used their method to date wood samples from tombs in Egypt whose historical date was known in terms of the Egyptian calendar, and found a tolerably good agreement.

Here then was a method which could date organic samples — whether bone, or charcoal or wood or indeed any plant or animal material — and which needed only a small sample of uncontaminated material. Today twenty grams of pure charcoal is sufficient. Of course the laboratory procedures are elaborate, and the method is expensive, nor will it work for samples older than about 60,000 years, since the radioactivity left in them is too weak to measure. But the method has been shown to have a world-wide validity, and its impact on archaeology throughout the world has been enormous.

The method determines the age of the sample, measured in years before the present (BP). To avoid the confusion of changing dates every year, the 'present' is defined as AD 1950 for the purposes of calculation, so that to obtain a date in years BC the figure of 1950 must be subtracted from the age in years BP (see columns 1 and 2 of Table 1). Unfortunately, however, there are statistical problems involved in measuring the radioactivity of the sample in the laboratory, and it is necessary to assign an estimate of the statistical uncertainty to each date. For example the date 2550 ± 150 BC means that the most likely correct value of the determination is indeed 2550 BC, and the probability of the correct value lying within one standard deviation of that date (i.e between 2700 and 2400 BC) is 66 per cent. The probability of its lying within two standard deviations (in this case between 2850 and 2250 BC) is 95 per cent. And the probability of its lying within three standard deviations (in this case between 3000 and 2100 BC) is 99.5 per cent. There remains, then, a very small chance that the correct value may lie outside these limits. For this reason it is preferable to have a number of radiocarbon dates from any specific archaeological context, so that the risks of error of this kind can be reduced.

An additional complication is that since Libby's early work, the half-life of radiocarbon has been re-measured. The correct value for the half life is now thought to be about 5730 years instead of 5568 years. This means that in order to obtain dates based on the new half-life a recalculation is necessary. Fortunately it is a simple one: a date in years BP calculated on the 5568 half-life may be converted to one on the 5730 half-life by multiplying by 1.03. All dates are, however, by international convention, published on the basis of the old 5568 half-life, in order that there should be no confusion about the procedure used for calculating them. In serious discussions they are always published accompanied by the standard deviation and by the laboratory code number, so that there is no risk of ambiguity. The periodical *Radiocarbon* regularly publishes date lists from all the radiocarbon laboratories of the world.

It was, no doubt, complications such as these, as well as the novelty of the method, which led archaeologists at first to view it with scepticism — especially when it did not agree with dates obtained by the conventional archaeological method of cross-dating. The story of their reactions, and of their gradual conversion, is an interesting one.[30] Professor Stuart Piggott, for instance, called the radiocarbon date of 2600 bc obtained for Durrington Walls 'archaeologically inacceptable', on the grounds that it was far earlier than existing archaeological estimates. But of course he, like other British archaeologists, was quick to accept the method when it became clear that a coherent pattern of dates was being produced.

*The tree-ring calibration*

Just as the archaeological world was settling down to accept radiocarbon dating as a routine method — even if it did suggest a chronology for Europe a good deal older than had been thought — a further problem arose. For some years it had been clear that the radiocarbon dates for historically dated Egyptian samples were not working out as neatly as Libby had at first thought: the radiocarbon dates were consistently too recent. The explanation for this came from an unexpected quarter: from the White Mountains of California, on which grows the incredibly long-lived bristlecone pine. Tree-ring work at the University of Arizona, undertaken mainly by Professor C.W. Ferguson, produced a continuous sequence of tree-rings, first in living trees, and then in trees long dead, extending back to before 5000 BC. Samples from these well-dated rings were then sent to radiocarbon laboratories at Tucson in Arizona, at Philadelphia and at La Jolla. As the Egyptian samples had suggested, the radiocarbon dates obtained were not the same as the true or calendar dates established by the tree-ring work: the radiocarbon dates before about 1000 BC were all too recent.

There has been a good deal of discussion about the reasons

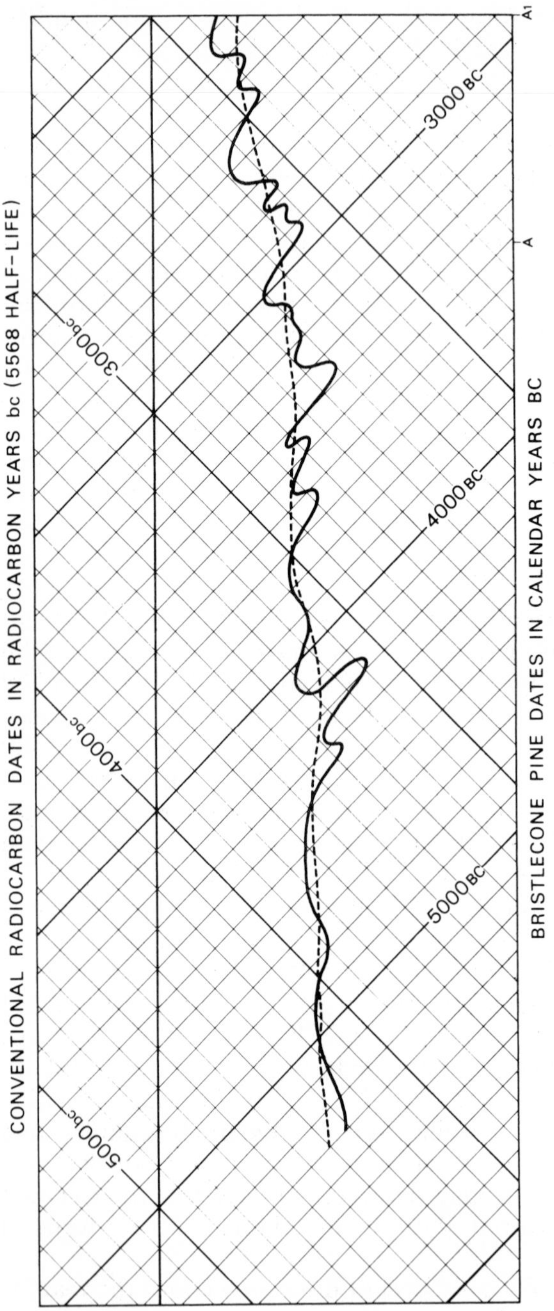

Figure 1. The bristlecone pine calibration of radiocarbon as proposed by Suess (continuous line) and as modified using a smoothing function (broken line). The dates running across the top and the lines to which they refer indicate radiocarbon dates measured in radiocarbon years bc; the dates running across the bottom and the lines to which they refer indicate bristlecone pine dates in calendar years BC. The curve indicates the deviation of the radiocarbon time scale.

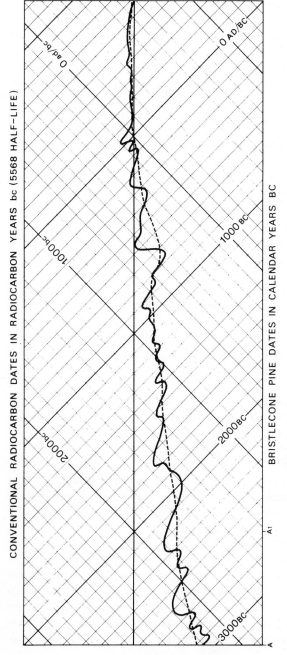

CONVENTIONAL RADIOCARBON DATES IN RADIOCARBON YEARS bc (5568 HALF-LIFE)

BRISTLECONE PINE DATES IN CALENDAR YEARS BC

To calibrate a radiocarbon date, say 2000 bc, follow the line for that date until it meets the curve. Now follow the line below the curve perpendicular to the previous line and read off the calendar date on the bottom scale. The radiocarbon date of 2000 bc gives a calibrated date of about 2500 BC. Note that all calibrated dates are at present approximate only, and that the final curve will probably be nearly as kinky as the Suess curve shown here.

for this discrepancy:[31] what is now clear is that it is there, and it applies on a world-wide basis. It is therefore necessary to correct radiocarbon dates in order to obtain true dates measured in calendar years BC. Professor H.E. Suess of La Jolla was the first to propose a calibration curve, and his more recent revision of it is seen in Fig. 1.[32] For each calendar date there is a single radiocarbon date, which samples of that age should yield on analysis. Unfortunately the curve has a number of kinks in it, so that a single radiocarbon date is obtained for samples of several different ages. It is consequently not possible to give a single equivalent in calendar years for each radiocarbon date — sometimes it is instead necessary to give a range within which the true date should fall.

This procedure has been adopted in Table 1, where column 4 shows the calibrated dates obtained by reading from Suess's curve: in some cases a date range has to be given because of such kinks in that part of the curve.

All this is tiresomely complicated, but it need not be confusing. Indeed a recently suggested convention does make life a little easier. On this convention, radiocarbon dates expressed in radiocarbon years are followed by ad, bc or bp in *lower case* letters. When the date has been converted to true, calendar years, expressed as AD, BC or BP, *capital* letters are used. This convention is used throughout this book. It is important to remember, however, that there are several possible calibration procedures proposed by different workers, and each of these will produce a slightly different calibrated date. Each will inevitably start from the radiocarbon determination provided by the laboratory, however, so that in detailed discussions the calibrated date should always be accompanied by the radiocarbon determination itself, in years bp or bc, with its standard deviation and its laboratory number.

Scientists in general do now seem agreed that the radiocarbon time scale has to be calibrated in this kind of way. The detailed shape of the calibration curve is still a matter for dispute, but the general magnitude of the calibration, which involves the correction of radiocarbon dates by up to eight centuries, is widely accepted. The most obvious objective test is again to compare radiocarbon dates of Egyptian material, after calibration, with Egyptian historical dates for that material. In fact, on statistical grounds, it is preferable to compare radiocarbon dates of historically dated Egyptian material (uncalibrated) with radiocarbon dates for tree-ring dated material: this offers a more satisfactory procedure for comparing the Egyptian chronology and the tree-ring calibration. Fortunately two laboratories, at the British Museum and the University of California at Los Angeles, have carried out a series of radiocarbon determinations on Egyptian samples for this purpose.[33] And despite suggestions to the contrary, notably by McKerrell,[34] a detailed statistical analysis of the results shows the calibration and the Egyptian chronology to be in adequate agreement, within the limits of error of the determinations.[35] This is an important result, since it encourages us to apply the calibration to British radiocarbon dates.

Although the tree-ring data and the Egyptian data are in adequate agreement, it is not yet clear what precise calibration curve should be used. Suess's curve has been criticised, since it is full of kinks, and was drawn by eye through the data, and not by any objective procedure. The calibrated dates in column 4 of Table 1 have been read off Suess's curve, which is seen as a continuous line in Fig. 1.

An alternative is to use some mathematical procedure to produce a smoothing function, which will plot a less 'kinky' line through the data. Several workers have in fact done this,[36] and the calibrated dates in column 5 of Table 1 are in fact the arithmetical mean obtained by Dr V.R. Switsur from two such smoothing functions proposed by workers at Philadelphia and Tucson, Arizona. This smoothing function is represented by a broken line in Fig. 1. It is simply a mathematical device to smooth out the kinks in the curve.[37]

Unfortunately, it is far from clear that we are justified in smoothing out the kinks: the calibration curve may indeed ultimately prove to have a lot of kinks in it. Recent statistical work at the University of Sheffield by Malcolm Clark has shown that many smoothing functions, including polynomial ones, do differ significantly from the tree-ring/radiocarbon data,[38] and I suspect that the same may be true of the other smoothing functions recently proposed. Suess may well be right, although some more objective procedure is needed to

| Radiocarbon date bc (5568 half-life) | Radiocarbon date bp (5568 half-life) | Radiocarbon date bc (5730 half-life) | Calendar date range BC (Suess calibration) | Mean calendar date BC (Arizona/Pennsylvania) |
|---|---|---|---|---|
| 0 | 1950 | 60 | 50 AD | 15 |
| 100 | 2050 | 160 | 130 (BC)-40 AD | 140 |
| 200 | 2150 | 270 | 180 (BC) | 270 |
| 300 | 2250 | 370 | 400 | 400 |
| 400 | 2350 | 470 | 470 | 530 |
| 500 | 2450 | 580 | 780-550 | 630 |
| 600 | 2550 | 680 | 790 | 780 |
| 700 | 2650 | 780 | 870 | 890 |
| 800 | 2750 | 880 | 960-890 | 980 |
| 900 | 2850 | 990 | 1100 | 1120 |
| 1000 | 2950 | 1090 | 1330-1220 | 1260 |
| 1100 | 3050 | 1190 | 1450-1340 | 1400 |
| 1200 | 3150 | 1300 | 1480 | 1500 |
| 1300 | 3250 | 1400 | 1620 | 1640 |
| 1400 | 3350 | 1500 | 1660 | 1750 |
| 1500 | 3450 | 1610 | 2000-1720 | 1880 |
| 1600 | 3550 | 1710 | 2060 | 2070 |
| 1700 | 3650 | 1810 | 2130 | 2160 |
| 1800 | 3750 | 1910 | 2160 | 2270 |
| 1900 | 3850 | 2020 | 2470-2220 | 2360 |
| 2000 | 3950 | 2120 | 2500 | 2540 |
| 2100 | 4050 | 2220 | 2760-2540 | 2730 |
| 2200 | 4150 | 2330 | 2940-2630 | 2830 |
| 2300 | 4250 | 2430 | 2960 | 2990 |
| 2400 | 4350 | 2530 | 3350-2970 | 3080 |
| 2500 | 4450 | 2640 | 3390-3260 | 3210 |

| Radiocarbon date bc (5568 half-life) | Radiocarbon date bc (5568 half-life) | Radiocarbon date bc (5730 half-life) | Calendar date range BC (Suess calibration) | Mean calendar date BC (Arizona/Pennsylvania) |
|---|---|---|---|---|
| 2600 | 4550 | 2740 | 3400 | 3340 |
| 2700 | 4650 | 2840 | 3500-3410 | 3430 |
| 2800 | 4750 | 2940 | 3650-3540 | 3510 |
| 2900 | 4850 | 3050 | 3690 | 3610 |
| 3000 | 4950 | 3150 | 3710 | 3730 |
| 3100 | 5050 | 3250 | 4190-3900 | 3890 |
| 3200 | 5150 | 3360 | 4210-3970 | 4040 |
| 3300 | 5250 | 3460 | 4230-4010 | 4170 |
| 3400 | 5350 | 3560 | 4340-4270 | 4240 |
| 3500 | 5450 | 3670 | 4350 | 4310 |
| 3600 | 5550 | 3770 | 4400 | 4420 |
| 3700 | 5650 | 3870 | 4470 | 4520 |
| 3800 | 5750 | 3970 | 4580 | 4640 |
| 3900 | 5850 | 4080 | 4800 | 4740 |
| 4000 | 5950 | 4180 | 4850 | 4850 |
| 4100 | 6050 | 4280 | 4950 | 4960 |
| 4200 | 6150 | 4390 | 5060 | 5070 |
| 4300 | 6250 | 4490 | 5290 | 5160 |
| 4400 | 6350 | 4590 | - | 5210 |
| 4500 | 6450 | 4700 | - | 5310 |

Table 1. The bristlecone pine calibration of radiocarbon. In the first three columns the same radiocarbon date is expressed in different forms. Column 4 gives the range of calibrated dates read from Suess's curve[32] (see Fig. 1). Column 5 indicates the date obtained using a smoothed version of this curve[37] (broken line in Fig. 1). Note, however, that calibrated dates are at present *approximate* only and may be in error by at least 200 years.

produce a curve than simply drawing it in by eye to fit the data.

At the moment, therefore, we have widespread agreement about the general form of the calibration, and differing views about its detail. It will be seen from Fig. 1 that the differences are no more than a century or two. At the moment, however, Suess's curve is perhaps the most realistic precisely because it *does* have kinks, and emphasises for us that individual radiocarbon dates may yield two or three alternative calendar dates differing by a century or two. The elegantly smooth curves may well give an erroneous impression of accuracy.

For this reason, Suess's curve has been used in the date lists in this book to give an approximate estimate for dates in calendar years BC. (Dr Burgess was emphatic that he wished the radiocarbon dates for his chapter to be accompanied also by calibrated dates proposed by Dr McKerrell.[39]) It must be realised clearly that until more physical and statistical work is undertaken on the precise form of the calibration, it is to be regarded as an approximation only, acceptable in its broad outlines but unreliable still for points of detail. Already, however, it can be used to show how fundamentally some of the major issues of British prehistory are affected.

## Phase 3: towards the study of culture process

*The radiocarbon revolution: the decline of diffusionism*
In the late 1950s the first radiocarbon dates for prehistoric Britain were becoming available. This was, of course, long before the tree-ring calibration of radiocarbon, which did not become established until 1969 or 1970. But already dates for the neolithic period were emerging centuries earlier than the supposed beginning of the period, which had been set at around 2000 BC by Stuart Piggott in 1954 in his standard work. As Glyn Daniel wrote at the time: 'We are now entering a new era of prehistory, and many of us are forgetting the drama of the moment ... Radiocarbon dating is the great revolution in 20th-century prehistory.'[41] The method was not without its critics, however, with Piggott himself at first understandably among them.

It was in about 1960 that the general validity of the method became widely recognised in archaeological circles. In that year Hallam Movius published the first radiocarbon-based account of the upper palaeolithic period of Europe,[42] and Godwin in a lecture to the Royal Society stressed that the radiocarbon evidence harmonised with varve dating in setting the beginning of postglacial times around 8000 B C.[43] Already in the previous year the *American Journal of Science* had started a new radiocarbon supplement, the journal now called *Radiocarbon*. And Grahame Clark was writing a new synthesis, *World Prehistory*, published in 1961, in which prehistoric developments in different continents could for the first time be compared using a radiocarbon chronology.

For British readers H.T. Waterbolk's account of the 1959 carbon 14 Symposium at Groningen was very influential in setting many doubts to rest.[44] And in September 1960, Daniel wrote in an editorial in *Antiquity*:[45]

There are still some archaeologists who are loth to accept Carbon-14 dates ... Some point to the apparent gap of a thousand years between the archaeological and radiocarbon dates, but often on examination this gap is an illusory one. We could say in Britain that there was a gap of a thousand years between the date of the Neolithic given in Piggott's *Neolithic Cultures* and the radiocarbon dates for the beginning of Windmill Hill (Piggott's Early Neolithic), but this gap was due entirely to the fact that our archaeological dates before 1400 B.C. had no firm basis whatsoever. The same is true of Eastern Europe.

I believe that we can date the third phase in the development of British prehistoric archaeology from that general real-isation in 1960 of the validity of the radiocarbon method. For the implication was not simply a chronological one. It had profound implications for the whole structure of the subject.

In the first place, of course, it meant an immensely longer duration for the British neolithic than had been proposed previously. And this itself made the distinction drawn by Piggott between a 'primary' and a 'secondary' neolithic more difficult to accept, at least insofar as the secondary neolithic was regarded as due to the resurgence of mesolithic traditions. In 1962 a paper by Clark and Godwin indicated that the British neolithic had lasted at least 1500 years.[46]

At the same time, however, doubts were gathering about the foreign nature of several elements in British neolithic culture. No one seriously doubted that the neolithic way of life was brought to Britain by immigrants, since the principal domesticated plants and animals did not have wild prototypes in northern Europe. But with the collapse of the traditional chronology came doubts about some of the arguments which had sustained it. In 1965 Childe's basic idea that the megalithic tombs of Iberia were derived from the east Mediterranean was seriously questioned.[47] Soon the very early radiocarbon dates for the Breton megalithic tombs made an independent north-west European origin for them even more probable.[48] In 1967 Daniel was able to write: 'Research on the European megaliths has been proceeding for a hundred years, and I think we do know that they did not have a single origin, and that 'megaliths' came into existence independently in Malta, Portugal, Denmark and probably western Britain and Ireland.'[49] Here the new dating was profoundly transforming the traditional patterns of explanation. And the fundamental link, forged by Montelius and strengthened by Childe — the east Mediterranean origin of the megalithic tombs of north-western Europe — was snapped. The tree-ring calibration of radiocarbon makes all this even clearer — evidently there were megalithic tombs in Britain fully a millennium before their supposed Aegean prototypes, the round tombs of Crete dated by Aegean scholars to around 2700 BC.

With the calibration of radiocarbon, the second basic link of the traditional chronology also came into question. We saw above that Montelius had set dates for the British early bronze age, including what was subsequently termed the 'Wessex culture' from 2000 to 1650 BC, and that Sir Arthur Evans, on the strength of its supposed Aegean connections, instead preferred to begin this period about 1500 BC, his view being followed by most subsequent workers. By 1968, although there were no radiocarbon dates available from early bronze age Wessex, several dated samples for the north German and Breton early bronze age were available from contexts which most scholars had considered as contemporary with Wessex. The calibration of these dates suggested that the Wessex culture might now be dated between 2100 and 1700 BC[50] — in much closer accord, indeed, with the view originally propounded by Montelius. This would be far too early for the genesis of the Wessex culture to be influenced from Mycenaean Greece, since the beginning of the Mycenaean civilisation may be set around 1650 BC. At the same time the evidence for links between the Aegean and Britain provided by the faience beads was called into question, when a reinterpretation of the evidence suggested that they were of local manufacture.[51]

Both these suggestions have been contested by McKerrell.[52] And three early bronze age dagger graves from south Britain (Hove, Earls Barton and Edmondsham) have yielded radiocarbon dates around 1200 bc, implying a calibrated date of c. 1500 BC, so that it must now, I think, be agreed that the British early bronze age persisted until that time, although an early date for its beginning still seems likely. The source of the British faience beads remains a matter of dispute, although the recent demonstration that the early faience beads of Czechoslovakia were locally made[53] is an indication that they were being made in at least one region of Europe at this time.

In the recent discussions on these related topics, however, it has become clear that no-one is seriously arguing for strong and significant Aegean influence upon early bronze age Britain, whether or not there may have been some contacts between the two regions. No-one today would *explain* the developments of the British early bronze age in these terms. Nor would it be safe to use such contacts to date the Wessex culture: instead a safe chronology will one day be provided by radiocarbon dating, although unfortunately there are still no dates available from south Britain for the early part of the period. The Wessex-Mycenae link is no longer regarded, as it was by Evans and Childe, as a lynch-pin for British chronology, nor are the accompanying diffusionist arguments accepted any longer.

The traditional view of the iron age has fared no better. In 1960 F.R. Hodson published a penetrating paper[54] in which he examined the traditional ABC schema, and in two subsequent articles argued that such a system of classification was inadequate, and the simple picture of three continental invasions an unsuitable explanation: 'The first step should be to define groups in their own right, without immediately interpreting their significance, or encumbering them with continental labels. The ancestry and affiliation of the groups should only be sought after their definition.'[55] Hodson's views did not, of course, arise as the consequence of radiocarbon dates. They were based simply on a shrewd consideration of the archaeological evidence. Radiocarbon dates have, however, been used by Euan MacKie to give a fresh assessment of the Scottish iron age, which differs substantially from the traditional one.[56]

The general moral underlying these specific changes was lucidly brought out in 1966 by Grahame Clarke in an article in *Antiquity*, 'The invasion hypothesis in British archaeology'.[57] In it he presented with devastating clarity the bankruptcy of the invasionist model, 'the invasion neurosis', as he termed it, which we have here recognised as characteristic of the second phase of British prehistoric studies.

Taking each period in turn he showed that changes previously interpreted as the consequence of invasion could now be seen in other terms:

> To sum up, whereas for the first half of the 20th century it was common form to try to explain every change in the culture of the first 3,000 years or so of peasant culture in the south of England in terms of invasion, the younger school of prehistorians has been more inclined to seek the explanation for change in terms of indigenous evolution ... Invasions and minor intrusions have undoubtedly occurred, even if far less often than other forms of culture contact, but their existence has to be demonstrated, not assumed.

This new outlook for prehistoric Britain is very much in harmony with recent developments in the prehistory of continental Europe also,[58] and indeed beyond. Some of them are the direct result of the new radiocarbon time scale, which indicates some of the fallacies in the old diffusionist structure for European prehistory. But it would be a mistake to see them simply as the consequence of the radiocarbon revolution. For the diffusionist assumptions were always open to question, and a good number of them were already being looked at critically, quite independent of radiocarbon, as Hodson's 1960 paper shows. In the long term the real significance of radiocarbon dating will not be to allow us to talk more about prehistoric chronology, but to encourage us to talk less. For chronology will be removed from the field of general discussion: radiocarbon dates will be among the basic factual data.

In the last analysis the insupportable burden borne by the archaeological reasoning of the second phase of British prehistoric studies was the need to make the material yield a chronology as well as an explanation of change. It could offer both only by distorting each. In this situation the analysis of diffusion, which gave the hope both of a chronology and an explanation, seemed the most profitable approach. At the beginning of this phase, as we have seen, it did indeed offer the means of breaking the confines of a rigid three age system. By 1960 it too had become a rigid and confining framework, out of which it was necessary to break. Radiocarbon dating facilitated that rupture, offering at last an independent chronology against which culture change could be measured.

*The study of process*
The present decade promises to be a fascinating one for British prehistory, indeed for prehistory in general. The collapse of the traditional view, the diffusionist paradigm, leaves a void which has not yet been filled. How, in fact, are we to explain culture change and the various developments in prehistoric Britain, without putting undue weight on the arrival of invaders or — unless their influence is analysed in detail — the effects of cross-Channel contacts? The simple answer, of course, is that we have to be willing to explain such changes in local terms, by discussing the social and economic processes which led to innovation and to the acceptance of innovation in the various communities of prehistoric Britain.

I believe that several lines of investigation can already be discerned: indeed they have been opened for us over the past fifty years by studies which at the time seemed just a little off the mainstream of current research. Yet these can now be recognised as the precursors of the more detailed study of culture process which I think will distinguish our work for some years. Lewis Binford has analysed the general problem illuminatingly: 'Archaeologists . . . are measuring along several dimensions simultaneously . . . culture is neither simple nor additive.'[59] The point here is that it is meaningless holistically to compare two cultures and suggest that they are alike or not, or to try to measure their similarity. Instead we have to analyse different fields of activity, different subsystems of the culture system. We have to think in terms of five or six different (although related) areas of investigation, different subsystems, which if properly understood should give us the information which we need in order to understand the working of the culture as a whole. I have tried to do this for the prehistoric Aegean,[60] and the same model is clearly applicable to prehistoric Britain. The fields which may conveniently be distinguished are:

1. subsistence
2. technology
3. social organisation
4. cognitive basis, implying the symbolic means which the culture has at its disposal for comprehending and using the world, including religion and other projective systems
5. trade and communication
6. population and population density.

It is in the interactions between these different fields or subsystems that culture change is produced, in the impact of bronze metallurgy on the social organisation, for instance, or of rising population on the subsistence basis.

Among the precursors in this field, of course, we can recognise Gordon Childe, who wrote in such terms as these in books like *Man Makes Himself* and *What Happened in History*. Curiously enough he developed his most interesting explanations to account for changes in the Near East, and often regarded Britain as a backwater, a passive receptor of such innovations. In his book *The Bronze Age*, however, he did illuminatingly relate the changing technology of the time to developments in other fields. One of the most promising paths for further research is in this field of prehistoric technology: so far we have too few papers such as Dennis Britton's penetrating study of the development of metallurgy at the beginning of the bronze age.[61]

In this country progress in the study of the prehistoric environment and of the subsistence base has been outstanding, due largely to the influence of our Scandinavian colleagues, and the lessons they have taught in the field of pollen analysis and palaeoethnobotany. Grahame Clark's *Prehistoric Europe: the Economic Basis*, published in 1952, was of course a landmark in the application of the ecological approach to archaeology, and his publication of the excavations at Star Carr in 1954 a model for the reconstruction of the environment and subsistence of a single site. The papers offered at a recent symposium in Leicester reflect some of the best of recent work.[62]

In the field of trade it is necessary to refer only to the impressive body of information which has been painstakingly won through the petrological study of neolithic axes,[63] and to the similar information obtained from pottery.[64] The reconstruction of social organisation is a much more difficult problem, but the papers in two recent symposia, in Southampton and in Sheffield,[65] reflect how geographical and locational models are once again being found useful, some forty years after the pioneering work of Fox, Crawford and Hawkes.

The merit of all these contributions is obvious enough, but it is worth emphasising that what they have in common is that they decline to measure along several dimensions at once. They do not compare artefact with artefact in elaborate typologies, impressive in themselves but impossible to interpret since the patterns among the artefacts are the product of so many variables operating simultaneously. Instead, each of these studies singles out one single aspect of the evidence, including the artefacts themselves, and examines it in terms of intelligible human activities. Archaeology has for too long thought in terms of patterns among artefacts in time and space. Instead the relevant dimensions are different ones, different *kinds* of human activity indicated in the five or six fields or subsystems listed above, all of which can simultaneously operate to define the form, composition and function of even a single artefact. Thinking in these terms we can recognise the wrong turning taken thirty or forty years ago during the second phase of British prehistory. It was to think of assemblages as a whole, these 'constantly recurring assemblages of artefacts', as defining cultures which could be discussed at this general level. The concept of culture is still a useful one, but only as defining limits of time and space *within* which more detailed studies are profitable.

The problem of formulating an acceptable explanation for the changes seen in a prehistoric culture over a few centuries is regrettably far from solved. In the first instance it must clearly require a detailed analysis of the changes in the fields or subsystems listed above. The interaction between them, which must evidently be decisive, is something as yet little understood. Already, however, it is clear that the answer should if possible be in quantitative terms. How much, how many, how big, how long? And the next major advance in field archaeology must surely be to develop the ability to use sampling techniques effectively to answer quantitative questions of this kind. We badly need estimates of population in different areas over specified periods, so that economic prehistory can work on some sort of demographic basis, as economic history is now trying to do.

The theme of this book is chronological. It is an attempt to draw the outlines of the new chronology of British prehistory, itself the essential first step before undertaking more ambitious research. But it would be a mistake to think that the interest of any of the authors is primarily chronological. Indeed I have tried to show that one of the most unfortunate aspects of the second phase of prehistoric research in this country was precisely a preoccupation with chronological questions. At the time this was understandable, but radiocarbon dating now allows us to make these a matter of routine, to determine the chronology and move on to more interesting matters. At the moment, of course, it is fascinating for us to learn that hillforts were already being constructed in the late bronze age, if not sooner. But this is, as iron age specialists have been quick to realise, only a first step towards the better understanding of how they came about at all. In just the same sense the aim of this book is simply to clear the decks, chronologically speaking, so that we can all go on, the chronological problems being solved, to talk of something more important.

The moral here is that this more important objective, namely the adequate explanation of the changes taking place in British prehistory rather than their mere description, will only be achieved by asking the right questions. Many of the questions are quantitative ones, making especially desireable the total excavation of sites, and the intensive examination of large areas of land, both with defined aims within the five or six fields or subsystems listed above. These are ambitious requirements, but it is a remarkable circumstance that they *can* be fulfilled now, indeed that they can *only* be fulfilled now, at the present time. Both the Department of the Environment, with its laudable initiative in setting up regional archaeological units in Britain, and the Rescue organisation, have stressed the extreme rapidity with which urban development, deep ploughing and other undertakings are destroying the existing archaeological evidence. Both have emphasised that the present decade is a crucial one for British archaeology, in that much of the evidence will soon be destroyed. This realisation has made large sums of money available for rescue excavation, making possible precisely those undertakings which now seem desirable, namely the total excavation of sites, and the intensive study of specific areas, for instance in the path of motorways.

The tragedy is that this wonderful and unrepeatable opportunity may have come too early. We are not yet ready for it. Our thinking is still largely governed by the concepts and ideas of the second phase of British prehistoric research, by typologies and culture names and cross-cultural parallels. Many archaeologists feel today that we now know how to excavate a settlement site, that it can be done adequately following recognised procedures. The truth is the opposite. Any archaeological site contains so much potential information that *any* kind of excavation is simply a sampling procedure, and a very partial one at that. A decision has to be made about what to sample — shall we sieve all the soil from these pits for animal bones, after flotation, or would it be better to record accurately in two dimensions the precise location of every sherd found in order to understand something more of the way pottery was being used and the spatial organisation of that activity? It may not be practicable, in terms of time and money, to do both. And because we do not in all cases know what we are looking for, in the sense that we have not yet formulated all the questions to which we shall desire an answer, we shall not find it.

David Clarke has written, in an article full of illuminating insights, of a 'loss of innocence' among archaeologists, although several reactions to it indicate that innocence in some cases has been retained.[66] To a large extent this loss coincides with the passing of the second phase of prehistoric studies in Britain, when the innocent confidence that archaeologists knew what they were doing and should get on with it has been replaced by the uncomfortable awareness that they didn't, and that we ourselves are none too sure. It is unfortunate that the great opportunities at present before us should have come before we are sufficiently experienced, before we have worked out the research techniques needed to give us a greater insight into the processes of culture change.

The new outline, which it is the purpose of this book to sketch, is in one sense a conclusion — a re-organisation of the familiar data in terms of the new radiocarbon chronology in a form which may prove durable. But even if this turns out to be the case, it is still in reality only a beginning. For with the attainment of that long-sought goal of dating and narrating Britain's past, we can now see how very far we are from the more important objective of explaining the changes observed. That I see as the task before us in this third phase of British prehistoric research. But it will only be achieved if archaeologists think out for themselves, anew, the archaeological methods, in both excavation and research, which it demands. Without this, much of the digging will simply be a waste of time, an accumulation of data fit only to answer yesterday's questions which no-one is asking any longer.

# 2. The palaeolithic and mesolithic

## PAUL A. MELLARS

### Pleistocene chronology and environments

The effective range of radiocarbon dating is in the region of 60,000 to 70,000 years, and in fact the earliest C14 determinations which can be related directly to archaeological horizons in Britain date from around 30,000 years before the present. Consequently, any attempt to provide a chronological framework for British prehistory prior to this time must be based on geological evidence — primarily on the well-documented succession of 'glacial' and 'interglacial' periods which collectively make up the 'Pleistocene' epoch.[1]

Owing to the often serious uncertainties involved in correlating geological and climatic events over large areas it is preferable for archaeological chronologies to be constructed in the first instance on the basis of purely local geological successions, in which at least the *relative* positions of the different deposits are firmly established. For the purposes of the present survey therefore the sequence of glacial and interglacial stages currently employed by British geologists has been adopted in preference to the better-known Günz-Mindel-Riss-Würm succession based on the glacial deposits of the Alpine areas. The most likely correlations between the British and Alpine successions are indicated in Table 2, but it is important to remember that these correlations remain to a large extent hypothetical.

As the evidence stands at present we know far more about the various interglacial periods of the Pleistocene than about the intervening glacial episodes. Through the application of pollen analysis to a series of extinct river and lake deposits it has been possible to recognise three major interglacial periods in Britain, and to document the patterns of vegetational development within these periods in remarkable detail. The three interglacials have been termed, in decreasing order of

| *Approximate dates bc* | *British glaciations and interglacials* | *Alpine glaciations* |
|---|---|---|
| | Flandrian ('postglacial') | |
| 8,300 | | |
| | Devensian Glaciation | Würm |
| 70,000 | | |
| | Ipswichian Interglacial | |
| 125,000 | | |
| | Wolstonian Glaciation | Riss |
| ?200,000 | | |
| | Hoxnian Interglacial | |
| ?250,000 | | |
| | Anglian Glaciation | Mindel |
| ?350,000 | | |
| | Cromerian Interglacial | |
| ? | | |
| | Beestonian Glaciation | Günz |

Table 2   Sequence of British glacial and interglacial periods, with possible Alpine equivalents. The dates quoted for periods earlier than the last (Devensian) glaciation should be regarded as highly tentative.

age, Cromerian, Hoxnian and Ipswichian, after a series of type-localities in East Anglia.[2] The pollen evidence shows that the development of the vegetation during each of the three periods was broadly similar leading to the appearance of temperate 'mixed oak forest' around the middle of the interglacial. All of the available evidence suggests that climatic conditions at the height of each interglacial were at least as warm as those of the present day. When examined in detail, however, the patterns of forest development during the three periods are sufficiently distinctive to allow individual deposits to be attributed to one or other of the interglacials with a high degree of confidence. For example, Hoxnian pollen diagrams are distinguished by a comparative abundance of lime and by a pronounced rise in the frequencies of silver fir during the later stages of the interglacial; Ipswichian diagrams on the other hand are characterised by a marked scarcity of both of these species, and by an unusual abundance of hazel towards the middle of the interglacial.[3] Comparative studies of pollen diagrams have also enabled a detailed system of vegetational 'zones' to be worked out for each interglacial, similar to those established for the postglacial period. These systems of zonation provide an extremely sensitive framework of relative chronology for any archaeological remains encountered *in situ* in pollen-bearing interglacial deposits.

In contrast to the detailed information available for the interglacial periods, evidence bearing on climatic and vegetational conditions during the various glacial phases in Britain is extremely sparse. Glacial environments are notoriously unfavourable to the preservation of organic deposits, and in fact botanical evidence relating to 'full glacial' environmental conditions in Britain prior to the last glaciation is virtually nonexistent. Even the maximum extensions of the ice-sheets during the different glaciations remain to be clearly established. The maximum glaciation of Britain (as far south as the Thames valley) is believed to have occurred during the Anglian glaciation, while the last major ice advance during the Devensian glaciation appears to have reached to around the latitude of York;[4] but the total extent of glaciation during the intervening Wolstonian glaciation is at present subject to considerable debate. The identification of milder 'inter-stadial' episodes within the earlier glaciations has given rise to equally difficult problems.

The character of animal populations in Britain during different stages of the Pleistocene varied in response to changes in climate and, above all, vegetation. Characteristic species during the glacial periods included reindeer, horse, bison, and musk-ox, as well as the extinct mammoth (*Elephas primigenius*) and woolly rhinoceros (*Tichorhinus antiquitatis*). During the interglacial periods these were replaced by a wide range of typically woodland forms including the straight-tusked elephant (*Elephas antiquus*), red deer, roe deer, wild oxen and wild boar.[5] There are some indications that certain mammalian species may be diagnostic of particular interglacial periods; thus an unusually large species of fallow deer (*Dama clactoniana*) appears to be restricted to Hoxnian interglacial deposits in southern England, while remains of hippopotamus are thought to be especially characteristic of the Ipswichian interglacial.[6] However, the value of these species as reliable chronological indicators is less well documented than is that of the pollen evidence discussed above.

Variations in sea levels during the Pleistocene have not been so thoroughly documented in Britain as in some other parts of the world, but the major features of these fluctuations nevertheless seem reasonably clear. At several localities there are indications that sea levels during the Ipswichian interglacial rose to at least 8 metres above the present-day level, and heights in the region of 30-35 metres seem firmly established for the preceding Hoxnian interglacial. Still greater elevations were possibly attained during the Cromerian interglacial. The exceptionally low sea levels experienced during the glacial periods (caused by the locking up of vast quantities of water in the ice sheets) are inevitably more difficult to ascertain, but estimates in the region of 100-150 metres are generally quoted for the maximum fall in sea level during the coldest part of the last glaciation.[7] The automatic effect of this lowering of sea level was to cause large areas of what are at present the English Channel and the North Sea basin to become dry land, and to make Britain in effect a part of the main European land-mass. During the interglacial periods on the other hand Britain would have become an island with coastlines broadly similar to those of the present day. In considering the movement of human groups into and out of Britain, these factors must clearly be kept in mind.

Finally, reference should be made to the question of absolute dating. As yet, absolute age determinations have not been obtained for any geological deposits in Britain older than the last glaciation and any attempts at providing an absolute time-scale for the earlier glacials and interglacials must therefore rest on inferred correlations with dated successions in other areas. Inevitably, different lines of correlation lead to different age estimates. For example, the age of the Hoxnian interglacial may be estimated at around 150,000 years on the basis of correlations with the potassium-argon dated terraces of the river Rhine, or at greater than 200,000 years on the basis of more long-range correlations with the raised beach deposits of the Mediterranean area.[8] In view of these ambiguities any attempts to assign absolute dates to the earlier stages of the British palaeolithic must be regarded as nothing more than approximate 'order of magnitude' estimates at the present time.

## Lower palaeolithic settlement

Any survey of the lower palaeolithic period in Britain must unfortunately begin by acknowledging the limitations of the available evidence. Despite the very large number of localities from which lower palaeolithic artefacts have been recovered — certainly running into several thousands — the number of sites which have yielded information of substantial scientific value remains pitifully small. The difficulties stem from three major sources: firstly, the overwhelming majority of lower palaeolithic artefacts derive from geologically disturbed contexts (principally river gravel deposits) in which material from several distinct occupations has frequently been mixed together; the prospects of observing truly *in situ* occupation sites in these situations are of course virtually non-existent. Secondly, the bulk of the available material derives not from controlled archaeological excavations but from collections formed more or less casually in the course of quarrying operations; in these circumstances artefacts were generally collected on a selective basis and as a result, true 'assemblages' of archaeological material represent the exception rather than the rule. Thirdly, the complexities and uncertainties of Pleistocene geology are such that most sites can only be dated within very broad limits; at present, in fact, it is doubtful whether more than a score of lower palaeolithic sites in Britain can be assigned to even the correct glacial or interglacial period with anything approaching certainty.

Perhaps the most obvious danger inherent in working with a very limited body of data in prehistory is that of over-simplifying the true pattern of events. The account of the British lower palaeolithic given below should therefore be regarded essentially as a 'minimum' reconstruction, which is likely to require further elaboration, and no doubt revision, as further evidence comes to light.[9]

## Hoxnian and pre-Hoxnian occupation

As several authors have recently pointed out, the earliest firmly-documented evidence for human occupation in Britain dates from the time of the Hoxnian interglacial.[10] There are however a number of fairly strong hints that human groups manufacturing well-characterised hand-axe industries reached Britain at some time before this period, most probably during

Figure 2. Lower and middle palaeolithic sites in Britain.

a warmer interstadial phase of the preceding Anglian glaciation. Perhaps the clearest indications of this are provided by the metrical analyses undertaken by D.A. Roe on the large series of hand-axes from the site of Fordwich in Kent.[11] The data obtained by Roe show that the hand-axes from this site are both thicker in cross-section and more coarsely worked than those from any of the sites which are known to belong to the Hoxnian interglacial in southern Britain. Some geological support for these typological indications is provided by the fact that the hand-axes were recovered from a high-level terrace deposit of the river Stour, at a height of approximately 40 metres above present sea level; hand-axes resembling those from known Hoxnian sites in Britain were obtained from a lower terrace feature of the Stour, only 30 metres above sea level.[12]

The evidence from Fordwich is supported by that obtained in the course of the 19th-century excavations at Kent's Cavern (near Torquay) in south Devon.[13] The lowermost 'breccia' deposits at this site yielded a series of thick, coarsely-worked hand-axes which, to judge by the published description, closely resemble the specimens from Fordwich. From the same deposits were obtained remains of at least three faunal species (*Homotherium latidens, Pitymys gregaloides* and *Arvicola greeni*) which are thought to have become extinct before the end of the Anglian glaciation. Other hand-axe industries which may possibly belong to this pre-Hoxnian phase of occupation have been reported from Farnham (Terrace A) in Surrey, Warren Hill in Suffolk and the Winter Hill terrace of the River Thames,[14] but the geological evidence for dating these occurrences is at present very uncertain.

There is of course nothing inherently unlikely in this evidence for pre-Hoxnian hand-axe manufacture in Britain. Clear traces of hand-axe industries attributed on geological grounds to the time of the 'Mindel' or 'Elster' glaciation have been recorded from a number of localities in western Europe, including the sites of Torralba and Ambrona in central Spain, Terra Amata in south-east France and Abbeville in northern France.[15] Still earlier traces of human occupation are known from southern Europe (notably from the cave of Vallonet on the French riviera, tentatively attributed to the 'Günz' glaciation), but these sites have not so far yielded evidence of hand-axe manufacture.[16]

With the commencement of the Hoxnian interglacial evidence for human occupation in Britain immediately comes into much sharper focus. Indeed, there are some grounds for thinking that the density of population in southern England during certain stages of this interglacial may have been greater than at any time prior to the mesolithic period. Evidently, environmental conditions at this time were very favourable for human groups practising a hunter-gatherer economy.

Probably the most thoroughly documented site from a chronological point of view is that of Hoxne itself, where hand-axes were first recorded by John Frere as long ago as 1797.[17] Geologically the site consists of a series of lake deposits laid down within a depression in the underlying 'Lowestoft' (= Anglian period) boulder clay; as already indicated, pollen analysis of these lake sediments has provided a remarkably detailed picture of vegetational and climatic conditions throughout the whole of the Hoxnian interglacial.[18] The current excavations of J. Wymer have revealed that there are in fact two distinct levels of occupation within the interglacial deposits at Hoxne, which can be dated with some precision in terms of the vegetational succession. Thus the earlier occupation level can be shown to date from around the middle of the Hoxnian (pollen zone IId), while the upper level belongs to a slightly later stage (zone III) of the same interglacial. Unfortunately the earlier horizon has so far yielded only a very small number of artefacts, but the upper level has produced a series of oval, heart-shaped and 'cleaver'-type hand-axes together with a number of carefully retouched flake implements.[19] The stratigraphic provenance of the large numbers of sharply pointed hand-axes found during the earlier quarrying operations at Hoxne remains to be established, although there are some indications that these may derive from the Wolstonian-period glacial deposits which overlie the Hoxnian levels.[20]

Hand-axe assemblages apparently belonging to the Hoxnian interglacial are particularly well represented in the gravel deposits of the so-called '100-foot' or 'Boyn Hill' terrace of the River Thames. These sites evidently date from a time when the river was flowing at approximately 30-35 metres above its present level. By far the most instructive section through these deposits is preserved at Swanscombe on the south bank of the Thames approximately 18 miles to the east of London. The bulk of the hand-axes from Swanscombe come from the 'Middle Gravel' deposits of the Barnfield Pit and evidently represent the accumulated sweepings from a succession of Acheulian camp sites situated close to the river's edge.[21] Recent geological work suggests that these deposits date from a relatively late stage of the Hoxnian interglacial, probably during the post-temperate stage (zone IV) of the vegetational development.[22] The hand-axes from this level show a marked predominance of pointed forms (Fig. 3: 1-2) with much smaller proportions of ovate and heart-shaped specimens.[23] Carefully retouched flake-tools

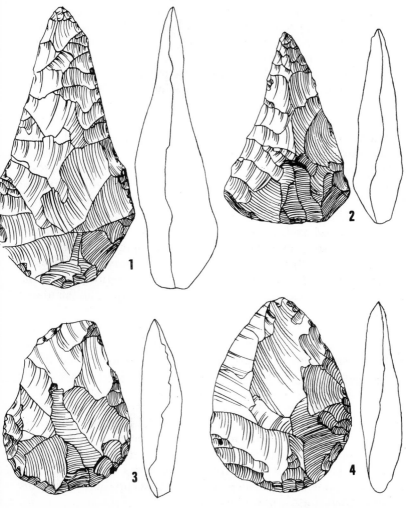

Figure 3. Acheulian hand-axes from Swanscombe; 1-2, from Middle
    Gravels; 3-4, probably from Upper Loam; no. 4 is a 'twisted ovate'.
    *After Wymer* (1/2).

appear to be rather less frequent than at Hoxne, possibly
indicating a difference in the activities undertaken at the two
sites. It was in these deposits that the famous Swanscombe
skull was discovered by A.T. Marston in 1935; although only
the rear portion of the skull is preserved this is sufficient to
show that the type of Man responsible for the Acheulian

industry belonged almost certainly to *Homo sapiens*.[24]

A somewhat later stage of hand-axe manufacture is represented by the material recovered from the 'Upper Loam' deposit in the Barnfield Pit at Swanscombe. The hand-axes from this level contrast rather sharply with those from the underlying Middle Gravels in showing a much smaller proportion of pointed types and a clear predominance of ovate and heart-shaped forms (Fig 3: 3-4). A further distinctive feature of the axes from this level is the occurrence of several specimens which show markedly 'twisted' edges.[25] Stratigraphically, this horizon must date either from the extreme end of the Hoxnian interglacial or, more probably, from an early stage of the succeeding Wolstonian glaciation.[26] It has been suggested that the differences between the shapes of the hand-axes from the two levels at Swanscombe might represent two general stages in the development of Acheulian industries in Britain,[27] but the recent discoveries at Hoxne would seem to cast doubt on this interpretation; hence the precise significance of the observed variations in hand-axe shapes is at present difficult to assess.[28]

One further hand-axe industry which can be attributed with some confidence to the Hoxnian interglacial is that recovered from the surface of the '135-foot' raised beach deposits at Slindon Park in Sussex.[29] At least seven of the hand-axes from this site are heavily abraded and clearly date from a time when the sea stood close to the 30–35 metre level. A larger collection of artefacts (27 hand-axes plus 280 waste flakes) was recovered from what seems to have been an undisturbed occupation surface immediately on top of the raised beach deposits. This site provides one of the few well-documented instances of coastal occupation during the lower palaeolithic period in Europe.

Present indications suggest that Acheulian industries occupy only the second half of the Hoxnian interglacial in Britain. The earlier part of the interglacial appears to be occupied by a series of assemblages from which true hand-axes are entirely absent. These are known as 'Clactonian' after a type-site on the foreshore at Clacton-on-Sea, Essex. Clactonian industries are at present known with certainty from only three, or possibly four, sites in south-east England. The best dated occurrences are those from Clacton itself and from the 'Lower Gravel' and 'Lower Loam' deposits at Swans-combe. At Clacton the industry occurs in the deposits of an ancient channel of the Thames formed at a time when the river flowed some way to the north of its present course.[30] Pollen obtained from the overlying deposits suggest that the industry dates from no later than zone II of the Hoxnian interglacial.[31] At Swanscombe the Clactonian levels lie immediately beneath the Middle Gravel deposits which con-tained the Acheulian industry and evidently relate to a period of river aggradation during the earlier part of the inter-glacial;[32] once again the geological evidence suggests a dating during zone II of the Hoxnian.[33] A stratigraphic situation similar to that at Swanscombe (i.e. Clactonian overlain by Acheulian) has been recorded at the site of Barnham St Gregory in Suffolk,[34] but the geological dating of this succession remains to be established.[35]

Clactonian assemblages consist of relatively thick, heavy flakes showing large striking platforms and prominent bulbs of percussion, accompanied by the nodules from which these were struck. Although the latter have often been regarded as merely waste-products of the industry it is now recognised that many of these Clactonian 'cores' are in fact identical to the 'pebble-tools' and 'chopping-tools' which play such a prominent role in the lower palaeolithic industries of Africa and the Far East.[36] The possibility of some direct con-nection between the Clactonian and the Asian chopping-tool industries has been considerably strengthened by the recent discovery of similar industries at a number of localities in central and eastern Europe — most notably at the site of Vertesszöllös in Hungary.[37] Many authorities therefore believe that the Clactonian may represent a cultural tradition quite separate from the Acheulian which occupied Britain briefly — and possibly exclusively — during the earlier part of the Hoxnian interglacial. Indeed, the two traditions may well have been adapted to rather different environmental condi-tions, the Clactonian groups exploiting the heavily forested environment during the first half of the Hoxnian, while the Acheulian groups were adapted to the more open conditions which characterised the later stages of the interglacial.[38]

## Post-Hoxnian developments

One of the most significant features which emerges from a study of well-dated Hoxnian sites in Britain is the general lack of evidence for use of the 'prepared core' or 'Levallois' technique of flake production. It is true that faint traces of this technique have occasionally been claimed from such sites as Swanscombe and Slindon, but all of these occurrences seem 'atypical' or otherwise questionable to some degree.[39] It is not until the succeeding Wolstonian glaciation that entirely convincing evidence for use of the Levallois technique can be identified.

In Britain the earliest traces of industries employing fully developed Levallois methods are recorded from a number of sites in the neighbourhood of Northfleet, less than one mile to the east of Swanscombe. The first stage in the Northfleet succession appears to be represented by the extremely rich site of Baker's Hole, discovered in the course of quarrying operations during the opening years of the present century.[40] The characteristic products of this site consist of large and exceptionally fine Levallois flakes which were struck from extensively prepared 'tortoise cores'; the majority of the flakes are relatively broad, but a number of more elongated, blade-like flakes are also represented in the industry (Fig. 4: 1-3, 7). In all probability the site represents a 'workshop' location intended to exploit the excellent supplies of raw material which outcropped along the banks of the river. It has sometimes been questioned whether the hand-axes also found at Baker's Hole are truly associated with the Levallois material, but these doubts seem largely unfounded; evidence from various parts of Europe suggests that Levallois flakes form a normal component of Acheulian industries from the time of the penultimate glaciation onwards.[41] Indeed, it may well be that the Levallois technique was invented by Acheulian groups towards the beginning of this period.

Similar associations of Levallois flakes and Acheulian-style hand-axes have been recorded in the other sites at Northfleet, which are believed to be somewhat younger than the Baker's Hole occurrence. At these sites the industries occur chiefly in a series of chalky solifluction horizons separated by deposits of wind-blown loess.[42] Presumably the occupation levels

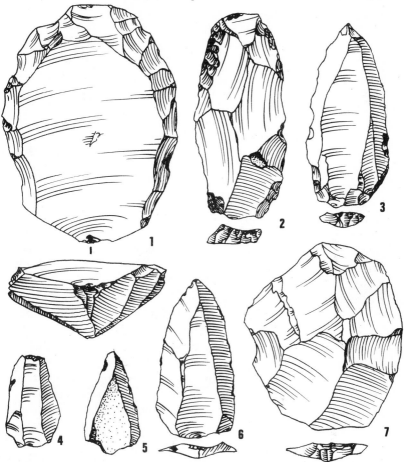

Figure 4. Artefacts produced by 'prepared core' ('Levalloisian') techniques from Baker's Hole, Northfleet (1-3, 7) and Creffield Road, Acton (4-6); 1, 'tortoise core'; 2-7 flakes. *After Wymer* (1/3)

represent short visits to Britain by human groups during the milder interstadial phases of the Wolstonian glaciation. As at Baker's Hole, the assemblages comprise not only broad Levallois flakes but also blade-like forms which must have been struck from specially prepared 'prismatic' cores. The ten or eleven hand-axes found in association with the Levallois material consist mainly of fairly small, pointed forms.

A further site which appears to date from an interstadial of the penultimate glaciation has been excavated recently by G. de G. Sieveking at High Lodge in west Suffolk. The existence of at least two, and possibly three, distinct industries at this site provides some indication of the complexity of industrial developments during this period.[43] The uppermost industry comprises abundant hand-axes and clearly belongs to the Acheulian tradition; unlike the specimens from Northfleet, however, the majority of the hand-axes from High Lodge are of finely-worked ovate and heart-shaped forms.[44] Whether or not this industry is earlier or later than the Northfleet succession would seem on present evidence to be an open question.

The earlier occupation horizon at High Lodge has not so far produced any hand-axes and is thought by some workers to represent an entirely separate industrial tradition. The majority of the artefacts consist of carefully retouched flake implements (side scrapers, points etc.) manufactured on rather thick non-Levallois flakes.[45] The assemblage shows distinct similarities to a number of industries from sites in southern France (notably La Micoque and Baume Bonne) which are also attributed to the penultimate glaciation, and which are often grouped together under the term 'Proto-Charentian'. It is just conceivable that this type of industry represents a continuation of the Clactonian/Chopping-tool tradition represented in Britain during the earlier part of the Hoxnian interglacial, but this suggestion must be regarded as entirely speculative at the present time. The alternative view is that the absence of hand-axes and the other idiosyncratic features of the industry reflect simply the specialised nature of the activities undertaken on the site.

Industries which can be dated with certainty to the last interglacial period are conspicuously scarce in all parts of Europe. In Britain it is doubtful whether more than two or three sites can be ascribed with any measure of confidence to this interval. By far the richest site was discovered in the 1870s at the base of the 'brick-earth' deposits at Crayford in Kent.[46] The character of the Crayford assemblage is of particular interest; the overwhelming majority of the artefacts appear to consist of elongated 'flake-blades' which, like the earlier specimens from Northfleet, were unquestionably struck from deliberately prepared blade cores. Probably, although not certainly, associated with these pieces are four heart-shaped hand-axes, so the industry can perhaps be seen as a continuation of the earlier Acheulian tradition.[47] At first sight the Crayford assemblage looks more like an upper palaeolithic than a middle palaeolithic industry; similar assemblages are however known from a number of sites attributed to the last interglacial in northern France, and the geological evidence for dating the Crayford section seems beyond question. The association of the industry with remains of mammoth and woolly rhinoceros probably indicates a date towards the end of the interglacial when the vegetation is known to have become fairly open.[48]

Other traces of Ipswichian occupation in Britain are exceedingly sparse. A few flakes obtained from a cliff section at Selsey in Sussex can be dated fairly closely by pollen analysis to around the middle of the interglacial (pollen zone $e$)[49] and a similar or slightly later date can perhaps be inferred for the larger collection of Levallois flakes and flake-blades from the site of Brundon in Suffolk.[50] Whether or not the occasional hand-axes obtained from the latter site are truly associated with the Levallois material would appear to be debatable.

*Geographical/economic aspects of the lower palaeolithic*
Evidence for lower palaeolithic occupation is effectively confined to southern and eastern Britain. A recent survey has revealed than out of a total of over 3,000 separate find-spots of lower palaeolithic implements in Britain, less than 100 — i.e. approximately 3 per cent — lie to the north-west of a line extending from the Bristol Channel to the Wash. If the calculations were based on the total numbers of artefacts rather than numbers of sites, the proportion would fall to around 0.3 per cent.[51]

The overriding problem, of course, is to assess how far this pattern of discoveries represents the true distribution of lower palaeolithic settlement in Britain and how far it reflects simply the destructive effects of the last two glaciations over the northern and western parts of the country. If the distribution is taken at its face value, two factors may help to explain the concentration of settlement in south-eastern England: (1) a deliberate preference on the part of early palaeolithic groups for relatively low-lying terrain; and (2) the occurrence of abundant and high-quality supplies of raw material for tool manufacture in the flint-bearing chalk deposits of the south-east. To human groups who were in the habit of manufacturing relatively large implements the latter consideration must have been of particular importance.

The other feature of lower palaeolithic settlement patterns which requires explanation is the marked concentration of occupation sites in close proximity to large bodies of water; this is evidenced on the one hand by the dense clustering of sites along major river valleys (for example, the Thames and the Medway) and on the other hand by the occurrence of well-documented lake-side settlements at such sites as Hoxne and High Lodge in Suffolk and Round Green in Bedfordshire. In addition to providing essential supplies of fresh water, these locations may have played a critical role in the hunting strategies of the human groups. Of particular interest in this connection is the evidence recorded from a number of lower palaeolithic sites in Africa and Spain which suggests that large animals were deliberately driven into swampy areas along the edges of rivers and lakes where they became bogged down and could be more easily attacked. Alternatively, animals could have been killed while they were drinking at the water's edge.

It has already been pointed out that the overwhelming majority of lower palaeolithic sites in Britain occur in contexts which have been disturbed to varying degrees by geological processes, and that fully *in situ* occupation sites are conspicuously scarce. A number of undisturbed 'living floors' were however encountered in the course of quarrying operations during the later years of the 19th century and we are fortunate in having relatively detailed accounts of these discoveries preserved in the contemporary literature. The best known of these sites were observed and recorded by Worthington G. Smith at Caddington in Bedfordshire and Stoke Newington in north-west London; full accounts of both sites were included in Smith's book *Man the Primeval Savage*, published in 1894.[52] The undisturbed nature of the occupation levels was indicated not only by the completely fresh and sharp condition of the artefacts, but also by the occurrence of localised clusters of flakes which could be fitted together. In one famous instance Smith was able to recombine all the flakes struck off in the course of manufacturing a hand-axe and obtain a plaster cast of the missing implement. At Stoke Newington conditions of preservation in certain parts of the site were so good that dense accumulations of ferns could be identified which Smith suggested might have served as beds for the Acheulian occupants. In the same area he also encountered two four-foot-long poles of birch, each of which was artificially sharpened at one end and which might have acted as supports for some kind of flimsy shelter or wind-break.[53] A somewhat later occupation site of the same calibre was recorded by F.C. Spurrel in 1880 at the base of the brick earth deposits at Crayford in Kent.[54] Here, the assemblage of Levallois flakes and blades was found in close association with the bones of mammoth, woolly rhinoceros and several other animals which had evidently been butchered on the spot. Needless to say, the excavation of sites of this nature with the aid of modern techniques would make an enormous contribution to our knowledge of the activities and ways of life of lower palaeolithic communities in Britain.

Reliable information on the hunting activities of lower palaeolithic groups is at present available from not more than seven or eight sites in southern Britain. Even when faunal remains are preserved in substantial numbers in archaeological deposits it is often difficult to be certain that these are truly associated with the archaeological material. For obvious reasons, particular caution is required in considering collections obtained from river gravel deposits.

Substantial faunal assemblages have been recovered from the Clactonian horizons at both Swanscombe (Lower Gravels) and Clacton itself, and these may well provide an accurate reflection of the hunting activities of Clactonian communities during the earlier stages of the Hoxnian interglacial. In these sites the most abundant mammalian species were the straight-tusked elephant (*Elephas antiquus*) and the Clacton fallow deer (*Dama clactoniana*), although remains of horse, wild oxen, red deer and rhinoceros were also well represented.[55] More explicit associations of Clactonian artefacts with remains of elephant, rhinoceros, bear, red deer, fallow deer and wild ox have been recorded in the recent excavations of J. Waechter in the Lower Loam deposit at Swanscombe, but as yet little information on the relative abundance of these species is available.[56]

The current excavations of J. Wymer in the Hoxne lake deposits are likely to yield extremely valuable information on the economic activities of Acheulian groups during the second half of the Hoxnian interglacial. Faunal remains so far recovered from the uppermost occupation level show a predominance of horse accompanied by smaller proportions of red deer, ox and elephant.[57] A similar faunal assemblage, dominated by remains of horse and ox, was found in association with the rich Acheulian industry in the Middle Gravel deposits at Swanscombe. The composition of these faunas is believed to indicate that the Acheulian occupations took place under more open vegetational conditions than those which prevailed during the occupation of the Clactonian levels in the earlier part of the interglacial.[58] In this context it is particularly interesting to recall that Hoxnian pollen diagrams from two sites in south-east England (Hoxne itself and Mark's Tey in Essex) have revealed evidence of a brief but well-defined phase of deforestation towards the middle of the interglacial which appears to coincide closely with the earlier of the two occupation levels at Hoxne.[59] The possibility that the Acheulian groups themselves may have been responsible for this event – for example, by deliberately setting fire to the forest to improve the grazing qualities of the vegetation for animal populations – should certainly be borne in mind.

Finally, faunal remains found in association with Levallois-type assemblages at Baker's Hole (Northfleet), Crayford and Brundon suggest that the specialised hunting of mammoth may have been practised by certain human groups during the Wolstonian glaciation and the Ipswichian interglacial.[60] The discovery of a pointed Levalloisian flake lying amongst the bones of what appears to have been a complete mammoth skeleton at a depth of four metres below the surface at Ealing (north London) may provide a rare glimpse of an actual 'kill' site belonging to this period.[61]

The importance of plant foods in the diet of lower palaeolithic societies inevitably remains an almost totally unknown quantity. Recent ethnographic studies of such groups as the Bushmen and the Hadza have emphasised the dangers of assuming that all non-agricultural communities are primarily 'hunters'; indeed, it has been found that amongst present-day hunter-gatherers vegetable foods may account for up to 80 per cent of the total calorie intake, and it is only in groups occupying extreme arctic and subarctic environments (such as the Eskimo and Yukaghir) that hunting normally provides the major part of the food supply.[62] There are in fact indications that the importance of vegetable foods tends to increase progressively as one moves from the poles towards the equator. The obvious inference to be drawn from this is that plants are likely to have played a particularly important — possibly dominant — role in the food-supply of palaeolithic groups during the warmer interglacial episodes of the Pleistocene. However, in the absence of any direct evidence for the consumption of vegetable food one can do no more than speculate on this point.

## The last glacial period

In contrast to the situation in the earlier stages of the Pleistocene, a comparatively detailed and firm reconstruction of both geological and archaeological events has been established for the last glacial period in Britain. The basis of this reconstruction is provided by a framework of radiocarbon determinations extending back over 60,000 years. From this point on we can therefore begin to speak, with varying degrees of confidence, in terms of an absolute chronology of British prehistory.[63]

The total time-span of the last glaciation appears to extend from approximately 70,000 to 8,300 bc. Abundant evidence is now available to show that this period cannot be envisaged as a single episode of uniformly cold climate. Research in both Britain and on the continent has shown that the last glaciation embraces a relatively complex sequence of climatic fluctuations which can be divided broadly into colder 'stadial' and warmer 'interstadial' phases. The clear definition of interstadial periods is a comparatively recent development in northern Europe and has come about chiefly through the investigation of pollen-bearing deposits stratified within typical glacial sediments. An early interstadial episode, dated by radiocarbon to around 59,000 bc, has been recognised at Chelford in Cheshire and more recently at Wretton in Norfolk.[64] The pollen evidence indicates that this interval was characterised by a type of northern coniferous forest similar to that found at the present day in parts of Finland. On the basis of both the pollen and the radiocarbon evidence, the Chelford deposit appears to correlate with the well known 'Brørup' interstadial as identified in Denmark and adjacent areas of the continent.

A second interstadial, dated to around 36,000-40,000 bc, is best represented by an exposure in the Main Terrace deposits of the river Severn at Upton Warren in Worcestershire.[65] Although this episode does not appear to have been characterised by any significant increase in tree growth, studies of the contemporary insect faunas suggest that average summer temperatures rose to within $2°C$ of those of the present day. Investigations of pollen-bearing deposits on the continent have suggested a rather more complicated sequence of climatic fluctuations around this time; a minor warm oscillation dated to around 42,000-44,000 bc (the 'Moershoofd' interstadial) was followed by more pronounced ameliorations at 35,000-37,000 bc (the 'Hengelo' interstadial) and 27,000-30,000 bc (the 'Denekamp' or 'Paudorf' interstadial).[66] It remains to be seen whether the recovery of more complete evidence for this time range will reveal a similarly complex series of fluctuations at British sites.

Climatic and vegetational conditions during the colder 'stadial' intervals of the last glaciation are less fully documented. The limited botanical evidence at present available suggests that these phases were characterised by extremely harsh, tundra-like conditions in which average annual temperatures fell to between $10°C$ and $15°C$ below present-day levels.[67] The positions of the ice margins during different stages of the glaciation remain to be established, but there is widespread agreement that the maximum extension of the ice sheets occurred towards the end of the glaciation, probably between 18,000 and 14,000 bc.[68] At this time the ice margin in central England appears to have stood at around the level of York, but to have extended further to the south in the more elevated areas of western Britain.[69]

By far the best known part of the last glaciation is the

'late-glacial' period, extending from approximately 12,000 to 8,300 bc.[70] This evidently represents the recessional stage of the glaciation when temperatures were rapidly warming up and the ice sheets were retreating towards the north. Studies of pollen-bearing deposits in many parts of Europe have led to the recognition of a well defined interstadial episode within the late-glacial period, dated by radiocarbon to around 10,000-8,800 bc. Conditions during this 'Allerød' interstadial were evidently mild enough to permit the migration of scattered birch woodland into the south-eastern parts of Britain. A slightly different picture of this interval is given by studies of the contemporary insect faunas.[71] According to this line of evidence the maximum temperatures were attained towards the end of the preceding 'Older Dryas' phase at a time when the landscape of northern Europe was still dominated by open tundra vegetation. Indeed, it has been suggested that summer temperatures at this time may have reached as high, or even slightly higher, than those of the present day. The explanation offered for this apparent conflict between the botanical and faunal evidence is that the insects were able to respond more rapidly to the improvement in climatic conditions than were the trees, which required an appreciable time to migrate to north-west Europe from their refuge areas further to the south. In any event, it is clear that the Allerød interstadial was brought to an end by a brief but very sharp return to cold conditions during the 'Younger Dryas' phase. Although only 500 years in length this led to a temporary reappearance of tundra vegetation and, apparently, a minor readvance of the ice sheets in northern Scotland. The end of the late-glacial period was marked by a further increase in temperatures which resulted in the establishment of fully forested conditions over most areas of Britain.

Substantial animal populations were undoubtedly present in southern Britain during certain stages of the last glaciation, and were presumably most abundant during the milder interstadial phases. The expansion of grassland during these periods would have provided rich grazing for such species as mammoth, wild horse, bison and reindeer. To judge by the evidence from continental sites it would appear that particularly large herds of wild horse and reindeer entered north-west Europe during the late-glacial period.[72] One of the most difficult problems is to assess whether these species remained permanently in Britain or whether they represent merely summer visitors who migrated further south during the winter months.

Finally, the formation of large ice sheets during the last glaciation resulted in a world-wide reduction in sea level which is estimated to have attained at least 100 metres.[73] As pointed out in an earlier section, the automatic effect of this drop in sea level was to make Britain in effect a part of the European mainland. Although a substantial rise in sea level must have occurred during the late-glacial period it is known that both human and animal populations were able to enter Britain across a wide land bridge until well into the ensuing postglacial era.

### Mousterian occupation

On purely *a priori* grounds it would appear highly unlikely that Britain was occupied continuously throughout the last glaciation. During much of this period large areas of Britain would have been covered by ice sheets, and conditions in the rest of the country must have been far too barren and inhospitable to permit any kind of permanent settlement. Traces of occupation are therefore to be expected only during the milder stages of the last glaciation — that is, at the very beginning and very end of the glaciation and during one or two major 'interstadial' periods. This is, in fact, very much the pattern suggested by the surviving archaeological remains.

The earliest sites which can be attributed with some measure of confidence to the last glaciation appear to be characterised by the presence of carefully worked hand-axes of a rather distinctive shape to which the term *bout coupé* has often been applied (Fig. 5: 1-2).[74] These are basically heart-shaped hand-axes which differ from the normal 'cordiform' types in having the bases worked to a distinctively angular outline. Hand-axes of this type have a fairly wide distribution over southern England, but the most fully documented discoveries come from Little Paxton in Huntingdonshire,[75] Christchurch in Hampshire,[76] the Coygan Cave in Camarthenshire[77] and Kent's Cavern in Devonshire.[78] The

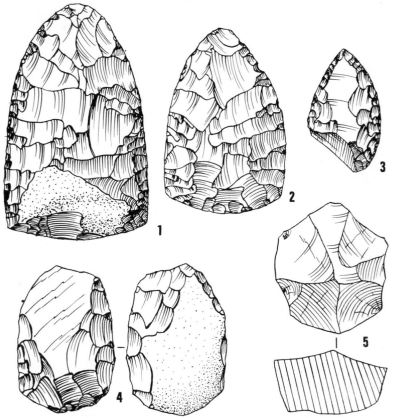

Figure 5. Early last glacial artefacts from British sites; 1, Christchurch; 2, Little Paxton; 3, Pinhole Cave: 4-5, Robin Hood's Cave; 1-2, 'bout coupé' hand-axes; 3, Mousterian point; 4, cordiform hand-axe manufactured from split quartzite pebble; 5, disc core of quartzite. *After Calkin and Green, Paterson and Tebbutt* (1/2)

clearest dating evidence comes from the Little Paxton site, where the axes were recovered from a low-level terrace of the Great Ouse river in association with remains of reindeer and a number of other typically 'glacial' species. Similar associations have been recorded at Kent's Cavern and (rather less reliably) at the Coygan Cave. On the basis of continental parallels, these *bout coupé* hand-axes are most likely to date from a very early stage of the last glaciation, possibly during the initial cold episode which preceded the Brørup/Chelford interstadial.[79]

Associations of these hand-axes with other archaeological material are at present poorly known. Possibly the most instructive site in this connection is the famous 'workshop floor' discovered by J. Allen Brown towards the end of the nineteenth century at Creffield Road, Acton, in north-west London.[80] The industry occurred at a height of approximately 30 metres above sea level and was overlain by a thick accumulation of 'brick-earth' which almost certainly represents a wind-blown loess deposit formed during the last glaciation. The majority of the artefacts from the site appear to consist of elongated blade-like and pointed flakes similar to those recorded from the site of Crayford referred to in an earlier section (Fig. 4: 4-6). In apparent association with these pieces were found two hand-axes which according to Wymer[81] approach closely to the *bout coupé* form. Taking into account both the geological and typological indications this assemblage could date from either the beginning of the last glaciation or from a very late stage of the Ipswichian interglacial.

The dating of certain other occurrences of 'Mousterian' industries in Britain remains problematic. Among these may be included the finds from the Oldbury 'rock-shelters' in Kent,[82] Wookey Hole in Somerset,[83] the Pont Newydd cave in Denbighshire and Creswell Crags in Derbyshire.[84] It is of particular interest that in all of these sites — as in the sites discussed above — well made hand-axes of more or less cordiform type have been recorded. The problem is to decide whether these sites belong to precisely the same episode of occupation as that represented by the *bout coupé* axes, or whether they represent a distinct and somewhat later phase of settlement. On balance, the weight of the present evidence seems in favour of the second alternative. Although one or two examples of *bout coupé* hand-axes have been reported from the site of Oldbury, the bulk of the hand-axes from the sites under consideration exhibit more rounded outlines and are in general much smaller in size than those encountered in the true 'Paxton type' industries. The overall forms of the hand-axes are in fact very similar to those found in the classic 'Mousterian of Acheulian tradition' assemblages from south-west French sites. The strength of the latter comparisons is enhanced by the fact that the French industries appear to date from a relatively late stage of the Mousterian which can probably be correlated with the Hengelo interstadial (c. 35,000 - 37,000 bc) of the Netherlands.[85] In terms of the British succession this would equate with the well-defined Upton Warren interstadial, during which summer temperatures are thought to have risen to within a few degrees of those of the present day. A short-lived occupation of southern Britain at this time would certainly make very good sense in ecological terms.

The material obtained from these later Mousterian levels is fairly scanty. By far the richest site is Oldbury, which appears to have produced approximately 40 hand-axes together with 600—700 flakes.[86] The retouched flake implements from Oldbury include typical Mousterian side scrapers, points, backed knives and denticulated forms. The material obtained from three separate cave sites at Creswell Crags (Robin Hood's Cave, Pinhole Cave and Church Hole) is largely unpublished[87] but includes at least five or six hand-axes (mostly manufactured from quartzite pebbles) as well as occasional specimens of side scrapers, points and discoidal cores (Fig. 5: 3-5). Of the finds from the remaining sites little is known apart from the presence of at least six cordiform hand-axes at Wookey Hole[88] and two or three similar specimens from the Pont Newydd cave. With the exception of the Oldbury assemblage, none of the material recovered from these sites suggests more than very brief — possibly seasonal — occupation by very small human groups. Unfortunately, the faunal associations of the industries are too poorly documented to provide any reliable information on the economic activities of the Mousterian populations.

## Upper palaeolithic settlement

The classic work on the British upper palaeolithic is D.A. Garrod's *Upper Palaeolithic Age in Britain* published in 1926. Recently, the whole subject has been exhaustively reinvestigated by J.B. Campbell, who has drawn not only on the material obtained during the earlier excavations but also on the results of his own re-excavations at many of the most important sites. I am indebted to Dr Campbell for allowing me to incorporate the results of his important studies in advance of full publication.[89]

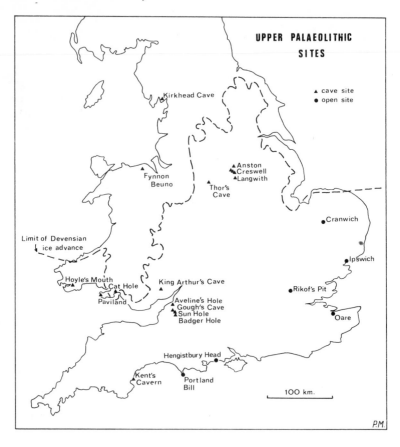

Figure 6. Upper palaeolithic sites in Britain.

It is now clear that there are two major episodes of upper palaeolithic occupation in Britain. The earlier phase of settlement appears to coincide with the Denekamp/Paudorf interstadial as defined by continental geologists, while the later phase corresponds with the late-glacial period when the extremely harsh conditions which characterised the 'full glacial' stages were beginning to ameliorate. These two episodes appear to be separated by an interval of around 10,000 - 15,000 years during which the most severe conditions of the last glaciation — with the maximum extension of the ice sheets — were attained.

*Early upper palaeolithic*

Well-documented traces of early upper palaeolithic industries are at present known from 12-15 sites in Britain.[90]
The best-known occurrences are recorded from Kent's Cavern
in Devonshire, Badger Hole and Soldier's Hole in Somerset,
Ffynnon Beuno in Flintshire, Paviland Cave in Glamorganshire and Robin Hood's Cave and Pinhole Cave (both in
Creswell Crags) in Derbyshire.[91] To these may be added a
number of more dubious occurrences at open air localities,
including the Forty-acres gravel pit in Gloucestershire,
Rikof's Pit in Hertfordshire[92] and Bramford Road, Ipswich,
in Suffolk.[93] The highly distinctive 'type-fossils' of these
industries are comparatively large (generally 10-20 cm. long)
leaf-shaped implements which are shaped by means of a
characteristically shallow, invasive form of retouch not dissimilar to the 'pressure-flaking' found on Solutrian implements (Fig. 7: 1-3). In a few instances this invasive retouch
covers the whole of both faces of the tool so that the result is
a totally bifacial implement; in most cases however the
retouching is confined to limited areas of one or both faces in
such a way as to achieve the desired shape without unnecessary expenditure of effort. Reconstructing the functions of
stone implements is notoriously difficult, but it is probably
safe to assume that these pieces represent missile heads
(probably spear heads) of some kind.

The remainder of the early upper palaeolithic tool-kit is
poorly known, principally owing to the fact that most of the
sites were excavated during the 19th century when the
importance of separating finds from different archaeological
horizons was not generally recognised. However, the careful
records kept during William Pengelly's excavations in Kent's
Cavern appear to indicate that the seven leaf-points from this
site were associated with at least 16 end scrapers, 3 nosed
scrapers, 12 miscellaneous retouched implements and 84
waste flakes;[94] the only trace of bone working from this
level of the site is provided by a single bone pin (Fig. 7: 5).
Of particular interest is the presence in this assemblage of one
piece identified by Campbell as a typical 'busked burin'. At
least one further very well-characterised example of this type
is known from the cave of Ffynnon Beuno in North Wales,
and at this site too the implement appears to have been

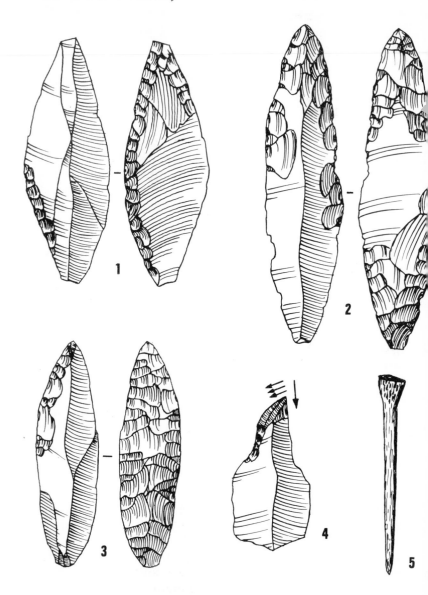

Figure 7. Early upper palaeolithic artefacts from Robin Hood's Cave, Creswell (1, 3); Ffynnon Beuno (2, 4); and Kent's Cavern (5). 1-3, bifacially-worked 'leaf-points'; 4, buskate burin; 5, bone pin. *After Garrod* (2/3)

associated with a bifacially-worked leaf-point (Fig. 7: 2,4).[95] Chronologically, the presence of these tools in the British early upper palaeolithic horizons is of considerable interest, since in western France the *burin busqué* type is bighly characteristic of a single narrowly-defined phase of the upper palaeolithic succession – namely the Aurignacian II stage. The latter episode has now been firmly dated by radiocarbon to around 30,000-27,000 bc.[96]

The chronological hint provided by the busked burins from Kent's Cavern and Ffynnon Beuno has been confirmed recently by two radiocarbon determinations of 26,770 and 26,210 bc obtained on samples of animal bone recovered from the early palaeolithic level at Kent's Cavern during Pengelly's excavations.[97] A further date is available for what appears to be an early upper palaeolithic horizon at Badger Hole in Somerset, but this merely provides a figure of more than 18,000 years.[98] All the evidence therefore points to a date for this initial episode of upper palaeolithic occupation in Britain very close to the time of the Denekamp/Paudorf interstadial as recorded at continental sites.

Much discussion has centred on the cultural affinities of these early upper palaeolithic industries. Early workers[99] were impressed by the presence of partially-retouched leaf-points in the earliest Solutrian levels in south-west France and assumed that the British industries were related to this 'Proto-Solutrian' phase. This view was endorsed by Garrod in 1926[100] and the term Proto-Solutrian has remained firmly attached to the British finds up to the present day. However, the dating evidence discussed above suggests strongly that the early upper palaeolithic industries in Britain are separated from the French Solutrian assemblages by a time-span in the region of 6,000 - 7,000 years; at the same time it has become apparent that the similarities between the British leaf-points and the Solutrian *pointes-à-face-plane* are not so close as was originally thought. The weight of the evidence now suggests that the British 'Proto-Solutrian' assemblages are in fact much more closely related to the *Blattspitzen* industries which characterise the earlier stages of the upper palaeolithic over large areas of central and eastern Europe. However, the possibility that the British industries may have contributed in some way to the origins of the French

Solutrian, as suggested by McBurney, should perhaps be kept in mind.[101]

In connection with the earlier phase of upper palaeolithic settlement brief reference should be made to the famous human skeleton discovered by Dean Buckland in the Paviland Cave (Glamorganshire) in 1823.[102] This was clearly an intentional burial (probably of a young man and not of a 'lady' as originally thought) which had been sprinkled liberally with powdered red ochre at the time of interment. The burial was associated with an interesting series of ivory ornaments for which convincing parallels are at present difficult to find.[103] Unfortunately, the records kept at the time of the original discovery are so inadequate that the stratigraphic relationships between the burial and the lithic industries recovered from the site are impossible to ascertain. However, a radiocarbon determination carried out on the actual bones of the skeleton has yielded a figure of 16,510 ± 340 bc.[104] If this date is reliable it means that the burial was interred during what appears to have been the coldest part of the last glaciation, and moreover at a time when at least the northern parts of Wales are thought to have been covered by an ice sheet. An alternative, and perhaps more economical, view would be to associate the burial with the collection of early upper palaeolithic artefacts known to have been found in the cave and to assume that the radiocarbon date is somewhat too young. On the basis of the existing data it is clearly impossible to reach a firm decision on this question.

*Later upper palaeolithic*
Evidence for the later episode of upper palaeolithic occupation in Britain is both more abundant and in general better documented than that relating to the earlier phase of settlement. In all, at least 25 sites have yielded clear evidence of later upper palaeolithic occupation, and in several of these there are indications that the occupation may have extended over a considerable period. The overall distribution of the sites however remains the same; as before, caves appear to have been strongly preferred for habitation and the richest sites are in Devon (Kent's Cavern), Somerset (Gough's Cave, Aveline's Hole, Soldier's Hole), Herefordshire (King Arthur's Cave), South Wales (Paviland Cave, Cat Hole, Hoyle's Mouth)

and Derbyshire (Langwith Cave and at least three separate sites at Creswell Crags).[105] Novel elements in the distributional pattern are provided by a number of decidedly impoverished sites in the Peak District of Derbyshire and Staffordshire (Dowel Cave, Fox Hole Cave, Thor's Cave), and by the recently excavated Kirkhead Cave in north Lancashire.[106] Evidence for open-air occupation is confined to a few scanty traces from sites in southern and eastern England — for example at Portland Bill in Dorset,[107] Hengistbury Head in Hampshire,[108] Oare in Kent[109] and Cranwich in Norfolk.[110]

The flint assemblages recovered from these sites convey for the most part a strong impression of homogeneity. The 'type fossils' of the industries consist of medium to large-sized blades which are blunted down the whole of one edge in such a way as to produce a characteristically angular form. Two sub-types can be distinguished within this general category of 'angle-backed blades'; in the case of the 'Creswell point' only a single angle appears on the blunted edge, whereas in the case of the 'Cheddar point' angles are worked at both ends of the implement to produce an elongated trapeze-like form (Fig. 8).[111] Other elements common to most if not all of the later upper palaeolithic assemblages include both curved and straight backed blades, steeply retouched awls, burins, and end scrapers manufactured on both flakes and blades.

Certain quantitative differences in the composition of the later upper palaeolithic assemblages have been documented by both Bohmers and Campbell. In 1957 Bohmers[112] proposed to divide the industries into distinct 'Creswellian' and 'Cheddarian' variants based respectively on the assemblages from Mother Grundy's Parlour in Creswell Crags and Gough's Cave in Cheddar Gorge. The Creswellian variant differed from the Cheddarian principally in possessing higher proportions of 'short' as opposed to 'long' end scrapers, and in the presence of small, basally-retouched 'penknife points' (Fig. 8: 7-8). Bohmers felt that the Creswellian and Cheddarian variants could be taken to represent two distinct 'cultures', and proceeded to identify representatives of the same cultures at a number of open-air sites in the Netherlands. However, Campbell has collected a substantial body of evidence which suggests that the assemblages from Gough's

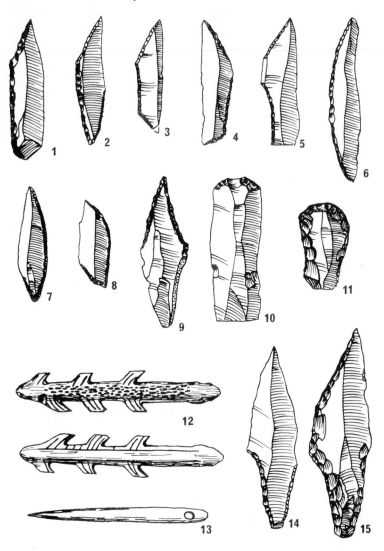

Figure 8. Later upper palaeolithic artefacts from Anston Cave (1), Mother Grundy's Parlour, Creswell (2-3, 5, 7-8, 10-11), Aveline's Hole (4, 6, 13), Gough's Cave (9), Church Hole, Creswell (13), Hengistbury Head (14) and Cranwich (15). 1-2, 'Creswell points'; 3-4, 'Cheddar points'; 5, shouldered point; 6, curved backed blade; 7-8, 'penknife points'; 9, awl; 10-11 end scrapers; 12, 'harpoon' head; 13, bone pin; 14-15, tanged points. *After Armstrong, Davies, Parry, Mace and Wymer (2/3)*

Cave and Mother Grundy's Parlour may represent simply two chronological stages in the development of a single industrial tradition. If the latter inference is correct, we might well adhere to Garrod's original suggestion in linking together all the industries characterised by the presence of angle-backed blades under the single term 'Creswellian'.[113]

When Garrod was writing in 1926 the closest parallels which she could find for the British Creswellian assemblages were provided by the 'Upper Aurignacian' (i.e. 'Gravettian') industries of south-west France.[114] Research undertaken over the past 40 years however has brought to light a whole series of industries distributed from northern France to Germany which show much closer resemblances to those from the British sites. Probably the closest overall parallels for the Creswellian assemblages are to be found in the 'Tjongerian' industries of Belgium and the Netherlands.[115] Certainly, examples of both Creswell and Cheddar points identical to those found in the British sites have been recorded − sometimes in substantial numbers − in many of the continental assemblages. From a chronological view-point it is therefore interesting to recall that the Tjongerian industries have been securely dated in at least ten sites to around the time of the Allerød interstadial.[116] At the same time, however, it may be significant that more sporadic elements in the Creswellian industries − for example, the typical *zinken* from Gough's Cave and the 'shouldered points' from the basal zone at Mother Grundy's Parlour − find their closest parallels in the Hamburgian assemblages of Germany and the Low Countries which appear to date largely if not entirely from the preceding Older Dryas phase (i.e. zone I) of the late-glacial. These well-documented affinities between the Creswellian and continental industries must of course be taken into account when the chronological position of the British sites is being assessed.

More wide-ranging connections between Britain and the continent are suggested by the artefacts of bone and antler which have been recovered from Creswellian levels. A small, biserially-barbed 'harpoon-head' found in close association with Creswellian flint-work at Aveline's Hole in Somerset is identical to specimens encountered in the latest Magdalenian levels ('Magdelenian VIb') in western France (Fig. 8: 12).[117]

A similar specimen, together with two simpler pieces barbed along a single edge, was recovered during the 19th-century excavations in the 'black band' horizon at Kent's Cavern.[118] The two perforated *batons* from Gough's Cave, the eyed sewing needles from the Church Hole at Creswell, Kent's Cavern and the Cathole Cave in south Wales, and the double-bevelled javelin head from the Pinhole Cave (Creswell) can also be paralleled closely in late Magdalenian contexts.[119] In assessing the significance of these parallels, however, it must be remembered that similar elements of Magdalenian-style bone-work have a relatively wide distribution over western and central Europe, extending from north-western Spain to Czechoslovakia.[120,121]

Unfortunately the available radiocarbon dates are not sufficient to provide a detailed chronological framework for the British industries. Perhaps the most instructive dates are those of 12,323 and 10,230 bc for the later upper palaeolithic levels at Kent's Cavern, which confirm that the earlier stages of this occupation extend back into zone I of the late-glacial period.[122] As we have seen, certain features of the archaeological evidence — notably the Hamburgian and Magdalenian elements referred to above — are fully in accord with this conclusion. The geological evidence for exceptionally mild climatic conditions towards the end of the Older Dryas phase makes it particularly easy to see why Britain should have been occupied at this time. A further date within the time-span of zone I has been obtained for the site of Sun Hole in Cheddar Gorge, but the associations of this date with the Creswellian artefacts from the site are less well established.[123] The only other radiocarbon determinations which relate unambiguously to later upper palaeolithic occupation levels are those for Robin Hood's Cave in Creswell Crags,[124] and the Anston Cave in south Yorkshire.[125] Of these the two dates for Robin Hood's Cave (8,440 and 8,640 bc) fall towards the end of the Younger Dryas phase (zone III) while the three dates for the Anston Cave (7,990, 7,900 and 7,800 bc) fall around the middle of the ensuing pre-Boreal stage (zone IV) of the postglacial period. Interpretation of these dates must however take into account the results of pollen analysis undertaken by J. Campbell which point rather strongly to the conclusion that the Creswellian horizons at both of these sites extend well back into the late-glacial period.[126] Taking into account all of the available evidence it would appear most likely that the majority of the later upper palaeolithic occupation horizons in Britain occupy a comparatively short span of time which coincides with the later part of the Older Dryas phase and the succeeding Allerød interstadial (i.e. late zone I plus zone II of the late-glacial). Nevertheless the possibility of a later survival in certain areas — conceivably until the beginning of the post-glacial era — should certainly be kept in mind.[127]

The faunal remains recovered from Creswellian levels help to substantiate the dating evidence discussed above and at the same time provide some insight into the economic activities of the human groups. The most abundant mammalian species encountered in the majority of Creswellian horizons for which reliable information is available (e.g. Gough's Cave, Kent's Cavern, Robin Hood's Cave and Mother Grundy's Parlour) appears to have been horse; at all of the sites, however, this was accompanied by a range of more specifically 'glacial' species including reindeer (recorded from at least ten sites), giant Irish deer (*Megaceros giganteus*), arctic fox, woolly rhinoceros and even mammoth. The faunas from Aveline's Hole and King Arthur's Cave differ from the above in showing a predominance of what is said to have been an exceptionally large form of red deer, but even at these sites such typically 'cold-loving' forms as reindeer and the cave pika (*Ochonta spelaea*) were clearly represented.[128] However, it would be unwise to conclude that the Creswellian communities subsisted entirely by the hunting of large animals; remains of hare are said to have been abundant in the Creswellian levels at both Gough's Cave[129] and Robin Hood's Cave,[130] and bones representing several species of birds have been recovered from almost all of the cave sites. The contributions of fish and plant foods to the diet can only be guessed at.[131] Perhaps the most difficult question to answer on the basis of the present evidence is whether the Creswellian sites were occupied exclusively during the summer months, in the manner of the Hamburgian and Ahrensburgian settlements on the continent, or whether they were inhabited on a more permanent, year-round basis.

To what extent the Creswellian assemblages constitute the

sole evidence for later upper palaeolithic occupation in Britain remains open to speculation. Suggestions of a quite different industrial tradition are provided by a series of discoveries of well characterised 'tanged points' reported from a number of open-air localities in southern Britain (Fig. 5: 14-15). The most fully investigated site is at Hengistbury Head in Hampshire, where according to Mace the tanged pieces were found in association with end scrapers, burins and a series of medium-sized backed blades.[132] More isolated discoveries of similar implements have been reported from Portland Bill in Dorset, Cranwich in Norfolk and Mildenhall in Suffolk.[133] Parallels for these pieces might be found in the Ahrensburgian industries of north Germany and the Netherlands (dated to zone III of the late-glacial)[134] or, perhaps more easily, in the Bromme industry of Denmark (dated to zone II).[135] In any event, it is significant that no trace whatever of true tanged points has so far been identified among the large collections of flint work recovered from later upper palaeolithic horizons in the British cave sites.[136] However, until these tanged forms have been obtained from securely datable contexts it would perhaps be unwise to accept them without reservation as evidence of late-glacial occupation.

It remains to mention two further discoveries from open-air localities, both of which occurred in association with deposits which can be dated on the basis of pollen analysis to around the time of the Allerød interstadial. At Flixton Carr in east Yorkshire a single shouldered point of microlithic proportions was found a depth of one and a half metres below the surface in association with bones representing at least three wild horses. More recently, two spear heads of antler, each barbed along a single edge, have been found lying in contact with the bones of a complete skeleton of an elk (*Alces alces*) at Poulton-le-Fylde in west Lancashire. Both of these discoveries presumably represent casual losses by late-glacial groups in the course of hunting expeditions. The finds help to fill out the picture of occupation in Britain during the Allerød phase, but their relationships with the material recovered from the cave sites are difficult at present to assess.

## The mesolithic period: early postglacial environments

Although the improvement in climate which brought the last glaciation to an end probably commenced as early as 14,000 BC the effects of this climatic amelioration continued for a long time into the postglacial (or 'Flandrian') period. Within the first 5,000 years or so of the postglacial, ice sheets are known to have retreated from the north-western parts of Scotland to something approaching their present.limits, and correspondingly large-scale changes are apparent in many other aspects of the natural environment. It is against this background of changing environmental conditions that the mesolithic occupation of Britain must be seen.[139]

Precisely how temperature conditions varied throughout the postglacial period is at present subject to some debate amongst Quaternary specialists; but from the viewpoint of the contemporary human groups the secondary effects of these changes — especially on vegetation and fauna — were probably of much greater importance than the climatic changes themselves. In any event it is now clear that the major modifications in the environment occurred during the earlier part of the mesolithic period between *c.* 8,300 and 5,000 bc. The critical feature which marked the transition from the late-glacial to the postglacial periods in northern Europe was of course the replacement of open tundra-like vegetation by forests at the time of the zone III-IV boundary. The changes which subsequently occurred in the composition of the postglacial forests, clearly documented by pollen analysis, are summarised in Table 3.[140] A rapid and pronounced rise in temperature at the end of the Younger Dryas episode led to the establishment of full birch forests over the whole of north-western Europe during the pre-Boreal phase; it is likely that relatively large areas of open vegetation would have persisted at the beginning of this period but these would rapidly have diminished as the forest cover thickened. The transition from the pre-Boreal to the Boreal periods was marked by a substantial increase in the frequency of pine, and it is possible that for a short period towards the beginning of the Boreal large areas of Britain were covered by true coniferous forests. Towards the middle of the Boreal phase however pine was overtaken by hazel as the dominant

Figure 9. Mesolithic sites in Britain.

tree species; the frequencies in which hazel has been encountered in certain late Boreal pollen diagrams (up to 90 per cent of the total tree pollen) has sometimes been taken to suggest the possibility of some form of human interference in the vegetation cover.[141] To what extent the appearance of such species as oak, elm and lime towards the end of the

Boreal period reflects a further increase in temperature at this time seems open to debate. However there appears to be widespread agreement that the ensuing Atlantic phase represents a period when climatic conditions over the whole of northern Europe were appreciably warmer than at the present day — probably by as much as 2½°C. This period, known as the 'climatic optimum', saw the establishment of true deciduous forests throughout Britain, in which oak, elm, alder and hazel were the dominant species. There are nevertheless certain indications that the climate may have been somewhat wetter than that experienced during the Boreal phase, possibly as a consequence of Britain becoming an island around this time. The end of the Atlantic period is marked in most pollen diagrams by a sharp fall in the frequency of elm pollen, accompanied in many cases by the

| *Approximate Dates bc* | *Zones* | *Periods* | *Characteristic Vegetation* | |
|---|---|---|---|---|
| | VIII | Sub-Atlantic | Alder, Oak, Birch | |
| 500 | | | | |
| | VIIb | Sub-Boreal | Alder, Oak, Lime 'Elm decline' | |
| 3,000 | | | | |
| | VIIa | Atlantic | Alder, Oak, Elm, Lime ('Mixed Oak forest') | |
| 5,500 | | | | |
| | VI | Later Boreal | Hazel, Pine | c. Oak, Elm, Lime b. Oak, Elm a. Elm, Hazel |
| 7,000 | | | | |
| | V | Early Boreal | Hazel, Birch, Pine | |
| 7,600 | | | | |
| | IV | Pre-Boreal | Birch, Pine forest | |
| 8,300 | | | | |
| | III | Younger Dryas | Park tundra | |
| 8,800 | | | | |
| | II | Allerød Interstadial | Birch with Park tundra | |
| 10,000 | | | | |
| | I | Older Dryas | Park tundra | |
| 12,000 | | | | |

Table 3   Late-glacial and postglacial vegetational zones in southern Britain, based on pollen analysis and radiocarbon dating. *After West, 1968, 282-3*

appearance of certain weeds characteristic of cultivated areas. By common consent, both of these features are now attributed to the agricultural activities of neolithic man.[142]

Probably of more immediate concern to the human communities were the changes in animal populations at the transition from the glacial to the postglacial periods. Open country forms such as horse, reindeer, bison and mammoth seem to have disappeared with remarkable abruptness at the end of the late-glacial period to be replaced by typically woodland species such as red deer, roe deer, elk, wild oxen ('aurochs') and wild boar.[143] Two aspects of these faunal changes must have been of crucial importance to the contemporary human societies; on the one hand the overall density of animal populations (the 'biomass') in forested areas is normally much less than that encountered in open tundra and grassland environments; and on the other hand forest species such as red deer and wild boar tend to be less gregarious in their habits than open country forms like reindeer and horse. In other words mesolithic communities had to adapt themselves not only to a substantially reduced food supply but also to the pursuit of animals whose behaviour was significantly different from that of the pre-existing glacial species.

Lastly, as a result of the melting of large quantities of ice, world-wide sea levels are known to have risen by at least 50 metres during the earlier stages of the postglacial era.[144] During the pre-Boreal period Britain was still connected to the continent by a corridor of dry land several hundred miles wide, allowing easy access to both animal and human populations. The precise date of the insulation has still to be established by geologists, but most authorities would place this event towards the end of the Boreal period. It is important to remember that the dramatic rise in sea level which occurred during the Boreal and early Atlantic periods had the effect not only of separating Britain from the continent but also of substantially reducing the areas of dry land available for occupation. It is equally important to remember that the contemporary coastlines of the earlier mesolithic period — together with any traces of coastal occupation — are now submerged beneath the sea.

Over the northern parts of Britain, in the areas which had

been covered by the glaciers, the effects of this 'eustatic' rise in sea level were compensated for to a large extent by the 'isostatic' recoil of the land itself as the weight of the ice sheets was removed. In Scotland and north-western England the continuation of this isostatic uplift after the rise in sea level was completed (around 3,500 bc) resulted in the later mesolithic coastlines emerging as a prominent raised beach feature at heights of up to 12 metres above present sea level.[145] Settlements associated with this so-called 'main postglacial strandline' provide virtually the only evidence at present available for the exploitation of coastal resources during the mesolithic period in Britain.

*Earlier mesolithic settlement*
The present chronological framework of the British mesolithic must be constructed on the basis of 23 sites for which radiocarbon dates are available, together with a further 10-15 sites which have been dated with varying degrees of accuracy by means of pollen analysis.[146] On the basis of this rather limited body of evidence it would appear that the typological development of mesolithic industries can be divided into two principal stages. On present evidence the major typological changes which mark the transition from the 'earlier' to the 'later' mesolithic would seem to have occurred towards the middle of the Boreal climatic phase, probably around 6,500 bc. In environmental terms this corresponds with the point at which the major components of the 'mixed oak forest' (notably oak and elm) were beginning to form a conspicuous element in the British vegetation.

The earlier stages of the British mesolithic are represented most clearly at the sites of Star Carr[147] and Flixton[148] in east Yorkshire, Broxbourne in Hertfordshire,[149] Sandstone in Buckinghamshire,[150] Thatcham[151] and Greenham Dairy Farm[152] in Berkshire, and Iping Common[153] in Sussex. The earliest dated sites are those of Star Carr and Thatcham. Five radiocarbon dates for sites I-V at Thatcham range from 8,415 to 7,530 bc, while Star Carr is dated by two determinations of 7,607 and 7,538 bc; both sites can be shown by pollen analysis to have been occupied during the pre-Boreal period. Flixton is assigned on the basis of pollen evidence to around the time of the pre-Boreal/Boreal transition, which in

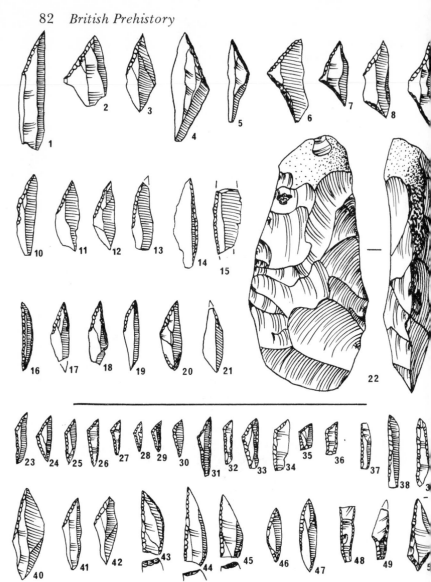

Figure 10. Above: earlier mesolithic artefacts from Star Carr (1-9), Broxbourne (10-21) and Thatcham (22). Below: later mesolithic tools from Farnham (23-50). 1-5, 10-13, 40-42, simple obliquely blunted points; 17-20, Obliquely blunted points with opposed retouch at tip; 6-7, isosceles triangles; 8-9, trapezes; 14-16, 37-39, rod-like forms; 23-31, scalene triangles; 32-34, 'sub triangles'; 35-36, micro-trapezoids; 43-45, hollow based 'Horsham' points; 46-47, crescent; 48-49, 'ultra-narrow tranchets'; 50, tanged form; 22, transversely-shaped flint axe. *After Clark and Wymer* (2/3)

northern England is dated at around 7,500 bc. Greenham Dairy Farm has a single radiocarbon date of 6,829 bc. The remaining sites of Broxbourne, Sandstone and Iping Common cannot be precisely dated but can be shown by pollen evidence to have been occupied no later than the end of the Boreal period.

The flint industries from these six sites differ in certain details but nevertheless share many basic elements in common. Carefully-shaped 'microliths' play a prominent role in all of the industries, and for the most part these are of comparatively large, simple forms (Fig. 10: 1-21). The most abundant microlithic type at all of the sites is the 'obliquely blunted point', a form which is sometimes modified by a short length of 'opposed' retouch towards the tip. These types are generally accompanied by large triangular microliths (generally of 'isosceles' rather than 'scalene' form) and by elongated points blunted down the whole of one edge. The microliths from Star Carr and Flixton differ from those found on the southern sites in showing an apparent absence of obliquely blunted points with opposed retouch at the tip and in the presence of substantial numbers of broad trapeze-like forms. In functional terms the microliths from all these sites can probably be divided into the barbs (obliquely blunted points) and tips (triangle, trapeze and rod-like forms) of wooden arrows.[154]

Larger implements encountered in these assemblages include end-scrapers manufactured on both flakes and blades, variable proportions of burins, awls, and occasional specimens of finely-denticulated saws. Of particular significance is the occurrence at five out of the six sites of heavy flint axes which were sharpened (and resharpened) by means of blows struck transversely to the long axis of the implement (Fig. 10: 22); even when the axes themselves are not represented (as at Iping Common) the use of these tools may often be inferred from the presence of the distinctive resharpening flakes. The appearance of these 'tranchet'-type axes in the early mesolithic industries of north-western Europe is generally seen as a direct response to the spread of forests which characterised the transition from the glacial to the postglacial periods.[155]

The obvious affinities between these early mesolithic

industries in Britain and the Maglemosian industries of Denmark, north Germany and south Sweden were first pointed out by Peake and Crawford in 1922.[156] During the pre-Boreal and Boreal periods Britain is in fact known to have been connected to these areas by large stretches of dry land, and it is perhaps to be expected that colonists should have reached eastern England from these sources during the initial stages of the postglacial era. Accordingly, the terms 'Maglemosian' and 'Proto-Maglemosian' have frequently been attached to the British industries.

Until comparatively recently it was believed that these assemblages of Maglemosian affinities were confined to the lowlying areas of southern and eastern England.[157] Research undertaken over the past 15 years however has shown that such industries are in fact much more widely distributed over both the lowland and upland areas of Britain. In 1960 Wainwright pointed out that the assemblages from Shapwick and Middlezoy in Somerset and Dozmare Pool in Cornwall are almost identical to those from Broxbourne and Thatcham.[158] Soon afterwards very similar industries were identified at a number of sites in the southern Pennines (most notably Deepcar) at heights of up to 450 metres above sea level.[159] The only conspicuous difference between these industries and those from the low-lying sites in south-east England lies in the marked scarcity of axes at the upland sites, but this feature may be explicable largely by reference to environmental differences between the upland and lowland habitats.[160] Clark[161] has recently put forward the interesting suggestion that both the upland and lowland sites may in fact have been occupied by essentially the same social groups in the course of regular seasonal movements based on the migrations of red deer.

To what extent similar industries can be identified in Wales and Scotland is a more problematic issue. The sites of Nab Head in Pembrokeshire and Aberystwyth in Cardiganshire have produced industries dominated by relatively large, simple microlithic forms and at the former site these were associated with three transversely-sharpened flint axes.[162] However, the microlithic forms in these assemblages are by no means identical to those found further to the east and the age of the sites is completely unknown. In Scotland similar industries have been reported from Morton in Fifeshire[163] and Lussa Bay on the island of Jura in the Inner Hebrides.[164] Radiocarbon determinations for the former site fall mainly in the 5th millennium bc but there are strong indications that the initial occupation on the site extends back to at least 6,000 bc. At Lussa Bay the industry occurs in a derived condition and is believed to date from a phase of marine transgression prior to the formation of the main postglacial raised beach in western Scotland; if so this would probably imply a minimum age for the assemblage of around 5,500 bc. On the basis of these occurrences therefore it may well be that human groups closely related to the early mesolithic communities of southern Britain reached parts of Scotland before the end of the Boreal period.

The types of bone and antler implements in use during the earlier part of the British mesolithic are known exclusively from the excavated discoveries at Star Carr and Thatcham, and from a series of isolated finds of antler and bone artefacts mostly recovered in the course of commercial quarrying and river-dredging operations. The abundant and well-preserved discoveries at Star Carr include a large number of antler spear heads barbed along a single edge (Fig. 11: 1-2) as well as 'mattock heads' manufactured from elk antler, skin-scraping tools made from the split metapodial bones of wild oxen, bone awls or pins, and a series of red deer antler 'frontlets' which may have served either as hunting disguises or as head-dresses in some ceremonial activity.[165] Detailed studies of the waste products of bone and antler working at Star Carr threw interesting light on the 'groove and splinter' technique by which suitable blanks for manufacturing barbed spear points were obtained from red deer antlers; this technique involved cutting parallel, V-shaped grooves along the length of the antler with a flint burin and prising out the intervening splinter. The bone and antler artefacts recovered from Thatcham are more limited than those from Star Carr and of rather different character.[166] The most interesting pieces are three missile-heads of bone, sharply pointed at one or both extremities, but showing no trace of barbs (Fig. 11:5). These were accompanied by two large implements of red deer antler which may have functioned as crude chisels or wedges.

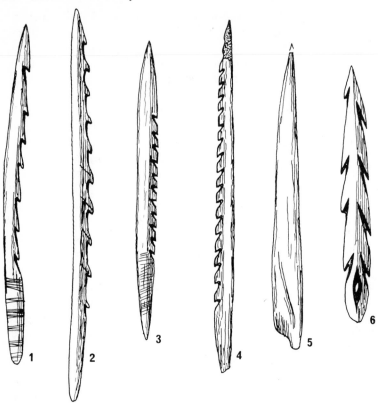

Figure 11. Projectile heads of bone and antler from British mesolithic
    sites; 1-2, Star Carr; 3, Hornsea; 4, Brandesburton; 5, Thatcham; 6,
    MacArthur's Cave (Oban). *After Clark, Bartlett, Wymer and
    Anderson* (approx. 1/2)

Barbed spear heads similar to those found at Star Carr have
been recovered as stray finds from at least seven separate
localities in eastern England (Fig. 11: 3-4); these include 13
specimens from the Holderness area of east Yorkshire (one
from Skipsea, two from Hornsea and ten from the neighbourhood of Brandesburton), a single specimen from Royston in
Hertfordshire and two specimens from the bed of the river
Thames at Battersea and Wandsworth. To these finds should
be added the famous specimen dredged up by a trawler from
the bed of the North Sea, at a point 25 miles off the Norfolk

coast, in 1931.[167] Unfortunately, none of these stray finds can be accurately dated, but there are strong circumstantial grounds for attributing the two specimens from Skipsea and the bed of the North Sea to some point within the Boreal period. The technique of manufacture of these pieces differs in certain respects from that of the Star Carr find — notably in the 'criss-cross' technique of shaping the barbs — and has been taken by Clark to represent a somewhat later stage in the development of the 'Maglemosian' tradition in eastern England.[168]

The exceptional conditions of preservation at Star Carr even led to the survival of some wooden objects. One piece is evidently a fragment of a wooden paddle; it resembles specimens recovered from early postglacial sites on the continent and presumably allows one to infer the use of boats on the site. Of equal interest are the tightly-wound rolls of birch bark encountered at several points in the cultural level; these may represent either supplies of easily combustible fuel (possible for use as tapers) or alternatively sources of raw material for the production of birch bark resin. (The latter material is known to have been used, among other things, for attaching microliths to wooden arrow shafts.)[169] These discoveries provide a rare glimpse into what must have been major aspects of the technology of mesolithic groups in Britain.

### Later mesolithic settlement

Towards the middle of the Boreal period there are indications of important changes in the form of British mesolithic industries. These changes are reflected most clearly in the appearance of new forms of microliths which are both smaller than the earlier 'broad blade' types and of more varied shapes. Probably the most characteristic and widespread of these new microlithic shapes is the small scalene triangle, but in rich assemblages this is usually accompanied by a wide range of other 'geometric' forms such as narrow 'rods' (blunted along one or both edges), 'trapezoids' (blunted on three edges), 'crescents' and a curious 'ultra-narrow' form of trapeze (Fig. 10: 23-50). It is probably fair to assume that the appearance of these new shapes of microliths reflects the introduction of new varieties of missile heads, but in the absence of any direct evidence for the functions of the different microlithic forms one can only speculate on this point.

The precise date of the appearance of these new microlithic types in Britain remains to be established. The earliest radiocarbon date for an assemblage comprising these forms is that of 6,623 bc for the site of Broomhead Moor 5 in the southern Pennines. A somewhat later date of 6,150 bc comes from the site of Ickornshaw Moor in the central Pennines.[170] The assemblages from both these sites comprise a range of small scalene triangles and rod-like forms manufactured from locally-obtained chert. On the evidence from these two sites it would seem that the 'geometric' pattern of microlith manufacture was established in at least certain areas of Britain appreciably before the end of the 7th millennium bc.

The microlithic forms which characterise the later mesolithic industries have a wide distribution over large areas of northern and western Europe. In 1955 Clark drew attention to certain similarities between the British assemblages and those from the classic 'Sauveterrian' sites of Sauveterre-la-Lémance in south-west France,[171] but equally close parallels for the British industries could be found in other areas further to the north and east (notably Belgium and Holland) which retained a direct land connection with Britain until well into the Boreal period. How far these parallels can be taken to imply an actual movement of new human groups into Britain at this time of course remains a debatable issue; the alternative view is that the similarities between the British and continental industries reflect merely the adoption of similar methods for the construction of barbed projectile heads, possibly stimulated by the continuing changes in ecological and environmental conditions. Hence the application of any specific cultural label to the later mesolithic industries of Britain is perhaps best avoided for the time being.

Industries of essentially geometric type evidently continued to be manufactured throughout the later part of the mesolithic period. Dates which range from the 6th to the 4th millennium bc have been obtained for geometric industries from Peacock's Farm in Cambridgeshire (5,650 bc),[172] Cherhill in Wiltshire (5,280 bc),[173] Culver Well in Dorset

(5,200 bc),[174] Westward Ho! in Devon (4,635 bc),[175] Thorpe Common in Yorkshire (4,483, 3,730 bc),[176] Barsalloch in Wigtownshire (4,050 bc),[177] High Rocks in Kent (3,780, 3,710 bc),[178] Dunford Bridge in Yorkshire (3,430 bc)[179] and Wawcott site I in Berkshire (3,310 bc).[180] In addition at least four more sites may be referred to which, although lacking radiocarbon dates, have been assigned on the basis of pollen analysis to some point within the Atlantic (zone VIIa) vegetational phase (Glaisdale Moor and White Gill on the north Yorkshire Moors, Hard Hill in the Pennines and Lealt Bay on the Island of Jura).[181] Perhaps the most interesting question in this connection concerns the extent of the chronological overlap between the latest mesolithic and earliest neolithic communities in Britain. Of particular relevance to this issue are the two radiocarbon dates of 2,670 and 2,250 bc obtained in association with a typical geometric microlithic assemblage (dominated by small scalene triangles and rods) recently excavated by Mercer at the site of Lussa River on the Island of Jura in the Inner Hebrides.[182] These dates are later by a factor of at least 600-700 years than those for the earliest neolithic settlements in southern Britain. Hardly less interesting are the small copies of late neolithic barbed and tanged arrowheads, executed in characteristic microlithic technique, found in apparent association with mesolithic industries at Shewalton Moor in Ayrshire, Risby Warren in Lincolnshire and at a number of sites in the Tweed valley.[183] On the basis of these occurrences we must clearly allow for the possibility that groups practising an essentially mesolithic technology – and presumably economy – persisted for a considerable period alongside the earliest farming communities in certain areas of Britain.

Although linked by the presence of small geometric microliths the later mesolithic industries nevertheless exhibit considerable diversity. A basic dichotomy can be recognised between the assemblages in which the microliths consist *exclusively* of geometric forms and those in which the latter types are accompanied by the larger, non-geometric types which characterise the earlier stages of the mesolithic. Industries of 'pure' geometric type are particularly well represented over the northern half of Britain. The well known 'narrow blade' industries of the Pennines and north-east Yorkshire moors fall clearly into this category,[184] and the same appears to be true of at least some of the assemblages from the Durham coast[185] and Scotland.[186] South of these areas comparable industries are less widespread but appear to be represented at Oakhanger site VIII in Hampshire[187] and (less certainly) at the coastal site of Culver Well on the Isle of Portland in Dorset.[188] It should perhaps be noted that the very large assemblages recovered from some of these sites rule out the possibility that the absence of large microlithic forms is due simply to sampling errors; hence an explanation for this pattern must be found in either cultural or functional terms.[189]

Assemblages in which geometric microliths are associated with larger non-geometric forms are distributed mostly over southern and eastern Britain.[190] Well-documented industries of this type include those from Farnham[191] and Selmeston[192] in Surrey, Downton in Wiltshire,[193] Peacock's Farm in Cambridgeshire[194] and Sheffield's Hill in Lincolnshire.[195] Further to the north and west similar industries have been recorded from King Arthur's Cave in Herefordshire,[196] Prestatyn in Flintshire[197] and Glen Wyllan on the Isle of Man.[198] Within this broad 'geometric plus non-geometric' grouping one rather clear sub-grouping appears to be defined by the occurrence of a distinctive form of 'hollow-based' microlith to which the name 'Horsham point' has been given. Assemblages characterised by this type are confined largely to the Greensand areas of Kent, Surrey and Sussex and include the industries from the famous 'pit-dwelling' sites of Selmeston, Farnham and Abinger Common (Fig. 10: 23-50). In 1939 Clark suggested that these assemblages were sufficiently distinctive to warrant their isolation as a discrete 'Horsham culture',[199] although it seems doubtful whether this view should be maintained at the present day. The occurrence of hollow-based microliths closely resembling the Horsham point at a number of sites on the Isle of Man provides one of the more intriguing features of the British mesolithic.[200]

The persistence of non-geometric microliths in the assemblages discussed above clearly hints at a strong element of continuity between the earlier and later stages of the mesolithic in southern Britain. This impression is considerably strengthened by the widespread occurrence in the same industries of transversely-sharpened flint axes identical to those encountered in the earlier assemblages of Boreal and pre-Boreal age. The distribution of these axes was at one time thought to be confined to the Horsham-type industries to the south of the Thames, but more recent discoveries suggest that they are in fact more widely distributed over southern and eastern England. The marked scarcity of similar axes over northern and western areas of Britain seems difficult to account for in purely environmental terms and remains to be satisfactorily explained.

Perhaps the most enigmatic aspect of later mesolithic occupation in Britain is represented by a series of shell midden settlements along the western coast of Scotland. These sites are generally referred to as 'Obanian' after the original discoveries at Oban in Argyllshire; but the most fully documented sites are on the islands of Oronsay in the Inner Hebrides and Risga in Loch Sunart.[201] The shell middens cluster around the level of the 'main postglacial strandline' in western Scotland, and evidently date from some time around, or shortly after, the maximum sea-level stand which gave rise to this feature. The relatively late dating suggested by this position has been confirmed recently by a series of six radiocarbon dates for the sites of Cnoc Sligeach and Caisteal-nan-Gillean II on Oronsay, all of which fall within the range 3,065-3,900 bc.[202] Owing to the strongly alkaline environment provided by the shell middens, artefacts of bone and antler are extremely well preserved in these sites. The most distinctive forms comprise a series of flattened 'harpoon-heads', sharply barbed along both edges and (in at least one instance) perforated towards the base (Fig. 11: 6). With these are associated a number of broad, chisel-like objects made of red deer antler, a variety of bone awls and pins and large quantities of finger-shaped objects, roughly bevelled at one or both ends, to which the term 'limpet scoop' has generally been applied.[203] A rarer type is represented by two perforated 'mattock heads' of red·deer antler from the sites of Risga and Cnoc Sligeach. In contrast to the wealth of the bone and antler artefacts, the flint industries recovered from the Obanian middens are exceptionally impoverished. The only definitely retouched forms so far recorded include a number of crudely worked scrapers and large quantities of heavily 'scaled' pieces (*lames ecaillés*). Clearly, the whole of the Obanian artefact assemblage represents a highly specialised tool-kit adapted to the intensive exploitation of coastal economic resources. But the relationships between the human groups who occupied the shell middens and those who manufactured the typical microlithic industries represented abundantly at other sites in western Scotland are extremely difficult to assess.

Bone and antler implements similar to those found in the Obanian middens would appear to have a fairly wide distribution over the northern parts of Britain. Double-barbed harpoon-heads of typical Obanian form have been recovered as stray finds from Cumstoun in Kirkcudbrightshire, Shewalton in Ayrshire[204] and even as far afield as Whitburn on the Durham coast.[205] Perforated mattock-heads of red deer antler similar to the specimens from Risga and Cnoc Sligeach have been found in association with the skeletons of stranded whales at several points within the 'Carse Clay' deposits of the Firth of Forth;[206] on geological grounds these discoveries must be of broadly similar age to the Obanian sites. And finally, recent excavations of a shell midden deposit at Morton Tayport in Fifeshire (radiocarbon dated to around 4,400–4,200 bc) have produced a series of bone artefacts which appear to belong to the 'limpet scoop' category.[207] It is worth recalling that the objects listed above constitute virtually the only evidence at present available for the manufacture of bone and antler implements during the second half of the mesolithic period in Britain.

*DATE LIST: Radiocarbon dates for the palaeolithic and mesolithic*

## 1. PALAEOLITHIC DATES

| Site | Feature | Lab. No. | Radiocarbon date bc (5568 half-life) | Calibrated date BC (approx.) |
|---|---|---|---|---|
| Kent's Cavern | Early upper palaeolithic 'leaf-point' level in Great Chamber (bone collagen) | GrN 6201 | 26,210 ± 435 | |
| | Early upper palaeolithic 'leaf-point' level in Gallery (bone collagen) | GrN 6202 | 26,770 ± 450 | |
| | Later upper palaeolithic 'black band' level in Vestibule: associated with uniserial 'harpoon' (bone collagen) | GrN 6203 | 12,325 ± 120 | |
| | Later upper palaeolithic level in Vestibule; associated with biserial 'harpoon' (bone collagen) | GrN 6204 | 10,230 ± 100 | |
| Paviland Cave | Human burial ('Red Lady'); archaeological associations uncertain (bone collagen) | BM 374 | 16,510 ± 340 | |
| Badger Hole | Early upper palaeolithic level, with 'leaf-point' (burnt bone fragments) | BM 497 | >16,050 | |
| Sun Hole | Apparently from later upper palaeolithic 'Creswellian' level (bone collagen) | BM 524 | 10,428 ± 150 | |
| Robin Hood's Cave | Later upper palaeolithic 'Creswellian' level (bone collagen) | BM 603 | 8,440 ± 90 | |

## 1. PALAEOLITHIC DATES (continued)

| Site | Feature | Lab. No. | Radiocarbon date bc (5568 half-life) | Calibrated date BC (approx.) |
|------|---------|----------|--------------------------------------|------------------------------|
| | Later upper palaeolithic 'Creswellian' level (bone collagen) | BM 604 | 8,640 ± 90 | |
| Anston Cave | Later upper palaeolithic 'Creswellian' level (bone collagen) | BM 439 | 7,900 ± 115 | |
| | Later upper palaeolithic 'Creswellian' level (bone collagen) | BM 440A | 7,990 ± 115 | |
| | Probably from same level as BM 439 and 440A (antler collagen) | BM 440B | 7,800 ± 110 | |

## 2. MESOLITHIC DATES

| | | | | |
|------|---------|----------|--------------------------------------|------------------------------|
| Thatcham | Site III, second hearth; associated with 'Maglemosian' industry (charcoal) | Q 659 | 8,415 ± 170 | |
| | Site III, hearth; 'Maglemosian' industry (charcoal) | Q 658 | 8,080 ± 170 | |
| | Site V, lowest horizon with artefacts; 'Maglemosian' industry (wood) | Q 651 | 7,890 ± 160 | |
| | Site V, from level with birch-bark roll; 'Maglemosian' industry (wood) | Q677 | 7,830 ± 200 | |

| Site | Description | Lab no. | Date |
|---|---|---|---|
| | Site V, from same level as Q 677 (wood) | Q 650 | 7,720 ± 160 |
| | Site V, from 'within occupation sequence'; 'Maglemosian' industry (wood) | Q 652 | 7,530 ± 160 |
| | Site II, layer 2; 'Maglemosian' industry (?contaminated) (charcoal) | BM 65 | 6,140 ± 180 |
| Star Carr | Wooden platform associated with 'Maglemosian' industry (wood) | C 353 | 7,538 ± 350 |
| | Wooden platform; 'Maglemosian' industry (wood) | Q 14 | 7,607 ± 210 |
| Greenham Dairy Farm | Red deer bone associated with 'Maglemosian' industry (bone collagen) | Q 973 | 6,829 ± 110 |
| West Hartlepool | Outer layer of antler associated with undiagnostic mesolithic industry | BM 81 | 6,730 ± 180 |
| | Same antler, intermediate zone | BM 80 | 6,750 ± 180 |
| | Same antler, spongy central zone | BM 90 | 6,150 ± 180 |
| | Central zone of same antler with further pre-treatment | BM 83 | 6,160 ± 180 |
| Broomhead Moor Site 5 | Charcoal from level with geometric microliths | Q 800 | 6,623 ± 110 |
| Stump Cross | Organic level associated with undiagnostic mesolithic artefacts (charcoal) | Q 141 | 6,500 ± 310 |

## 2. MESOLITHIC DATES *(continued)*

| Site | Feature | Lab. No. | Radiocarbon date bc (5568 half-life) | Calibrated date BC (approx.) |
|---|---|---|---|---|
| Ickornshaw | Burnt hazelnut shells associated with geometric microliths | Q 707 | 6,150 ± 150 | |
| Morton | Site A, T46 occupation; associated with non-geometric microlithic industry (charcoal) | NZ 1191 | 6,100 ± 255 | |
| | Site A, T43/44/46 occupation; non-geometric industry (composite sample, charcoal) | NZ 1302 | 5,380 ± 200 | |
| | Site A, T47/55/56 occupation; non-geometric industry (composite sample, charcoal) | NZ 1192 | 4,840 ± 150 | |
| | Site A, T53 hearth; non-geometric industry (charcoal) | NZ 1193 | 4,450 ± 125 | |
| | Site A, T53 hearth; non-geometric industry (charcoal) | Q 989 | 4,500 ± 80 | |
| | Site A, T43/44 occupation; non-geometric industry (composite sample, charcoal) | Q 948 | 4,785 ± 180 | |
| | Site A, stake in T42 occupation; non-geometric industry (charcoal) | GaK 2404 | 4,350 ± 150 | 5,300 |
| | Site B, lower midden deposit; undiagnostic mesolithic industry (charcoal) | Q 981 | 4,432 ± 120 | |

| Site | Description | Lab no. | Date | |
|---|---|---|---|---|
| | Site B, lower midden deposit (charcoal) | Q 988 | 4,197 ± 90 | 5,050 |
| | Site B, upper midden deposit; undiagnostic mesolithic industry (charcoal) | Q 928 | 4,165 ± 110 | 5,000 |
| Peaock's Farm | Peat from approximately same level as geometric industry | Q 587 | 5,650 ± 150 | |
| Cherhill | Base of tufa deposit overlying level with geometric microliths (bone collagen) | BM 447 | 5,280 ± 140 | |
| Culver Well | Basal portion of shell-midden; associated with Geometric microliths (charcoal) | BM 473 | 5,200 ± 135 | |
| Westward Ho! | Base of peat deposit overlying shell-midden with Geometric microliths (peat) | Q 672 | 4,635 ± 130 | |
| Thorpe Common | Hearth associated with geometric microliths (charcoal) | Q 1116 | 4,483 ± 115 | |
| | Red deer bone from layer overlying Q 1116; associated with geometric microliths (bone collagen) | Q 1118 | 3,730 ± 150 | 4,520 |
| Blashenwell | Tufa deposit containing undiagnostic mesolithic industry (bone collagen) | BM 89 | 4,500 ± 150 | |
| Oakhanger | Site VII, phase 2; burnt hazelnut shells associated with non-geometric microlithic industry | F 67 | 4,350 ± 110 | 5,300 |
| | Same level as F 67 (charcoal) | F 68 | 4,430 ± 115 | |

## 2. MESOLITHIC DATES *(continued)*

| Site | Feature | Lab. No. | Radiocarbon date bc (5568 half-life) | Calibrated date BC (approx.) |
|---|---|---|---|---|
| Barsalloch | Hearth in scooped dwelling associated with geometric microliths (charcoal) | GaK 1601 | 4,050 ± 110 | 4,900 |
| Freshwater West | Peat associated with undiagnostic mesolithic industry | Q 530 | 4,010 ± 120 | 4,850 |
| High Rocks | Site F, layer 2, apparently associated with geometric microliths (charcoal) | BM 40 | 3,710 ± 150 | 4,470 |
| | Site F, layer 2, apparently associated with geometric microliths (charcoal) | BM 91 | 3,780 ± 150 | 4,550 |
| Caisteal-nan-Gillean II | Basal portion of shell-midden on Island of Oronsay (charcoal) | Birm 347 | 3,500 ± 140 | 4,350 |
| | Same level as Birm 347: 'inner fraction' of limpet shells (probably too old owing to hard water error) | Birm 348 | 3,900 ± 310 | 4,800 |
| | Upper portion of same shell-midden (charcoal) | Birm 346 | 3,200 ± 380 | 3,970/4,210 |
| Cnoc Sligeach | 'Obanian' shell midden on Island of Oronsay (shell) | GX 1903 | 3,065 ± 210 | 3,750/4,160 |
| | 'Obanian' shell midden (bone) | GX 1904 | 3,805 ± 180 | 4,580 |
| Wawcott Farm | Hearth in pit dwelling; ?associated with geometric microliths (wood) | BM 449 | 3,310 ± 130 | 4,230/4,010 |

| | | | | |
|---|---|---|---|---|
| Dunford Bridge Site B | Hearth associated with geometric microliths (charcoal) | Q 799 | 3,430 ± 80 | 4,330 |
| Lussa River | Level containing geometric microlithic industry (charcoal) | BM 555 | 2,250 ± 100 | 2,950 |
| | Same level as BM 555 (charcoal) | BM 556 | 2,670 ± 140 | 3,480/3,400 |

### 3. DATES WITH UNCERTAIN ASSOCIATIONS

| | | | |
|---|---|---|---|
| Gough's Cave | Skeleton of 'Cheddar Man'; possibly associated with later upper palaeolithic 'Creswellian' industry, but mesolithic artefacts also present on site (bone collagen) | BM 525 | 7,130 ± 150 |
| Aveline's Hole | Bones of human skeleton; could be associated with either later upper palaeolithic 'Creswellian' or Mesolithic artefacts from site (bone collagen) | BM 471 | 7,164 ± 110 |
| | Stalagmite from inside human skull – presumably post-dates deposition of skeleton | GrN 5393 | 6,160 ± 150 |
| Mother Grundy's Parlour | Layer B; could be associated with either later upper palaeolithic 'Creswellian' or mesolithic artefacts (charcoal) | Q 551 | 6,850 ± 300 |
| | Layer C/B interface; apparently associated with mesolithic artefacts (charcoal) | Q 552 | 5,652 ± 140 |
| | Layer C; associated with undiagnostic mesolithic artefacts (charcoal) | Q 553 | 4,965 ± 140 |
| | Same layer as Q 553 (charcoal) | Q 554 | 4,755 ± 140 |

# 3. The neolithic

## I. F. SMITH

At the time of writing some 150 radiocarbon dates are available for the neolithic of the British Isles,[1] but the distribution of dated material and monuments is very uneven. Three-fifths of the dates relate to sites in southern England and one-fifth to Ireland. The few determinations that can be considered for northern England, Scotland and Wales permit useful, if sporadic, correlations with the two regions for which there are longer runs. There are convincing series of dates for causewayed enclosures and for earthen long barrows, but for henges and, above all, for chambered tombs (the most numerous of surviving neolithic structures) many more will be needed before there is satisfactory objective evidence of sequence to serve as a control for hypothetical sequences based on typology. One effect of the new chronology has been to invalidate criteria formerly employed to define a 'middle' neolithic;[2] for immediate purposes the material is therefore divided into an earlier and a later phase, imprecisely separated around the second quarter of the 3rd millennium bc. Thus this paper offers no neat, new, all-embracing cultural/chronological scheme for the neolithic, but rather a series of comments on the changing perspectives introduced by radiocarbon dating and on the reorientations of approach to some of the old problems that are suggested by recent discoveries and by reappraisals of finds and monuments already familiar.

### The introduction and establishment of neolithic economy[3]

When composing *The Neolithic Cultures of the British Isles* some twenty years ago, Professor Piggott envisaged an early neolithic represented by the 'Windmill Hill culture' and first appearing at the typesite in Wiltshire shortly after 2000 BC (reckoned in terms of calendar years). The introduction of neolithic culture to other parts of the British Isles could be attributed partly to diffusion from southern England and partly to the arrival of colonies of chambered tomb builders; the whole span of the neolithic then seemed unlikely to exceed four centuries. The concepts of a primary 'Windmill Hill culture' based in the chalklands of Wessex, of 'Severn-Cotswold', 'Clyde-Carlingford' and similar 'cultures' find no places in the new configurations that are emerging.

Radiocarbon dates now indicate that many parts of Britain and Ireland had been settled by farmers before 3000 bc (Fig. 12) and that the duration of the neolithic, as attested by the earliest and latest determinations obtained for material that is formally assigned to this 'period', may have to be reckoned as at least 23 centuries in radiocarbon years or 28 calendrical centuries (Fig. 17). As yet it is impossible to detect a pattern of expansion from any nuclear area of colonisation, but this is of minor consequence in view of the more fundamental implications of the evidence that a homogeneous material culture had been spread over widely separated regions and established in very diverse environments long before the end of the 4th millennium bc.

The earliest radiocarbon dates so far obtained come from the settlement at Ballynagilly, Tyrone, where a hearth, pits, and associated pottery represent initial occupation within the range 3795–3675 bc.[4] These dates are three to four centuries older than any others certainly associated with neolithic material[5] and it is probably significant that in the bog adjacent to the settlement a landnam horizon does not appear until *c.* 3200 bc,[6] when it can be correlated with a later stage of occupation and the building of a substantial house.[7] Clearance horizons falling within the date brackets 3400–3000 bc have been identified in a number of peat deposits elsewhere in Ireland and in England and it is evident that this was the time when neolithic farming made its first real impact on the environment.[8] In Scotland and in England it was during these centuries that the first field monuments were constructed.

Although no site in Scotland or in England has yet yielded a date comparable with the three earliest from Ballynagilly, there are firm indications of settlement in these regions antecedent to the sites that have given the oldest dates. Apart

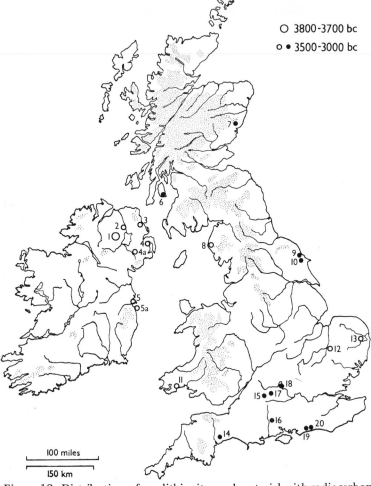

Figure 12. Distribution of neolithic sites and material with radiocarbon
dates falling before 3000 bc. Open circles represent settlements or
occupation; black spots denote field monuments. Key to sites: 1.
Ballynagilly, Tyrone; 2. Newferry, Antrim; 3. Madman's Window,
Glenarm, Antrim; 4. Ringneill Quay, Down; 5. Sutton, Dublin; 5a.
Dalkey Island, Dublin; 6. Monamore chambered tomb, Arran; 7.
Dalladies long barrow, Kincardineshire; 8. Ehenside Tarn, Cumberland; 9. Seamer Moor long barrow, N. R. Yorkshire; 10. Willerby
Wold long barrow, E. R. Yorkshire; 11. Coygan Camp, Carmarthen-
shire; 12. Shippea Hill, Cambridgeshire; 13. Broome Heath, Ditching-
ham, Norfolk; 14. Hembury causewayed enclosure, Devon; 15.
Horslip long barrow, Wiltshire; 16. Fussell's Lodge long barrow,
Wiltshire; 17. Lambourn long barrow, Berkshire; 18. Abingdon
causewayed enclosure, Berkshire; 19. Church Hill flint-mine, Sussex;
20. Blackpatch flint-mine, Sussex.

from the practical consideration that pioneers with a stone technology are unlikely to have been in a position to construct large funerary monuments or communal centres immediately upon arrival, there is direct evidence that such constructions were preceded by an interval, perhaps lengthy, devoted to prospection, forest clearance and the establishment of trade networks. Earthen long barrows, for example, seem always to have been built in an open environment, often on grassland.[9] Stacked turves, frequently incorporated in the mounds, could already be employed around 3400 bc in the mound of the Lambourn long barrow in Berkshire.[10] Finds from the causewayed enclosure at Hembury, Devon, dated 3330—3150 bc, have similar implications. They include axes of Cornish rocks and pottery made in Cornwall, 100 miles to the west; axes of grey flint, from a source as yet unidentified but probably at least as far to the east; and other artefacts made of non-local substances. Taken together, these must attest the prior existence of an extensive network of contacts or trading relationships, which again must have required time for its organisation.

As more evidence becomes available, it may be possible to distinguish an initial phase in the earlier part of the 4th millennium when neolithic colonists spread rapidly over the British Isles, establishing small settlements but not yet producing marked alterations in the natural environment, followed by a phase beginning in the latter half of the millennium when well-established and expanding communities started to transform the landscape by extensive forest clearances and by building the first monuments of earth and stone. Such phases might seem appropriate to an early and a middle neolithic.[11]

## Material culture: earler neolithic

### The economic basis

Most of the information about stock-breeding and cereal cultivation in the neolithic of the British Isles has been summarised in a recent work by Murray.[12] Windmill Hill is still the only site where the data can be treated statistically, but the indications are that they epitomise the situation, at least for southern England. At Windmill Hill the cattle/

ovicaprid/pig ratios for the pre-enclosure occupation, dated 2950 bc, were 66:12:16; amongst bones recovered from the enclosure ditches, dated 2580 bc, the proportions had altered to 60:25:15, possibly reflecting an increase in grassland. The ages of animals at death do not support the earlier idea of autumnal decimations and there is no real evidence that cattle were slaughtered by pole-axing.[13] The consistently low proportions of wild animal bones from all sites permit the conclusion that hunting made a minimal contribution to subsistence.

Wheat (emmer with a little eincorn) constituted the main cereal crop, accounting for over 90 per cent of grain impressions on pottery from Windmill Hill. Barley, mainly of the naked variety, made up the rest. The problem posed by the identification of charred grains of spelt at Hembury has been discussed elsewhere.[14] It has usually been assumed that hoe-cultivation was practised throughout the neolithic, but furrows produced by cross-ploughing, preserved beneath the South Street long barrow within sight of Windmill Hill, imply a more advanced system of husbandry and raise the question whether oxen may have provided the traction. A thin turf-line had formed in the interval between the ploughing and construction of the barrow; charcoal from the surface of this turf-line gave a radiocarbon date of 2810 bc.[15]

## Settlements

The most important addition to the short list of early houses published by Piggott in 1954[16] is the one at Ballynagilly, Tyrone, referred to above and dated 3215 bc. It was almost square in plan (6.5 by 6 m.); the longer walls had consisted of split oak planks set in trenches and supported by packing stones; there were two internal hearths. Tenuous traces of what may have been a dwelling of comparable size and proportions, but defined by shallow trenches on all four sides, were recovered together with abundant sherds and flints of earlier neolithic types at Peterborough, Northamptonshire, in the summer of 1972.[17] Extensive stripping round both these sites failed to reveal any other buildings and the circumstances seem to support the idea that the settlement pattern of the earlier neolithic was one of isolated farmsteads. Pits, either single or in clusters, constitute the most frequent structures indicative of settlement; at Hazard Hill, Devon, and Hurst Fen, Mildenhall, Suffolk, ditches of uncertain function (though clearly not defensive) were associated with clusters of pits and post-holes which yielded no coherent plan.[18]

## Flint and stone industries

Until recently flintwork has received far less systematic attention than other aspects of neolithic culture, despite the obvious fact that tools and weapons are basic equipment upon which survival depends and, within the limitations of a stone technology, are likely to be closely adapted to the maintenance of a traditional mode of existence. An obstacle to comprehensive analyses of flint industries is, of course, the virtual absence of large assemblages from closely identifiable contexts except in southern England. Nevertheless, the information that can be pieced together about earlier neolithic flintwork consistently attests a unity of tradition that underlies all such variables as pottery styles and tomb types or presence/absence of other kinds of monuments (e.g. causewayed enclosures). Over the whole of southern England, from East Anglia to Cornwall, the flint industry is to all appearances homogeneous, although associated with five or six distinctive regional pottery styles, and this observation seems to hold good for the rest of the British Isles. The recurrent appearance of the bifacially retouched leaf-shaped arrowhead requires no emphasis; other recurrent types are larger bifacially retouched foliate forms (laurel-leaves), found in Ireland as in England; single-piece sickle-blades; various forms of knives; convex scrapers; and the highly characteristic narrow-flake industry, adaptable to the utilisation of any available supply of flint.[19] (The early adoption in Ireland of a specialised form, the hollow scraper, represents an addition to the basic equipment.)

The need for reliable sources of material for axes was met in southern England by flint-mining; radiocarbon dates suggest that mining had begun at Church Hill, Findon, Sussex, by 3390 bc and at the nearby Blackpatch mine by 3140 bc. Other dates from Sussex mines range from 2980 to 2700 bc. On present evidence, Grimes Graves, Norfolk, came into use considerably later. Stone axes from Hembury,

Devon, show that the Cornish axe-industry had begun, if only in a small way, at the same time as the Sussex flint-mines.[20] The first indications of land-clearance in the vicinity of the 'axe-factory' sites in the Great Langdale district of Westmorland appear at 3300-3200 bc and it is a reasonable inference that the exploitation of the Langdale tuff began then,[21] though determinations from a chipping-floor gave results of 2730 and 2524 bc and seem to relate to the period of maximum expansion of the industry as suggested by the contexts of many Langdale axes. In south Wales a tuff, probably from Pembrokeshire, was used for an axe indirectly dated 3050 bc at Coygan Camp, Carmarthenshire; axes of the same rock, though not numerous, have been found from East Anglia to Devon. The better-known Graig Lwyd rock of north Wales seems not to have been used before the 3rd millennium, but it is probable that the porcellanite of Tievebulliagh/Rathlin Island in Antrim was exploited at an earlier time.[22]

### Pottery

Owing to its variability and to the circumstance that it constitutes the most widespread of surviving traces of neolithic material culture, pottery offers convenient pegs upon which to hang the rudiments of a new chronological framework (Fig. 13). In constructing this diagram, preference has been accorded to ceramic styles and, where possible, to single sites for which there are series of radiocarbon dates, since a consistent pattern inspires more confidence than a patchwork of isolated determinations. Some kinds of pottery for which only one or two dates are available have necessarily been omitted. In the light of recent developments, generic terms formerly employed in connection with the round-based pottery of the earlier neolithic — neolithic A, western neolithic or Windmill Hill ware — seem no longer appropriate; but there is no reason to abandon the familiar type-site nomenclature for individual styles and this is retained in the following pages.

The pottery with the earliest dates, referred to here as the Grimston/Lyles Hill series, is also the most widely distributed (Fig. 14) and seems to have survived as a recognisable entity for a longer period than any other. It is dated 3795-2960 bc

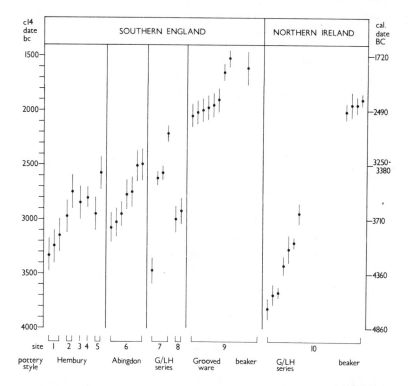

Figure 13. Radiocarbon dates for some neolithic pottery styles in southern England and in northern Ireland; beaker dates included for comparison. Key to sites: 1. Hembury, Devon; 2. Hazard Hill, Devon; 3. High Peak, Devon; 4. Hambledon Hill; Dorset; 5. Windmill Hill, Wiltshire; 6. Abingdon, Berkshire; 7. Broome Heath, Ditchingham, Norfolk; 8. Shippea Hill, Cambridgeshire; 9. Durrington Walls, Wiltshire; 10. Ballynagilly, Tyrone.

at Ballynagilly, Tyrone, and 3474-2217 bc at Broome Heath, Ditchingham, Norfolk. Some other relevant determinations are: 3000-2920 bc at Shippea Hill, Cambridgeshire; 3050 bc at Coygan Camp, Carmarthenshire; 3080 to 2880 bc in the Seamer Moor, Willerby Wold and Kilham long barrows in Yorkshire; 2860 bc in a round cairn at Pitnacree in Perthshire; and 2750 bc at Aston-on-Trent, Derbyshire. In Ireland the Lyles Hill facies of the series may have gone out of use around the middle of the 3rd millennium bc; the late date from Broome Heath, combined with evidence for association with beakers at a number of sites in Yorkshire and in Scotland, suggest a long survival in Britain.[23]

Since Piggott defined the 'Grimston ware' of Yorkshire, the 'Lyles Hill ware' of Ulster, and drew attention to related pottery elsewhere in eastern Britain and in the Irish Sea province, the range and density of the known distribution have increased considerably and it has now become evident that this ceramic series represents the pottery used by the great majority of the earlier neolithic communities of the British Isles. Although details of shape exhibit regional variations, the whole series is linked by a number of distinctive attributes and by continuity of geographical distribution.[24] The compound 'Grimston/Lyles Hill' embraces the two most familiar sub-styles; 'series' has been added to allow for the recognition of further variants. But a new name is clearly required for a ceramic style that is found in Ireland, Wales, Scotland and in eastern England from Northumberland to Sussex, and that appears not only on settlements but also in association with burials by inhumation and cremation in earthen long barrows, round barrows or cairns, several classes of chambered tombs, and with a variety of ceremonial monuments.[25]

In southern England other ceramic styles with more or less clearly defined regional distributions can now be seen to have come into use before 3000 bc. The most important of these is the Hembury style, with dates ranging from 3330-3150 bc at the type-site to 2580 bc at Windmill Hill (Fig. 13); the distribution extends from Cornwall into Wessex and southern Sussex (Fig. 14). The appearance of decorated pottery within and eastwards from Wessex, once thought to mark the opening of a 'middle' neolithic phase, can now be placed almost as early as those of the plain Grimston/Lyles Hill and Hembury styles. The ornamented vessels from the Fussell's Lodge long barrow in Wiltshire may be taken (on the strength of a single radiocarbon date) to have been deposited before 3230 bc;[26] and a series of dates for the Abingdon style at the type-site in Berkshire covers the period 3110-2500 bc.

A new approach to the problem posed by the co-existence of these regional pottery styles in southern England (all in use by communities with an otherwise homogeneous material culture)[27] is offered by Peacock's work on the petrology of

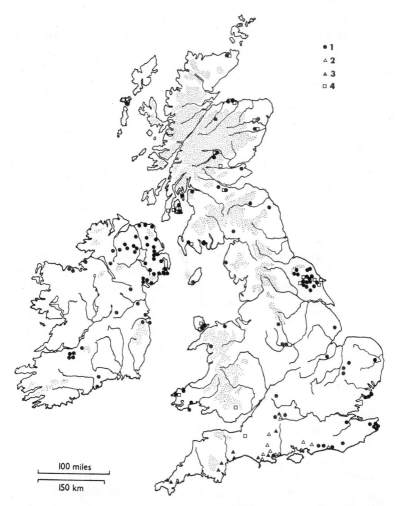

Figure 14. Distribution of plain round-base neolithic pottery. 1. Grimston/Lyles Hill series (Irish distribution mainly after Case); 2. Hembury style, gabbroic ware not present; 3. Hembury style, including gabbroic ware; 4. Other pots with lugs. (Some unclassified assemblages omitted.)

Hembury-style assemblages. He has been able to show that the finer vessels from ten such assemblages in Cornwall, Devon, Dorset and Wiltshire are made of a gabbroic clay that is found only on the Lizard Head in Cornwall, and suggests that these vessels were made on the Lizard by professional potters and dispersed eastwards along channels of trade. The distinctive attributes of the coarser vessels which form the bulk of Hembury-style assemblages show them to be locally-made imitations of gabbroic-ware prototypes; it therefore appears that the style of the pottery used in the south-west and over much of Wessex was set in workshops situated in a remote corner of the region.[28] The inferred system was not, it seems, a short-term arrangement but one that persisted for several centuries; gabbroic ware of Cornish origin is recorded from contexts bracketed by the dates 3330-2580 bc.

In Wiltshire pottery was also being imported from another region. Vessels shown by their content of fossil shell and oolites to have been made of clay from the Jurassic limestone, perhaps in the Bath/Frome area, account for nearly a third of all the pottery from Windmill Hill, and are known from several other sites on the chalk. At Windmill Hill the oolitic ware appears as Hembury-style vessels, imitating the gabbroic prototypes, and also as ornamented bowls closely comparable with the Abingdon and other decorated styles.[29] The pottery from the deeper levels of the ditches can be broadly classed as: (1) Hembury style: (*a*) gabbroic prototypes (two sherds only), (*b*) imitations in oolitic ware, (*c*) imitations apparently made locally; (2) Abingdon and other decorated styles: (*a*) in oolitic ware, (*b*) made locally; (3) Ebbsfleet style: (*a*) in oolitic ware, (*b*) in local ware; and (4) various other stylistic groups in local ware, including vessels with Hembury forms with added decoration.[30]

The mixed character of the pottery from sites in Sussex, and especially at Whitehawk, can perhaps be interpreted along the same lines. At Whitehawk the Hembury style reaches the eastern limit of its known distribution, and there is associated with two groups of decorated bowls which owe their forms respectively to Hembury and to Grimston/Lyles Hill, and with a number of Ebbsfleet bowls.[31]

In the past much confusion about the identities and origins of neolithic communities has arisen from the conventional approach to pottery, which proceeds from the assumption that pot-making must invariably have been a domestic or communal industry and that pottery styles must necessarily express communal traditions. The new model for pottery production suggested. by Peacock's work seems to resolve satisfactorily for southern England the apparent anomaly of the co-existence of multiple 'traditions' within a comparatively restricted territory. Mutually exclusive or partially over-lapping distributions and minor stylistic variations might now be explained in terms of trade competition[32] and of innovations introduced by perhaps just a few inventive or mobile potters.[33] The general applicability of this model to other parts of the British Isles is clearly a matter for detailed investigation, both petrological and typological. It will also be necessary to attempt to distinguish possible instances of diffusion of ceramic styles that may represent actual folk movements. One example may be mentioned: in Yorkshire, Wales and Scotland plain vessels with lugs (Fig. 14) have been more or less explicitly interpreted as evidence of colonisation from southern England.[34] The lug types are very simple in comparison with the considerable variety seen in the Hembury style (which should provide their source) and they may occur in association with or even on vessels attributable to the Grimston/Lyles Hill series or its specialised derivatives. The question that arises is whether, outside its area of origin, a simplified version of the Hembury style may have been transmitted as a 'tradition' carried by communities in process of expansion.

## Material culture: later neolithic

### Pottery

Against a background of earlier styles, both plain and decorated and variously surviving through part or all of the 3rd millennium bc, developments beginning around the turn of that millennium's first and second quarters exhibit complex patterns of divergence and convergence in England and Wales, in Ireland and in Scotland. Innovations within the round-based bowl series may be considered first; unfortunately, there are very few radiocarbon dates to provide a detailed time-scale for these.

The significant development in England south of the River Tees and in Wales was the appearance of the sequence of styles known collectively as Peterborough ware.[35] In broad outline the stages seem to have been as follows:

1. Emergence of Ebbsfleet bowls, apparently as a variant of the Grimston/Lyles Hill series, in and around the lower Thames valley. Decoration was comparatively restrained and clearly related to that of other southern English regional styles, although already exhibiting distinctive characteristics that were to persist throughout the whole series; cord impressions were rarely employed and a proportion of the pottery was plain. For this stage the radiocarbon date of 2710 bc from Ebbsfleet, Kent, provides a *terminus ante quem*.[36]

2. Impressions of twisted or whipped cord tended to supersede other decorative techniques and to cover larger areas of the bowls' surfaces. Ebbsfleet bowls of this stage have a wider distribution, reaching Dorset in the west and Yorkshire in the north. At Windmill Hill their chronological position is roughly fixed by the date of 2580 bc for the lower fill of the enclosure ditches.[37]

3. Development of Mortlake bowls, still more profusely ornamented; complex impressions ('bird-bone') and finger-nailing frequently employed. Morphological changes include expansion of rims to accommodate decoration, and some rims assume the form of incipient collars. It has been inferred that a tendency to zonal arrangement of the decoration was inspired by beaker styles; in their mature form Mortlake bowls are sometimes associated with beakers. Stage 3 may therefore be placed at the close of the third millennium or later.[38]

4. During the first quarter of the 2nd millennium bc two partially parallel developments can be traced, each combining perpetuation of traits derived from the earlier stages with further reaction to beaker styles. As domestic pottery, the Fengate style carried on the formally neolithic tradition, but flat bases, often disproportionately narrow, and evolved collars produce urn-like forms.[39] There is a radiocarbon date of 1640 bc for Fengate and beaker pottery associated in a pit at Letchworth, Hertfordshire. Collared urns of the primary series, formally of the bronze age, appear to have sprung from a fusion of Mortlake/Fengate and beaker traditions.[40]

The Peterborough series clearly represents a ceramic tradition in the specific sense defined by Longworth.[41] In the discussion of earlier neolithic pottery the term has been employed circumspectly for reasons made obvious there. Within the Peterborough series continuity through an evolutionary sequence together with a distribution pattern that differs significantly from that of other decorated styles indicate a change in the organisation of pottery production. The purpose of Fig. 15 is to illustrate the overall distribution of the Peterborough tradition in relation to other decorated neolithic pottery; on a single map it is obviously impossible to represent numerous stylistic variations. It will be seen that in the south Peterborough ware extends as far west as Dorset and Somerset and in the north hardly reaches beyond Yorkshire and Cumberland. The dynamic expansion and development of this tradition, already evident at a time anterior to beaker contacts, contrasts with the apparently static character of most other ceramic styles. It also contrasts strangely with a gradual loss of cultural status (at least in archaeological terms); with the exception of the Ebbsfleet style, Peterborough pottery rarely occurs in closed association with other diagnostic artefacts or in a primary context in any kind of structure other than pits. Ebbsfleet bowls appear as one facet of earlier neolithic culture and the Mortlake and Fengate bowls as facets of later neolithic culture, but there was no 'Peterborough culture' as such.

In Ireland ceramic innovations exhibit a different pattern; with the exception of the Limerick style, known only from the vicinity of Lough Gur and representing a decorated variant of the Lyles Hill facies of the Grimston/Lyles Hill series, geographically delimited pottery styles seem not to occur. In Case's recent survey of Irish neolithic pottery,[42] all the other decorated round-based vessels are classed together as Sandhills ware. This ware is subdivided by him into Sandhills Western and five individual bowl types, all with interlocking if not quite identical distributions. Sandhills Western assemblages comprise carinated bowls of Lyles Hill derivation, accompanied by an increased proportion of simple bowls, often with lugs. Decorative techniques are in general comparable with those employed on Peterborough ware and these also appear on four of the recurrent bowl types. Two of the latter (Ballyalton[43] and Murlough bowls) represent highly specialised versions of carinated forms

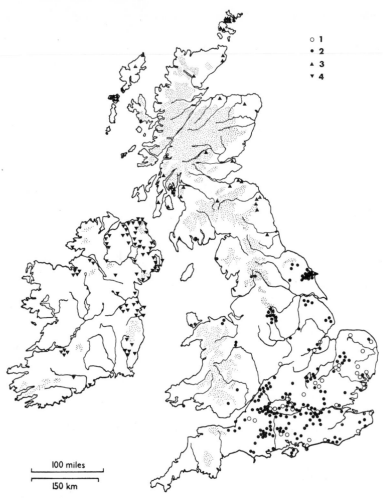

Figure 15. Distribution of decorated round-base neolithic pottery. 1. Southern English styles; 2. Peterborough series; 3. North British and Scottish styles; 4. Limerick style and Sandhills ware. *Mainly after Case*

selected from the Lyles Hill range; and two are of simple semi-globular shape (Goodland and Dundrum bowls, the latter with massive rims and frequently provided with lugs). Carrowkeel bowls (otherwise Loughcrew or passage-grave ware) are of simple form, characteristically ornamented by stab-and-drag and related techniques, and consistently differ in fabric from other Sandhills pottery. But techniques of decoration were to some extent interchangeable throughout the whole range of Sandhills ware.

The sequence in which these bowl forms appeared has not yet been determined; evidence now available indicates a chronological range for the series as a whole extending from the first quarter of the 3rd millennium bc[44] to the middle of the 2nd. Numerous fragments of Sandhills Western, Dundrum, Goodland and Carrowkeel bowls, together with one from a plain carinated vessel and part of a flat base, were recovered from a settlement sealed beneath a small passage-grave, Townleyhall II in Louth, dated 2730 bc; the circumstances suggest that the whole range represents the pottery used by one family or other small social unit.[45] A further date for mature Sandhills ware, 2625 bc, comes from Goodland, Antrim. Survival of some of the individual bowl types for a millennium or more thereafter is suggested by a date of 1530 bc from Fourknocks II, Meath (for a Carrowkeel bowl) and another of 1430 bc from an occupation layer at Island MacHugh, Tyrone (for Goodland and Murlough bowls). But evidence from Goodland seems to indicate that Sandhills Western went out of fashion much earlier.[46]

Despite the occurrence, as at Townleyhall II, of apparently contemporary assemblages comprising various Sandhills ware forms, there is a marked degree of segregation overall with respect to the contexts in which individual bowl types appear. Ballyalton and Carrowkeel bowls occur uncommonly on occupation sites; the former are found most frequently in court cairns and in portal dolmens, the latter in passage-graves and related monuments. Sandhills Western, Dundrum, Goodland and Murlough bowls are well represented on occupation sites (notably on coastal sandhills and lakeside settlements), and all except Murlough bowls appear in court cairns.

Case explains Sandhills ware in terms of the acculturation and eventual dominance of the native mesolithic population of Ireland; some of the decorative motifs and techniques may, he suggests, have been borrowed from other contemporary pottery styles within as well as outside the British Isles as a result of widely-ranging contacts established in the course of seasonal voyages and trade in stone axes.[47]

For Scotland the establishment of an outline chronology of the complex pattern of ceramic developments is largely a matter for the future. Innovations seem essentially to represent elaborations, some of them highly specialised, of forms derived from the Grimston/Lyles Hill series and from the putative Hembury contribution previously mentioned (p. 111). In her recent detailed analysis of the pottery from chambered tombs, Henshall[48] points to significant resemblances between specific types of decorated carinated bowls in western Scotland and in Ireland (Achnacree and Beacharra bowls, the latter being the Scottish counterparts of Ballyalton bowls). At Townhead, Rothesay, Bute, fragments of an Achnacree bowl, two Beacharra bowls, and others which Henshall finds comparable to Irish Dundrum bowls, are dated 2120 bc. In the typological sequence proposed by Scott for his 'Beacharra style', which includes Beacharra bowls (*sensu* Henshall), simple bowls and cups, as well as deep bag-shaped pots with lugs, the pottery from Rothesay is considered to represent an important formative influence. He has constructed (on, it may seem, somewhat slender foundations) a series of stages for the evolution of the 'Beacharra style' before and after 'Rothesay' influence, with successive extrapolations to the Hebrides and to Ireland. For Scott the Achnacree bowl and other vessels with heavy rims from Rothesay represent an intrusive element in the Clyde region; for its inspiration he looks to the decorated pottery of southern England rather than to Ireland.[49] Henshall's Hebridean style, known from North Uist and Harris, comprises an even wider variety of forms, amongst which can be recognised Achnacree and Beacharra carinated bowls, Unstan bowls (occurring otherwise in Orkney and northern Scotland), collared vessels reminiscent of Irish Murlough bowls, and others which appear to be local inventions.[50] With the single exception of a cord-impressed Beacharra bowl, the decoration of all the pottery mentioned above is executed by channelling, incision, stab-and-drag (rare in the Hebrides, but characteristic of Unstan bowls in Orkney), and punctulation. Stratification at the settlement at Northton, Harris,[51] shows that the Hebridean style and Unstan bowls antedate the arrival of beakers.

In Scotland pottery with impressed decoration (cord, 'bird-bone', fingernail, etc.) is confined almost exclusively to occupation sites; known find-spots are predominantly coastal (e.g., Glenluce, Wigtownshire, and Hedderwick, East Lothian), but the probability of a wider inland distribution is indicated by a discovery at Grandtully, Perthshire. In the east the distribution extends southwards to Northumberland, where pottery from Ford and other sites is now seen to find its best parallels in Scotland. The impressed pottery exhibits generalised resemblances to Irish Sandhills ware and to Peterborough ware (but true Peterborough sherds are known from one site only).[52] In discussing this pottery, McInnes has remarked: 'The impressed wares of Scotland have a common denominator in their decoration and in their fabric, but the forms are innumerable and their decoration follows no classifiable pattern.' Individual assemblages are, however, differentiated by marked preferences for particular forms and decorative techniques.[53] The only radiocarbon dates, 2030 bc and 1870 bc, are from Grandtully.

The last class of neolithic pottery to be considered, grooved ware, presents a contrasting facet of later neolithic culture. First recognised at Clacton, Essex, and defined as grooved ware in 1936, this flat-based pottery was renamed Rinyo-Clacton by Piggott in 1954 when the known distribution still indicated a northern province centred in Orkney and a southern in England south of The Wash. Discoveries made since 1954, notably in Yorkshire, have blurred the distinction, but this was not taken into account by Clarke in his recent attempt to divorce the Orcadian pottery from that of southern England.[54] Clarke's arguments have now been refuted by Wainwright and Longworth after detailed analysis of all the pottery and its associations in connection with their publication of the finds from Durrington Walls, Wiltshire.[55] Although Wainwright and Longworth have distinguished four sub-styles, differentiated by preferences for particular combinations of decorative motifs and techniques (grooving and applied cordons), they have shown that the interlocking geographical distributions of these sub-styles do not support the idea of a dichotomy between north and south (as implied by the name Rinyo-Clacton) and therefore recommend a return to the more general term grooved ware.

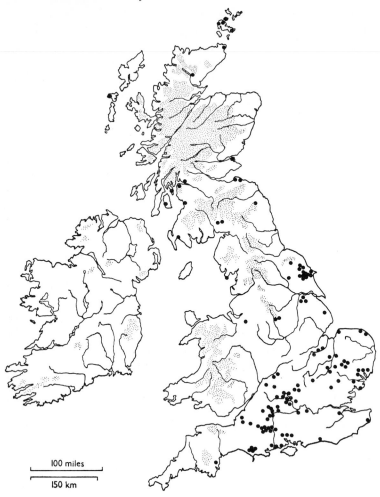

Figure 16. Distribution of grooved ware.

As will be seen from Fig. 16, the distribution pattern contrasts markedly with those indicated in Fig. 15, and extends across the territorial limits of all other decorated Neolithic styles in Scotland and in England. Wainwright and Longworth do not recognise grooved ware in Ireland; it may, however, be represented by a few sherds at Dalkey Island, Dublin, and at the Grange circle in Limerick.[56] Connections with Ireland, direct or indirect, are implied by the occurrence on vessels from Skara Brae and from several sites in southern England of motifs that can be matched precisely in the art of the Boyne passage-graves.[57] Indeed, circumstantial evidence suggests that the passage-graves of the Maes Howe group in Orkney, closely linked with the Boyne group, were built by the communities who used grooved ware.[58]

Nine radiocarbon dates are available for grooved ware, all from Wiltshire. The earliest, 2180 bc, relates to sherds from the ditch at Stonehenge; six from Durrington Walls range from 2050 to 1900 bc (Fig. 13); a single determination from Marden, 1988 bc, falls neatly amongst the latter. Finally, two from a settlement adjacent to Durrington Walls, 1647 bc and 1523 bc, indicate survival through the first half of the second millennium bc.[59] Further north, two grooved ware pots are known to have been used as cinerary urns. One from Eddisbury, Delamere, Cheshire, is the single surviving member of a cremation cemetery.[60] The other, from Winhill, Derbyshire, known only from a sketch by Thomas Bateman, may have been under a cairn.[61] Both belong to the Durrington Walls sub-style, a fact that lends support to the hypothesis that this sub-style, with its emphasis on deep bucket-shaped vessels and applied cordons, may have contributed significantly to the development of bronze age pottery.[62]

As yet it is not possible to isolate any developmental sequence for grooved ware or its sub-styles; the occasional appearance of cord and comb-impressed decoration indicates incidental absorption of Peterborough and beaker techniques, but formative influences from any recognised class of pottery are not certainly detectable. For the present the style seems best interpreted as a ceramic innovation within the British Isles involving the translation into clay of a tradition of wicker basketry. However, it is conceivable that a link may eventually be established between grooved ware and other flat-based vessels which occur sporadically with round-based bowls in Britain and Ireland. At Windmill Hill fragments of flat bases came from deep in the enclosure ditches and long antedate the appearance of grooved ware on the site.[63]

Fig. 17 illustrates schematically the duration and chronological relationships of well-dated neolithic pottery styles, with the range of beaker dates added for comparison.

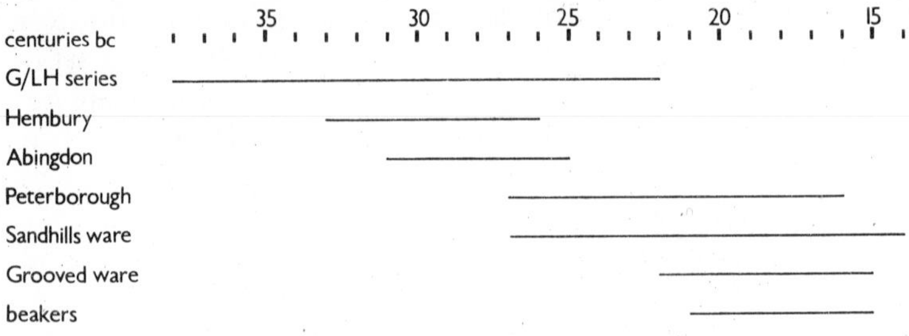

| centuries bc | | 35 | | 30 | | 25 | | 20 | | 15 |
|---|---|---|---|---|---|---|---|---|---|---|

G/LH series ——————————————————————

Hembury ——————————————————

Abingdon ————————————————

Peterborough ——————————————————————

Sandhills ware ——————————————————————————

Grooved ware ——————————————————

beakers ———————————————

Figure 17. Diagram illustrating the probable life-spans of neolithic and beaker pottery. Based on means of earliest and latest radiocarbon dates, each rounded off to the nearest century.

## Flint and stone industries

Much uncertainty remains about the processes and chronology of the changes in flint-working during the 3rd millennium; the two most clearly documented changes are the substitution of transverse for leaf arrowheads and the replacement of the narrow-flake industry by one in which broader forms predominate.

In Ireland transverse arrowheads had come into use before the middle of the 3rd millennium bc; they are present in assemblages associated with Sandhills ware at Townleyhall II[64] (2730 bc) and at Goodland[65] (2625 bc). Local mesolithic[66] or earlier neolithic prototypes are apparently unknown. The Townleyhall arrowheads are made on flakes, as are the other later neolithic examples in Ireland and in Britain, and are thus differentiated from the mesolithic *petit tranchet* arrowheads of Britain, which are made on blade segments. At Goodland the transverse arrowheads were associated with other neolithic implement types, but the flint-working technique was in the Larnian tradition, with leaf- and plunging-flakes. Case interprets this as evidence for the assimilation of basic elements of neolithic economy and culture by the aboriginal population. Earlier stages in this process of acculturation are seen in the association of Larnian flints with bones of domesticated animals in the south midden at Dalkey Island, Dublin, and at Ringneill Quay, Devon,[67] or with polished stone axes at Sutton, Dublin, and Newferry, Antrim,[68] all dated 3400-3300 bc. Thus there may have emerged in northern Ireland a 'secondary neolithic' culture of the type envisaged by Piggott.[69] Case has discussed the very special circumstances that could have facilitated this development: a strongly entrenched meso-lithic population, perhaps already of semi-sedentary habits and enjoying a monopoly of the restricted sources of good flint and of the best (Tievebulliagh) rock for axe-manufac-ture.[70] Such conditions would be likely to result in early and continuing contacts with neolithic settlers; Mitchell has offered the further suggestion that the farmers may also have provided a market for fish and other game supplied by Larnian fishers and hunters.[71]

In south-eastern England single specimens of transverse arrowheads are known from four or five sites in earlier neolithic contexts.[72] Unambiguous associations are other-wise almost exclusively with grooved ware, and specimens from Durrington Walls are tied in with the dates 2050-1900 bc. In their comprehensive analysis of artefacts found with grooved ware, Wainwright and Longworth have demon-strated that, apart from convex scrapers, transverse arrow-heads are the commonest type of implement, present in over 50 per cent of closed finds.[73] The contrasting rarity of distinctive artefacts in closed finds with the Peterborough series has been referred to above. Sherds in the Fengate style occurred once in certain association with a transverse arrowhead[74] and there are a few other instances where the balance of probability falls in favour of a link with the Mortlake or Fengate styles.[75] In other words, transverse arrowheads can be related to Peterborough ware only at a late stage in its development. The flint-working technique of the later neolithic industries in southern England is charac-terised by the production of a high proportion of broad, squat flakes,[76] totally dissimilar to the controlled blade production of the local mesolithic industries, and evidence for any continuing mesolithic tradition is not obvious. The convex scrapers of the later neolithic, thinner and more elegant than those of the earlier neolithic, were frequently struck from prepared cores.[77]

As mentioned above (p. 106), the 3rd millennium bc was the period of most intensive exploitation of igneous and meta-morphic rocks for axe manufacture; the distribution patterns of axes from identified sources provide evidence of a kind not otherwise available for inter-communal contacts. On the whole the model that seems to fit the known facts most satisfactorily is one involving straightforward trading operations,[78] even if the basis on which these were organised remains obscure. Unfortunately, there are still no up-to-date and comprehensive distribution maps for the British Isles as a whole and systematic petrological surveys have not yet covered all regions. Nevertheless, intensive surveys conducted within limited areas[79] show clearly that there were four 'axe-factories' of outstanding importance. The most widely distributed axes are those made of the Tievebulliagh/Rathlin Island porcellanite of Antrim (petrological group IX); the bulk of these axes is clustered in north-eastern Ireland, with a thinner scatter elsewhere in the country; at least 50 are known from Scotland, including the Hebrides and Orkney; in England find-spots extend from Lancashire and Yorkshire to Dorset and Kent. In Britain the Great Langdale axes of Westmorland (group VI) are by far the most numerous; large numbers have been identified in Scotland, Yorkshire and East Anglia, and specimens are known from Devon, Cornwall and northern Ireland. The output of the Graig Lwyd (group VII) working-sites in Caernarvonshire seems to have been less prolific; in Britain the distribution outside Wales follows that of group VI axes. The dating evidence for the inception of activity at these sources is discussed on p. 105. The associations of group I axes, from the Mount's Bay area of Cornwall, suggest that this 'factory' may not have come into operation much before 2000 bc. Important numbers of group I axes reached Wessex, East Anglia and Yorkshire and a lesser quantity is recorded from Wales.

Continuity of exploitation into the earlier part of the 2nd millennium is attested by mace-heads attributable to groups I, VI and VII. Roe[80] has shown that stone mace-heads are not demonstrably earlier than the typologically earliest forms of battle-axes and the technique of producing more or less cylindrical shaft-holes in stone seems likely to have been acquired through contacts with beaker craftsmen. But antler mace-heads, the presumed prototypes of the stone series, may be of earlier origin and so represent a native invention. Roe's detailed analysis of the associations of stone mace-heads reveals a preponderance of grooved ware contexts;

there is one closed find with sherds of Mortlake and Fengate bowls.[81]

## Economy and settlements

By the late 3rd millennium bc the subsistence economy may have been essentially pastoral. Wainwright and Longworth note the absence of grain impressions on grooved ware from Durrington Walls and elsewhere;[82] corn-grinding equipment, found recurrently in earlier neolithic contexts, is also lacking. In southern England there are indications of an increased emphasis on pig-breeding.[83] As in the earlier neolithic, bones of wild animals constitute a small fraction of the total food refuse, suggesting that game was hunted primarily for sport or to vary the diet. A predilection for sea-food may be evidenced by marine shells from grooved ware sites in Wessex; as might be expected in a coastal situation, it was collected in considerably quantities at Skara Brae.

Most of the existing information about later neolithic settlements and houses has been conveniently assembled by McInnes.[84] As for the earlier neolithic, the evidence recovered consists mainly of pits or 'occupation floors'. The plans and dimensions of the houses at Mount Pleasant, Glamorganshire, and Ronaldsway, Isle of Man, are comparable to those of the earlier houses at Haldon, Devon, and Clegyr Boia, Pembrokeshire. An oval setting of stake-holes enclosing an area 12 feet by 7½ feet at Cefn Cilsanws, Brecknockshire, has been interpreted as a hut; sherds of Mortlake and indeterminate vessels were scattered over the floor.[85] The complex site C at Barford, Warwickshire,[86] gave evidence of several successive structures that may have been domestic. The main feature was a trench of sub-rectangular plan which may have supported upright posts; post-holes within the enclosure suggest perhaps two successive timber buildings; Ebbsfleet/Mortlake pottery was clearly related to one of the structural phases. Attention may also be drawn to the curious resemblances between site D at Barford[87] and the two sites at Townleyhall, Louth. In each instance dense clusters of stake-holes appear to represent impermanent structures, several times renewed. Barford D and Townleyhall I[88] were surrounded by penannular ditches, the former with an external, the latter with an internal bank; Townleyhall II had no enclosing ditch.[89] Here the occupation area was subsequently sealed beneath a small passage-grave; at Townleyhall I a secondary mound seems to have been related to deposits of cremated bones, but there is no obvious explanation for the mound which eventually covered Barford D. If the pre-monumental occupation at these sites was of a domestic nature, the structural evidence may suggest temporary visits, perhaps in connection with seasonal activities.

In the Somerset levels continuing investigation of timber trackways is bringing to light a system of communications maintained over the greater part of the 3rd millenium bc between settlements which must have been situated on either side of the bog and on islands of higher ground within it.[90]

### Funerary monuments

Since the new approaches to the problems of neolithic tombs in Scotland, discussed in Chapter 4, are relevant to the problems of tombs (both chambered and 'unchambered') in other parts of the British Isles, it is necessary here only to draw attention to recent synoptic studies of these monuments in England,[91] Wales,[92] and Ireland,[93] and to present the dating evidence (Fig. 18), including for completeness dates from Scotland, with a minimum of further comment.

The radiocarbon chronology for earthen long barrows[94] indicates that they were constructed over a period of at least a millennium. The known sequence starts with the incompletely excavated Lambourn long barrow, dated 3415 bc from charcoal on the floor of its ditch; it has been grouped with the earthen long barrows owing to lack of certain evidence that it contained a stone chamber.[95] Beaker sherds in the mound of the Skendleby barrow imply that it may have been built nearer the end of the 3rd millennium bc than the two radiocarbon dates of *c*. 2400 bc would indicate. The dated sites (which include the barrowless long mortuary enclosure at Normanton) exhibit much variation in burial rite[96] and in the remains of former structures of timber or turf (mortuary houses, façades, revetments); their number is still too small to show any significant trends. Even the four earliest barrows are of monumental dimensions, 170 to 200

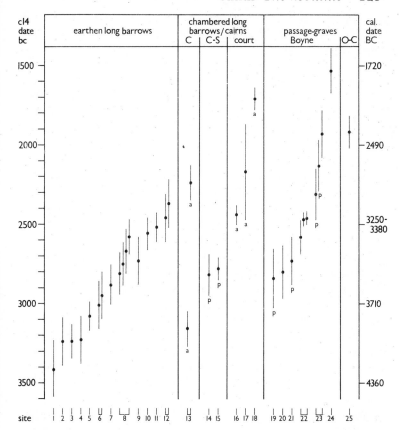

Figure 18. Radiocarbon dates for earthen long barrows and chambered tombs. Abbreviations are as follows: C, Clyde group; C-S, Cotswold-Severn group; court, court cairns (Ireland); O-C, Orkney-Cromarty group. The letters a and p indicate that the dates so qualified offer only *termini ante* or *post quos* for the actual date of construction. Key to sites: 1. Lambourn, Berkshire; 2. Horslip, Wiltshire; 3. Dalladies, Kincardineshire; 4. Fussell's Lodge, Wiltshire; 5. Seamer Moor, N. R. Yorkshire; 6. Willerby Wold, E. R. Yorkshire; 7. Kilham, E.R. Yorkshire; 8. South Street, Wiltshire; 9. Nutbane, Hampshire; 10. Normanton Down, Wiltshire (long mortuary enclosure without barrow); 11. Beckhampton Road, Wiltshire; 12. Giants Hills, Lincolnshire; 13. Monamore, Arran; 14. Wayland's Smithy, Berkshire; 15. Ascott-under-Wychwood, Oxfordshire; 16. Annaghmare, Armagh; 17. Ballyutoag, Antrim; 18. Ballymacdermot, Armagh; 19. small mound, Knowth, Meath; 20. main mound, Knowth, Meath; 21. Townleyhall II, Louth; 22. Newgrange, Meath; 23. Mound of the Hostages, Tara, Meath; 24. Fourknocks II, Meath; 25. Embo, Sutherland.

feet in length, and are therefore more likely to have been built by well-established communities than at the pioneering stage of settlement.

As will be seen from Fig. 18, dates for chambered long barrows/cairns[97] are as yet too few to support any general inferences about their chronological relationship to earthen long barrows. The three Irish court cairns, for example, represent only about 1 per cent of the known tombs of this group and in each instance the date given refers to an episode during the period of use; except perhaps at Annaghmare, the dated material may have been deposited long after the time when the tomb was built. Both earthen and chambered long barrows can now be seen to constitute a morphologically and in part spatially interlocking series of regional groups and in the present state of knowledge arguments about relative priority are likely to be circular and may turn out to be irrelevant. (The sequence at Wayland's Smithy demonstrates only that at a single site a chambered barrow replaced one with a timber mortuary house.) The uniformity of earlier neolithic material culture has been emphasised in the previous section; the artefacts of this culture (with local variations in pottery) comprise the grave-goods, offerings or occupation debris deposited in earthen long barrows and the oldest amongst those surviving in their chambered counterparts.

Dates for Irish passage-graves of the Boyne group suggest that this new cult[98] was introduced at the beginning of the later neolithic. Charcoal from the basal layer of the great mound at Knowth[99] gave a determination of 2795 bc, and specimens from ground surfaces beneath a small mound in the same cemetery and beneath another at Townleyhall II are statistically indistinguishable from this. At Newgrange[100] two almost identical results, 2475 and 2465 bc, were obtained from material used to caulk the passage roof. Fourknocks II,[101] which gave a date of 1530 bc from a cremation-pit approached by a megalithic passage, is clearly linked by grave-goods and other small finds to the main passage-grave tradition.

## Causewayed enclosures and henges

Both causewayed enclosures[102] and henges[103] have recently been reviewed at length; therefore only the dating evidence will be considered here. Determinations from Hembury, Devon, and Abingdon, Berkshire, indicate that both came into use in the latter part of the 4th millennium bc. The fairly compact series of three dates from Hembury, 3330, 3240 and 3150 bc (two from the ditch and one from an occupation area) suggest that this site may have been frequented for a comparatively brief period. But the seven dates obtained from deposits in the inner ditch at Abingdon, ranging from 3110 to 2500 bc, imply not only that some enclosures continued in use over much longer periods but also that single determinations from ditches (e.g. at Windmill Hill) are of limited value.[104]

The range of dates for the class I henge at Llandegai, Caernarvonshire,[105] 2790, 2530 and 2470 bc, suggests that its period of use overlapped that of causewayed enclosures in Wessex, and perhaps also that of the anomalous class I henge at Arminghall, Norfolk,[106] (2490 bc), and that for a late stage of the small multi-phase monument at Barford, Warwickshire,[107] (2416 bc). The date from the Stonehenge ditch (2180 bc) suggests that the first constructional phase of this class I henge was not far removed from the building of the huge class II henges at Durrington Walls (specimens from the bottom of the ditch, 2050, 2015 and 1977 bc)[108] and Marden (1988 bc).[109]

Finally, the result of 2145 bc obtained for Silbury Hill[110] confirms its contemporaneity with the other great ceremonial monuments of the late 3rd millennium bc.

## DATE LIST: *Radiocarbon dates for the neolithic*

### 1. SETTLEMENTS AND OCCUPATION MATERIAL

| Site | Feature | Lab. No. | Radiocarbon date bc (5568 half-life) | Calibrated date BC (approx.) |
|---|---|---|---|---|
| Aston-on-Trent, Derbyshire | Pit | BM 271 | 2750 ± 150 | 3520 |
| Ballynagilly, Tyrone | Hearth | UB 305 | 3795 ± 90 | 4580 |
| | Pit/gully complex | UB 307 | 3690 ± 90 | 4480 |
| | Pit | UB 197 | 3675 ± 50 | 4470 |
| | Layer 5b, pit complex | UB 304 | 3420 ± 85 | 4340 |
| | Post-hole inside house | UB 199 | 3280 ± 125 | 4220-4000 |
| | Plank wall of house | UB 201 | 3215 ± 50 | 4200-3970 |
| | Pit | UB 301 | 2960 ± 90 | 3690 |
| Broome Heath, Ditchingham, Norfolk | B horizon of soil under bank of earthwork | BM 679 | 3474 ± 117 | 4350 |
| | Pit 40, layer 6 | BM 757 | 2629 ± 65 | 3400 |
| | Pit 29, layer 4 | BM 756 | 2573 ± 67 | 3390 |
| | Top of soil under bank | BM 755 | 2217 ± 78 | 2950 |
| Coygan Camp, Carmarthenshire | Pit | NPL 132 | 3050 ± 95 | 3740 |

| Site | Context | Lab no. | Date | |
|---|---|---|---|---|
| Durrington Walls, Wiltshire | Pit 27 | BM 702 | 1647 ± 76 | 2070 |
| | Pit 27 | BM 703 | 1523 ± 72 | 2000-1720 |
| Ebbsfleet, Kent | Wood from base of peat | BM 113 | 2710 ± 150 | 3500-3410 |
| Goodland, Antrim | Pit | UB 320E | 2625 ± 135 | 3400 |
| Grandtully, Perthshire | Pit | GaK 1398 | 2130 ± 190 | 2920-2530 |
| | Hollow | GaK 1396 | 1970 ± 100 | 2510 |
| Hazard Hill, Devon | Pit | BM 149 | 2970 ± 150 | 3700 |
| | Occupation level | BM 150 | 2750 ± 150 | 3520 |
| Hembury, Devon | Occupation level | BM 136 | 3240 ± 150 | 4210-3990 |
| High Peak, Sidmouth, Devon | Pit | BM 214 | 2860 ± 150 | 3670 |
| Island MacHugh, Tyrone | Occupation level | D 47 | 1430 ± 120 | 1670 |
| Letchworth, Hertfordshire | Pit 1, layer 4 | BM 284 | 1640 ± 130 | 2070 |
| Madman's Window, Glenarm, Antrim | Hearth | UB 205 | 3145 ± 120 | 4200-3950 |

## 1. SETTLEMENTS AND OCCUPATION MATERIAL (continued)

| Site | Feature | Lab. No. | Radiocarbon date bc (5568 half-life) | Calibrated date BC (approx.) |
|---|---|---|---|---|
| Shippea Hill, Cambridgeshire | Occupation level | Q 527/8 | 3000 ± 120 | 3710 |
| | Occupation level | Q 525/6 | 2920 ± 120 | 3680 |
| Townhead, Rothesay, Bute | Hearth? | GaK 1714 | 2120 ± 100 | 2920-2530 |
| Townleyhall (II), Louth | Occupation beneath passage-grave | BM 170 | 2730 ± 150 | 3500-3410 |
| Windmill Hill, Wiltshire | Occupation beneath enclosure bank | BM 73 | 2960 ± 150 | 3700 |

## 2. FLINT MINES AND AXE-FACTORY

| Site | Feature | Lab. No. | Radiocarbon date bc (5568 half-life) | Calibrated date BC (approx.) |
|---|---|---|---|---|
| Church Hill, Findon, Sussex | Antler picks | BM 181 | 3390 ± 150 | 4340-4250 |
| Blackpatch, Worthing, Sussex | Antler from shaft 4 | BM 290 | 3140 ± 130 | 4200-3950 |
| Langdale, Westmorland | Chipping floor | BM 281 | 2730 ± 135 | 3500-3410 |
| | Chipping floor | BM 676 | 2524 ± 52 | 3390 |

## 3. EARTHEN LONG BARROWS

| | | | | |
|---|---|---|---|---|
| Beckhampton Road, Wiltshire | Antler pick under mound | BM 506b | 2517 ± 90 | 3380-3250 |
| Dalladies, Fettercairn, Kincardineshire | Second phase of primary mortuary house | I 6113 | 3240 ± 105 | 4200-3980 |
| Fussell's Lodge, Wiltshire | Collapsed mortuary house | BM 134 | 3230 ± 150 | 4200-3980 |
| Giants Hills, Skendleby, Lincolnshire | Antler | BM 191 | 2460 ± 150 | 3380-3210 |
| | Antler | BM 192 | 2370 ± 150 | 2970 |
| Horslip, Avebury, Wiltshire | Antler from primary fill of ditch | BM 180 | 3240 ± 150 | 4200-3980 |
| Kilham, Bridlington, E. R. Yorkshire | Facade bedding-trench | BM 293 | 2880 ± 125 | 3670 |
| Lambourn, Berkshire | Burnt wood on bottom of ditch | GX 1178 | 3415 ± 180 | 4340 |
| Normanton Down, Amesbury, Wiltshire | Antler from bedding-trench | BM 505 | 2560 ± 103 | 3390 |

## 3. EARTHEN LONG BARROWS (continued)

| Site | Feature | Lab. No. | Radiocarbon date bc (5568 half-life) | Calibrated date BC (approx.) |
|---|---|---|---|---|
| Nutbane, Andover, Hampshire | Second forecourt building | BM 49 | 2730 ± 150 | 3500-3410 |
| Seamer Moor, East Ayton, N. R. Yorkshire | Ground surface beneath mound | NPL 73 | 3080 ± 90 | 4180-3880 |
| South Street, Avebury, Wiltshire | Ground surface beneath mound | BM 356 | 2810 ± 130 | 3650-3540 |
| | Bone on ditch bottom | BM 357 | 2750 ± 135 | 3510 |
| | Antler on ditch bottom | BM 358a | 2670 ± 140 | 3480-3400 |
| | Antler in mound | BM 358b | 2580 ± 110 | 3400 |
| Willerby Wold, Bridlington, E. R. Yorkshire | Facade bedding-trench | BM 189 | 3010 ± 150 | 3710 |
| | Base of crematorium deposit | BM 188 | 2950 ± 150 | 3690 |

## 4. CHAMBERED LONG BARROWS AND CAIRNS

| Site | Feature | Lab. No. | Radiocarbon date bc (5568 half-life) | Calibrated date BC (approx.) |
|---|---|---|---|---|
| *Clyde group* Monamore, Arran, Bute | Hearth (?) in forecourt under blocking | Q 675 | 3160 ± 110 | 4200-3950 |
| | Hearth in forecourt, end of tomb use | Q 676 | 2240 ± 110 | 2950 |

*Cotswold-Severn group*

| | | | | |
|---|---|---|---|---|
| Ascott-under-Wychwood, Oxfordshire | Ground surface beneath mound | BM 492 | $2785 \pm 70$ | 3640-3530 |
| Wayland's Smithy, Ashbury, Berkshire | Surface of soil overlying earthen barrow and underlying chambered barrow | I 1468 | $2820 \pm 130$ | 3650-3540 |

*Court cairns*

| | | | | |
|---|---|---|---|---|
| Annaghmare, Armagh | Charcoal sealed behind primary blocking of forecourt | UB 241 | $2445 \pm 55$ | 3380-3210 |
| Ballymacdermot, Armagh | Charcoal beneath blocking of inner forecourt | UB 207 | $1710 \pm 60$ | 2130 |
| Ballyutoag, Antrim | Charcoal from forecourt | D 48 | $2170 \pm 300$ | 2940-2580 |

5. PASSAGE-GRAVES

*Boyne group*

| | | | | |
|---|---|---|---|---|
| Fourknocks II, Meath | Crematorium | D 45 | $1530 \pm 140$ | 2010-1710 |
| Knowth, Meath (large tomb) | Basal layer of mound | UB 337 | $2795 \pm 165$ | 3650-3530 |
| Knowth, Meath (smaller tomb) | Ground surface beneath mound | UB 319 | $2845 \pm 185$ | 3670 |

## 5. PASSAGE GRAVES (continued)

| Site | Feature | Lab. No. | Radiocarbon date bc (5568 half-life) | Calibrated date BC (approx.) |
|---|---|---|---|---|
| Mound of the Hostages, Tara, Meath | Ground surface beneath mound | D 43 | 2310 ± 160 | 2960 |
| | Ditch ante-dating mound | D 42 | 2130 ± 160 | 2920-2530 |
| | Charcoal contemporary with construction | D 44 | 1930 ± 150 | 2480-2250 |
| Newgrange, Meath | Basal sod layer | UB 361 | 2585 ± 105 | 3390 |
| | Caulking of roof-slab 3 | GrN 5462-C | 2475 ± 45 | 3380-3220 |
| | Caulking under cross-lintel | GrN 5463 | 2465 ± 40 | 3380-3220 |
| Townleyhall (II), Louth | Occupation ante-dating tomb | BM 170 | 2730 ± 150 | 3500-3410 |
| *Orkney-Cromarty group* | | | | |
| Embo, Sutherland | Bones contemporary with cairn-building | BM 442 | 1920 ± 100 | 2490-2240 |

## 6. OTHER ROUND MOUNDS

| Site | Feature | Lab. No. | Radiocarbon date bc (5568 half-life) | Calibrated date BC (approx.) |
|---|---|---|---|---|
| Pitnacree, Aberfeldy, Perthshire | Ground surface beneath mound | GaK 601 | 2860 ± 90 | 3650-3540 |
| | Stone-hole on summit of mound | GaK 602 | 2270 ± 90 | 2950 |
| Silbury Hill, Avebury, Wiltshire | Core of primary mound | I 4136 | 2145 ± 95 | 2930-2560 |

## 7. CAUSEWAYED ENCLOSURES

| | | | | |
|---|---|---|---|---|
| Abingdon, Berkshire | Specimens from inner ditch | BM 351 | 3110 ± 130 | 4190-3910 |
| | | BM 353 | 3020 ± 130 | 3710 |
| | | BM 350 | 2960 ± 110 | 3700 |
| | | BM 348 | 2780 ± 135 | 3660-3560 |
| | | BM 352 | 2760 ± 135 | 3520 |
| | | BM 355 | 2510 ± 140 | 3380-3250 |
| | | BM 354 | 2500 ± 145 | 3380-3250 |
| Hambledon Hill, Dorset | Bottom of ditch | NPL 76 | 2790 ± 90 | 3640-3530 |
| Hembury, Devon | Burnt layer in ditch | BM 138 | 3330 ± 150 | 4220-4050 |
| | Bottom of ditch | BM 130 | 3150 ± 150 | 4200-3950 |
| Knap Hill, Wiltshire | Bottom of ditch | BM 205 | 2760 ± 115 | 3520 |
| Windmill Hill, Wiltshire | Lower fill of ditch | BM 74 | 2580 ± 150 | 3400 |

## 8. HENGES

| | | | | |
|---|---|---|---|---|
| *Class I* | | | | |
| Arminghall, Norfolk | Base of post-hole 7 | BM 129 | 2490 ± 150 | 3380-3210 |

*8. HENGES (continued)*

| Site | Feature | Lab. No. | Radiocarbon date bc (5568 half-life) | Calibrated date BC (approx.) |
|---|---|---|---|---|
| Barford, Warwickshire | Last phase | Birm 7 | 2416 ± 64 | 3350-2980 |
| Llandegai, Caernarvonshire | Primary fire-pit | NPL 220 | 2790 ± 150 | 3650-3530 |
| | Cremation circle outside entrance | NPL 224 | 2530 ± 145 | 3390 |
| | End of primary silting in ditch | NPL 221 | 2470 ± 140 | 3380-3210 |
| Stonehenge, Wiltshire | Construction of ditch | I 2328 | 2180 ± 105 | 2940-2590 |
| | Aubrey Hole 32 | C 602 | 1848 ± 275 | 2350-2190 |
| *Class II* Durrington Walls, Wiltshire | Bottom of ditch | BM 400 | 2050 ± 90 | 2520 |
| | Bottom of ditch | BM 399 | 2015 ± 90 | 2520 |
| | Bottom of ditch | BM 398 | 1977 ± 90 | 2500 |
| | South Circle, phase II | BM 396 | 2000 ± 90 | 2510 |
| | South Circle, phase II | BM 395 | 1950 ± 90 | 2500-2400 |
| | South Circle, phase II | BM 397 | 1900 ± 90 | 2490-2220 |
| Marden, Wiltshire | Bottom of ditch | BM 557 | 1988 ± 48 | 2510 |

# 4. *Scottish chambered tombs and long mounds*

## AUDREY S. HENSHALL

These two classes of monuments, the chambered tombs and the long barrows/cairns, provide the largest body of material remains from the pre-beaker period in Scotland, and indeed the only structures belonging to this period with the exception of a few henges and one or two habitation sites in Orkney. The chambered tombs and the long mounds appeared in Scotland at not very different dates, towards the end of the 4th millennium þc, the one concentrated in the west of the country but soon extending northwards, the other occupying the east and south of the country but spreading to the south-west and the north mainland. Essentially the monuments fall into three groups with different origins, for there are two distinct groups of chambered tombs. These three groups presumably reflect the presence of culturally distinct peoples. Their histories in Scotland are interwoven, and their relationships, as represented by their funerary and ritual monuments, are indeed very puzzling.

During the first half of this century study of the Scottish chambered tombs was largely concerned with classification in two typological series.[1] The first series, now known as the Clyde group of south-west Scotland,[2] was distinguished by long rectangular chambers opening straight from the outside of the cairn, which was normally a rectangle or trapeze in plan, much longer than needed to cover the chamber. At the chamber entrance the cairn was often recessed and faced by an imposing setting of tall stones, or orthostats. But in the same region there are small rectangular or square chambers, sometimes under more or less round cairns. Between these two extremes lie the majority of tombs with chambers of intermediate size, and there are many complications including cairns which cover more than one chamber.

The second series of tombs, in the Outer Isles, the

Figure 19. The distribution of chambered tombs in
   Scotland. 1. O-C-H passage-graves; 2. Clyde-type
   chambers; 3. Bargrennan-type chambers; 4. Clava-
   type chambers; 5. Maes Howe-type chambers;
   6. unclassifiable chambers.

1
2
3
4
5
6

mainland north of the Caledonian Canal, Orkney and Shetland, comprises various groups of passage-graves. Their chambers vary even more widely in size, plan, and .construction techniques, seemingly having little in common other than entry down a passage. The majority are under round cairns, but heel-shaped cairns, square cairns, and long cairns occur, all with or without forecourts, and most combinations of chamber plan and cairn plan are now known.

Consideration of this bewildering variety of tombs during the first half of the century was naturally dominated by the current diffusionist concepts involving assumptions that our prehistoric cultures were likely to derive from the Mediterranean area. It was thus natural to stress features in the Scottish tombs which could be paralleled in tombs to the south and east of Britain. These features, which then seemed so significant, such as forecourts with imposing concave façades, known in Scotland, in the Balearics, and in southern Spain, were only part of a tomb, the other parts requiring comparison with tombs in other regions of the continent or having no continental parallels at all. These selective comparisons seemed unsound to Piggott writing in the early fifties,[3] and today are largely rejected. From the ensuing rather negative phase in the study of the tombs it is now possible to approach the subject more positively, largely due to the work of Scott and Corcoran, recasting the questions and assumptions uppermost in our minds in the light of current chronology and recent excavation, and utilising a recently completed field survey of the monuments.

The first factor to be considered is the greatly extended time-scale within which the tombs developed structurally and spread spatially. The new chronology has been discussed in Chapter 1, and here it suffices to emphasise that writers in the fifties were thinking in terms of seven hundred years for the whole span of British tomb-building, whereas today the building of the Scottish tombs probably covers some fourteen centuries on radiocarbon dates, and as much as some twenty-two centuries on calibrated dates.

The enormously extended time-span within which chambered tombs were used and developed makes another new factor much more acceptable. This is that many tombs are composite monuments: they were first built as relatively

Figure 20. The distribution of long cairns in Scotland: 1. without stone chambers (including some intact examples which may contain chambers); 2. uncertain long cairns (including sites with and without chambers); 3. with Clyde-type chambers; 4. with O-C-H passage-graves; 5. with unclassifiable chambers; 6. with Bargrennan-type chambers.

small and simple structures, later added to, altered and embellished.[4] An example of these processes was demonstrated by Corcoran at Mid Gleniron[5] (WIG 1 and 2)[6] (Fig. 21:2). At Mid Gleniron I the first structure was a simple rectangular chamber build of heavy split boulders set within a roughly circular small cairn. This was followed by a second similar tomb built in front of the first. A third chamber was built between the other two, probably in a third building phase, and the whole complex was covered by a trapezoidal cairn.[7] When this was done access to the front chamber was provided by linking it with the front of the cairn by a passage-like entry, but the rear chamber was completely sealed and inaccessible. Here the complex history of a chambered cairn has been revealed by excavation, built in three or four separate phases and embodying two distinct funerary traditions, the rectangular chambers in their round cairns and the superimposed long cairn. Two further points should be noted, that the chamber was structurally extended to allow access when the cairn was enlarged, and that the forms of the earlier cairns had been completely masked by the latest cairn.

Similar processes may be deduced at a site of different type, Camster Long (CAT 12) (Fig. 21: 3). Here the long narrow cairn, edged by a double wall-face, contains two chambers and probably more. The two excavated chambers are approached by fairly long passages, but are otherwise unalike. The excavator's plan of 1866 may be re-interpreted: the first structure on the site was probably the small simple polygonal east chamber built with a relatively short passage, presumptively in a small round cairn; a later chamber was built beside it, also presumptively in a round cairn, and in another building phase a long cairn was superimposed on the earlier structures. Access to the chambers was provided by extending the passages. As the passage of the east chamber was not at right angles to the main axis of the long cairn, the finished passage had an angle at the original entrance. At the west chamber a straight joint in the wall-face, and a corbelled roof in contrast to the inner lintelled roof, indicate that the outer part was indeed an extension of the inner part. Even in ruin the profile of the long cairn indicates the position of the earlier cairns which were higher in order to cover the chambers.[8]

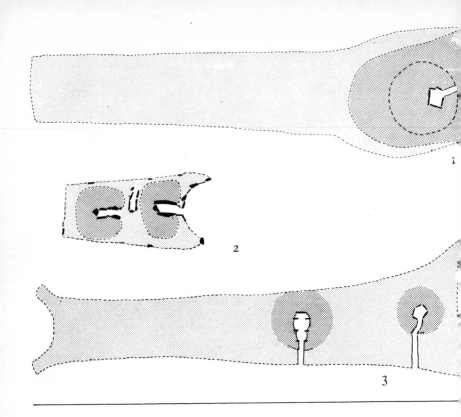

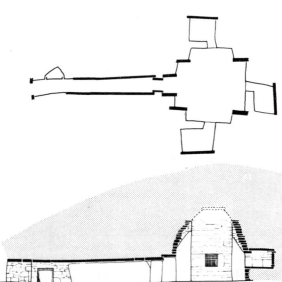

Figure 21. Above: 1. Tulach an t'Sionnaich, CAT 58; 2. Mid Gleniron I, WIG 1; 3. Camster Long, CAT 12. Scale 1: 480. Below: Maes Howe chamber, ORK 36. Scale 1:240.

Another Scottish site, this time containing only one chamber, has had its structural history revealed by Corcoran's campaign of excavation. Tulach an t'Sionnaich (CAT 58) (Fig. 21: 1) consisted in the first place of a small simple passage-grave set in a small round cairn. It was later enclosed within a heel-shaped cairn; the unbroken kerb at the front of this cairn should be noted, there being no extension of the passage to the exterior in the second phase, presumably meaning that the passage-grave was no longer to be used. Later still a long cairn was added on a slightly skew axis.[9]

These processes of adding to the original monument may happen intermittently over a long period, and may be in the hands of a group of people of different origins and traditions from the first builders.

Once it is accepted that some tombs may be composite monuments, there is the problem of how extensively this concept can be applied, whether it is possible to dissect individual tombs into their significant component parts without total modern excavation undertaken with these problems specifically in mind. Structural analysis has been used with caution by Corcoran and Scott who have pioneered this approach in Scotland, and the writer is inclined to go further and regard all tombs as potentially multi-period constructions, believing that most eccentric plans are due to difficulties of adapting or incorporating earlier structures in later additions. Such analysis is, after all, an everyday tool in the hands of architectural historians, and there is plenty of evidence, once it is looked for, that this is a valid line of enquiry. There are, however, dangers and difficulties. It is easy to misinterpret half-observed features at unexcavated sites, such as walling within cairns which can be claimed as evidence of an earlier phase when it is no more than a structural device during building. And it is a sobering thought that if the earliest sites are most likely to have gathered extensive additions they will be all the more difficult to recognise and isolate.

With these matters in mind, the Scottish chambered tombs can be considered anew. The established two-fold division into Clyde cairns and passage-graves obviously stands, but there must be radical changes within these groups. The distribution of the five main types of tomb has been plotted in Fig. 19.

## The Clyde cairns

The Clyde cairns, comprising nearly a hundred sites, have been the subject of a recent study by J.G. Scott[10] who has shown conclusively that the formerly accepted typological series in which the largest and most elaborate were held to be the earliest with a degeneration series to the smallest, must be reversed. The writer, feeling that the dissection of sites should be taken further, would favour a less precise typology for these tombs, and the inclusion of a wider range of simple rectangular chambers in the earliest phases.[11]

The development of chamber plans is illustrated Fig. 22. The earliest are small quadrangular structures built of close-fitting orthostats needing little dry walling to fill the gaps between the stones. The roofing is by a capstone, in the main resting directly on the side slabs at a low level giving an internal height of about 3-4 ft. The structure is a very simple box-like affair even if the size of the stones handled may be surprising. The chamber at Mid Gleniron I (WIG 1) (Fig. 22: 1) is the simplest of all with no elaboration of the entrance. Another version, illustrated by Glecknabae (BUT 4) (Fig. 22: 2), has transverse portal stones and a low sill across the entrance. This is the form which gives rise to the classic Clyde chamber. Yet another form, Ardmarnock (ARG 17) (Fig. 22: 3) being an example, has the chamber inaccessible, the 'entrance' being sealed by a high transverse slab built between the portal stones (here set lengthwise) and the chamber.

The next stage in development is the enlargement of the simple single-compartment chamber by the addition of an outer compartment. This process is easily recognisable at Cairnholy (KRK 2, 3) (Fig. 22: 4-5). The chambers had been of the Ardmarnock form but were subsequently doubled in size. Brackley (ARG 28) (Fig. 22: 7) appears to have started as a single-compartment chamber with a low sill across the entrance and to have received an additional compartment in front; this interpretation cannot be proved because of the removal of the surrounding cairn, but the difference in construction of the two parts strongly suggests it. This two-compartment chamber had a pair of low portal stones, and later still large portal stones were added and linked to the front of the chamber by walling.

The genesis of the two-compartment Clyde chamber plan

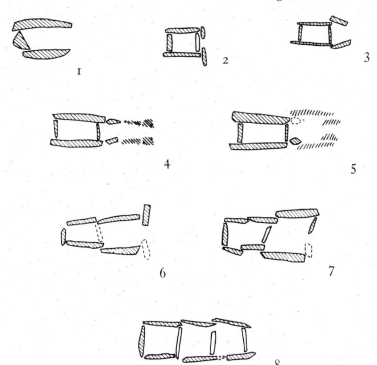

Figure 22. Above: 1. Mid Gleniron, WIG 1; 2. Glecknabae, BUT 4; 3. Ardmarnock, ARG 17; 4-5. Cairnholy (KRK 2-3) (shaded stones without outline, additions); 6. Gort na h'Ulaidhe, ARG 30; 7. Brackley, ARG 28; 8. Beacharra, ARG 27. Scale 1:180. Below: 9. Ardacheranbeg, ARG 15; 10. Water of Deugh, KRK 13; 11. Mid Gleniron I, WIG 1. Scale 1:480.

can be seen in the plans of such sites as Cairnholy and Brackley. The main chamber at Gort na h'Ulaidhe (ARG 30) (Fig. 22: 6) represents the largest group of Clyde chambers, those with two compartments built as a unit. Once this stage of development had been reached, the way was open, given the desire and the resources, to build three-compartment, four-compartment and even five-compartment chambers. These larger chambers are represented here by the still quite modest Beacharra (ARG 27) (Fig. 22: 8), but the longest chamber extended for over 10 m. In some two-compartment chambers, but especially in the longer chambers, dry walling heightened the walls above the orthostats and bore a series of capstones which might be as much as 3 m. above the ground. In the most carefully constructed chambers the orthostats were paired, their ends overlapping, with low transverse slabs across the chambers acting as struts to counteract any inward thrust from the cairn.

The cairns of the early chambers were small and round, revealed by excavation at Mid Gleniron (WIG 1, 2) (Fig. 22: 11), and still visible at Ardacheranbeg (ARG 15) (FIG. 22: 9). But generally the cairns have been removed or have been incorporated within later additions. The long cairns typical of the Clyde group are an acquired feature from a quite different funerary tradition. The obvious questions, at what stage of the development of Clyde chambers long cairns were first imposed on the tombs, and at what stage they were first built as a unit with the chambers, must be left open until there have been excavations of the cairns covering developed chambers. At Mid Gleniron II the long cairn seems to be contemporary with one of the single-compartment chambers whilst at Dunan Mor (ARN 8) a two-compartment and possibly a three-compartment chamber are under a round cairn.

Besides the secondary enlargement of small early chambers, presumably because more space was needed for burials, there was also a tendency to build a second chamber, or more, in the immediate vicinity of an existing chamber, subsequently incorporating all in one long cairn, as exemplified by Mid Gleniron. There is abundant structural evidence at other sites that the chambers of one or two compartments are earlier than the cairns under which they now lie.

Besides the desire to build larger chambers, there was an ever increasing interest in the external appearance of the tombs, perhaps reflecting changing attitudes, with the tomb acquiring sanctity, with resultant veneration and ritual activity. Generally early chambers were built either without portal stones or with small portal stones, but more imposing entrances became desirable. Very large portal stones were sometimes added, as in the case of Brackley (ARG 28) already mentioned. The long cairns became larger, and the early straight façades became deeper in plan. In the latest phases orthostats linked by panels of dry walling were used to create handsome post-and-panel façades and occasionally were continued round the edge of the whole cairn. It seems likely that modest long cairns were sometimes enlarged or embellished according to later fashion. The addition of large portal stones or of orthostatic façades was liable to produce the so-called complex entrance with two pairs of portal stones.

Reversal of the former typological sequence of Clyde cairns means the abandonment of the theories deriving them from the continent. The chambers developed from simple structures into the characteristic long subdivided chamber without any external influences. The origins of the chamber are likely to lie in the Irish Sea area, for in many of the peripheral areas, North Wales, South Wales, Cornwall, eastern and northern Ireland, there may be found simple single-compartment chambers, sometimes of the specific type known as portal dolmens, sometimes of a less distinctive kind and easily overlooked, especially if incorporated into a composite monument.

Consideration of the development of the Clyde tombs leads to a general proposition which is probably applicable to other large groups of tombs and in particular to the main group of Scottish passage-graves next to be described. The chambers start as small simple structures in minimal functional cairns. The first chambers must be very early in date, going back almost to the time of the establishment of the earliest farming communities in the region. Apart from all other considerations, peoples in a pioneering situation would not have the resources to build anything but modest tombs. Development of the two-compartment plan was the consequence of a desire for more space for burials, and having invented this structure there was no technical limit to the length of the chamber built. With the larger chamber there went a desire for an impressive exterior, and elaboration of the cairns may even have continued after chamber-building had ceased.

## The passage-graves

### The O-C-H group

The main group of Scottish passage-graves, now known as the O-C-H (Orkney-Cromarty-Hebridean) group,[12] comprises about three hundred sites. Amongst these it is again necessary to resort to dissection, for small early chambers are liable to be found under enlarged cairns sometimes with elaborate external features, as at Tulach an t'Sionnaich and Camster Long (CAT 58, 12) already referred to. The small simple passage-graves are polygonal in plan, some only 1.5 m. in diameter, constructed of orthostats and roofed by a single capstone generally raised above the orthostats by a row or two of flat slabs slightly overhanging the interior to make a relatively low false vault, for instance Unival (UST 34) (Fig. 23: 1). Entry is by a narrow passage, typically quite short. There are a few chambers of this type surrounded by small minimal cairns 8 or 9 m. in diameter.

In the Outer Isles there are large round cairns containing small polygonal chambers, some having deep V-shaped forecourts, and indications can be found that the chambers were originally under smaller cairns. For instance at Oban nam Fiadh (UST 25) (Fig. 24: 6) part of a setting of upright stones surrounding the chamber within the cairn is likely to be the kerb of the first period cairn, the very short orthostatic passage ending in line with the setting. At the excavated site of Rudh' an Dunain (SKY 7) (Fig. 24: 7) the small chamber has a short passage narrowed by a portal, and an outer section of passage with a second portal. A likely interpretation of this site, and others with V-shaped forecourts, is that the inner section of passage is original, indicating the small size of the original cairn, and that subsequent enlargement of the cairn involved difficulties of access, a problem solved by providing the forecourt and linking this with the earlier structure by a small outer section of passage.

Development of the chamber seems to have aimed, in the first place, at producing larger chambers of similar single-compartment plan (Fig. 23: 2). The large number of passage-graves in the Outer Isles and Skye are almost monotonous in their similarity, at any rate in unexcavated ruins, though some impressive chambers were built, the largest measuring 6 by 3.8 m. Chambers of this type also appeared on the mainland. Nor can a tomb be claimed as early because it has a simple plan, for in the west particularly they were still being built when more elaborate forms were emerging in the far north-east.

On the mainland there was a tendency for the entry into the passage, and the entry from passage to chamber, to be marked by a pair of transversely set slabs. One unique chamber plan, Kilcoy (ROS 24) (Fig. 23: 4), invites hypothetical dissection. The passage of the completed structure is almost certainly an addition to allow access after the cairn was enlarged with the V-shaped forecourt. The main part of the tomb, the so-called ante-chamber and chamber, may be regarded as an example of the type of single-compartment chamber with transversely-set stones just mentioned. But the so-called cell, set awkwardly on a different axis and linked to the main chamber by a very short passage, is likely to be a small chamber of early date, the first structure on the site. If this analysis be accepted, the Kilcoy chamber provides a sequence of small passage-grave, larger but still simple passage-grave, with a still later extension of the passage. The two later phases are of further interest, for arrangements such as this give rise to the bipartite plan, such as Tulloch of Assery A (CAT 69) (Fig. 23: 3).

One other variant of the simple plan may be mentioned, that with a small cell built to one side, as seen at Kyleoag (SUT 37) (Fig. 23: 5). These cells are no more than a shallow bay roofed at a low level. They become significant when the cell is arranged on the axis of a bipartite chamber producing the tripartite plan typical of Caithness (Fig. 23: 6). Mainly because of the high quality of the local flagstone for building, there was an increased use of dry walling in the far north, the orthostats taking on a special function, dividing the parts of

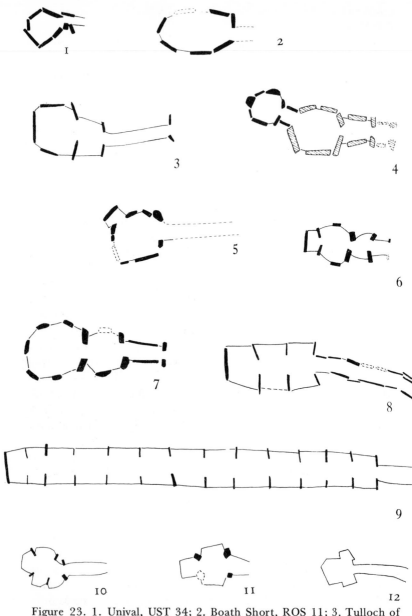

Figure 23. 1. Unival, UST 34; 2. Boath Short, ROS 11; 3. Tulloch of Assery A, CAT 69; 4. Kilcoy S. ROS 24; 5. Kyleoag, SUT 37; 6. Kinbrace Burn, SUT 65; 7. Skelpick Long, SUT 53; 8. Tulloch of Assery B, CAT 70; 9. Midhowe, ORK 37; 10. Calf of Eday SE, ORK 10; 11. March Cairn, ZET 27; 12. Vementry, ZET 45. Scale 1:240.

the chamber and stabilising the walling. Also due to this stone, high vaults could be built over the main part of the chamber. There are three variations of the roofing arrangements of the tripartite plan. First, the ante-chamber and the cell at the rear were roofed relatively low with lintels resting on the wallheads and the paired transverse slabs, the central area only having a vault; but the two developments in response to a desire for a larger chamber were to roof either the ante-chamber and main chamber together under a vault, or the main chamber and cell, though retaining the unnecessary pair of transverse orthostats as sub-divisions of the chamber.[13]

In striving for a larger chamber still, the limiting factor was the circular vault. One solution was to build two connecting vaulted compartments, as at Skelpick Long (SUT 53) (Fig. 23: 7). Another solution was the construction of a barrel vault, the side walls all oversailing, the transverse orthostats acting both as divisions of the chamber and supports to the overhang, the roofing by a series of lintels at a height of 2.5 or more metres. These stalled chambers could be much larger even whilst retaining the tripartite ground plan, as at Tulloch of Assery B (CAT 70) (Fig. 23: 8), but having achieved the barrel vault there was no limit to the length of chamber which could be built. The main development of the stalled chamber was on Orkney, with extreme versions of the plan on the island of Rousay (Fig. 23: 9), the largest of all at the Knowe of Ramsay (ORK 30) reaching the astonishing length of nearly 27 m. with fourteen compartments, and a probable roof height of over 3 m.

Besides the stalled chambers, there also evolved in Orkney another chamber plan based on the tripartite chamber, named after the site of Bookan (ORK 4). The chambers are small, consisting of a number of recesses with dry built walls generally rounded in plan, and divided by orthostats set radially (Fig. 23: 10). At two sites in Orkney there is the unique arrangement of one chamber built directly on top of another. This chamber plan (but not the double-decker arrangement) migrated to Shetland and gave rise to the trefoil chamber plans in those islands. The Shetland chambers also have dry-built recesses, but arranged symmetrically, and in two or three instances such as March Cairn (ZET 27) retain the orthostats between the recesses (Fig. 23: 11). But the difficult building stone of Shetland affected the construction methods, orthostats were abandoned and the chambers were built of massive crude masonry, as at Vementry (ZET 45) (Fig. 23: 12), and were often rather irregular in plan. This construction obscures their ancestry, but two details add confirmation. In both Bookan and Zetland trefoil chambers the roofing is fairly low, by a slab set across each recess, and by a further slab or slabs resting on these to cover the central area. There also appear in both groups of tombs stone benches built into the recesses.

It thus appears that this whole complex group of O-C-H passage-graves has evolved from small simple chambers without any outside influences, except that possibly the pairs of transversely-set orthostats at the chamber entrance may derive from any early stage of the Clyde group. There were two stimuli to development. One was the desire for larger chambers, culminating in the astonishing and bizarre stalled chambers of Orkney. The other was the availability of flagstone for building in Orkney and Caithness, contrasting with the split boulders and igneous rocks of the highlands, the Outer Isles and Shetland. The passage-graves can be arranged in a typological series, the most elegant and extravagant being restricted to Caithness and particularly to Orkney. As these were the result of the building material they need be no later in date than some of the less sophisticated tombs elsewhere. The simple early passage-graves appear to be of an international type: they can be paralleled in Ireland and less closely in France and Iberia. It is difficult to be specific about their origins, but probably we should look to north-west France.

Small round cairns are appropriate to the O-C-H tombs, and large round cairns are in the main attributable to later enlargements. With the very long chambers in Orkney the round plan was abandoned for a casing of cairn material echoing the rectangular shape of the chamber (Fig. 24: 1). But passage-graves are also found under long cairns, more frequently at eastern sites but known in the Outer Isles. The long cairns, deriving from the long cairn/barrow series without stone chambers, were generally, if not always, additions to existing tombs. The building of long cairns seems to have been in decline by the time the Orcadian stalled chambers were being built. Another imposed cairn type was the heel-shaped cairn, and its more developed forms, the short-horned and square cairns. They have a widespread distribution in the region occupied by the passage-graves, but are not numerous except in Shetland where they are the normal covering of the Zetland chambers.

## The Bargrennan group

There remain three groups of passage-graves which do not come within the O-C-H group. The Bargrennan group of SW Scotland consists of about twelve rather disparate sites, but all having a relatively small single-compartment chamber and a passage element giving access, normally under a round cairn. Their distribution overlaps with the Clyde tombs, and the two have much in common. The Bargrennan chambers may be grouped together with two or more under one cairn (Fig. 22: 10), in two or three cases the grouped chambers are under a long cairn which is almost certainly a later addition, and the plan of some chambers is close to the early single-compartment rectangular chambers of the Clyde group. The recognition that early Clyde chambers were under round cairns, and that early chambers in this group might acquire short passage-like additions for access after cairn enlargements, makes the distinction between Bargrennan and early Clyde sites less clear-cut. On the other hand some chambers are polygonal in plan, and at some sites the passages can be shown to be integral with the chambers, making them indistinguishable from early passage-graves of the O-C-H group. Yet another variation of the chamber has paired orthostats in a long wedge-shaped plan; this can be regarded either as an enlargement of the simple rectangular chamber with more than one orthostat in each wall, as found at Mid Gleniron I (WIG 1), or as derived from passage-graves with orthostatic passages which do occur within the group (e.g. AYR 4), and so comparable with the Irish entrance graves such as those at Knowth, Co. Meath.[14] Altogether the Bargrennan group poses problems, but seems best explained as the result of local hybridisation between early Clyde tombs and early O-C-H passage-graves.

*The Clava group*

The Clava passage-graves, again comprising only about twelve sites, are a distinct group with a relatively restricted distribution around Inverness and in the Spey valley. The chambers are round in plan, dry-built with a heavy foundation course, the upper courses oversailing for the roof which was closed by a capstone at a height of about 3 m. above the floor (Fig. 24: 4). The passages are fairly long, for the chambers are set centrally within quite large round cairns edged by a heavy kerb. Round the cairn is a circle of standing stones. In the past these passage-graves were claimed as early in date, of simple international type. This now seems most unlikely, for they have several highly individual features. Most passage-graves face the eastern half of the compass, but this group consistently faces the south-west quarter. The stones of the foundation course of the chamber, and of the kerb, and the circle of standing stones, are all graduated in height with the tallest to the south-west. Most of the sites incorporate stones decorated with cupmarks, otherwise unknown among Scottish tombs, and rare on tombs elsewhere. Only one other tomb in western Europe is encircled by standing stones, but the chamber at this site is unrelated to the Clava group. Nor does the group show any signs of the multiperiod construction work which has been observed elsewhere.

The Clava passage-graves thus seem distinct from the other Scottish passage-graves, and from continental passage-graves also, and therefore appear to be a locally evolved group. The question of their ancestry is difficult, as the existing tombs are very similar with few hints of evolution or devolution: they seem to appear on the scene fully developed. But they are closely related to the local ring-cairns, and these in turn relate to the homegrown traditions of circular ritual enclosures and henges, a tradition quite separate from that of the chambered tomb. This tradition appears to be the dominant parent of the Clava passage-graves, and the presence of stone circles in particular suggests a late date for the group, but not so late that the technique of building a roofed chamber could not be observed at O-C-H chambers which occur within the northern limit of the Clava distribution.[15]

*The Maes Howe group*

The Maes Howe group of passage-graves, with only ten or eleven sites, is confined to the Orkney Islands. Clearly these tombs do not belong to the main Scottish series of passage-graves for the whole conception is different. The large chambers are square or rectangular in plan, dry built without orthostats (except at Maes Howe itself (ORK 36) (Fig. 21) where they are used in a special way). Off each chamber there open a number of cells, as many as fourteen at the largest chamber, which is nearly 14 m. long (ORK 22). The entries to the cells are minimised so as not to detract from the splendour of the main chamber. The chambers have long passages from the exterior of the large cairns which are of complex construction. As with Clava cairns, there is little sign of later enlargement or elaboration: chamber and cairn are one magnificent conception and achievement. The earliest and finest tomb is Maes Howe (Fig. 21: 4); the brilliance of the designer and the skill of the builders have produced here one of the outstanding buildings of prehistoric Europe.

The origin of this group of tombs almost certainly lies in Ireland, among the few corbelled cruciform chambers of which the most famous is New Grange.[16] But it must be admitted that the comparison is not all that close, and when the crudity of the actual construction of New Grange is compared with the sophistication of Maes Howe one is forced to suppose that there must have been at least one lost earlier tomb in Orkney.

## The long cairns

Besides the chambered tombs, the other great tradition of funerary monuments in Britain was the long cairns/barrows. These are better known from England and have been discussed in Chapter 3. Many English examples have been excavated, showing that normally they contained structures built of wood or turf designed to receive bodies, but unlike chambered tombs, access was not possible once construction work was completed. In Scotland the monuments are more often cairns than barrows, but in external appearance and size some at least compare well with English sites.[17] Recently a Scottish cairn, Lochhill (KRK 14), and a Scottish barrow, Dalladies (KNC 8), have been totally and near-totally excavated, producing the first information on the internal arrangements at Scottish sites.[18]

At Lochhill Masters identified a timber mortuary structure containing cremated bones. The structure measured 7.5 by 1.4 m., having three large oval pits at either end and midway which had held timber uprights. There had also been a free-standing timber façade across one end, and in front of it four slabs set as sides of a 'porch'. The wooden structures had been burnt down, and after burning the cairn had been begun. This was long, with the mortuary structure on the axis at the wider end. It had an orthostatic façade (placed in front of the timber façade) which was connected to the four slabs to form a small 'chamber'.

At Dalladies Piggott found the mortuary structure askew to the axis of the barrow with its entry from the side near the wider end. The first structure, 8 by 3.5 m., was identified by two large post-holes at the entrance and three large D-shaped pits, one at the rear and the others equally spaced between it and the pair of posts. The pits had held unburnt timbers which had rotted *in situ*, and are probably to be interpreted as supports for some kind of gabled structure. This was replaced by another structure built concurrently with the mound. It had a pair of posts incorporated into the revetment wall of the mound, and side walls of boulders, but was open at the rear. Within this was a slight timber structure roofed with birch bark under slabs. This had been burnt down and the mound completed over it. The only evidence for burials was a piece of unburnt skull.

Besides the long mounds with a simple trapezoidal or rectangular plan and a profile sloping down uniformly from the higher end, as at Dalladies before destruction, there are also a variety of sites which appear to have been built in two or more phases. At certain sites the long cairn appears to have been an addition to a large heel-shaped or round cairn standing some 3 m. or more high, the two parts being distinguishable either in ground plan, or in profile, or both, giving a head-and-tail effect. In the parts of Scotland where chambered tombs do not occur the nature of these primary mounds is uncertain, but it is suggestive that when Knapperty Hillock (ABN 5) was destroyed no chamber but only masses of burnt wood were observed. A large round mound at Pitnacree, Perthshire, excavated in 1964, produced a central pair of large pits which had held timber uprights, and had been followed by an overlying rectangular enclosure, measuring about 7 by 12 m., built at the same time as the covering mound through part of which there was a passage-like entry. Three cremations underlay the enclosure wall. The precise interpretation of the structure is not clear, and it is without exact parallel, but it must be related to the timber structures under long barrows, the excavators instancing the earlier phase at Wayland's Smithy, Berkshire.[19]

The long cairn/barrows which have been discussed mostly lie in the south and east of the country. North of the Moray Firth is a region well supplied with passage-graves, and at least half of the long cairns in this region are known to cover such tombs. The excavation of Tulach an t'Sionnaich (CAT 58) showed that the long cairn was an addition to a passage-grave which had already been sealed within a heel-shaped cairn. Other examples of a long cairn sealing an earlier passage-grave are known. Alternatively a long cairn might be added to a passage-grave in such a way that access was provided: the odd case of Camster Long (CAT 12) has been described already, but at other sites the chambers lie on the main axis with the entry in the centre of the forecourt, the whole having sometimes the appearance of a unitary design as at South Yarrows North (CAT 59) (Fig. 24: 3). The development of plan in the north of Scotland was towards wider and deeper forecourts, edged by neat dry walling where the stone was suitable, and to double-ended cairns, the rear reproducing the front on a small scale.

In the south-west of Scotland the situation was comparable, long cairns being added to tombs of the Clyde and Bargrennan groups. In the Clyde group, however, there seems to have been a real fusion of the two traditions, at least by the time the latest chambers were being built. The development of cairn plans was also parallel, with wider deeper forecourts appearing, though in the last stages with post-and-panel orthostatic façades (Fig. 24: 5).

It is perhaps strange that there was no provision for burials in the long cairn at Tulach an t'Sionnaich. In this respect the long cairn can be compared with a few English sites,[20] and it may be noted how slight was the evidence for burials at Dalladies, and for that matter nonexistent in the enclosure at Pitnacree. This suggests that the long cairns/barrows were not primarily funerary monuments at all, and that in some cases the structures within them were not designed as the permanent repositories for the dead. The purpose of the great mounds is difficult to envisage, but at least this view of the long mounds makes their imposition on alien burial monuments slightly less incomprehensible.

### Heel-shaped and square cairns

The curious heel-shaped and square cairns present another problem. Their behaviour in relation to passage-graves is comparable to that of long cairns, for at some sites they are certainly later additions, and they may or may not seal the pre-existing tomb (Fig. 24: 8, 11-12). The important façade element is common to both. The development of the plans of heel-shaped and long cairns is similar, for the double short-horned plan, such as Ormiegill (CAT 42) (Fig. 24: 10), echoes the double-ended long cairns such as South Yarrows (CAT 54, 55). The heel-shaped and long cairns frequently appear at the same sites in the north mainland. Yet the two cairn types are distinct, and in one case at least, at Tulach an t'Sionnaich (CAT 58), the heel-shaped cairn predated the long cairn by an appreciable time. Heel-shaped cairns occasionally and square cairns frequently appear apart from long cairns on the mainland and the Hebrides; and most telling of all, in Shetland, where heel-shaped and square cairns are the normal covering of chambers, there is not a single long cairn. Though the origin of the heel-shaped cairn is obscure, it seems that it should be sought among the builders of long cairns/barrows rather than amongst the passage-grave builders. A connection is likely with the Yorkshire neolithic round barrows amongst which wooden façades are known, and the mortuary structure with free-standing façade already mentioned at Lochhill (KRK 14).[21]

### Finds
The chambered tombs and the long cairns/barrows have

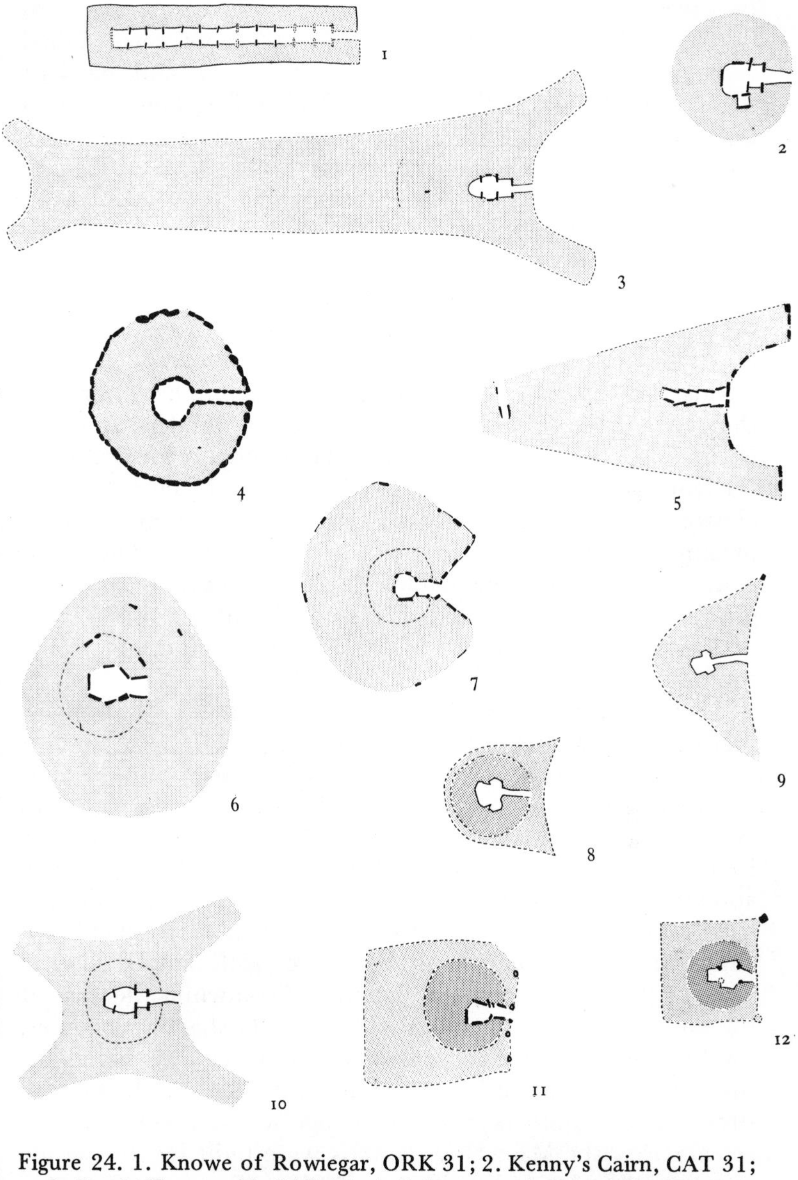

Figure 24. 1. Knowe of Rowiegar, ORK 31; 2. Kenny's Cairn, CAT 31; 3. South Yarrows N, CAT 54; 4. Balnuaran of Clava NE, INV 9; 5. East Bennan, ARN 14; 6. Oban nam Fiadh, UST 25; 7. Rudh' an Dunain, SKY 7; 8. Vementry, ZET 45; 9. Punds Water, ZET 33; 10. Ormiegill, CAT 42; 11. Balvraid, INV 51; 12. March Cairn, ZET 27. Scale 1:480.

produced on the whole a disappointingly meagre quantity of finds, and these, with such exceptions as the Orcadian stalled cairns, tend to be rather diverse in character, and many of them certainly datable to the 2nd millennium. If it is accepted that most of the tombs had a long and sometimes complex history including structural additions, it is difficult to avoid the conclusion that the chambers were emptied and re-used time and again. If so, the greater part of the grave-goods belong only to the last burial phase, or sometimes to the penultimate and last phases. If by chance some of the original grave-goods have survived, probably as no more than fragments, our knowledge of material culture during the first half of our period is so slight that at present they give little help in identifying the tomb-builders. And this is true also, of course, of the skeletal material recovered from the tombs. The exceptions to this sombrely negative conclusion are the relatively few really late tombs which presumably had a short period of use. In Orkney, for instance, some of the stalled chambers have been fairly productive of pottery, and this is consistent in type, known as Unstan ware, and is likely to have belonged to the tomb-builders or their close descendants.

This situation presents one of the ironies of Scottish prehistory, for the Clyde tombs and the O-C-H passage-graves were built by two dynamic peoples who came to Scotland as our first farmers, who established themselves and prospered, and pioneered between them the whole west coast and the Hebrides, the area north of the Caledonian Canal, Orkney and Shetland; yet except for their tombs these peoples are hardly known to us — we have little of their material culture, apparently only one habitation site with any structural remains,[22] probably not a skeleton. Meanwhile the east of the country was being colonised by equally shadowy peoples, the builders of long cairns. It is probably only at the end of the tomb-building and in the far north that the habitation sites of the builders can be recognised. It seems almost certain that the Maes Howe tombs were built by the people known to us from the villages of Skara Brae and Rinyo in Orkney,[23] and that the latest of the Shetland tombs belonged to the inhabitants of identifiable homesteads.[24]

## Chronology

The discussion of the tombs and long mounds has been largely typological, and is intended as a statement in very general terms. Unfortunately there are few radiocarbon dates bearing directly on the monuments. The two long mounds have dates as early as the comparable English sites, Dalladies (KNC 8) 3240 bc and Lochhill (KRK 14) 2130 bc. The earliest chambered tombs, the small rectangular chambers of the Clyde and Bargrennan groups, are likely to be of similar date. At Glenvoidean the axial chamber, which is of the curious closed type, has a date of 2910 bc. Probably long cairns first began to be added to Clyde chambers about the time two-compartment chambers were being built, but the enlargement and elaboration of sites was an intermittent and haphazard process. The development of the chambers, and of the long cairn plans which may have continued longer, may well have spanned most of the 3rd millenium bc. There are two dates from the tomb of Monamore (ARN 9): that of 3160 bc from below the forecourt blocking but post-dating the whole construction seems too early for a three-compartment chamber with an added slightly concave façade;[25] the second date of 2240 bc for the end of the use of the chamber is satisfactory. The whole Bargrennan group appear to be relatively early with their small simple chambers and the imposition of long cairns which do not have the developed Clyde plan. If a comparison of the wedge-shaped chamber plan such as Bargrenna itself (KRK 5) and the satellites at Knowth is valid, we may note the dates of 2925-2845 bc for one of the latter.

The O-C-H passage-graves are likely to have appeared in west Scotland only a little after the first Clyde chambers: their relative dating is implied by their more northerly distribution suggesting that the builders of Clyde tombs were already established in the south-west. But the appearance of a few simple passage-graves in the south-west as an element in the Bargrennan group indicates they are not much later than the early Clyde tombs, and a starting date of about 3000 bc may be estimated. The O-C-H tombs span the whole 3rd millennium bc with the last tombs on the periphery of their area later still. Whatever the exact origin of the Clava passage-graves, an overlap with ring-cairns and stone circles has to be allowed, and they are unlikely to begin earlier than the end of the 3rd millennium bc. An overlap with the nearby O-C-H passage-graves also has to be allowed, and there is in fact the surprisingly late date of 1920 bc from Embo (SUT 63).

In Orkney the later stalled chambers of the O-C-H group form a parallel and presumptively contemporary development series with the Maes Howe tombs, sharing such technical tricks as rock-cutting to allow the chambers to be built into the hillside, rings of cairn material added round the core of the cairn, and excessive lengthening of the chamber. If Maes Howe is to be linked with New Grange with its dates of 2550-2465 bc, then the group cannot start much later than the middle of the millennium. With the small number of Maes Howe-type tombs it is difficult to suppose they span a very long period, and one would expect them all to lie within the 3rd millennium. On the other hand, the rock scribings, especially at the typologically latest tomb (ORK 22), suggest a date two or three centuries later.

The building of long cairns seems to have ceased about the middle of the millennium, for though they cover typologically early and middle O-C-H chambers, there is only one certain instance of association with a stalled tripartite chamber and a doubtful association with a long stalled chamber, and no known connection with Maes Howe-type and Clava tombs.

The Shetland tombs present difficulties, for the chambers appear to be quite late, deriving from Orcadian Bookan-type chambers which were contemporary with the stalled and Maes-Howe-type chambers, but their heel-shaped cairns are no later than long cairns in the north of Scotland. Shetland chamber tombs, producing a development series in isolation, are twice certainly associated with Calder's house-sites. These have produced beaker-derived pottery and other material appropriate to the mid 2nd millennium bc, and the house at Ness of Grunting (admittedly not provided with a tomb) has a date of 1564 bc.

In the Hebrides we may guess that the simple but large passage-graves, and the enlargement of their cairns, continued through the 3rd millennium bc. Certainly one strange little tomb, not of local type but derived from the tripartite plan, was secondary to the great complex of standing stones at Callanish (LWS 3). This can hardly be earlier than the 18th century bc.

But even if tomb building had ceased by the early 2nd millennium bc except in very remote areas, the tombs often continued in use. Those tombs which have produced definite evidence show the last burials and the ritual final sealing of the tomb generally to have been in the hands of late neolithic or beaker peoples, in the 18th-16th centuries bc.

*DATE LIST: Radiocarbon dates relating to the Scottish tombs*

| Site | Feature | Lab. No. | Radiocarbon date bc (5568 half-life) | Calibrated date BC (approx.) |
|---|---|---|---|---|
| Achategan | The upper of two occupation levels, with neolithic A pottery | I 4765 | 2300 | 2950 |
| Dalladies | Mortuary structure contemporary with long barrow | I 6113 | 3240 ± 105 | 4200-4000 |
| Embo | Contemporary with building passage-grave chamber | B 442 | 1920 ± 100 | 2500-2250 |
| Glenvoidean | Below the structure of the axial chamber of a multi-chamber Clyde cairn | I 5974 | 2910 ± 115 | 3700 |
| Knowth 1 | Beneath passage-grave mound | UB 318 | 2925 ± 150 | 3700 |
| 2 | Beneath passage-grave mound | UB 319 | 2845 ± 185 | 3650-3550 |
| Lochhill | Mortuary structure immediately pre-dating long cairn | I 6409 | 3120 ± 105 | 3900 |
| Monamore 1 | Hearth in forecourt of Clyde cairn, under blocking | Q 675 | 3160 ± 110 | 3950 |
| 2 | Hearth over forecourt blocking | Q 676 | 2240 ± 110 | 2950 |
| Ness of Gruting | Barley cache in base of house wall | BM 441 | 1564 ± 120 | 2050-1950 |
| New Grange 1 | Contemporary with building of passage-grave | GrN 5463 | 2465 ± 40 | 3400-3200 |
| 2 | Contemporary with building of passage-grave | GrN 5462 | 2550 ± 45 | 3400 |
| Pitnacree | Beneath mound with rectangular enclosure | GaK 601 | 2860 ± 90 | 3700 |

# 5. The bronze age [1]

## COLIN BURGESS

In the centuries around the middle of the 3rd millennium BC the appearance of exotic pottery in neolithic contexts marks the arrival of continental migrants in Britain. These new-comers, the beaker folk, while essentially neolithic in their way of life, nevertheless set in motion the changes which brought long-established neolithic traditions to an end, and ushered in the bronze age.

Study of the British bronze age has always been hampered by a lack of settlement evidence, a problem which persists despite recent recognition that many supposedly iron age sites and their associated cultural material had bronze age beginnings. Most of our knowledge of the period is derived from burial and ritual sites and unassociated artefacts, which give a biased picture, too much concerned with matters sepulchral, religious and technological, and not enough with more mundane aspects.

### Physical background

The relevance of Fox's highland and lowland zones in the bronze age must be stressed in view of the growing tendency to dispute this division. For the bronze age a simpler dividing line than that of Fox's can be drawn, taking all of Yorkshire into a highland zone more alien to the lowland zone than the latter was to north-west France.[2] The physical similarity between southern England and north-west France was reflected in remarkable cross-Channel contacts that were one of the most enduring and interesting features of the bronze age.

Altitudinal extremes apart, much of the two zones is separated by only small differences in height, precipitation and temperature, but such is the geographical position of these islands that even such minor variations are critical for crop-ripening and congenial living. Thus from prehistoric times a predominantly pastoral highland zone has contrasted with a more arable lowland zone. The lower tracts of the highland zone are individually too small or scattered, their soil too often poor, to provide a basis for agricultural wealth and dense population, contrasting strongly with the broad arable expanses of the lowland zone so rich in the tractable soils sought by prehistoric farmers. Hence the enduring gulf between the two, which is reflected in population densities.[3] Domesday figures may already have been approached by the end of the bronze age.[4]

Geographical position ensures further advantages for the lowland zone, which, lying close to the continent, was more open to outside influences than the highland zone, and quicker to change. The west at least received influences via the Atlantic sea routes, whereas northern Britain not only had the poorest climate and settlement potential but was also furthest from the outside world and exotic influences.

## Climatic change

The bronze age climate of Britain and the continent seems to have been warmer and drier than now,[5] as is reflected in the drying up of bogs and the spread of settlement into now inhospital upland areas. The Irish climate may have been more oceanic, and a development of moister conditions from the beginning of the period seems likely. In Britain such climatic deterioration has been postulated only at the late bronze age/iron age transition.[5] The effect of climatic change in the bronze age has received little attention. The deterioration was probably at least as marked as that which brought the Mediaeval climatic optimum to an end *c.* AD 1300 with such disastrous consequences.[6] The poor climate of the 14th-17th centuries saw the limits of cereal cultivation in marginal upland areas fall by as much as several hundred feet, enormous tracts of arable land reverting to rough grazing. The social and economic consequences of the resulting land pressures have hardly begun to be appreciated, nor their relevance to such historical phenomena as the abandonment of Mediaeval farms and villages, and the onset of clan troubles and border strife. If anything the effects of the later prehistoric deterioration would have been magnified by the more primitive landscape and conditions of the time. One imagines not only the loss of great tracts of marginal arable land in upland areas but also the water logging of land at all levels. Pressure on land must have grown, and those who possessed it would increasingly need to guard against the dispossessed who coveted it. This may have had great significance for the development of hillforts and settlements.

The chronology of this climatic deterioration thus becomes a matter of importance. It seems likely that the process was gradual, with an initial deterioration leading into a period of poorer weather, culminating in a second more serious deterioration. Calibrated C14 dates for the initial onset centre on *c.* 1100-1000 BC,[7] with one as early as *c.* 1460 BC.[8] Thus climatic deterioration began much earlier than has hitherto been believed, certainly during the middle bronze age, and possible late in the early bronze age in some areas. The later deterioration is more securely fixed around the 7th-6th centuries.

## The nature of the evidence: division of the period

Because the site evidence has such a sepulchral/ritual bias, one has to turn to artefacts to find a basis for dividing up the period. Pottery and metalwork make up the bulk of bronze age finds, but the pottery has for long been misused as a chronological and cultural indicator. Much of it is too insular, too undistinguished or too much tied to one type of site to be used as it has been in the past. This emphasises the importance of metalwork which alone has undiminishing relevance throughout the period, shows regional variations and clear typological development, and can be related to continental evidence. Unfortunately most Irish — British metalwork consists of stray finds, which are difficult to relate to other material, and to the site evidence.

The fundamental divisions of the period remain those of Hawkes' 1960 scheme,[9] modified by several later authors,[10] who have substituted industrial phases, named after distinct metalworking traditions, for Hawkes' numbered phases. This is a more flexible system, though it fails to deal with the difficulty of different regional rates of development. The

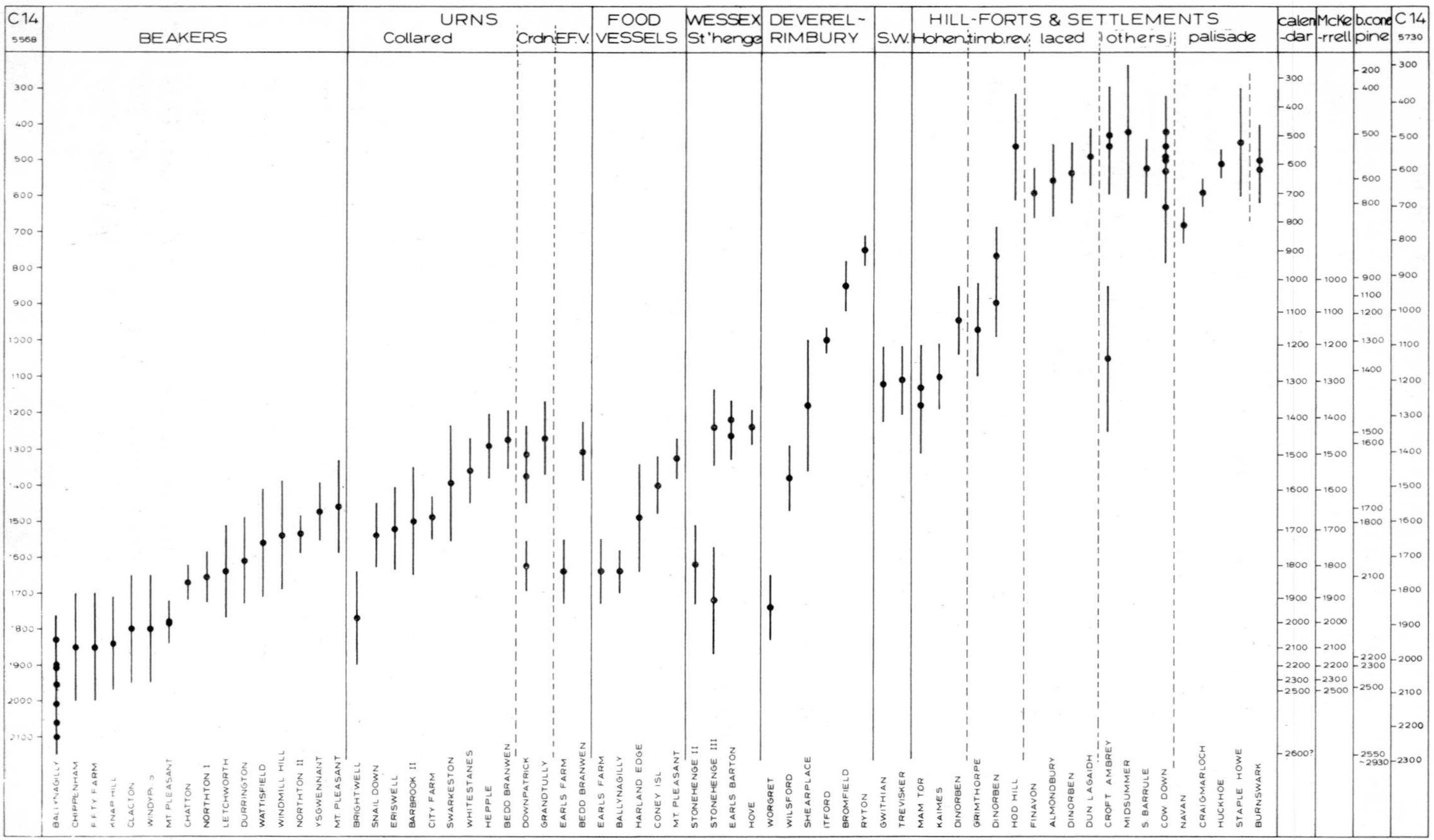

Figure 25. Radiocarbon dates for the bronze age in Britain and Ireland.

basic four-fold division of the period now rests largely on a techno-typological basis, with traditional ceramic and cultural criteria of less importance than previously.[11] The technological developments signalling the onset of the late neolithic copper-working phase and the early bronze age are self-explanatory. The change from early to middle bronze age constitutes one of the most important watersheds in the bronze age, marked by the disappearance of the last neolithic survivals (p. 194), a striking sepulchral/religious hiatus, significant shifts in the bases and centres of wealth and power, and the adoption of a new tool kit and weaponry.[12] The late bronze age is best divided from the middle bronze age by the adoption of lead-bronze, and of the three classic late bronze age types, leaf-shaped swords, socketed axes and pegged spearheads.[13] Such traditional late bronze age features as developed urns[14] now belong to earlier periods.

## Absolute chronology

The chronology of the middle and late bronze age still rests largely on cross-dating, but C14 dating, for long used reluctantly in bronze age contexts, has become increasingly important, pushing back the beginnings of the early bronze age at one end, and, at the other, bringing into the bronze age a mass of sites and material traditionally regarded as iron age. The problems of C14 dating are particularly acute in the bronze age, when a century of two can make all the difference to interpretation of phenomena such as the Wessex culture. A basic C14 date can be calibrated in several ways, which may give wildly different values. The absolute chronology used here (Figs. 25 and 26) takes account of these options, utilising the adjustments which conform best with historical expectation. Thus tree-ring calibration suffices for the 3rd and 1st millennia, but McKerrell's historical scale[15] is here preferred for much of the 2nd millennium. The resulting chronology pushes beaker immigration and copper metallurgy back at least to the mid-3rd millennium BC, while bronze-working may have started around the 20th century. The transition from early to middle bronze age still falls around 1400 however, with the late bronze age beginning in

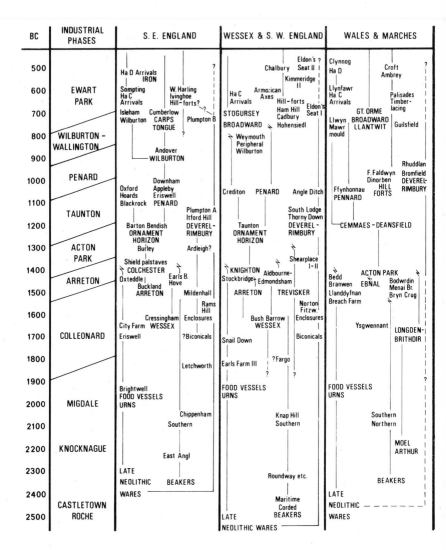

Figure 26. Chronological table for the bronze age of Britain and Ireland (dates in calendar years BC).

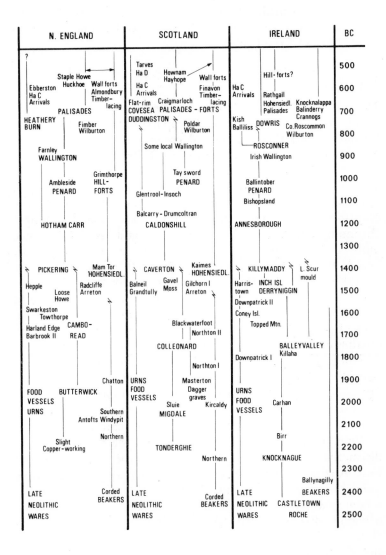

the 10th century in the lowland zone and in the 8th century elsewhere. Hallstatt penetration occurred in the 7th century, bringing iron-working to restricted areas by its close. In the century or two after 600, iron will have become known in most regions of the British Isles.

## The beaker folk

There is still no agreement on the origins of the beaker folk, which have been placed as far apart as Iberia and eastern Europe,[16] but there is general concurrence that the Rhine basin was the immediate source of British beaker settlement.[17] Attitudes to British beakers require drastic review in the light of the recent major publications of Clarke[18] and Lanting and van der Waals,[19] and the doubling of the duration of the beaker phase by C14 calibration. This longer chronology makes beaker settlement and its consequence more comprehensible, and it becomes easier to see how beaker folk could be contemporaries both of indigenous late neolithic groups and their early bronze age descendants.

The traditional and easily understood three-fold division of British beakers — α, β, γ; A, B, C; long-necked, bell, short-necked — is rejected totally by recent writers, though obstinate shadows of it persist in their more complex schemes. In many respects the approaches of Clarke and Lanting and van der Waals to the subject are diametrically opposed. Clarke sees British beaker developments resulting from seven major immigrations in two main waves, with small dispersed groups of settlers arriving over considerable spans of time. These successive arrivals shaped the development of distinctive insular beaker traditions, northern, southern and East Anglian. There are crucial arguments against multiple immigrations and in favour of the Lanting and van der Waals scheme, which envisages only a single, initial immigration, bringing all-over-corded (AOC) beakers. These alone have abundant 'pot-for-pot' parallels on the continent. With other British beakers, one can usually only match component features amongst the continental material. This is a major obstacle to later immigrations, though there must have been repeated contact with continental beaker groups to account for subsequent British developments.[20] The further novelty of the Lanting and van der Waals scheme is to treat British beakers on a regional basis, with local development through successive 'steps'. The extent to which these are represented varies from region to region, only Wessex showing uninterrupted development through all seven steps. Outside Wessex early steps are more indifferently represented, and AOC beakers may have lasted longer and the development of local combed beakers been delayed. Against such a framework Clarke's East Anglian, northern and southern insular traditions retain broad validity, developing in that order, with least continental influence in the last.[21] C14 dates push the early settlements, marked by AOC beakers and limited maritime beaker penetration, well back into the 3rd millennium. The prompt development of comb-decorated vessels in Wessex was not matched elsewhere. The barrel-shaped vessels so typical of the East Anglican tradition were rare until step 3, around 2200 BC, while the northern tradition emerged only in step 4, towards 2000. The southern tradition belonged essentially to the centuries after 2000, but by this time indigenous groups were growing stronger. In the south beaker groups survived long enough to overlap with the Wessex culture,[22] but by *c.* 1500 the last beaker elements had everywhere been absorbed.

The traditional distinction between sturdy brachycephalic beaker settlers and the slighter dolichocephalic neolithic people requires fresh re-appraisal. Sparse settlement evidence makes the relationship between beaker and indigenous societies uncertain, though the lack of hybridisation between their ceramics suggests prolonged beaker aloofness. An initial beaker superiority seems likely, yet beaker communities here, as on the continent, assimilated many aspects of local culture, in farming practice, ritual, and perhaps domestic architecture.[23] In return they brought metallurgy (p. 191 below), flat-based pottery,[24] possibly textiles,[25] a new burial concept, emphasising individual inhumation, and a whole range of new equipment. They embellished local ritual architecture, and brought new concepts of political power, organisation and social stratification.

The elusiveness of beaker houses and settlements[26] has led to a widespread belief that beaker folk were nomadic pastoralists. While this is a convenient over-simplification it is true that large-scale excavation of beaker settlements such as Ballynagilly, Co. Tyrone,[27] or the many East Anglian sites, such as Lakenheath, Suffolk,[28] have uncovered extensive occupation deposits, but no house plans. Suggestions that beaker settlements lie deeply buried in valleys[29] must await future discoveries. Meanwhile the evidence in many areas suggests beaker houses were flimsy, generally oval or circular,[30] grouping in small open or enclosed settlements,[31] and contrasting with the substantial rectangular houses of the neolithic.[32] The nomadic pastoralist concept should not be exaggerated in view of the evidence for renewed forest clearance in this period.[33] Beaker farmers may have borrowed many local techniques,[34] but they seem to have instituted a swing from wheat to barley cultivation.[35]

The beaker folk are normally regarded as practising individual inhumation burial under a round mound, but this is a gross over-simplification. This was a common beaker rite, but two or more bodies were sometimes placed in graves,[36] and cremations were fairly common, both alone,[37] and with inhumations. This hints at contact with indigenous cremating groups. Occasionally social stratification is suggested, with a lesser (a native?) receiving a different rite and subordinate position in the grave. Major regional contrasts exist, between the burials under round mounds south of the Tees,[38] the flat cist graves north of it, and the scarcity of any beaker single grave tradition in Ireland, though these rules are not invariable.[39]

Native religion was widely adopted by the beaker folk, who helped to transform the henge tradition,[46] adding embellishments such as stone settings, which led on to the whole stone circle development. Similarly the cursus was adopted,[41] leading to other linear monuments, such as embanked and stone avenues and alignments. These show the beaker folk as skilled engineers, surveyors and perhaps even mathematicians and astronomers,[42] skills largely derived from the native population with its long tradition of field engineering. The extent to which natives and newcomers worked together on these great projects is problematic, but they were clearly present together at many sites.

Beaker pottery had varying influences on local neolithic wares, affecting mostly decoration (from domestic beakers?)

and the base. Most of the native forms showed logical development from earlier traditions, though the mysterious grooved ware has an uncertain background.[43] Fengate ware,[44] a distinctive southern style, evolved before 2000 in the Ebbsfleet-Mortlake tradition under beaker influence. Rather later, and to the north, collared urns may have been developed from the same Mortlake background under different beaker influence,[45] a parallel tradition to Fengate, eventually to flourish and expand as the latter declined. In many areas the diverse bowl and vase forms lumped together in the heterogeneous 'food vessel' classification were evolved from local neolithic ceramics by native communities reacting to whatever beaker influences were prevalent in their area. After long co-existence, the beaker groups themselves were absorbed.

## Indigenous groups of the early bronze age

The traditional cultures of the early bronze age may reflect only sepulchral differences, which need not have affected other aspects of life. An immediate distinction can be made between inhuming and cremating groups, and those using both rites, altogether a more complex situation than the traditional contrast between cremating urn cultures and inhuming food vessel cultures. Urns are almost invariably associated with cremation, but food vessels have no similar total association with inhumation.

Neither 'urns' nor 'food vessels' are coherent entities, but show great variation in form, origins and associated cultural material and ritual. Both divide into regional groups. Some of the food vessel groups were almost invariably associated with inhumation,[46] most notably in east Yorkshire. Inhumation is still strong in adjoining regions, in the Peak, north-east England and eastern Scotland, but cremation increases markedly to the west, and predominates in Ireland and Wales. Whether some chronological difference or ritual option is implied can only be determined by further discoveries.

Inhuming food vessel communities were probably the most strongly beaker-influenced element in the native population, and their distribution coincides with the major beaker concentrations in the east.[47] Equally, as beaker densities fall moving westwards, so cremation increases. The rarity of food vessel inhumation in the great southern beaker strongholds may be accounted for by local neolithic burial customs. Whereas inhumation was still prevalent in the east when the beaker folk arrived,[48] in the south it may have been largely replaced by cremation.[49] This tradition was continued by the urn groups. Round mounds, over cremations and inhumations, are usually regarded as a beaker contribution, but the growing number of neolithic round mound burials shows that local development cannot always be discounted.[50]

The fallacy of the traditional bronze age pottery sequence — beakers with inhumation, followed by food vessels with inhumation in the early bronze age, enlarged food vessels and collared urns with cremations in the middle bronze age, and late collared, cordoned and encrusted urns in the late bronze age — has long been apparent, but has proved very resistant to attack. All were used by early bronze age communities on the evidence of associations[51] and C14 dates, and there is no evidence for later survival.[52] The best illustration of contemporaneity is provided by the Corkragh grave, Co. Tyrone (Fig. 27), with Irish vase, pygmy cup, encrusted and cordoned urns all in the same cist.[53] Given this overlap it is legitimate to ask why the familiar beaker/food vessel/urn stratigraphic sequence is almost never upset. The answer must lie in the inter-relationship of these various groups, in their attitude to burial, and in *local* sequences. Beakers and food vessels have sometimes been found in the same grave,[54] and innumerable times under the same mound with the beaker in a primary position. But such stratigraphic differences may often indicate not a secondary but a satellite food vessel burial, the gap being a social, not chronological one.[55] Beaker folk, socially pre-eminent, built their own burial monuments and occupied the important positions within them. Food vessel users, at least beaker influenced, and perhaps occupying some undefined, lower niche in the beaker social order, were allowed to place their dead in less important positions. If no beaker burial was involved, they too preferred to build their own burial monument.[56] Urn users were not nearly so fussy, and seem to have been equally at home building their own tombs or

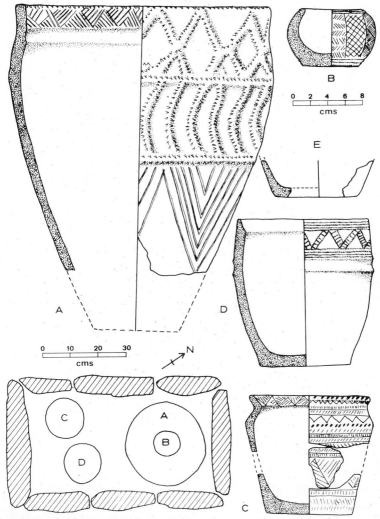

Figure 27. Grave group in cist, Kilskeery, Corkragh, Co. Tyrone:[1] A. 'Encrusted urn'; B. Pygmy cup; C. Irish-Scottish vase; D. Cordoned urn: E. Base of another urn.

digging their cremations into any mound available. The beaker or food vessel builders of such mounds may have departed the scene only days or hours before.

Local events may also have produced this sequence in some areas, where urn users may have arrived late on the scene. In the early bronze age, cremation groups ultimately became the major expansive force, moving into areas previously dominated by beaker and food vessel communities.

As with beaker interments, only a small proportion of urn and food vessel burials were provided with grave goods other than the pot, and these were usually few and simple.[57] A large proportion of burials lacked even an accompanying pot, though the possibility of organic grave furniture remains an unknown factor.[58] Rich graves stand out amidst the general poverty, and may reflect a passing fashion for rich burial, which was magnified in the Wessex culture (p. 184).

*Urns and cremating groups*
Only one of the five main cinerary urn groups, Cornish urns, shows a marked regional concentration. Enlarged food vessels and cordoned urns were a highland zone, biconical urns a lowland zone, phenomenon. Collared urns, the most numerous, are distributed throughout the British Isles.[59] 'Encrusted urns' are now interpreted as relief-decorated enlarged food vessels,[60] while bucket-shaped urns are so generalised as to present problems of chronology and relationships.

Cornish and biconical urns occur on settlements,[61] but it is uncertain to what extent other urn types were used domestically. Like beaker settlements, urn settlements all too often show considerably spreads of occupation but no house plans.[62] Surviving houses, mostly from western sites, are circular or oval timber structures.[63] Bank and ditch enclosures, of uncertain function, were also built, as at Rams Hill, Berkshire,[64] and Norton Fitzwarren, Somerset.[65] The urn folk have often been regarded as pastoralists, but frequent grain impressions on their pottery, of barley, wheat, spelt and flax, attest arable interests.[66] The familiar north-south agricultural contrast is repeated, northern urns producing scarcely any impressions, suggesting a greater emphasis on pastoralism.

Urn folk, with their cremation rite and cemeteries, were the most assiduous of the indigenous communities in preserving neolithic burial and .ritual traditions. Sometimes they used existing neolithic henges for their burials, as at

Cairnpapple, West Lothian,[67] but other henges, such as Loanhead of Daviot, Aberdeen,[68] were specially built. They built a whole range of enclosed cemeteries in the henge tradition.[69] What seem to be unenclosed cemeteries may sometimes betray early or incomplete excavation. Use of stone settings and circles could well show beaker influence, but rare cave burials, as at Goatscrag, Northumberland,[70] echo another indigenous tradition.

Urn burials show marked north-south differences, with barrow burial predominant south of a Mersey-Tees line and flat cemeteries common to the north. Sometimes the mound was erected over a single burial,[71] sometimes over a cemetery,[72] but secondaries were frequently inserted into any mound available.[73] Pond 'barrows', in reality enclosures, were an exception to the southern barrow tradition. Flat cemeteries may have been more common in the south than appears at first glance, their numbers obscured by the mass of barrow burials.[74]

The lack of regionalisation among the urn groups raises difficult questions of relationships. Do the different forms represent different cultures, communities or merely altern-atives within one community? The problem is most acute where the urns show the greatest overlap, in the west and north. The Anglesey evidence, provided by cemeteries such as Bedd Branwen,[75] suggests that a single community might produce variously decorated and shaped pots. Such cemeteries imply survival of neolithic family-oriented atti-tudes, as expressed in collective burial.[76] The alternative would be to envisage separate enlarged food vessel, collared urn and cordoned urn communities within a general cremat-ing tradition, co-existing in the same areas, sometimes using common cemeteries,[77] their lives touching at some points and diverging at others. This concept cannot be ruled out, since urn folk were clearly not fussy about sharing burial monuments, while the political situation in Wessex at this time shows that different cultural groupings could co-exist.[78]

Some highland zone urns were clearly counterparts of lowland zone forms, and even within a single group, such as collared urns, regional trends can be seen. Thus some biconical urns have good parallels among enlarged food vessels and cordoned urns in the highland zone,[79] while some of the early bronze age bucket-shaped urns of the north and west, the Largs type,[80] are indistinguishable from southern Deverel-Rimbury forms. As other highland zone urns exhibit Deverel-Rimbury features, the possibility of early bronze age Deverel-Rimbury beginnings is raised (p. 216).[81] This is all part of a general problem, a profusion of ceramic styles, each merging into others at its extremities. Thus the lines between collared and cordoned urns, or between short northern tripartite vessels and tall tripartite bowls are impossible to draw (Figs. 29-30).[82] Once such similarities would have provided the basis for complex typologies, but surely they illustrate rather 'a complex thread of connections, convergences and borrowings',[83] the potters of one community influencing those of another, but at a local level, with no significance for the whole class of pots which these individual examples represent.

Collared urns can be derived from the neolithic Peterborough tradition, modified by some beaker influences.[84] Features relating to other urns and to food vessels need be no more than local borrowings from contemporary traditions. A distinction has been made between primary and secondary series vessels, based on possession, or lack, of Peterborough traits, with the presence or absence of these theoretically having broad chronological significance. But this is not supported by recent C14 dates and excavations, which show pots of both series, exhibiting wide trait variation, in use contemporaneously.[85] This demands a completely fresh look at collared urn typology and relationships, set against the very much longer development period, from the 20th-15th centuries, implied by calibrated C14 dates (Figs. 25-26).

The origins of the Largs type bucket-shaped urns can be traced to the similarly shaped neolithic vessels of the north and west,[86] but how long such simple urns persisted, and their relationship to later flat-rim wares is unknown. A cordoned urn corpus is urgently needed because such a wide variety of vessels has been included in this category. There is broad contact with, but not necessarily influence from, certain collared urns, and late neolithic wares of the north and west provided a more likely basis for development,[87] with some contribution from beaker coarse wares.[88] In contrast, enlarged food vessels are what the term implies,

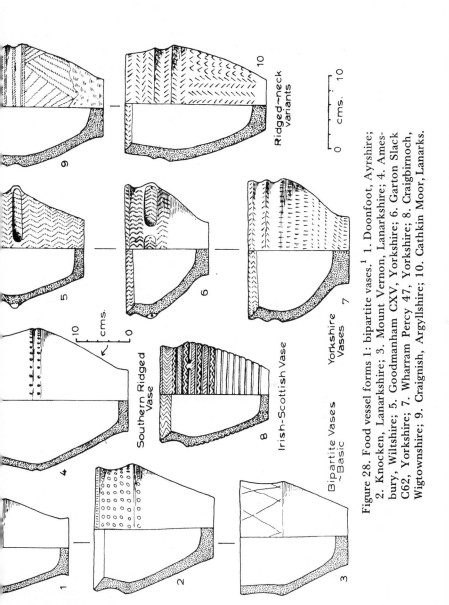

Figure 28. Food vessel forms 1: bipartite vases.[1] 1. Doonfoot, Ayrshire;
2. Knocken, Lanarkshire; 3. Mount Vernon, Lanarkshire; 4. Amesbury, Wiltshire; 5. Goodmanham CXV, Yorkshire; 6. Garton Slack
C62, Yorkshire; 7. Wharram Percy 47, Yorkshire; 8. Craigbirnoch,
Wigtownshire; 9. Craignish, Argyllshire; 10. Cathkin Moor, Lanarks.

illustrating the rising tide of early bronze age cremation, and its impact on a non-cinerary ceramic form.[89] The whole range of vase and ridged bucket food vessel shapes was used (Figs. 28-29), enlarged two or three times, for the cinerary role.[90] Their common 'encrusted' decoration has been related to grooved ware relief ornament. Objections to this[91] have been eased by removing the chronological gap between them,[92] and by better knowledge of northern relief-decorated grooved wares.[93]

Biconical urns are not a homogeneous group, falling into various subtypes, often of regional significance, with different origins and relationships. Unfortunately work on these vessels has been notoriously Wessex-oriented. The finds from Wessex, other southern counties, East Anglia and south Wales[94] are well known, but the distribution goes beyond this, through the midlands and eastern England up to the Humber.[95] While some may be local versions of bipartite enlarged food vessels,[96] other have been compared to cordoned urns.[97] Origins in Cornish (early Trevisker) urns[98] and grooved wares[99] have been most favoured for southern examples. There are similarities with bipartite collared urns[100] and Deverel-Rimbury vessels[101] to a point where distinction becomes difficult. They have generally been assigned to the middle bronze age, after early bronze age beginnings,[102] but their associations are wholly early bronze age,[103] the evidence for later survival uncertain.[104] The similar Hilversum urns of the Low Countries, betray a rare emigration from Britain to the continent,[105] but there is little accompanying material to throw light on the strength of this movement.[106]

### Food vessels

The various ceramic forms lumped together under the 'food vessel' label, united by variable association with inhumation burial, were developed from neolithic pottery traditions under beaker influence. Their diversity results from the marked regional variations shown by both contributory traditions.[107] In the absence of a modern corpus it is difficult to arrive at a meaningful food vessel classification. Abercromby's work[108] has remained the basis for recent schemes, which have been either too complex[109] or too

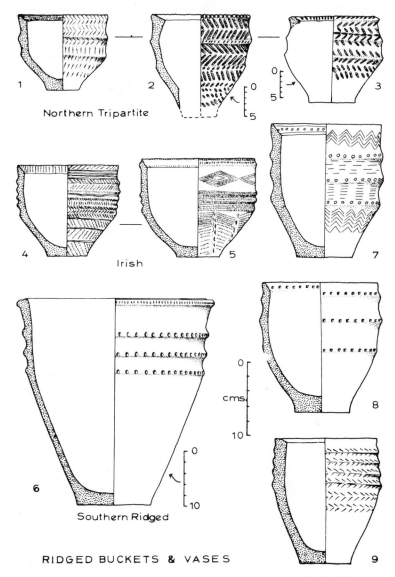

Northern Tripartite

Irish

Southern Ridged

RIDGED BUCKETS & VASES

Figure 29. Food vessel forms 2: ridged buckets and vases.[1] 1. Garton Slack 75, Yorkshire; 2. Hartington, Derbyshire; 3. Parwich, Derbyshire; 4. Rathbarron, Co. Sligo; 5. Killicarney, Co. Cavan; 6. Friar Mayne, Dorset; 7. Stevenston, Ayrshire; 8. Mount Vernon, Lanarkshire; 9. Knocken, Lanarkshire. Compare 4 and 5 with Fig. 30:5, illustrating the merging of forms. Scale of 7 unknown.

generalised[110] for satisfactory use, and the scheme suggested here is intended only as an interim guide. Shape must clearly figure large in considering such disparate vessels, but shows correspondence with ornament and distribution. The familiar division into *vase* and *bowl* forms holds good, the former essentially English, the latter Irish, with Scotland mixing vases and bowls.[111] The vases can be divided into two basic groups (Figs. 28 and 29), bipartite, and tripartite/ridged. Bowls can be divided into tripartite, simple and waisted forms (Fig. 30), with ridged variations, and should be contrasted with much simpler British globular bowls (Fig. 30: 6,7). Decoration, like form, shows regional variation, being richer in Ireland and Scotland than in England. The sparser English decoration employs cord-ornament, incision and impressed techniques, contrasting with the Irish tooth-comb, false relief and incised decoration.

Much of what has been said about beaker burial and ritual practices can be applied to food vessel users. Their burials show the same distinctions, between stone cists over much of the highland zone and dug graves in stone-free areas, with the Tees isotaph dividing flat graves in the north from barrow graves to the south. Individual interment was similarly emphasised, but two or more burials were sometimes placed in the same grave,[112] several different graves may be contemporary,[113] and cremations occur with inhumations.[114] Food vessel cemeteries are as familiar as urn cemeteries, usually in cists, either flat or with covering mound.[115] Food vessel users, like beaker folk, were interested in henges and stone circles,[116] and both communities have been linked with the enigmatic cup-and-ring marked rocks of the highland zone.[117]

### The Wessex culture

The most publicised exception to the general poverty of British early bronze age graves is the unique regional concentration of rich graves in Wessex, which provided the basis for Professor Piggott's creation of the Wessex culture.[118] For him this was clearly not a cultural entity, but a label applied to a small dominant aristocracy, founded by intrusive Breton warriors, which established a vigorous

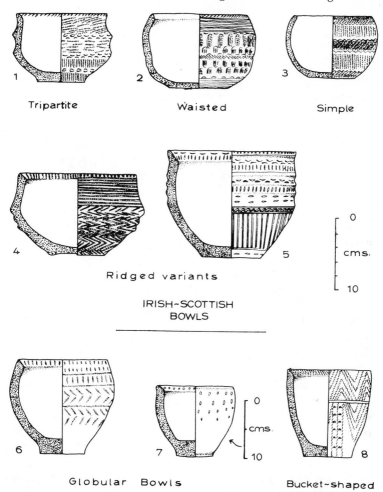

Figure 30. Food vessel forms 3; bowls and bucket-shaped vessels.[1] 1 Corky, Co. Antrim; 2. Newry, Co. Down; 3. Omagh, Co. Tyrone; 4. Corrower, Co. Mayo; 5. High Banks Farm, Kircudbrightshire; 6. Mount Vernon, Lanarkshire; 7. Arbor Low, Derbyshire; 8. Skeldon, Ayrshire.

hegemony over the native population. The power and wealth of these chieftains was based on their dynamism and their commercial success, in particular their skill as middlemen in channelling trade from Ireland, Europe and the Mediterranean through their territory. The abundance of exotic materials in their graves provided ample testimony of this mercantile ability. Eventually, like the beaker folk, they were absorbed by emerging, numerically stronger, indigeneous communities, after a *floruit* which spanned the whole early bronze age, succeeding beaker groups at one end and merging into middle bronze age communities at the other.

Piggott listed the artefact types he considered character- istic of Wessex culture graves,[119] thereby encompassing practically all the rich non-beaker graves from the region. On the same basis many rich graves from other regions could have been included. Two broad categories of burials seem to be represented. The first contain pottery of the urn and food vessel groups, together with a few simple items such as beads, buttons, flints, metal awls and knives.[120] Such burials, so often matched outside Wessex, seem merely to represent aggrandised elements in the indigenous early bronze age population. In this sense one can speak of Wessex cultures but certainly not a Wessex culture. They are less exceptional than second category burials, which normally lack such familiar pottery types, but are characterised by artefacts rare outside Wessex. Second category burials have grooved daggers, grape, Aldbourne and slotted cups, sheet-gold objects, halberd pendants, perforated whetstones, bone tweezers and dress pins of central European background. Such burials form a more valid Wessex grouping, focussing overwhelmingly on Dorset and Wiltshire, spilling out into adjoining counties, but only rarely beyond. Even this distinction is not simple, as is proved by burials combining second category grave goods with first category pots.[121] Similarly, the 'fancy' barrows, the only monuments concen- trated, like second category graves, in Wessex, often yield first category burials.

The Wessex culture, as a term of convenience, would only refer to these second category burials, which reduces Piggott's grave schedule alarmingly. Clearly this was not a culture at all, but one facet of a complex fabric of co-existent communities. There is more than a hint of social stratifi- cation, with second category graves suggesting a warrior aristocracy, whose lowlier women, and Hawkes' 'middle folk',[122] would claim the first category burials. The mass of unaccompanied or poorly furnished graves would then belong to Hawkes' 'lower folk'. Clearly much of this social picture can be explained in local terms, and recent interpretations of the Wessex culture have almost unanimously favoured local emergence and aggrandisement.[123] The basis for such developments already existed in the late neolithic, when Wessex was already wealthy, densely populated and well-organised, with evidence, implicit in its great henge monuments, for centralised political power and a well-developed administrative set-up. Old ideas of a great nodal commercial power clearly will no longer do.[124] The region had already grown rich and powerful on its agricultural and manpower resources, which remained the bases of wealth throughout the early bronze age. In this sense the Wessex phenomenon had nothing to do with fresh economic factors, but must relate to the religious and social differences implicit in the graves. These are already apparent in beaker contexts, with occasional rich graves, especially of warriors,[125] outstanding amidst a rather larger number of 'middle' graves,[126] with the mass of burials furnished only with a pot and occasional artefact. A similar late neolithic and beaker background existed in areas outside Wessex,[127] whose unique success therefore demands further explanation. In fact a catalyst is required to account for the dramatic spread in this one area of a minority burial rite. Whether it implies religious conversion, or a broadening of the economic and social bases which governed rich burial, remains unknown. But such a catalyst must surely have come from outside Britain, and there is no alternative but to seek it in Piggott's Breton warriors.[128] Only small numbers would have been needed to add the emphasis which made Wessex stand out in early bronze age Britain. Similarities between Breton and Wessex graves at this time are certainly striking,[129] differences no more than would be forced on an alien minority by 'sea change' and a strange environment, and such a connection must be viewed against the background of remarkable cross-Channel connections which are such a feature of the bronze age.

The Wessex culture, as represented by second category graves, was therefore a segment of indigenous early bronze age society, galvanised by an intrusive warrior element. Grasping the nettle, it could be equated with Fleming's wealthy, mobile pastoralists, dominating a population of more sedentary cultivators,[130] who comprised both the middle folk and the lower folk.

Traditionally, the Wessex culture spanned the whole early bronze age, contemporary with central European Únětice and shaft grave Mycenae, in absolute terms extending over the 17th-15th centuries BC.[131] Claims have been made on the strength of bristlecone pine-calibrated C14 dates that Únětice, Breton dagger graves and Wessex must pre-date shaft grave Mycenae quite appreciably.[132] This would necessitate reinterpretation of the supposedly Mycenaean elements in Wessex, the Bush Barrow sceptre mounts, sheet gold covering and gold pins, gold bound amber discs, amber spacer beads, faience beads and various features of Stonehenge III.[133] Some are certainly too generalised to admit much certainty, while others, the faience beads, for example, can be seen as native work.[134] At the same time Coles and Taylor have propounded a 'minimal view' of the Wessex culture, disputing its longevity, its traditional twofold division and its importance.[135] Their arguments are based on the present difficulty of separating chronologically the continental precursors of Wessex metalwork, the claim that most Wessex gold stemmed from a single craftsman, and the lack of any stratigraphic evidence for a two-phase culture.

Most of these arguments are now seen to be inconclusive or refutable. A much larger series of C14 dates is now available, including the first for Wessex graves, and McKerrell's historical calibration of these[136] gives a much less drastic separation of C14 and calendar years. The Wessex dates, for contexts with Camerton-Snowshill daggers, fall between 1300-1100 bc (see date list *infra*), not the 1700-1600 bc of the Únětice dates. Calibrated, these confirm that a traditionally late phase of the Wessex culture flourished around 1400 BC, matching exactly the horizon for the closest eastern parallels for British faience.[137] Mycenaean links again become chronologically possible. That they are probable is suggested both by McKerrell's re-affirmation of an eastern origin for British faience,[138] and by Branigan's survey of Mediterranean metal exports to Europe.[139] Unfortunately no C14 dates are available for earlier phases of the Wessex culture, but the numerous

Breton dates must be relevant here.[140] While the latest calibrate to *c.* 1400 BC and match available Wessex dates, others cover the whole period back to the 19th century BC confirming overlap both with Únětice and shaft grave Mycenae.

The C14 evidence thus suggests an even longer Wessex chronology than has hitherto been envisaged. This disposes of a chronologically 'minimal view'. As only a tiny minority of Wessex graves contain gold, the brevity of a 'gold phase' is irrelevant to the span of the whole culture. Similarly the lack of stratigraphic evidence for its subdivision is irrelevant, since no two Wessex graves have come from the same barrow,[141] while the undifferentiated continental background of its bronzes could admit a long chronology as much as a short one.[142] Coles and Taylor fail to dispose of the metallurgical evidence for a division into Bush Barrow and Camerton-Snowshill phases,[143] and pay little heed to the tendency for certain elements in the Wessex culture to group with some things and not others. Such groupings can be explained in various ways, but chronological differences seem most likely. The Wessex culture has for long been divided into two phases, I and II, following ApSimon's identification of Bush Barrow and Camerton-Snowshill daggers,[144] and Atkinson's more elaborate treatment of the material.[145] Two separate groups of burials may still be distinguished on grounds of association and typology, but their chronological separation is now less certain. The first, characterised by Dr Gerloff's Armorico-British (Bush Barrow) daggers,[146] has strong Breton connections and equates with the old Wessex I. Its burials include inhumations and cremations, associated with goldwork, small flat axes, amber spacer beads, grape cups, axe and halberd pendants and simple (Wilsford) stone battle-axes. This may be termed the Bush Barrow group. The second, or Aldbourne-Edmondsham,[147] group lacks the strong Breton element. Its connections are equally wide ranging, but none demand more than commercial contacts. It is characterised by Camerton-Snowshill daggers, cremation burial, Aldbourne cups, bone tweezers, developed stone battle-axes[148] and disc barrows. Its faience beads and dress pins of central European types (often copied in bone) show old contacts being maintained, but new links may have been developed with the Sögel group of north-west Europe. Here is a possible source for the Camerton-Snowshill daggers, and abundant parallels for bulb-headed pins and perforated whetstones, while two Sögel nicked-flanged axes have actually been found in Wessex.[149] Such connections could be important for the chronology of the Aldbourne-Edmondsham group, since Sögel is likely to be later than the Dieskau-Leubingen background of the Bush Barrow group.

Some features seem common to both groups of burials, such as bowl and bell barrows, handled cups, beads of various shapes and substances, awls, small riveted knives and collared urns. Considerable overlap between the two groups is suggested by graves containing elements drawn from both[150] but there still is insufficient mixing to allow a general contemporaneity. C14 dates for three Aldbourne-Edmondsham contexts (Hove, Earls Barton, Edmondsham) all calibrate to *c*. 1400 BC confirming other indications, especially of metal typology, that this was the later group. Breton dates suggest that the Bush Barrow group started as early as the 19th century. Its graves show how indigenous trends towards social stratification and rich burial were accentuated by the arrival of a small number of Breton adventurers. This Armorico-British aristocracy made use of local agricultural and religious importance to indulge in far-flung commercial contacts and attract all manner of exotic commodities. A few local craftsmen supplied limited amounts of bronze and goldwork. With the passage of time, and as new fashions were introduced, the Breton character of this group disappeared. New contacts and time brought increasing changes and Aldbourne-Edmondsham burials. The growth of extensive southern metalworking outside Wessex,[151] the Arreton tradition heralded a new age, and a new basis of wealth. The Wessex aristocracy was in no position to contend with the religious and economic revolution, whatever its cause, which set in around 1400 BC (p. 169), and it vanished from prehistory.

### Early bronze age metalworking traditions

The development of bronze-working in Britain and Ireland was preceded by a copper-working phase of disputed length and background,[152] yielding metalwork of two distinct groups. The first comprises mostly tanged knives and daggers and a few ornaments, sparsely scattered throughout these islands, and given a strong beaker/central European background by frequent occurrence in beaker graves. The second is enormously larger, comprises mainly flat axes and halberds, and is overwhelmingly concentrated in Ireland. It has few associations, and sepulchral and settlement contexts are almost unknown. Thus its background remains uncertain, though various sources have been suggested.[153] If opinion has recently hardened in favour of a beaker/central European connection[154] it is because this so obviously lies behind the first group, and because the evidence for alternatives is even more tenuous. Worrying anomalies remain, notably the contrast between the concentration of beakers in Britain and of copper-work in Ireland.[155] That this Irish metallurgy overlapped with beaker metallurgy is clear from the tanged knife in the Knocknague, Co. Galway, hoard,[156] but this hardly represents an early stage in local copper-working, or demands a direct beaker role. The earliest Irish metallurgy is likely to have developed in Munster,[157] poorest of the Irish provinces in beaker finds,[158] and another reason for urging caution in the question of origins.[159] The mass of British copper consists of flat axes and halberds, for which an Irish rather than beaker origin seems likely, though some of it was undoubtedly produced locally.[160]

The early copper and bronze-working of Britain and Ireland can be divided into five industrial stages, corresponding with five typological stages in axe development. Care must be taken in equating these stages with phases. Overlap of stages was clearly considerable, each tends to be better represented in some areas than others, and development may have proceeded at different rates in different regions. The axes divide firstly into copper broad-butt flat axes (Group A), bronze narrow-butt flat axes (Group B), and bronze flanged axes.[161] Group A subdivides into thick-butted and thin-butted (AB)[162] versions,[163] Group B into a basic simple form, and typologically more advanced implements with embellishments such as median bevel and hammered up edges.[164] These form a distinctive indigenous Irish/British flat/flanged axe series that is continuous and logical in its development, no matter what external influences may have played upon it at various times. From an early stage this sequence diverged from continental traditions. Most Irish/ British copper flat axes have a short, curved-sided form, which contrasts strongly with the Continental 'trapeze' form. Many in addition have thin butts (AB) and some even slight flanges.[165] Case explained these developments in terms of hybridisation, resulting from the impact of B axes on A. But the continuity of the Irish/British sequence favours Coles' view that such features could as well show transition as hybridisation,[166] and could have been a logical, local development.[167]

This concept admits the possibility of a much longer and more significant stage 1 in Irish metallurgy than that entertained by Case. This would have copper-working of uncertain geographical and cultural background, developing in Munster well back in the 3rd millennium. This earliest industry, named after the hoard from Castletown Roche, Co. Cork,[168] produced Group A axes with straight sides, based on the Continental 'trapeze' type, but soon developed a shorter, broader form with curved sides. This 'Irish' shape became dominant as copper-working spread through Ireland. Stage II, beginning well before 2000 BC, overlapped with Beaker influence, and equates with Case's 'impact phase' and Harbison's Knocknague and Frankford phases.[169] The axes of stage I were still produced. Many were now made with thin instead of thick butts, but whether this represents more local inventiveness or a reaction to beaker-introduced ideas remains uncertain. Admittedly much in stage II shows central European/beaker influence, notably tanged knives and daggers, gold ornaments, awls, halberds, and the first local experiments with bronze.[170] But all were compounded into an industry that was still distinctively Irish.

Copper artefacts in Britain, few by Irish standards,[171] concentrate mainly in the north and west. Group A axes and halberds make up the bulk of this material, and it seems sensible to see a connection with Irish industry rather than local beaker elements, though at least some were manufactured locally.[172] Stage II everywhere overlapped with stage III, which in some regions at least must have been underway by c. 2000 BC,[173] and was characterised by the adoption of bronze and the Group B narrow-butt ('thin-butt')[174] flat axes.[175] This stage, Case's II*b*, was regarded by him as broadly contemporary with Wessex I, but Coles has demonstrated the theoretical possibility of a pre-Wessex bronzeworking phase.[176] This primary bronze-working, represented by his Scottish Migdale industry, is characterised by material with a Reinecke A1 background in central Europe, whereas the Wessex culture apparently has nothing earlier than A2.[177] The Migdale industry used single valve stone moulds to produce the new Group B flat axes in simple versions.[178] Halberd manufacture continued, often still in copper, but much in the repertoire was new. Simple riveted knives and daggers, small tanged blades and razors,[179] and a whole range of ornaments are all attested in A1 contexts in central Europe.[180] Lunulae may also fit into this stage.[181] But, as always, exotic ideas were tempered with insular inventiveness, implicit in the form of the Group B axes, and in the Migdale plain bar and solid ribbed armlets.[182]

Much in stage III was still current in stage IV,[183] illustrating the chronological problems inherent in this material. Stage IV can be equated with Coles' Colleonard phase in Scotland, with the early part of the Wessex culture, with Harbison's Ballyvalley phase in Ireland,[184] and is still Case's stage II*b*. The continuing impingement of central European ideas on essentially insular industries shows in more sophisticated flat axes, often decorated, narrower, and with bevelled faces and hammered up edges designed to improve hafting qualities; also in more sophisticated and substantial daggers, frequently with blade grooves and ribs, e.g. the Bush Barrow type.

Stage V (Case's III), embodying significant developments in technology and fashions, probably began in the 16th century, but belonged mainly to the 15th. It is characterised above all by the Arreton industry of southern and eastern England,[185] which provided bronzes to the Aldbourne-Edmondsham group of the Wessex culture. Its continental contacts extended to northern as well as central Europe.[186] A whole new range of products was introduced, notably cast-flanged axes, ogival, grooved daggers (Camerton-Snowshill), tanged spearheads and socketed pegged spearheads,[187] the last indicating that core-casting, as well as bivalve casting, was now known.[188] Some other regions had equivalents of Arreton metalworking, notably Ireland, where the Inch Island/Derryniggin tradition[189] produced its own versions of flanged axes, ogival, grooved daggers and socketed spearheads ('end-looped').[190] Comparable metalwork in Scotland, best known in the Gavel Moss hoard, Renfrewshire,[191] and in Wales and the Marches, best represented by the hoards from Ebnal, Salop, and Menai Bridge, Anglesey,[192] shows contact with both Arreton and Inch Island/Derryniggin traditions. But finds are so few as to suggest that any local manufacture was severely limited, and over much of the north and west of Britain one can only conclude that older metalworking traditions, of stages III and IV, survived to the end of the early bronze age.[193]

### The end of the early bronze age and a hiatus

Many of the features which characterise the early bronze age can be traced down to *c.* 1400 BC, but then disappear from the archaeological record. A marked hiatus is evident in sepulchral and religious development, and to a certain extent in technological and economic aspects, touching, in fact, most of what is known of early bronze age life. Knowledge of settlements and domestic life is scanty, but it is hard to believe that these were not affected in some way.

The intensive exploitation of lowland flint and highland zone rocks was still important in the early bronze age,[194] but cannot be detected later. The most distinctive products of this stone technology, barbed and tanged arrowheads and perforated implements, can be traced thus far and no farther. Changing fashions, and the growth of metallurgy, banished stone to a lesser role. But metalworking itself was affected. All the major products of the early bronze age were replaced,[195] though technical advances were less sweeping.[196]

All the established pottery types, beakers, food vessels, enlarged food vessels, collared, cordoned, encrusted and biconical urns and pygmy cups, and the whole range of burial and ritual monuments and practices with which they are associated, vanished at this time. One must not assume that whole cultures passed with them, though clearly communities

subject to such profound changes must have been trans-
formed. So it appears in the south, the only region where
much is known of the communities which emerged from this
hiatus. Here the contrast between Deverel-Rimbury developments and anything familiar from the early bronze age seems
remarkable at first glance, though barrow burial and
cremation survived. Elsewhere everything connected with
established burial and ritual apparently vanished. Nowhere is
there any evidence that the old linear and circular ritual
monuments, the cursus, avenues, alignments, henges and
circles, survived. A convincing scientific case has now been
made out for linking these sites with a remarkable store of
engineering, mathematical and astronomical knowledge,[197]
which was presumably lost as the monuments themselves
were abandoned.

The passing of the Wessex culture graphically illustrates
the magnitude of this hiatus. It can be traced to the very end
of the early bronze age on C14 evidence, yet although rich
graves were its hallmark, none contains an undisputed middle
bronze age artefact. Its end could not therefore have been
long and lingering, but what, apart from some catastrophe,
could have induced it so rapidly, and could have brought
comparable changes not only throughout Britain and Ireland,
but even across the Channel in Brittany? The pattern hardly
suggests natural change, nor is there any evidence for
invasions or migrations. It is difficult to think of any other
human force which could have been more than contributory.
One is left with natural agencies, of which climatic change
seems likeliest.

Whereas the main climatic deterioration of the bronze age
belonged to its end, around the 7th-6th centuries BC, the
initial onset of wetter conditions came everywhere much
earlier, certainly by c. 1100 BC, possibly even earlier.[198] On
the Mediaeval evidence climatic deterioration would certainly
have produced changes of the order and scale envisaged.
While admitting that there is at present scarcely any scientific
evidence for or against change at this time, there is some
interesting, and possibly relevant, archaeological evidence.
The hiatus marks a religious metamorphosis beyond anything. Knowledge of early bronze age religion suggests that
it was everywhere associated with burial, and that its shafts,

pits,[199] circles and alignments evoke a pantheon both subterranean and celestial. All this apparently disappeared at the hiatus, and what knowledge there is of middle and late bronze age religion suggests that it was water-oriented.[200] Much of the finest metalwork of these phases comes from wet places such as rivers and bogs, and must represent offerings to water deities, anticipating the well-known custom of iron age Celts.[201] The abandonment of old gods and the rise of new ones could well follow from the flooding and waterlogging produced by worsening climate. Increased precipitation and rising water tables would inhibit both shaft digging and the use of stone circles and alignments. Some of the major concentrations of these monuments, as on Dartmoor and in parts of Co. Tyrone, are now on, and often buried in, peat moorland, yet this peat has clearly formed since the sites were built. Ruined settlements on Dartmoor and buried field walls in the Tyrone peat attest the former potential of such areas, before human interference and deteriorating climate turned them into moorland.[202] So in places the religious sites themselves gradually became water-logged. A second point is the effect of worsening climate on the careful observations and sightings implicit in many of these sites, which make sense only in a period warmer and drier than today, since they required prolonged, still, dry, warm air conditions both for establishment and use.[203] The onset of a poorer climate would have brought insuperable difficulties of visibility and refraction, only too evident when observing at these sites today. It is difficult to account for the passing of early bronze age mound and cemetery burial traditions in climatic terms, except against a background of general religious change.

Climatic deterioration would also seriously affect settlement and farming patterns, combining with human misuse to make extensive tracts marginal or unusable. The abandonment of upland farms in the south-west provides a good example (p. 218). Resulting land pressure might make it necessary to defend land and stock, i.e. to start building defensive settlements, and to occupy naturally defensible positions such as hilltops. As late as the early bronze age there seems to be no general tradition of defence building or hilltop occupation, and, indeed, the shifting pattern of farming probably precluded such developments in many areas. Norton Fitzwarren and Rams Hill may show the beginning of a trend, emphasised by deepening social stratification and by deteriorating climate. The occupation of highland zone hilltops may have begun at this time on the evidence of calibrated C14 dates from Mam Tor, Derbyshire and Kaimes Hill, Midlothian.[204] Hillforts, if not started now, were being built only three centuries later at sites such as Dinorben, Denbighshire, and Grimthorpe, Yorkshire (p. 207).

Many regions which were wealthy and important in the early bronze age emerged from the hiatus as comparative backwaters, for example Wessex and south-west Wales. Their decline is matched by the rise of new centres, notably north Wales, the Thames Valley and the Fens. The whole basis of power and wealth must have shifted away from the agricultural, manpower and religious factors which had hitherto prevailed. The new wealth was based on metallurgy and the new religion. Some of the emerging areas, such as north Wales, possessed the raw materials necessary for metallurgical development, but the success of the Thames Valley and Fens, both water-dominated, suggests they had become the centres of the new water-based religion.[205] Stonehenge in fact had moved eastwards, and commerce was attracted to the new holy lands as it had been to the old.

That north Wales was already important in the early bronze age is obscured by the brilliance of Wessex, and artificial archaeological pre-occupation with this and other areas such as east Yorkshire. Local metalworking had been established since copper-working days, and rich graves and metal finds show growing contact both with lowland England and Ireland.[206] This nodality became even more important after the hiatus, when local commerce can be seen reaching out far and wide (p. 199). Spectacular finds, such as the Beddgelert, Caernarvonshire rapier hoard, illustrate this success. One might have added the Mold burial, were its chronology more certain.[207]

Religious tergiversation, deepening social stratification, a changing basis of wealth and new continental contacts thus combined to produce a watershed in British prehistory. Climatic deterioration could account for many of the phenomena observed, but has yet to be clearly demonstrated.

### The middle and late bronze age

The hiatus marks the end of recognisable sepulchral practices in most regions, and as settlement evidence continues to be scanty, knowledge of subsequent phases rests heavily on stray finds of metalwork. Reciprocal connections with the con-

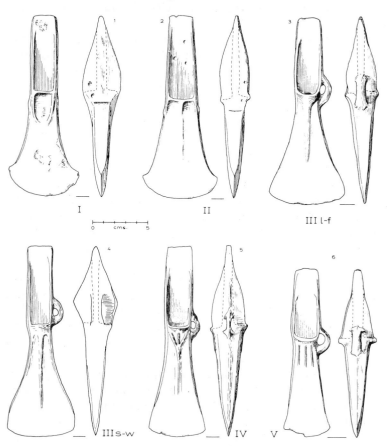

Figure 31. The Anglo-Welsh palstave series:[1] 1. Group I (shield-pattern), Llanidloes, Montgomeryshire; 2. Group II (early midribbed), St Harmon, Radnorshire; 3. Group III (low-flanged), Llanegryn, Merionethshire; 4. Group III (south-western, high-flanged), Buildwas, Shropshire; 5. Group IV (transitional), River Thames at Barnes; 6. Group V (late), Llantisilio, Denbighshire.

tinent, shifting with the passage of time, intensified in the middle bronze age and give lie to the popular idea that this was a period of insularity. The most constant and closest links were with north-west France, continuing the pattern evident from the Breton element in Wessex culture graves.

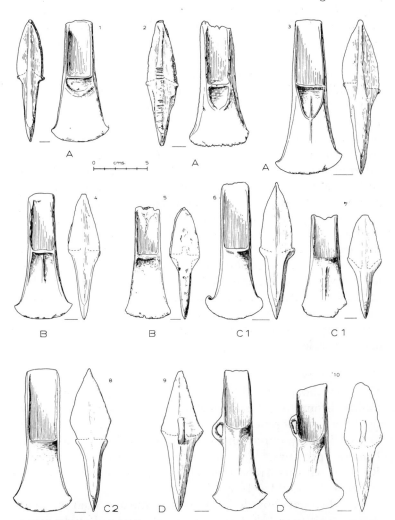

Figure 32. The Irish palstave series:[1] 1-3, Group A (shield-pattern); 4-5, Group B (flanges extend below stop); 6-8, Group C (continuous flange-stop line; 6-7, C1, low-flanged, 8, C2, high-flanged); 9-10, Group D (looped, narrow blade). All from 'Ireland', unprovenanced.

The middle bronze age hoard record is very uneven,[208] which places heavy reliance on the evidence gleaned from typology and continental contacts. Fortunately some key middle bronze age implements and weapons had their form changed at intervals, and these typological developments, regional variations in form, and the changing pattern of continental influences, provide a basis for isolating regional metalworking traditions and sub-dividing the period. Axes, dirks and rapiers are most useful in this respect, spearheads less so since they remained basically unchanged for centuries (Fig. 33).[209] There were two basic axe traditions, palstaves and short-flanged axes, the former characteristic of southern England and Wales, the latter of northern England and Scotland, with Ireland having both. The Anglo-Welsh and Irish palstave series developed along parallel lines, but differed markedly in character (Figs. 31 and 32).[210] Dirks and rapiers can be divided into four broadly sequential groups on a basis of cross-section (Fig. 34).[211]

As developments proceeded at different rates in different regions, inter-regional synchronisms present a difficult problem. Everywhere four distinct and inter-related industrial stages can be distinguished between the hiatus at the end of the early bronze age and the late bronze industrial revolution of the 8th century (p. 209), but these stages show considerable overlap, and varied in duration from region to region. Thus only in a broad sense can one speak of phases on a national scale.[212]

### The Acton Park phase

Very few hoards are known from the opening phase of the middle bronze age, but important continental contacts throw light on developments in the British Isles. Two regions are particularly important, north-west and Baltic Europe, the Ilsmoor province,[213] and north-west France, especially Brittany with its Tréboul group,[214] but connections can be traced as far afield as Italy.[215]

The Ilsmoor hoards of northern Europe contain many British-type axes.[216] Group I ('shield-pattern') palstaves of various forms are most common, but group II (early midribbed) palstaves, thin-bladed flanged 'axes' and a variety of bar-stop axes are all familiar in Britain. Here north

Wales is the only region to have yielded all these types, and a series of hoards of this period. The most important of these hoards, from Acton Park, Denbighshire,[217] finds a remarkable parallel in the Dutch Voorhout hoard,[218] sometimes interpreted as the property of an itinerant north Welsh trader.[219] Unfortunately the Acton Park group of hoards contains only tools,[220] and gives no indication of the weapons of the period, and relevant Ilsmoor hoards lack British weapons. However, the Orsdorf grave, Schleswig-Holstein,[221] Tréboul contexts in Brittany,[222] and the Cascina Ranza hoard in Italy,[223] all confirm the currency of group II dirks and rapiers. The Tréboul group also has ribbed and grooved rapiers identical with Irish/British group I weapons in all except butt shape and number of rivets.[224] Tréboul hoards, like Ilsmoor hoards, include numerous group I palstaves, including the heavy north Welsh form, some group II palstaves, bar-stop axes and thin-bladed flanged axes.[225] The rest of northern France is less well known than Brittany but had even closer English contacts. From the beginning the palstave series of Normandy and Picardy diverged from that of Brittany, and paralleled the Anglo-Welsh series. This makes it difficult to be certain of the source of western palstaves in areas such as Brittany and the Baltic.[226]

The repertoire of Acton Park smiths and their southern contemporaries thus included group I and II palstaves, bar-stop and thin-bladed flanged axes, and group I and II dirks and rapiers. The evidence for spearhead types is scanty, but side-looped and leaf-shaped basal-looped spearheads (Fig. 33) must have been current.[227] In other regions such material occurs almost entirely as stray finds. Irish smiths produced Group A and B palstaves, counterpart to the Anglo-Welsh group I and II implements, examples of which were actually imported from north Wales.[228] Haft-flanged axes were also standard Irish products,[229] though whether they complimented the palstaves or were used in different areas remains unknown.[230] The moulds from Inchnagree, Co. Cork, and Killymaddy, Co. Antrim,[231] show that socket-looped spearheads and group I and II dirks and rapiers were the current weapon types, probably with basal-looped spearheads.[232] Industrially, north English and Scottish

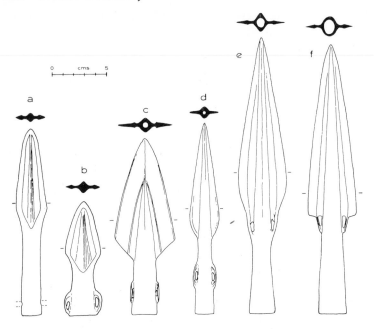

Figure 33. Some spearhead types of the early and middle bronze age: *a*, pegged, solid blade; *b*, end-looped; *c*, socket-looped; *d*, side-looped; *e*, leaf-shaped basal-looped; *f*, straight-based basal-looped.

industries looked to Ireland, rather than Wales or the south, in this, as in subsequent, periods. Production was based on stone moulds, haft-flanged axes were dominant, and local group I and II dirks and rapiers, including some very Irish in character, should belong here. But the British side-looped spearhead was preferred to its Irish socket-looped counterpart. Some palstaves were used, mostly Anglo-Welsh group I implements,[233] probably deriving from north Wales, but scattered Irish imports of Group A are also found.[234]

Wessex has produced little metalwork of this phase, and seems to have shrunk into industrial obscurity. The southwest was more important, the Knighton moulds, in the highland zone stone tradition, showing that group II rapiers could be numbered among local products.[235] South Wales was relatively unimportant,[236] and it is the Thames Valley and Fen areas which stand out as the southern rivals of north Wales.[237]

*The Taunton phase*

Acton Park developments must have lasted for much of the 14th and 13th centuries, but already, from around 1300, new trends were emerging. The Frøjk-Ostenfeld hoards of later Montelius II,[238] beginning about this time, contain British-type palstaves different from those in the Ilsmoor hoards, suggesting that somewhere in Britain a new industrial stage was setting in. Close examination of relevant Anglo-Welsh palstaves suggests that southern England took the lead in these changes, while older traditions lingered on in highland zone areas.[239] This seems to mark the beginning of a general economic and industrial resurgence of southern regions. Continental connections with northern regions such as the *Ilmenau Kreis* in Germany, and with France,[240] may have played some part in this, providing all those ornaments and tools which characterise M.A. Smith's 'ornament horizon',[241] the second stage of middle bronze age metal-working. Though beginning in Montelius II these developments relate mainly to Montelius III, and must thus have centred on the 12th century.

The imported ornaments[242] provoked a keen response in Irish-British smiths, who not only copied them in bronze and gold but were also inspired to invent ornaments of their own.[243] The new tools also provoked much local copying and experiment.[244] Southern England drew closer to north-western France, especially to Normandy/Picardy, whose palstaves, identical with the Anglo-Welsh low-flanged type,[245] contrast strongly with the Portrieux palstaves of Brittany. Some of the latter reached Britain, however.[246] A striking cross-Channel community of tradition clearly existed.[247]

Irish-British smiths continued to produce and modify well-established local types alongside the continental novelties. Spearheads remained unchanged, but group III and IV dirks and rapiers gradually ousted group II weapons.[248] New palstave types became general: group III, low-flanged and south-western, in the south and Wales, group C in Ireland, while highland zone haft-flanged axes were developed into wing-flanged axes. In the south and Wales production utilised bronze moulds, but in other areas stone moulds remained predominant.[249] South-west England, especially Somerset,

I    II    II    III    IV

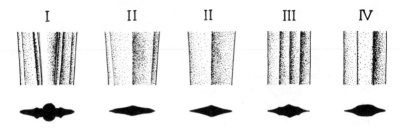

Figure 34. Dirks and rapiers of Britain and Ireland: classification according to blade cross-section. Group I, rounded midrib (usually with accompanying grooves and/or beadings); Group II, flattened lozenge section (with or without bevelled edges); Group III, triple ridge or arris; Group IV, flattened mid-section.

emerged as a region strong in the exotic elements of this new metalworking, and Wessex seems to have recovered something of its former strength. The Thames valley and Fens continued to display a remarkable quantity and range of metalwork, and the new hoard from Bulphan Fen, Essex, probably deposited towards the end of the period, illustrates the prevailing mixture of established and novel ideas.[250]

Developments in north Wales seem less dynamic than before.[251] The exotic innovations of the period had little impact in Wales, and it is not known whether a few gold versions of the new torcs[252] were made locally or in Ireland. Irish smiths made much of the new ornament forms, producing considerably quantities in gold as well as bronze.[253] The Bishopsland hoard, Co. Kildare,[254] shows that most of the new tool fashions also reached Ireland, perhaps via Britain, for the Annesborough find, Co. Armagh, has an Anglo-Welsh low-flanged palstave with its ornaments.[255] But the main volume of production in Ireland, as in Britain, continued along traditional lines,[256] though craftsmanship reached a peak.[257] Scotland, and especially northern England, were little affected by the exotic innovations, and can show just a few torcs, mostly in gold, and even fewer tools.[258] The Hotham Carr hoard, Yorkshire, demonstrates the mixture of influences touching the north at this time, local, Anglo-Welsh and Irish.[259]

*The Penard phase*

The rise of the urnfield groups of central Europe produced ripples felt in the most distant corners of the Old World.[260] Whether the scatter of urnfield bronzes in these islands, mostly swords and other warrior equipment, shows that urnfield adventurers were active here, as in so many other remote regions, or whether it merely represents commercial activity, is uncertain. The arrival of new stimuli from urnfield and Atlantic Europe, at a time when Irish and British smiths were still experimenting with Taunton novelties, produced an even more intensive climate of experiment. This led to developments in traditional areas ('transitional' and group D palstaves, notched-butt group IV dirks and rapiers, basal-looped spearheads of the triangular basal-looped form),[261] and completely new inventions, such as cylinder-socket sickles.[262] There was further work on Nordic ideas (socketed axes and hammers, torcs), and experiments with the new urnfield fashions started. A major event, the re-appearance of pegged spearheads,[263] is of uncertain background, but bifid razors probably reflect the closeness of French links.

The quantity of early urnfield imports is small, but they are widely scattered. The earliest, notably rod-tanged and Rixheim swords, are likely to be of Hallstatt Al;[264] some, such as the first leaf-shaped, flanged-hilt swords (Erbenheim and Hemigkofen types),[265] pointed ferrules and tanged, curved knives,[266] belong to Hallstatt phase A2, but others, such as tanged arrowheads[267] and possibly shields,[268] only have a more general early urnfield background. But all should have been brought in around the 11th century.[269] Quantitatively more important was the local response, in particular a variety of sword types, some with flanged hilts, other with hilt tangs. The latter, much more numerous, include Lambeth/Rosnöen, Chelsea and Ballintober forms, exhibiting a very mixed local rapier/Rixheim/rod-tanged ancestry.[270] Copies of flanged-hilt swords are not easily distinguishable from their Erbenheim and Hemigkofen prototypes,[271] but the U-shouldered weapons of Hammersmith type[272] constitute the first British standardised form.

The principal concentrations of these urnfield and urnfield-inspired bronzes[273] are in south-east England,

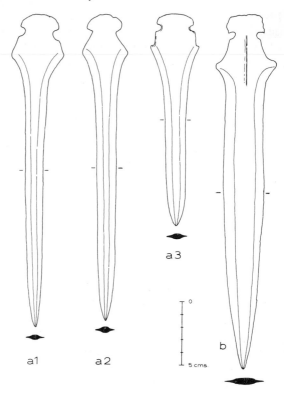

Figure 35. Notched-butt dirks and rapiers of Group IV: *a*, the Lisburn series, with straight blade: *a*1, Mildenhall form; *a*2, Portna form; *a*3, Imeroo form. *b*, the Cutts type, with leaf-shaped blade.

especially the Thames Valley, and Ireland, with important intermediate finds showing that traffic went via south Wales. The Thames/Ireland connection was unusually close judging from the material the two have in common, including flanged-hilt and tanged swords,[274] notched-butt dirks and rapiers,[275] triangular bas'al-looped spearheads, cylinder-socket sickles, and possibly, shields. The connecting Welsh hoards, from Penard, Glamorganshire, and Ffynhonnau, Breconshire have an appropriate mixture of urnfield, south-eastern, Irish and local types.[276] Ireland, while rich in relevant stray finds, lacks the important hoards of the south-east.[277] Outside this interesting axis, urnfield bronzes and derivatives are so few that they could have had little effect on local industry, but are nevertheless widely scattered.[278] The remarkable lost hoard from Ambleside, Westmorland,[279] with an impressive array of these novelties, looks out of place in an otherwise barren north.

Events across the Channel followed a parallel course to those in southern Britain, with a similar influx of early urnfield elements, and local response.[280] The resulting Rosnöen tradition is best known in Brittany, but clearly extended all over north-west France.[281] Parallels with Penard metalworking are striking, though there are inevitable differences in emphasis. Thus Lambeth/Rosnöen and Ballintober swords are found on both sides of the Channel, but whereas the latter were much preferred in Britain, Lambeth/Rosnöen swords predominated in France.

The nature of these early urnfield contacts presents a crucial, if at present insoluble, problem on both sides of the Channel. The scanty material includes nothing which demands more than trade, though its strongly martial character encourages those who have postulated urnfield incursions.[282] The upsurge in native weapon development, especially of swords, could have been provoked by intrusive urnfield swordsmen. The establishment of the Thames/south Wales/Ireland axis might reflect the opening of a new trade route in a time of intense industrial activity, but has such an unparalleled intensity and air of directness as to suggest urnfield warriors blazing an unconventional trail to the west. It is attractive to relate such possibilities to the first reasonable evidence for hill-fort building in Britain. In addition to the C14 dates which would place the Dinorben and Grimthorpe hill-forts in this phase,[283] there are pins of urnfield origin or inspiration from hill-forts or enclosures at Dinborben itself, the Breiddin, Montgomeryshire, and Totternhoe, Bedfordshire.[284] It is surely no coincidence that continental urnfield groups were such great hillfort builders.

*The Wilburton-Wallington phase*
Urnfield influence, whatever its nature, soon petered out, and the unusual Thames-Ireland connection was severed. Cross-channel links remained as strong as ever, however, and both in southern England and north-west France adoption of a new industrial repertoire and a new lead-bronze alloy in the

10th century ushered in the late bronze age.[285] The two representatives of the new metallurgy, the Wilburton tradition in England and the Saint-Brieuc-des-Iffs group in France, had many products and techniques in common while showing the familiar differences in emphasis. Wilburton smiths, for the first time in Britain, produced in quantity leaf-shaped swords, pegged spearheads and socketed axes, the traditional indicators of the late bronze age.[286] In both areas developed palstaves (termed 'late' in Britain) were the main axe type. Both industries used the free-flowing properties of lead-bronze to develop thin-walled products, notably tongue chapes, and both produced tubular spear ferrules, but there is no reflection in the Saint-Brieuc group of the range of 'fancy' spearheads[287] developed by Wilburton smiths. Much of the new repertoire followed on logically from Penard/Rosnöen developments, and this earliest late bronze age metalworking was more a question of changing emphasis and techniques than a sudden influx of novelties.

Southern England remained closer, metallurgically, to north-west France than to other regions of the British Isles. Throughout the two or three centuries of Wilburton domination, the highland zone experienced a lingering middle bronze age.[288] Associations of this period are rare over much of the north and west, which gives added importance to the Wallington hoards of northern England. These show that the old tin-bronze alloy, and middle bronze age products such as dirks, rapiers (of group IV), 'transitional' palstaves and looped spearheads, were still current. New developments, such as protected-loop and single-looped spearheads, followed middle bronze age traditions. Southern novelties were not entirely excluded; there was experimental production of socketed axes in particular. A more or less similar state of affairs prevailed throughout the highland zone, with Wilburton interests achieving only peripheral penetration. Wilburton products are practically absent beyond the southern fringes of northern England, for example, and in Wales show only isolated ingress via the Severn gap.[289] Ireland has more Wilburton material than other highland zone regions, but it is swamped by the mass of local Wallington bronzes, and not even here was there a Wilburton phase in the southern sense. Everywhere there is evidence that what little Wilburton material is present arrived late, and may be seen against a background of Wilburton decline and industrial unrest in the 8th century.[290] Whether this late dissemination represents export of outmoded scrap implements, or an actual movement of emigré Wilburton smiths under pressure, is difficult to determine. The widespread appearance of Wilburton elements in highland zone industries of the ensuing Ewart Park phase could suggest the latter.

## The Ewart Park phase

An industrial revolution spread late bronze age metallurgy throughout these islands in the 8th-7th centuries, ending the southern monopoly.[291] Diverse exotic influences, Mediterranean, Atlantic, late urnfield and north European, are discernible in the metalworking of the ensuing Ewart Park phase,[292] but nothing on a scale suggesting causative invasion or immigration. The extent of the changes is reflected in the wider range of products, and the greater quantities of metal, everywhere available, involving significant technological and marketing developments, yet Irish-British metallurgy retained its basically insular character. The vastly increased number of hoards deposited in this period is very much a sign of the times, reflecting both the security motive in troubled times and also votive deposition,[293] the two probably linked. Two developments in the 7th century may have combined to produce unsettled conditions, further climatic deterioration, and the rise of Hallstatt power in central Europe.[294] The great quantities of metal deposited in wet places in this period betoken renewed interest in the old-established water cult, a reaction both to worsening climate and troubled times. Hallstatt influence in the British Isles was considerable, but its nature has been hotly disputed. However it is surely no accident that the greatest numbers of hoards of this period come from where the Hallstatt presence was strongest, the lower Thames basin and Ireland.[295]

The apparent suddenness and totality of the break between Wilburton-Wallington and Ewart Park metalworking may be illusory. The lack of evidence of transition from one to the other may reflect the date of deposition of the great mass of Ewart Park hoards. If this was linked to Hallstatt pressure then it would not have begun before the mid-7th century, by which time Ewart Park metalworking traditions would have reached maturity, their transition from Wilburton-Wallington industries poorly attested in a period when few hoards were deposited.[296]

Carp's tongue metalworking, and French contacts, were mainly a south-eastern monopoly, though industries elsewhere managed to find limited markets in carp's tongue France.[297] Some exotic influences had a more widespread effect, notably the Mediterranean and central European urnfield ideas which inspired a great tradition of sheet metalworking, bringing buckets and cauldrons to the affluent.[298] Scandinavian contacts, restricted mainly to luxury lines, ornaments and horse gear, were strongest, surprisingly, with Irish Sea lands.[299] It was at this time that horse-riding and wheeled vehicles became familiar in the British Isles, evidenced by abundant harness and vehicle fittings drawn from urnfield, as well as northern, Europe.[300]

Regional industries are clearly differentiated in the Ewart Park phase, and are best approached through regional socketed axe types. The major industrial provinces were the carp's tongue south-east, the west of England and south-east Wales, covered by the Llantwit-Stogursey tradition, northern England, with its Heathery Burn tradition, and Ireland with its Dowris tradition.[301] Some areas, such as Scotland and north Wales, had no local socketed axe form, and drew instead on axes from other areas. Regional character naturally extended far beyond socketed axe forms.[302] Some products were common to all industries, notably the Ewart Park sword, plain spearheads and basic tools. Differences extended to technology,[303] methods and organisation, as well as products, dictated by relative proximity to supplies of raw material. The system in ore-bearing areas would have differed markedly from that in areas lacking ores. Thus founders' hoards abound in the south-east, full of broken, worn out and reject metalwork and ingot metal, indicating the local importance of the scrap trade. Contrast the traders' hoards, usually of socketed axes, from Lincolnshire and east Yorkshire, and the personal hoards, of tools and ornaments, of Ireland.[304] Hoard differences of course imply much else. The apparently votive weapon hoards of the Broadward complex extend over a great territory, with its apex in south Yorkshire, extending down the Marches, and spreading out into south-west and south-central England and the Thames Valley.[305] The overwhelming preponderance of spearheads in these hoards suggests that these great tracts were dominated by spear warriors, much given to ceremonial, and devotees of the water cult. The striking similarities between widely scattered finds, notably between the Broadward hoard, and the Thames Street and Broadness finds, suggests considerably industrial, political and religious cohesion over this great area. On the east the Broadward spearmen hemmed in the carp's tongue province, where swords and spearheads were used together. To the north, Broadward finds just touch another large province stretching from Yorkshire to Aberdeen, characterised by swordsmen's hoards, containing up to three swords, with accompanying chape or rings (belt or scabbard fittings?).[306] Spear and sword hoards have a strikingly complementary distribution. In both areas there are numerous less remarkable hoards with axes, tools and occasional weapons, suggesting the property of less martial elements in the community. There is again a hint of Hawkes' threefold division of society.[307]

Hallstatt expansion, at first directed southwards into France, subsequently spread westwards into the Low Countries[308] and northern France, as evidenced by the distribution of Gündlingen class *b* swords,[309] reaching eastern Britain by mid-7th century.[310] Penetration of Ireland and the west must have come later still, and via Britain, not direct from the continent, since classifiable Irish Gündlingen swords are of the distinctively insular classes *c* and *d*, almost unknown on the continent.

Unfortunately the mass of Irish, British and north French Hallstatt finds are stray finds, without context, so that the nature of the influences they represent is uncertain. Opinions have ranged from the traditional full-scale Hallstatt immigration, the foundation of British iron age settlement, through raiding, trading, the activities of travelling smiths, and exchange of gifts.[311] The first point to be made concerns the strength of the contacts, with nearly ninety Gündlingen swords, more than a third of the total known, coming from the British Isles. Thus although old ideas of invasion and

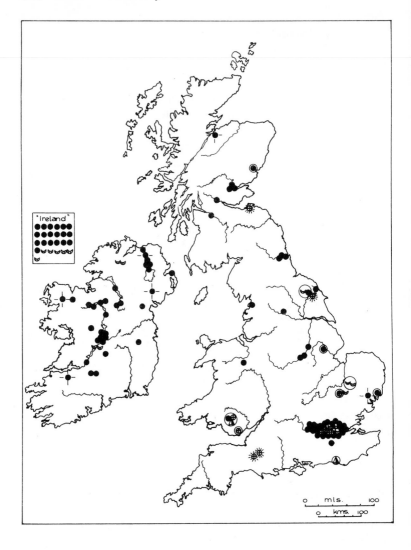

Figure 36. Distribution map of Hallstatt C material in Britain and Ireland.
- ● Swords (all bronze Gündlingen examples except for iron sword in Llynfawr hoard, Glamorganshire)
- ♆ Winged chapes
- ⊕ Razors
- ▲ Harness and vehicle bronzes
- ⁙ Hill-fort or settlement site: associations encircled

settlement have waned with the demise of the invasion hypothesis, nevertheless there is much against a purely commercial solution. Most of the material consists of warrior equipment, with a coastal-riverine distribution[312] which forms a classic raiding pattern, very different from familiar trade-based distributions. The near-absence of Hallstatt finds in native contexts argues strongly against trade, and makes some harrying of British shores all the more likely. At least some Hallstatt elements must have settled, if only to make and use the large number of class *c* and *d* Gündlingen swords.[313] These could hardly have been copies by local smiths since they are absent from indigenous contexts, and contrast so strongly with the widespread Gündlingen-influenced Ewart Park swords that represent the known local response to Hallstatt swords.[314]

So the likelihood is that Britain and Ireland were penetrated in the 7th century by Hallstatt adventurers, traders and smiths, usually untrammelled by women and all the cultural paraphernalia that would have made a broader-based immigration more noticeable. Some Hallstatt settlers may have come, as has been claimed at South Cadbury hill-fort, Somerset,[315] while other settlers may have been refugees from Hallstatt pressure on the continent. Razors alone amongst Hallstatt types regularly turn up on local hill-forts and settlements,[316] often in areas otherwise devoid of Hallstatt material. Conversely, they are rare in areas such as Ireland rich in Hallstatt warrior equipment. Their presence alone cannot betray Hallstatt settlers, and some at least should show the success of a luxury novelty in a difficult trading situation. Hallstatt contact with the natives could hardly have been friendly to judge from the lack of their material in local hoards, and their failure to influence local bronze-working. But they may have harassed metal supplies.[317] The importation of shoddy Armorican socketed axes, perhaps referred to in the Massaliote Periplus,[318] could betray a French attempt to provide hard-pressed friends with an emergency metal supply,[319] for French carp's tongue lands seem to have suffered little from Hallstatt pressure.[320] The only major innovation in Britain metalworking at this time, the massive Sompting socketed axes,[321] were strongly influenced by these Armorican axes. But this was the last gasp of British bronze-working, for by *c.* 600 BC, scattered iron-working was already under way.[322]

## Settlements and burial: middle and late bronze age

Because it is still so difficult to relate middle and late bronze age metalwork to site evidence, an account of these periods still lends itself to the dual approach.

### The Deverel-Rimbury culture

In spite of the technical imprecision of the term 'Deverel-Rimbury',[323] it is still widely retained as a convenient umbrella expression to cover all those southern groups characterised by coarse, bucket-shaped urns.[324] For long the Deverel-Rimbury culture was regarded as late bronze age and intrusive, the result of a continental immigration around 750 BC. But more recently an indigenous background and middle bronze age beginnings have seemed likely.[325]

Of the three classic Deverel-Rimbury pottery types, barrel, globular and bucket urns, only the last is found amongst all the scattered Deverel-Rimbury groups. Globular urns are widely distributed, but barrel urns are practically confined to wessex north of the Stour.[326] Because of artificial archaeological emphasis and differential survival, the Deverel-Rimbury groups of Wessex, Hampshire and Sussex have always been best known, indeed Deverel-Rimbury has too often been thought of as peculiar to those areas. Recent work has extended its distribution to the fringes of the highland zone, and shown just how many distinct regional groups existed. Even in the classic Wessex area, a distinction can be made between a western *Deverel-Rimbury group* proper, characterised by bucket urns, globular urns of Type II and barrow cemeteries, and an eastern *Cranborne Chase* or *Wessex general group*, characterised by bucket, barrel and Type I globular urns, and flat cemeteries, the two divided by the River Stour.[327] The *Sussex group* is best known from its enclosed settlements,[328] but other regional groups are much less well-known. The extensive *Thames Valley* material[329] may relate to several groups, but an *Eastern group* in Essex and Suffolk is more homogeneous.[330] A *West Midland group* has only come to light with recent finds such as those from

Bromfield, Shropshire, and Ryton-on-Dunsmore, Warwickshire,[331] and may have extended into north Wales.[332] An
*East Midland group* is represented by burial finds[333] lying
for the most part unpublished in local museums, and may
just have extended across the Humber into southern
Yorkshire.[334]

Most of what is known of Deverel-Rimbury relates to its
intensively studied southern branches. Domestic sites there
can be divided into enclosed settlements, simple enclosures,
and associated 'Celtic' field systems. The enclosed
settlements are best known in Sussex.[335] Type sites such as
Itford Hill and Plumpton Plain A[336] show that these
settlements consisted of a complex of embanked enclosures,
some containing circular timber buildings, with small pits for
cooking and storage,[337] associated with field systems. They
housed not more than large family groups, practising mixed
farming in a well-organised and manured field system,
spinning and weaving their own textiles. The simple enclosure
sites,[338] irregularly shaped and up to 2½ acres in extent, are
best known from Wessex. Their bank and ditch perimeter is
frequently discontinuous. The apparent absence of buildings
in examples excavated by Pitt Rivers,[339] and their association with the linear ditched 'ranch boundaries', has led to
their being interpreted as stock enclosures, but the Thorny
Down example was full of post structures,[340] suggesting that
not all served the same function. Some were clearly farmsteads, while others were animal pounds, mainly for cattle.

Deverel-Rimbury groups usually buried their dead in
cremation cemeteries, either in flat urnfields or in barrows,
containing up to a hundred or more burials. Some were
in-urned, some simply in pits. Some urns may lack bones
entirely, while others contain only token deposits, and urns
were sometimes incomplete when deposited. Grave goods are
very rare. Because of the extreme fragility of the pottery, and
the quantity of old, poorly recorded finds, many aspects of
Deverel-Rimbury burial tradition are imperfectly understood.
Both flat and barrow cemeteries may have early bronze age
beginnings, indicated by the presence of collared urn burials
(p. 220 below).[341] Where Deverel-Rimbury groups did raise
their own barrows, these were often small, low, and
sometimes ditchless.[342] Cemeteries in barrows were often

concentrated in the south-eastern/southern part of the mound. Deverel-Rimbury settlement wares are generally coarser, simpler versions of funerary pottery, but problems of relating the domestic and sepulchral aspects of the culture have been greatly alleviated by the discovery of parts of the same urn in the Itford Hill settlement and a nearby barrow cemetery.[343]

The problems of Deverel-Rimbury origins and chronology are interrelated. There is such a striking contrast with familiar early bronze age features that it is easy to see why continental origins were sought for so long. But the much favoured *Deverel-Urnen* prototypes have long since been turned into Hilversum and Drakenstein urns, representing migration from, not to, Britain. If an indigenous origin must prevail, then relationships with grooved wares, biconical and Trevisker urns must all be considered. Trevisker origins have been argued for biconical, bucket and even globular urns,[344] and there are sufficient numbers of Trevisker-influenced vessels in Wessex to indicate that potters there must have been affected by Trevisker styles. But whether this influence was formative or *en passant* is at present insoluble. Meanwhile, vastly increased knowledge of grooved wares[345] provides an alternative, more proximate possibility. The enormous grooved ware repertoire now available encompasses most of the shapes and decorative features of biconical, bucket, barrel and even globular urns. The problem is the chronological gap, not so much for the early bronze age biconical urns as for the supposedly middle bronze age Deverel-Rimbury urns. To see the biconicals as a bridge will not do, since they are further removed from grooved wares than the Deverel-Rimbury urns. The fault perhaps lies in the established view that biconical urns were ancestral to bucket urns, when morphologically no firm line separates them. Both are represented at sites such as Mildenhall.[346] Biconical urns, like Deverel-Rimbury urns, were once firmly middle bronze age, so the time has perhaps come to transfer some of the latter into the early bronze age, alongside the biconicals. While there is nothing tending to deny this possibility there is little evidence to support it, since most Deverel-Rimbury contexts lack datable finds. However, there is some supporting C14 evidence for early bronze age beginnings.[347] Further, the early Shearplace Hill farmers may have used Deverel-Rimbury, as well as collared and biconical, urns.[348] Deverel-Rimbury and collared urn burials frequently occupied the same site, and the latter are not always necessarily primary.[349] The compartmentalisation of early bronze age pottery types is a familiar phenomenon,[350] and the addition of another, Deverel-Rimbury, compartment should cause no extra problems.

Having argued a case for indigenous origins, the fact remains that the closest parallels for Deverel-Rimbury urns are to be found in France. The immigration view has always been strikingly supported by a classic seaborne landing distribution pattern, concentrating around Christchurch harbour, which still leaves nagging doubts about a migrant contribution. Good Breton parallels occur in the mound make-up covering early bronze age graves,[351] and in domestic sites such as La Roussellerie, Loire Atlantique,[352] and thus probably represents domestic pottery of the period.

Beyond Brittany similar wares have a wide distribution in northern France, but are less securely dated. Fort Harrouard, with so many parallels for British bronze age material, can even provide approximations to globular urn shapes.[353] The Trevisker pottery from Hardelot and biconical/Hilversum urn from Marguise, Pas-de-Calais,[354] hint at significant cross-Channel movements during the early bronze age, so that this whole question must await broader knowledge of the French ceramics.

The mistake is perhaps to search for a single Deveral-Rimbury/biconical urn origin when a more complex mixture of influences, as so often with British bronze age ceramics, is probably the right answer. Deverel-Rimbury pottery probably began life as the domestic ware of early bronze age communities in southern England, based essentially on the equally domestic local grooved wares,[355] but with possible French and Cornish contributions. It survived the religious upheaval at the end of the early bronze age in which sepulchral wares vanished, and emerged in the middle bronze age as both sepulchral and domestic pottery. There ensued the period of the classical Deverel-Rimbury culture, with a calibrated C14 date for the Itford Hill settlement of *c.* 1200 BC,[356] and metal finds placing numerous burials and settlements in the Taunton and Penard phases.[357] Too little is known of Deverel-Rimbury groups outside the south and east to be sure whether they developed contemporaneously, or represent middle bronze age expansion. Calibrated C14 dates attest cemeteries in the Midlands by the 10th-9th centuries.[358] Deverel-Rimbury developments after the Penard phase are everywhere difficult to plot. Sites such as Plumpton Plain B, Sussex, show it still vigorous in the Ewart Park phase, possibly rejuvenated by arrivals from France,[359] while the site at Eldon's Seat, Dorset, reveals a Deverel-Rimbury settlement on the eve of the iron age, with new shouldered vessels alongside its bucket urns.[360] Continuity with iron age settlement remains elusive, but the latter clearly derived much from the Deverel-Rimbury tradition: small enclosed settlements of round timber houses, storage pits, Celtic fields and the farming pattern they represent, and, possibly, weaving combs.[361] The early iron age lacks burials, but so too, at present, does the Deverel-Rimbury culture in its later stages.[362]

## Settlements in the south-west

Settlement studies in south-western England are complicated by unequal survival and lack of datable associations. The numerous stone-built settlements on moorlands and uplands, and their division into pastoral and arable units according to location, are well-known.[363] But the Trevisker excavations[364] show that comparable settlements, though with timber houses, must have been common at lower levels. The upland sites have generally been assigned to the early and middle bronze age, but the Trevisker evidence suggests that most should now fall in the early bronze age, and that it is difficult to continue their life beyond *c.* 1300 BC.[365] Such marginal lands would have been early affected by the climatic deterioration and ecological changes of the later 2nd millennium.[366] Deterioration of soil and pasture, and the spread of peat and moorland, caused as much by deforestation and cultivation as climatic change, would have brought widespread abandonment of these high farms as the Acton Park phase progressed. Later settlements, lower down and timber-built, would, like Trevisker, have been obliterated by subsequent land use.

*Hohensiedlungen, hillforts and palisades*

Realisation of the long bronze age development of hillforts and settlements, palisades, and much of their associated cultural material, has come from a combination of circumstances, but particularly from C14 dating, and the re-appraisal of old finds that it has occasioned. The situation should not cause surprise when it is realised that in central Europe hillforts go back at least to late Únĕtice times.[367] There was no general tradition of defence building in Britain before the bronze age, though many constituent elements of later defensive works were already anticipated in neolithic enclosures,[368] which may occupy relatively kind eminences in the south. Actual neolithic hilltop settlements (whether enclosed or open is usually uncertain) have been found beneath later defensive enclosures in many areas.[369]

Both bank and ditch enclosures and palisades are attested on hilltops in the early bronze age, the former at Rams Hill and Norton Fitzwarren,[370] underlying later hillforts, and the latter at Mount Pleasant, Dorset,[371] and Rams Hill again. They were also built in less defensible positions, for example at Castell Bryn Gwyn, Anglesey,[372] and Shearplace Hill.[373] Enclosures of Rams Hill type have been regarded as pastoral works on slight evidence, like the rather weak Deverel-Rimbury enclosures of Wessex, which enable the development of bank and ditch works to be followed through the middle bronze age. A similar function has been suggested for the slight enclosures which preceded many southern hillforts, as at Thundersbarrow Hill, Sussex, and Yarnbury, Wiltshire,[374] which may occupy stronger positions. These, and the extensive linear ditch and dyke systems of the chalk, the 'ranch boundaries' and plateau enclosures, being earlier than hillforts have presumptive bronze age beginnings. They must fit somewhere in the general pattern of Deverel-Rimbury settlement and farming, but have been little explored. From them may have grown some of the earliest southern hillforts.[375]

There is little sign of early bronze age hill-top occupation in the harsher highland zone, though it probably began at the end of this phase at sites such as Kaimes and Mam Tor (p. 197). The Mam Tor pottery includes shouldered and bipartite forms, some with relief horseshoe (?) ornament, strongly suggesting a local version of the biconical urn.[376] When such timber house *Hohensiedlungen* acquired their ramparts is uncertain. Actual hillforts may have needed an external stimulus, and the first may have been prompted by urnfield pressures in the Penard phase. The evidence from Grimthorpe and Dinorben (p. 207) suggests at least some of the earliest hillforts had timber-framed or revetted ramparts.[377] This technique had a long life, for at Ivinghoe Beacon, Buckinghamshire,[378] it was being used in the Ewart Park phase. Ivinghoe is one of a widespread group of hillforts which have produced metalwork of this phase. In some cases open settlements are indicated, as at South Cadbury, while in others, as at Ham Hill, Somerset, and Portfield Camp, Lancashire,[379] the relationship of bronzes and ramparts is unknown. But in all such cases the ramparts were probably built before the Ewart Park phase was over, for this period, the 7th-6th centuries, was a time of major disturbance, occasioned both by Hallstatt penetration and climatic deterioration. Defensive enclosures as far apart as the Isle of Man and Yorkshire, northern Scotland and Dorset, have given C14 dates blanketing this period (Fig. 25). Forms vary considerably, governed by local geographical and social factors. In many areas palisades precede actual ramparts,[380] a quick and convenient compromise, perhaps inspired by the timber revetments of proper ramparts.[381] Such palisades may soon have been converted to embanked or walled enclosures.[382] In the west, and especially in Scotland, timber-laced ramparts were common, often subsequently vitrified.[383] In Scotland these have been ascribed to an 8th-7th century immigration from north Germany, but the evidence is extremely slight.[384]

There must also be re-appraisal of the material culture associated with all these sites, especially the pottery. It is remarkable that so much has depended on pottery so plain and simple. Shouldered forms, and finger-tip decoration, characteristic of early hillfort pottery and for so long axiomatically iron age, can now be seen to have a long bronze age ancestry, stretching right back through Deverel-Rimbury and biconical urns to the early bronze age. Then shouldered forms were widespread, especially amongst enlarged food vessels[385] and domestic pottery.[386] Some of the Mam Tor pottery, perhaps as early as this, may point the moral, that simple shouldered pottery by itself has no dating value. Such shapes have been found in a wide variety of contexts right through the late bronze age.[387] By the Ewart Park phase they had been joined by the fine bowls so characteristic of Cunliffe's West Harling group.[388] The earliest iron age settlements have their ceramic novelties, but they cannot be considered here.[389]

## Epilogue

The British bronze age, with so many gaps in the available evidence, is particularly susceptible to changing interpretations in keeping with more general fluctuations in attitudes. Invasion hypotheses and insularity hypotheses may come and go, but the fact remains that so often in the British bronze age it is impossible to be certain whether indigenous development or immigration is the answer. At the root of the trouble is the 'sea change', that mysterious transmogrification that seems to have affected any traveller setting out to cross the narrow waters dividing the continent from Britain. The answers to many problems, one suspects, may lie beyond Britain, especially in France, most of which is still largely *terra incognita* in the bronze age as in other periods of prehistory. The strength of cross-channel links between southern England and north-west France is now plain for all to see, but just what these connections involved in human terms is another matter. There is more than a suggestion that the political and kinship ties so familiar from Caesar's day stretched right back through the bronze age. It is clear, too, that the transition from bronze age to iron age was not marked by the disruption that has always been claimed. To what extent newcomers were involved in this process is irrelevant. Quite clearly some were, but no matter who or how many, the essential point is that the mass of the native population, and at least some of their traditions and culture, survived, as they had survived so many other invasions. So the political dispositions of the iron age may well have long ancestry, as the cross-channel ties suggest, and can hardly reflect a new pattern created by iron age immigrants. There are hints that at least some of the tribal territories of Caesar's day already existed in the bronze age. The distribution of Trevisker pottery matches very well the territory of the Dumnonii, while later on the main spread of Yorkshire socketed axes corresponds remarkably with the lands of the Brigantes. In Wales late bronze age divisions made on an industrial basis accord very well with known tribal dispositions, the south Welsh axe province in the south-east matching the territory of the Silures, the north-west, marked out by long preference for late palstaves, coinciding with the Ordovician lands, and the northern Marches, heart of the Broadward province, coinciding with the territory of the Cornovii. A much more detailed examination of the bronze age material would be required to determine whether such correspondence is merely fortuitous, and it leads on to the whole thorny problem of the Celts. As so often in the British bronze age, a final answer remains elusive.[390]

## DATE LIST: Radiocarbon dates for the bronze age

### 1. BEAKERS

| Site | Feature | Lab. No. | Radiocarbon date bc (5568 half-life) | Calibrated date BC (approx.) McKerrell | Suess |
|---|---|---|---|---|---|
| Ballynagilly, Co. Tyrone | Occupation site | | | | |
| | (a) long pit | UB 555 | $2100 \pm 50$ | — | 2760-2540 |
| | (b) depression | UB 558 | $2060 \pm 80$ | — | 2520 |
| | (c) hearth | UB 316 | $2010 \pm 75$ | — | 2510 |
| | (d) hearth pit | UB 200 | $1955 \pm 120$ | 2400 | 2500-2410 |
| | (e) burnt area | UB 356 | $1955 \pm 75$ | 2400 | 2500-2410 |
| | (f) hearth pit | UB 556 | $1910 \pm 50$ | 2225 | 2480-2220 |
| | (g) pit | UB 309 | $1900 \pm 55$ | 2200 | 2480-2220 |
| | (h) pit | UB 557 | $1830 \pm 70$ | 2060 | 2180 |
| Chippenham, Cambridgeshire | Hearth of occupation site, Barrow 5 | BM 152 | $1850 \pm 150$ | 2090 | 2350-2190 |
| Fifty Farm, Mildenhall, Suffolk | Occupation site | BM 133 | $1850 \pm 150$ | 2090 | 2350-2190 |

## 1. BEAKERS (continued)

| Site | Feature | Lab. No. | Radiocarbon date bc (5568 half-life) | Calibrated date BC (approx.) McKerrell | Suess |
|------|---------|----------|--------------------------------------|----------------------------------------|-------|
| Knap Hill, Wiltshire | Upper fill of causewayed camp ditch | BM 208 | 1840 ± 130 | 2080 | 2190 |
| Lion Point, Clacton (Jaywick) Essex | 'Cooking Hole', site 114, area 2 | BM 172 | 1800 ± 150 | 2020 | 2160 |
| Antofts Windypit, Helmsley, N. R. Yorkshire | Burials and ritual or occupation material in fissure | BM 62 | 1800 ± 150 | 2020 | 2160 |
| Mount Pleasant, Dorset | Primary silt of main ditch of large enclosure ('henge') | BM 645 | 1784 ± 41 | 2000 | 2150 |
| | | BM 646 | 1778 ± 59 | 1995 | 2150 |
| Chatton Sandyford, Northumberland | Stake structure associated with primary pit burial under round cairn | GaK 800 | 1670 ± 50 | 1850 | 2090 |
| Northton, Harris | Beaker settlement phase I | BM 706 | 1654 ± 70 | 1830 | 2080 |
| Letchworth, Hertfordshire | Occupation site, pit I | BM 284 | 1640 ± 130 | 1825 | 2080 |

| Site | Description | Lab no. | | | |
|---|---|---|---|---|---|
| Durrington Walls, Wiltshire | Hearth overlying primary silt of ditch of large enclosure ('henge') | BM 285 | 1610 ± 120 | 1800 | 2060 |
| Wattisfield, Suffolk | Deep shaft | BM 77 | 1570 ± 150 | 1750 | 2050 |
| Windmill Hill, Wiltshire | Occupation associated with old turf line over filled outer ditch of causewayed camp | BM 75 | 1550 ± 150 | 1740 | 2040-1750 |
| Northton, Harris | Beaker settlement phase II | BM 707 | 1531 ± 54 | 1705 | 2030-1750 |
| Ysgwennant, Denbighshire | Burial pit under mound | Birm 85 | 1473 ± 82 | 1650 | 1700 |
| Mount Pleasant, Dorset | Occupation in partially silted main ditch of large enclosure ('henge') | BM 664 | 1460 ± 131 | 1645 | 1700 |

## 2. URNS AND PYGMY CUPS

| Site | Description | Lab no. | | | |
|---|---|---|---|---|---|
| Devil's Ring Barrow C, Brightwell, Suffolk | Primary burial with collared urn | NPL 133 | 1770 ± 130 | 1980 | 2150 |
| Earl's Farm Down, Amesbury, | Pyre associated with phase III of a cemetery mound, involving inhumation and cremation burials with food vessel, enlarged food vessel and collared urn | NPL 75 | 1640 ± 90 | 1825 | 2080 |

## 2. URNS AND PYGMY CUPS (continued)

| Site | Feature | Lab. No. | Radiocarbon date bc (5568 half-life) | Calibrated date BC (approx.) | |
| --- | --- | --- | --- | --- | --- |
| | | | | McKerrell | Suess |
| Snail Down, Everleigh, | Pyre under barrow. Probably associated with collared urn burial removed in 19th century | NPL 141 | $1540 \pm 90$ | 1725 | 2040-1750 |
| Eriswell, Suffolk | ? Bier on old ground surface, under barrow over primary cremation with collared urn | BM 315 | $1520 \pm 115$ | 1700 | 2030-1750 |
| Barbrook II, Ramsley Moor, Derbyshire | Cremation with collared urn under cairn inside enclosed cremation cemetery | BM 179 | $1500 \pm 150$ | 1690 | 2020-1720 |
| City Farm 3, Hanborough, Oxfordshire | Pit in ring-ditch cemetery, associated with collared urn | GrN 1686 | $1490 \pm 60$ | 1670 | 1990-1710 |
| Swarkeston, Derbyshire | Secondary cremation with collared urn, in barrow | NPL 17 | $1395 \pm 160$ | 1590 | 1660 |
| Whitestanes Moor, Dumfriesshire | Pit with pygmy cup, in enclosed cremation cemetery | GaK 461 | $1360 \pm 90$ | 1550 | 1640 |
| Bedd Branwen, Llanbabo, Anglesey | Cremation with cordoned urn in pit, in cremation cemetery | BM 455 | $1307 \pm 80$ | 1500 | 1610 |

| Site | Description | Lab no. | Date bc | | |
|---|---|---|---|---|---|
| Kirkhill, Hepple, Northumberland | Cremation with collared urn in pit, cremation cemetery | SRR 133 | 1292 ± 90 | 1490 | 1610-1520 |
| Bedd Branwen, Llanbabo, Anglesey | Cremation with collared urn and pygmy cup, phase I of cairn cemetery | BM 453 | 1274 ± 81 | 1460 | 1580-1510 |
| Grandtully, Perthshire | Cremation with cordoned urn in pit, in cremation cemetery | GaK 603 | 1270 ± 100 | 1460 | 1580-1510 |
| Downpatrick, Co. Down | Settlement of two main phases, both associated with cordoned urn, with a small beaker element also represented | | | | |
| | 1. Lower occupation level | UB 471 | 1625 ± 70 | 1810 | 2070 |
| | 2. Upper occupation level | UB 474 | 1375 ± 75 | 1570 | 1650 |
| | | UB 473 | 1315 ± 80 | 1510 | 1610 |

### 3. FOOD VESSELS

| Site | Description | Lab no. | Date bc | | |
|---|---|---|---|---|---|
| Ballynagilly, Co. Tyrone | Neolithic – EBA occupation site. Charcoal Mass with Irish bowl sherd | UB 198 | 1640 ± 60 | 1825 | 2080 |
| Harland Edge, Beeley Moor, Derbyshire | Multiple cremations in secondary grave pit under barrow, with food vessels and plano-convex flint knives | BM 178 | 1490 ± 150 | 1670 | 1990-1710 |
| Coney Island, Lough Neagh, Co. Armagh | Occupation site with Irish bowl material | UB 43 | 1400 ± 80 | 1590 | 1660 |

## 3. FOOD VESSELS (continued)

| Site | Feature | Lab. No. | Radiocarbon date bc (5568 half-life) | Calibrated date BC (approx.) McKerrell | Suess |
|------|---------|----------|----------|----------|----------|
| Mt. Pleasant, Dorset | Large late neolithic enclosure (henge). Hearth in later fill of site IV ditch, associated with food vessel and collared urn sherds | BM 669 | 1324 ± 51 | 1520 | 1610 |
| **4. STONEHENGE AND THE WESSEX CULTURE** | | | | | |
| Stonehenge, Wiltshire | Phase II | I 2384 | 1620 ± 110 | 1800 | 2070 |
| | Phase IIIa | BM 46 | 1720 ± 150 | 1910 | 2120 |
| | Phase IIIb/IIIc transition | I 2445 | 1240 ± 105 | 1430 | 1490 |
| Earls Barton, Northampton-shire | Burnt structure under bell-barrow, with Camerton-Snowshill dagger in uncertain relationship | BM 680 | 1219 ± 51 | 1405 | 1470 |
| | | BM 681 | 1264 ± 64 | 1455 | 1510 |
| Hove, Sussex | Barrow covering tree-trunk coffin, containing inhumation with amber cup, Camerton-Snowshill dagger, stone battle-axe, and perforated whetstone | BM 682 | 1239 ± 46 | 1430 | 1490 |
| **5. THE DEVEREL-RIMBURY CULTURE** | | | | | |
| Worgret, Arne, Dorset | Primary (?) cremation in pit under barrow. Upright bucket urn stood on contents of pit | NPL 199 | 1740 ± 90 | 1940 | 2140 |
| Wilsford, Wiltshire | Waterlogged wood from near bottom of shaft c. 100ft deep, with globular urn sherds some feet above, and bucket urn sherds higher still in the middle fill | NPL 74 | 1380 ± 90 | 1560 | 1650 |

| Site | Description | Lab. ref. | Date bc | | |
|---|---|---|---|---|---|
| Shearplace Hill, Dorset | Settlement, mainly of Deverel-Rimbury background. Date obtained from combined phase I-II sample | NPL 19 | 1180 ± 180 | 1380 | 1470 |
| Itford Hill, Sussex | Barley from settlement | GrN 6167 | 1000 ± 35 | 1190 | 1330-1220 |
| Bromfield, Shropshire | Cremation cemetery: urn burial | Birm 63 | 850 ± 71 | 1020 | 1070-1000 |
| | Urn burial | Birm 62 | 762 ± 75 | — | 890 |
| Ryton-on-Dunsmore, Warwickshire | Cremation cemetery: urn burial | Birm 26 | 751 ± 41 | — | 890 |

*6. SOUTH-WESTERN SETTLEMENTS*

| Site | Description | Lab. ref. | Date bc | | |
|---|---|---|---|---|---|
| Gwithian, Cornwall | Multi-period settlement. Cremation fire, site X, layer 5, with Trevisker associations | NPL 21 | 1120 ±103 | 1310 | 1440-1350 |
| Trevisker, St. Eval, Cornwall | Floor of hut A, probably end of settlement | NPL 134 | 1110 ± 95 | 1300 | 1440-1350 |

*7. HOHENSIEDLUNGEN*

| Site | Description | Lab. ref. | Date bc | | |
|---|---|---|---|---|---|
| Mam Tor, Derbyshire | Huts within, but unknown whether associated with, hill-fort | | | | |
| | Hut 2 | Birm 202 | 1180 ± 132 | 1380 | 1470 |
| | Hut 3 | Birm 192 | 1130 ± 115 | 1320 | 1450-1350 |
| Kaimes, Midlothian | Hut 3, within, but not known whether associated with, hill-fort | GaK 1970 | 1191 ± 90 | 1350 | 1480 |

## 7. HOHENSIEDLUNGEN (continued)

| Site | Feature | Lab. No. | Radiocarbon date bc (5568 half-life) | Calibrated date BC (approx.) McKerrell | Suess |
|------|---------|----------|--------------------------------------|----------------------------------------|-------|
| Dinorben, Denbighshire | Occupation material under period 1 rampart of hill-fort | V 123 | 945 ± 95 | 1120 | 1210–1130 |

### 8. HILLFORTS WITH TIMBER REVETTED OR FRAMED RAMPARTS

| Site | Feature | Lab. No. | Radiocarbon date bc (5568 half-life) | Calibrated date BC (approx.) McKerrell | Suess |
|------|---------|----------|--------------------------------------|----------------------------------------|-------|
| Grimthorpe, Yorkshire | Bones from primary silt of hillfort ditch | NPL 137 | 970 ± 130 | 1150 | 1220 |
| Dinorben, Denbighshire | Material from period I rampart | V 122 | 895 ± 95 | 1075 | 1100 |
| Dinorben, Denbighshire | Material between period I-II ramparts, 'probably derived from period I' | V 125 | 765 ± 85 | — | 890 |
| Hod Hill, Dorset | Occupation layer associated with phase II of hillfort defences | BM 47 | 460 ± 150 | — | 780–520 |

### 9. HILLFORTS WITH TIMBER-LACED AND VITRIFIED RAMPARTS

| Site | Feature | Lab. No. | Radiocarbon date bc (5568 half-life) | Calibrated date BC (approx.) McKerrell | Suess |
|------|---------|----------|--------------------------------------|----------------------------------------|-------|
| Finavon, Angus | Vitrified fort, beams along inner wall face | GaK 1224 | 590 ± 70 | — | 800 |
| Almondbury, Yorkshire | Hillfort, phase III, timber-laced rampart | | 555 ± | - | 790–560 |
| Dinorben, Denbighshire | Hillfort, material associated with phase II timber-laced rampart | V 124 | 535 ± 85 | — | 790–550 |

| | | | | | |
|---|---|---|---|---|---|
| Dun Lagaidh, Ross & Cromarty | Vitrified fort, branch under wall core | GX 1121 | 490 ± 80 | — | 790-540 |

## 10. OTHER HILLFORTS AND SETTLEMENTS

| | | | | | |
|---|---|---|---|---|---|
| Croft Ambrey, Herefordshire | Hillfort. Carbonised grain from main quarry ditch | Birm 144 | 1050 ± 200 | 1250 | 1330 |
| | Timber of period Vb guardroom | Birm 185 | 460 ± 135 | — | 780-520 |
| Midsummer Hill, Herefordshire | Hillfort. Wood from quarry ditch floor, associated with first gate | Birm 142 | 420 ± 190 | — | 480 |
| Cow Down, Longbridge, Deverill, Wiltshire | Settlement: House I, encl 2 | NPL 105 | 630 ± 155 | — | 860-820 |
| | House (unspecified) | NPL 104 | 530 ± 90 | — | 790-550 |
| | House 2, encl 2 | NPL 106 | 500 ± 90 | — | 790-540 |
| | Pit 37, encl 2 | NPL 109 | 490 ± 90 | — | 790-540 |
| | Pit 7, encl 2 | NPL 108 | 460 ± 140 | — | 780-520 |
| | Post hole, house 2, encl 2 | NPL 107 | 420 ± 95 | — | 480 . . |

## 11. PALISADE SETTLEMENTS

| | | | | | |
|---|---|---|---|---|---|
| Navan Fort, Co. Armagh | Farmstead enclosed by palisade and ditch. Charcoal from primary ditch fill | UB 188 | 680 ± 50 | — | 870 |
| Craigmarloch Wood, Renfrewshire | Palisade enclosure | GaK 995 | 590 ± 40 | — | 800 |

## 11. PALISADE SETTLEMENTS (continued)

| Site | Feature | Lab. No. | Radiocarbon date bc (5568 half-life) | Calibrated date BC (approx.) McKerrell | Suess |
|------|---------|----------|------|------|------|
| Huckhoe, Northumberland | Palisade settlement: charcoal from palisade trench (end?) | GaK 1388 | 510 ± 40 | — | 790-550 |
| Staple Howe, Yorkshire | Palisade farmstead, charred grain | BM 63 | 450 ± 150 | — | 780-520 |
| Burnswark, Dumfriesshire | Hillfort. Primary defences, either timber framed rampart or double palisade | I 5314 | 525 ± 90 | — | 790-550 |
|  |  | GaK 2203 | 500 ± 100 | — | 780-550 |

# 6. *The iron age*

## BARRY CUNLIFFE

The material available to those wishing to study the iron age is both rich and plentiful, ranging from settlement pattern evidence and structural sequences on the one hand, to elaborate ceramics, works of art and numismatics on the other.[1] Such a wide range has understandably encouraged a diverse approach to iron age studies, yet while the starting points have been widely separated the conclusions have usually converged, relying heavily upon a simple monocausal model of invasion from the European mainland to explain the observed cultural changes. The use of a simple invasionist model might at first sight seem surprisingly naive, but the reasons for widespread adherence to it should be examined.

A ready-made explanation for the end of the pre-Roman iron age is provided by classical literary sources, which describe in great detail the destruction of native government and its replacement by an alien European culture — in other words the Roman invasion initiated by Claudius in AD 43. Equally detailed and reliable records exist of another, though less successful, invasion mounted by Julius Caesar in 55 and 54 BC, while before that Caesar himself refers to a Belgic invasion brought about by people who, he says, came to raid and stayed to farm. Thus in the last century and a half of iron age Britain, three invasions are attested beyond dispute.[2] It is therefore hardly surprising that those writing of the earlier centuries should simply back-project this model to explain the changes which they observed amongst their essentially prehistoric material.

To clarify the present state of iron age studies, something will first be said, by way of background, of the direction in which the subject has so far developed; then follows a consideration of certain classes of data before, in the final section, some brief synthesis is offered of the influences, both internal and external, to which the country was subjected.

## Early theories and assumptions

Little of outstanding significance happened throughout most of the 19th century save for the gradual amassing of isolated finds, including some of our finest metalwork, dredged from rivers. But towards the end of the Victorian period, two advances were made: the development of excavation skills designed to answer specific questions concerning social and economic structure, and the adoption of an, albeit crude, chronological scheme based on the ordering of material from the continental sites of Hallstatt and La Tène. The first major breakthrough came in 1890 with the discovery and publication of the cemetery at Aylesford in Kent.[3] The material was discussed in detail and linked directly to continental sequences from which followed the conclusion that the cemetery was the burial place of Caesar's 'invaders from Belgium'.

The early decades of the 20th century saw the rapid accumulation of data from a flood of excavations of very varying quality; Glastonbury and Meare in Somerset, Hengistbury Head in Hampshire, All Cannings Cross in Wiltshire and a number of others.[4] The result of all this work was to show that the iron age was a very complex period, difficult to classify by the direct application of continental terminologies. In parallel with the acquisition of the new raw data, general works of synthesis were attempted, like Rice Holmes' *Ancient Britain and the Invasion of Julius Caesar* and Peake's now sadly overlooked writings, in which he integrated archaeology and linguistics to create models based on pan-European ethnic movements, the ripples from which were felt in Britain. By 1925, the year in which the British Museum guide to the iron age collection was published,[5] the simple invasionist model then in vogue proposed three incomings: a late urnfield invasion about 800 BC giving rise to the cultural elements apparent at All Cannings Cross; a La Tène invasion into Yorkshire in the 5th to 4th centuries, and a Belgic invasion submerging the south-east of England some time about 150 BC. To this Leeds later added another incursion into Cornwall from Spain during the La Tène period.[6]

This was the state when, at the beginning of the 1930s, Hawkes began to systematise the scattered material and theories. He believed that the British nomenclature should stand on its own, separated from continental terminologies; thus he renamed the Hallstatt invasion 'A', the two La Tène invasions 'B', and the Belgic invasion, which he split into two, 'C'.[7]

The decade of the 1930s saw an immense growth in the number of iron age excavations. Iron age studies were at this time fashionable. More than fifty hillforts were dug into, most of them within integrated regional policies. Even more remarkable is the fact that, with a few significant exceptions, the great bulk of the work was rapidly published. The result was the accumulation of masses of new data which had to be fitted often somewhat reluctantly into the ABC scheme. This was attempted by many workers, some of whom did not fully appreciate the nature of the original concept, nor for that matter did they correctly integrate their work with the additions and modifications of their fellows. Thus there emerged a complex of A1s and A2s, ABs and ABCs, in which the actual communities were sometimes lost sight of — one might refer to the resulting mêlée as the syndrome of the animated ceramics. Hawkes, indeed, saw these dangers, when he issued his stern warning in 1939 that now was the time to begin to define cultural groups in terms of time and space, as was then the more normal archaeological procedure.[8]

In the years following the war, the spearhead of iron age studies passed to the north, with the work of Piggott, Jobey and Hamilton, which was concerned largely with the siting and form of settlements, while in the west country and south Wales Lady Fox surveyed much of the relevant settlement evidence. This concern with the nature and implications of the socio-economic data has led to what now constitutes one of the most important areas of study at present being pursued.

The 1960s saw other changes. The general dissatisfaction felt by some for the ABC scheme, restated at the CBA conference in 1958, was voiced by Hodson in a series of papers in which, impressed by a strong element of continuity, he proposed the concept of an underlying *Woodbury Culture*, upon which were superimposed intrusive elements representing the *Arras Culture* of Yorkshire and the *Aylesford-Swarling Culture* of south-eastern England.[9] MacKie has since taken up this concept and applied it to Scotland.[10]

The situation in which we now find ourselves is one in which the major conceptual models for structuring the period have been generally discarded, while at the same time major advances are being made in acquisition and analysis of the data. In the following pages, a summary of a *selection* of these areas of rapid advance is offered.

## Ceramics

Pottery has always bulked large in discussions about the British iron age, but it is perhaps worth remembering that for more than half the country, pottery does not form a significant element in the material culture. Broadly speaking, Britain can be divided into three separate zones:

a) *North and west Scotland, including the Orkneys, Shetland and the Western Isles.* In this area, a ceramic tradition, rooted in the neolithic period, continued to flourish producing, in the iron age, a varied series of local styles which developed different characteristics with time. Here the raw material for both regional and chronological division is available.

b) *Northern Britain, Wales and parts of the Midlands and south-west.* Throughout most of the period, the communities of this area, while not aceramic, seem to have placed little significance on pottery as a medium for design and display. Accordingly, the material is sparse and lacks characteristics suitable for the definition of regional and chronological groups.

c) *The south-east of England, including the Welsh Marches.* In this area a vigorous ceramic tradition was maintained throughout the iron age, at frequent occasions reflecting the styles and developments of the contemporary continental mainland. It was also an area in which regional innovations and distinctive local styles appeared.

There are several possible explanations for these broad differences: traditions of native folk culture, economic basis, degree of technological advance and even, to a lesser extent, factors affecting the nature of data retrieval. The effect, however, has been to focus attention very strongly on the south-eastern ceramic zone, to such an extent that the northern evidence is often neglected, and the far north-western groups are regarded as isolated and irrelevant. This trend, is, to say the least, unfortunate, since it inflates the significance of the ceramic element of the culture, and obscures the vast blanket of underlying similarities. In short, the nature of a community's ceramic development should be seen in proper perspective, and we should ask of it only such questions as it may reasonably be expected to answer.

A pottery sequence from a site or region can, of course, provide a rough yardstick for measuring relative chronologies. This is an old established usage and will continue to be helpful, but little work has yet been done on establishing finer calibrations in local sequences, largely because the material at present available is pitifully inadequate. When large assemblages of closely stratified material have been amassed, however, there is no reason why statistical techniques should not be applied to refine the local sequences still further. Such an approach would be something of a hollow academic exercise unless it could be applied, for example, in defining the stage by stage development of a totally excavated settlement. Such a project may indeed be possible at Danebury (Hampshire), where a hillfort containing an estimated six to eight thousand pits is currently being excavated.

Another approach to ceramics has been ably demonstrated in recent years by Peacock.[11] Using a series of sophisticated analytical techniques geared to isolating the place of origin of both clay and filler, he has been able to offer an objective classification of certain groups of pottery, to identify their likely region of origin and to define the distribution of vessels from each source. It would be no exaggeration to say that this programme of analysis has totally revolutionised ceramic studies, focusing, as it does, attention on economic factors, and, incidentally, showing many of our old assessments to be inaccurate and incorrect.

Petrological analysis of this kind coupled with stylistic consideration is likely in future years to enable the south-eastern ceramic zone to be subdivided into a series of

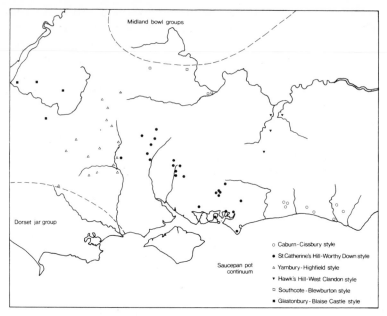

Figure 37. Distribution map of saucepan pot groups in southern Britain.

*style zones* overlapping both geographically and chronologically (Fig. 37). This has been attempted by the author using purely typological arguments, but each zone needs now to be tested against its petrological background.[12] The general results of the preliminary work have been discussed elsewhere and need not be repeated here, but in summary, the pottery of south-eastern Britain can be classified into a series of well-defined styles, the distribution of each of which can be plotted. The resulting style zones represent, by definition, the region within which the style was prevalent. Each style can also be defined in time by reference to local sequences.

This method, then, attempts merely to classify: interpretation· of the significance of each style zone, whether it is cultural, economic, or technological, must be left until the petrological work is more advanced, but already certain pointers are emerging. In Dorset, for example, it is possible to show that a fairly restricted territory retained a 'ceramic identity' throughout a period of time represented by several succeeding style zones. That the same territory can be distinguished numismatically, in terms of its defensive development and, ultimately, by its reactions to the Roman advance (below, p. 252), goes some way towards supporting the view that, *in this example*, style zones are related to social identity. Other examples can be given where the converse is true.

Another valid approach to pottery evidence is to ask whether the introduction of new forms can be associated with outside stimuli. There are several well-attested examples where this is likely. The appearance of small angular bipartite bowls often covered with a haematite slip in the 7th or 6th centuries may be reasonably interpreted as the local copying of imported bronze types like the vessel found in the Welby (Leicester) hoard. However, the sharply angled bowls with flared rims which appear in eastern England from the 5th century, are more readily understandable as the result of direct influence from the adjacent continent where similar ceramic forms were common. A further example, the occurrence of wheel-turned pottery known as Hengiştbury Class B ware and its derivatives in and near the Poole Harbour region, must represent trade associated perhaps with a movement of skilled potters into Britain, sometime about the beginning of the 1st century BC.

From the above discussion it will be seen that pottery can be used in a variety of ways to illuminate the complex nature of iron age society; it can provide evidence of sequence, production and distribution, it can help define areas of contact, and it can reflect technological advances; but it should not be used to reconstruct pseudo-history as it has been in the past. Pottery evidence cannot prove an invasion any more than it can disprove one.

## Sequence and chronology

Until recently, pottery has been the main source of dating for the iron age. Suitably arranged in stratified or typological sequences and calibrated by cross reference to a few distinctive metal objects, dating by means of pottery has been an acceptable and reasonably precise method in those areas in which finds are fairly prolific. But for most of the country outside the south-east, age-assessment has been based

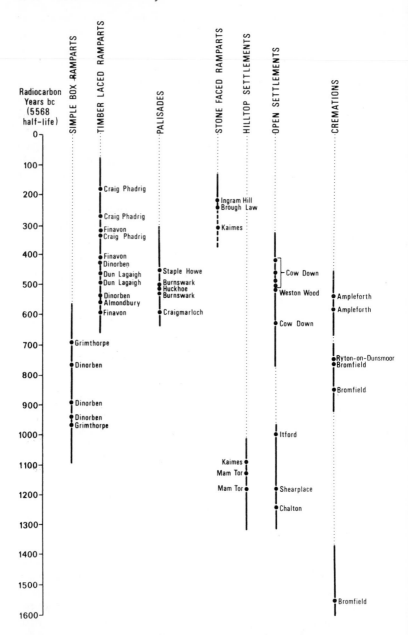

Figure 38. Radiocarbon date chart for the British iron age.

largely on inspired guesswork supported by arguments of analogy. The use of radiocarbon dating has, however, radically altered the situation, allowing a totally new independently dated sequence to be proposed for the north and west which, while it replaces earlier preconceptions, in no way contradicts the archaeological evidence.[13]

Most of the dates at present available come from defended structures of the hillfort or homestead category: many are isolated dates for phases within constructional sequences, but a few series of related assessments have recently been published. One of the most important groups comes from the hillfort of Dinorben (Denbighshire), for the earliest phase of which we have three radiocarbon dates, 945 bc (*c.* 1170 BC), 895 bc (*c.* 1100 BC) and 765 bc (*c.*880 BC), all related to a simple rampart constructed of two rows of vertical timbers tied together with horizontals. This box style rampart has been classed as the Ivinghoe type (Fig. 39) after the Buckinghamshire hillfort which, while undated, has produced a group of metalwork well within the late bronze age tradition of the 8th century. A third site, Grimthorpe (Yorkshire) was defended in much the same style.' Two assessments for bone found in the silting of the ditch, 970 bc (*c.* 1220 BC) and 690 bc (*c.* 880 BC) caused some disquiet at the time of their publication, but can now be seen to be perfectly consistent with the evidence from the other sites. A picture is therefore emerging which suggests that the Ivinghoe type of box rampart was being constructed throughout what is technically the late bronze age, between 1000 and 700 bc (*c.* 1260-900 BC after calibration).

In typological terms it can be argued that the next style in rampart development involved the addition of a sloping bank of soil behind the soil-filled box structure — a style which we can call the Hollingbury style of rampart after the famous Sussex type-site. Although no radiocarbon dates have been produced for sites of this category, the pottery evidence would suggest a range spanning the 6th to the 4th century. The subsequent stages, typified first by Hod Hill (Dorset) and later by Poundbury (Dorset), developments in which the rear row of timbers becomes gradually less important to the structure, best fit within the 5th to 3rd century bracket, again on the evidence of associated pottery. Thus a simple

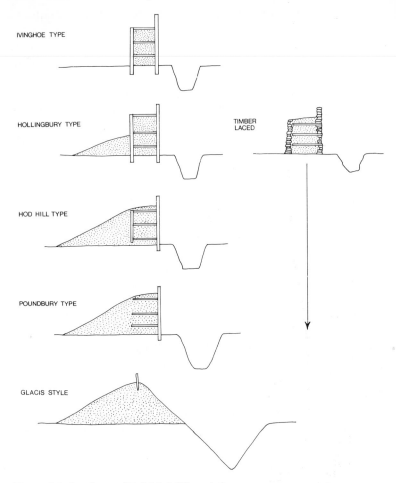

Figure 39. Sections of British hillfort defences.

sequence of box rampart development based on typology, with a little help from stratigraphy, and calibrated first by radiocarbon dates and later by pottery evidence, is internally consistent, all classes of evidence being in harmony.

In parallel with the construction of box ramparts, some sites were defended with single or double palisades. Several radiocarbon assessments have been published: Craigmarloch Wood (Renfrewshire), 590 bc (*c.* 800 BC); Burnswark (Northumberland), 500 bc (*c.* 630 BC); Huckhoe (Northum-

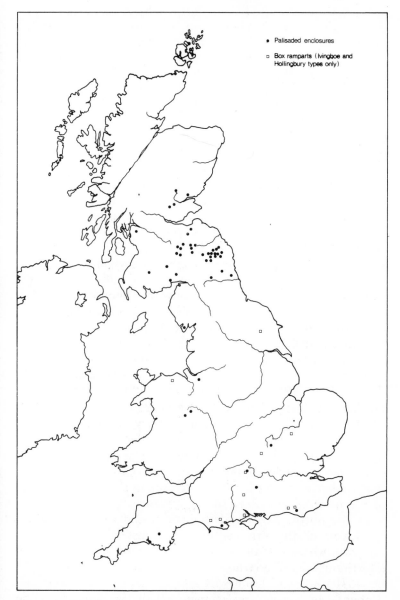

Figure 40. Distribution of palisaded enclosures and box ramparts.

berland), 510 bc (*c.* 650 BC); Ingram Hill (Northumberland), 220 bc (*c.* 250 BC), and Staple Howe (Yorkshire) 450 bc (*c.*

530 BC). In the first four cases palisades can be shown to precede rampart construction. However the late date for Ingram Hill is explained, the conclusion must be that palisaded enclosures were a feature of the 7th and 6th centuries in northern Britain. That some palisades in southern England were probably constructed during the 5th to 3rd centuries, for example Swallowcliffe (Wiltshire), Little Woodbury (Wiltshire), Meon Hill (Hampshire) (dated on the basis of their associated pottery), lends credence to the Ingram Hill assessment.

The third constructional technique in use involved the lacing of earth or rubble ramparts with horizontal timbers, usually laid in courses. In areas where stone was abundant, vertical facing of the front and rear was usual, sometimes with the ends of the timbers poking through the stone work.[14] In many examples in Scotland and northern and western Britain the timbers caught fire, giving rise to the characteristic 'vitrified forts'. A series of radiocarbon dates can now be quoted, beginning with Dinorben, where a timber-laced rampart could be shown to replace the earlier box structure: for the laced structure, dates of 535 bc (*c.* 670 BC) and 420 bc (520 BC) have been published. These compare closely with the northern group: Finavon (Angus) 590 bc (*c.* 780 BC) and 410 bc (510 BC), Dun Lagaidh (Wester Ross) 490 bc (*c.* 600 BC) and 460 bc (560 BC), Craig Phadrig (Inverness) 330 bc (400 BC), 270 bc (350 BC), 180 bc (180 BC) and Castle Hill, Almondbury (Yorkshire) 555 bc (*c.* 670 BC). To these can be added Kaimes hillfort (Midlothian), where the laced rampart was replaced by a simple stone faced rampart. The conclusion would seem to be that timber lacing was a technique used in the north and west of Britain from the 7th to the 4th century.

In the north, horizontal timbers ceased to be commonly employed in the 4th century, and instead simple dump ramparts with stone faces came into fashion. At Brough Law (Northumberland) a structure of this type was dated to 245 bc (310 BC); at Kaimes a simple rampart replaced the timber-laced version and at Ingram Hill the date of 220 bc (250 BC) represents the replacement of the palisade by a stone rampart; but a reminder that simple ramparts were being erected some centuries earlier is given by Huckhoe,

Figure 41. Distribution of box ramparts and timber-laced forts.

where the assessment of 510 bc (*c.* 660 BC) represents the change from palisade to rampart.

The dates which it is now possible to attach to hillforts are beginning to show just how complex the problems of development are, but already some generalisations can be offered. Simple box ramparts, which must have an ancestry back into the 2nd millenium, were widely established in Britain (though are not yet known in Scotland), and in the south formed an essential element in defensive architecture down to about the 4th century. In the north and west there developed a timber-laced style of construction alongside defences based on single and double palisades. The *floruit* for these two styles spans the 7th to the 4th century, after which simple dump ramparts, either stone-faced in the north and west or with a sloping front in the south-east, began to be widely adopted for most kinds of defence from massive hillforts to small farmsteads.

This simple interpretation, made possible by the dates now to hand, raises many questions, including that of the origins of the various classes of structures, which cannot be considered here.[14] There can, however, be little doubt that further programmes of excavation combined with the acquisition of more radiocarbon dates will provide the only sure means of major advance in this field.

Something must be said of the radiocarbon dates from settlement sites. As Fig. 38 will show, the dates for the occupation levels within the hillforts of Mam Tor and Kaimes are within the same late 2nd millennium range as those from the open farmsteads of the mid-late bronze age, such as Chalton (Hampshire), Itford (Sussex) and Shearplace Hill (Dorset). Clearly, many of these hilltop settlements have an ancestry which may well prove to pre-date the first phase of their defences. This need occasion no surprise when it is remembered that a number of hillforts have produced indisputable evidence, in the form of artefacts, of occupation extending back into the bronze age. Among the more significant of these should be listed Highdown (Sussex), South Cadbury (Somerset), Ham Hill (Somerset), The Breiddin (Montgomeryshire) and Norton Fitzwarren (Somerset). The implication would seem to be that some of our hillforts arose out of the need to defend already well established settlements.

A collection of dates from other settlement sites in various parts of the country is at last being amassed, but so far there is little to be said of them except that in the south they will allow the calibration of the pottery sequence to be checked, while in the north they are still the only reliable means of dating so far available.

One application for radiocarbon which will undoubtedly prove to be profitable is the dating of cremation burials. Only a few sites have so far been tested, for example Bromfield (Salop.), Ryton (Warwickshire) and Ampleforth Moor (Yorkshire), but clearly as a tool for studying cemetery topography and continuity, as well as dating pot styles, it is invaluable.

## Society and hillforts

When all is said and done, the approaches described above are only a means to an end, the end being to study iron age society and the dynamic processes at work within it. This, of course, is a vast and still virtually untouched field, but one about which something must be said.

One essential preliminary to the reconstruction of iron age society is the need to understand the meaning of hillforts — a major class of monuments about which there is still much confusion. The very term 'hillfort' obscures the issue, since it imposes an apparent unity on a group of enclosures which may well have different functions and different antecedents. The origins of hillforts have recently been discussed and need not delay us here,[15] except to reiterate that many potential beginnings can be listed, ranging from religious foci and meeting places to pastoral enclosures and settlements.

It is perhaps worth expanding on the first two categories, if only to speculate. It has been suggested that the neolithic causewayed camps served a socio-religious function as places where communities could assemble at certain times during the year. The basic need for such a focus is a theme running through the entire span of British social development, reappearing from time to time as the rural shrines and markets of the Roman period, the country fairs held on saints' days in Mediaeval and later times, and even the Bank Holiday fairs of today. The underlying features are entertainment, exchange and religious observance (though this last is difficult to perceive on the average Bank Holiday).

If the tradition behind communal meeting places is continuous, it might reasonably be suggested that some hillforts served this function. The presence of temples or shrines is now well attested within several defended enclosures, for example Heathrow (Middlesex), South Cadbury (Somerset) and probably Maiden Castle (Dorset), and a continuity of religious observance might be thought to be reflected in the large number of hillforts which house later Roman temples. In the case of Danebury (Hampshire) the hill-top seems to have been defined by a series of large pits, some of them containing upright timbers of considerable dimensions, and dating (on present estimates) to the beginning of the 1st millennium. Are we here seeing the tail end of the henge monument tradition? If so, Danebury provides the evidence for the transition from a purely 'ritual' centre to what was later to become a permanent settlement of some size.

If we allow ourselves the luxury of speculating further about continuity of these tribal foci, it is impossible not to be impressed by the physical re-use in the iron age of hill tops already enclosed by neolithic causewayed camps: Hembury (Devon), Maiden Castle (Dorset), Hambledon Hill (Dorset), Whitesheet Hill (Wiltshire), ? Knap Hill (Wiltshire), Trundle (Sussex), Crickley Hill (Gloucestershire) and Maiden Bower (Bedfordshire) — in fact eight of the fifteen known neolithic sites are re-used. It could be argued that this is little more than coincidence, the only common factor being that both types of site required hill-tops and further that there is no archaeological evidence of physical continuity. These may be valid arguments, but the possibility of continuity by socio-religious association should not be overlooked.

Although the origin and early development of hillforts is still somewhat obscure, evidence is rapidly accumulating to suggest that while some forts fell into disuse, others became gradually more significant. This is shown by an increase in labour invested in defence and by the dense packing within of dwellings and other structures.

Evidence for internal structures comes in two forms, from the surface observation of forts where physical remains of the houses are still apparent, as in many of the forts in Wales and northern Britain and occasionally in the south, for example Hod Hill, and by the large scale excavation of the defended interiors. The former method gives a picture biased towards the latest phase of construction: it can seldom allow sequence and development to be proposed with any degree of assurance. Large-scale excavation is a far more satisfactory way of tackling the problem, in that it removes many of the sources of misinterpretation which bedevil the study of surface features alone.[16]

Relatively few forts have been examined in this way. Maiden Castle (Dorset) and South Cadbury (Somerset) have yielded some evidence, but the major advances have been made by the series of excavations in the Welsh Marches at Credenhill, Croft Ambrey and Midsummer Hill, and by the current work at Crickley Hill (Gloucestershire) and Danebury. The three forts in the Welsh Marches have all produced indisputable evidence of ordered internal occupation. Similarly, the 1971 season of work at Danebury exposed four rows of six-post structures arranged along streets with the areas behind reserved for storage pits. Even more remarkable is the fact that each of the buildings had been reconstructed on the same site on several occasions, some of them showing in excess of five rebuildings. Much the same pattern was found at Credenhill, the only differences being that here the buildings were based on four posts and pits were absent.

Stanfield has suggested that the Credenhill buildings were houses, and has gone on to estimate the total population of the fort on this basis.[17] A note of caution is however sounded by the Danebury excavation where the area examined in the centre of the fort in 1972 proved to be devoid of the characteristic six-post structures. The conclusion, though necessarily tentative, would seem to be that those hillforts which were extensively occupied, were divided into zones reserved for differing functions. Thus any attempts to estimate population must await the results of very large-scale excavations.

The temples or shrines found at South Cadbury (Somerset) Maiden Castle (Dorset) and Heathrow (Middlesex),[18] usually sited in prominent positions, are a further indication of separate functional zones within the forts; so too is the bronzesmith's area discovered at South Cadbury. Finds of this kind, taken together with a study of the economic catchment areas of the forts, suggest that we should begin to consider some of the major structures as possessing proto-urban characteristics.

The excavation of hillfort interiors promises to provide one of the major growth points in iron age studies in the years to come, but hillforts should not be studied in isolation. They are, after all, merely one part of a complex social pattern which embraces the whole landscape. To understand them fully, it is necessary to know something of the other elements of the pattern.

It would be impossible here to discuss, even briefly, the widely ranging studies now in progress, but attention might be drawn to one aspect — the examination of farmsteads. It is a sobering thought that it was not until 1965 that a southern British farmstead, the example at Tolland Royal, (Dorset) was totally excavated.[19] Until then, knowledge of the nature of these sites had to rest upon the interpretation of partial plans often recovered under excavation conditions which would not be regarded as satisfactory today. The rest of Britain is, however, much better served. The work of local archaeologists and the Royal Commission on Historical Monuments has produced a wealth of settlement plans from highland areas where surface features survive and in some regions, notably Northumberland and Shetland,[20] a fine series of large scale excavations has been carried out. The result of all this work, when viewed together, is impressive. For iron age Britain we must possess one of the most extensive collections of settlement plans available for any area or period in prehistoric Europe. This material is badly in need of collation and further study, particularly by the methods now widely used by geographers.

### Towards an assessment of social change

We have already referred to the difficulties of using pottery to reconstruct a pseudo-history of the iron age, but this need not be taken to mean that no attempt should be made to define directional change. There are, in fact, many sources of overlapping information which, taken together, can be built into a cohesive pattern reflecting aspects of social, economic or political development.

The best way to understand the problems involved is to take a simple example – the south-eastern region of Britain from the 2nd century BC until the Roman invasion of AD 43. This area is particularly susceptible to study because of the wealth of surviving material, the large number of excavations carried out over the years, and its contacts with the literate Roman world.

By the second century BC the landscape had become dominated by hillforts, or more correctly those hillforts which survived the processes of selection which had led to the abandonment of many earlier fortified sites and the emergence of a few as strongly defended and continuously occupied locations approaching the complexity of urban centres. Some time towards the end of the 2nd century BC the entrances of many of these forts underwent extensive modifications, which were usually designed so as to create a long inturned approach. This was accomplished in a variety of ways, ranging from the inturning of the rampart ends to create a corridor with the gate at the end, to the construction of extensive foreworks forcing any attacker to wend his way between carefully designed mazes of earthworks, exemplified in their most advanced form by the gates of Maiden Castle (Dorset).

The question which immediately arises is, can the appearance of this type of specialised gate structure be regarded as a unified response to a single stimulus? While there can as yet be no decisive answer to this question, the dating evidence, where it exists, and the evident conceptual planning behind the gates together imply a phase of building activity restricted in time but widespread geographically. The simplest explanation is that a threat arose requiring greater security. The fact that several forts yield evidence of destruction at this time might be thought to support the idea.

During the 1st century BC it is possible to discern a marked difference in the development of the forts between those of the south-west, broadly Dorset and Somerset, and those of the south-east, the approximate divide being the Wiltshire Avon. The south-west group for the most part continued to be intensively occupied, while those of the south-east were abandoned. Other classes of evidence further underline this divergence. For example, the coinage of the south-west, that is the territory occupied by the Durotriges, was based on a silver standard, presumably to facilitate trade with the silver-using areas of Armorica, while the south-eastern group used a standard based on the gold staters. The principle tribal grouping.involved here was the Atrebates. There were also substantial differences in the styles of pottery adopted in the two areas, differences which can be traced back to the ceramic traditions of the previous centuries.

The abandonment of the hillforts of Hampshire and Sussex deserves further consideration since such a radical change in settlement pattern must surely imply some kind of social reorganisation. All that can safely be said at the moment is that at about this time there is evidence of a more intensive settlement of the countryside, while at the same time large oppida appear, as at Selsey (Sussex) and *Calleva* (Hampshire). Thus, whatever the causes of the change, it results in the abandonment of the smaller nucleated settlements (hillforts) in favour of a more dispersed settlement pattern on the one hand, and the growth of the large urban centres on the other. In the south-west the old hillfort-dominated landscape remained unchanged.

It is very tempting to link the divergent developments in the two areas with social differences implied by the coinage. Whereas the Atrebatic coins imply a dynastic rule by kings, the Durotrigian issues are strongly suggestive of a less cohesive form of government.[21] In summary, both the settlement pattern and the style of coinage in the Atrebatic area is consistent with the appearance of a unified system of government, while in the Durotrigian area the evidence combines to support the view that the old social order prevailed.

This difference becomes even more apparent at the time of the Claudian invasion in AD 43. While it is clear that a large part of the Atrebatic territory did not oppose the Roman advance, and indeed may even have welcomed it, the reverse is true in the Durotrigian area, where the hillforts held out as localised centres of resistance, each having to be subdued individually. This process is vividly documented by the writer Suetonius, who records how Vespasian and the second legion under his command overcame two powerful tribes and took more than twenty fortified native capitals. On a conservative estimate, the forts must have fallen at a rate of one every two or three days, a fact which reflects both the efficiency of the Roman army and the total unsuitability of hillforts for defence against seige attacks. There is much archaeological evidence for the advance in the form of a network of Claudian forts as well as clear traces of attack and destruction in a number of hillforts.

The Roman administration attempted, wherever possible, to retain something of the old native groupings by using them as the basis for the new system of local government. Thus the Durotriges remained an entity based on *Durnovaria* (Dorchester, Dorset), while the more diffuse Atrebatic territory was governed from *Noviomagus* (Chichester), *Venta* (Winchester) and *Calleva* (Silchester). Even after a century or two of Romanisation, the descendants of the Durotriges maintained their old-established individuality, which shows itself strongly in the retention of specialised elements of burial ritual and in the intensely native appearance of the locally made pottery, even into the 3rd and 4th centuries AD. In contrast, the territory once ruled by the Atrebatic dynasty was very rapidly assimilated into the Roman way of life.

This pattern of change, discernable in southern Britain in the last two centuries before the conquest and summarised all too briefly here, can be described more easily than it can be explained. Using one model, it could be argued that the phase of hillfort gate building was caused by the invasion of the Belgae who conquered the south-east and set up their own dynastic rule, introducing sweeping changes which resulted in the greatly changed settlement pattern. A perfectly acceptable alternative is to suggest that the defensive activity was the result of internal stresses for which there are many possible explanations, such as an increase in population. The change in settlement pattern, and presumably government, in the south-east, could then be seen as the result of acculturation consequent upon developing trading contacts between Britain and the adjacent coasts of Roman Gaul.

Clearly, monocausal explanations are no longer satisfactory. In all probability, all the factors mentioned above are likely to have been effective in differing degrees.

The example will have served its purpose if it demonstrates that directional changes can be recognised in the archaeological record of the iron age by comparing and contrasting various categories of evidence and by linking it to the processes and events recorded by the classical writers. This is a legitimate goal, but the desire to explain these changes in terms of simple historical events is unlikely ever to be satisfied. The best we can hope for is to arrive at a comprehensive and mutually supporting series of hypotheses.

## The nature of the British iron age

In this final section it is necessary to give a brief outline of the main developments discernable during the British Iron Age. The account is necessarily a highly simplified summary, but such a summary has a distinct value in that it emphasises the trends, forcing matters of detail and disagreement into the background, thus allowing the nature of the period to be understood more clearly.

The last thousand years BC are divisible into three broad phases, the first ending during the 8th century, the second towards the beginning of the 5th. In terms of the old technological model the 'iron age' begins during the second phase, but to understand it we must begin much earlier.

### *The phase of conservatism (c. 1000-750)*
During this quarter of a millennium society seems to have changed very little. Small farmsteads continued to be the principle type of settlement, but some of the old tribal foci were enclosed with simple box ramparts, a type of defence which' was also used to protect existing, and newly founded, hill-top settlements. The appearance of these communal works would suggest a greater tribal cohesion.

The material culture remains largely traditional, with bronze and pottery technology deeply rooted in the indigenous folk culture of the 2nd millennium.

*The phase of innovation (c. 750-500)*

During the 8th century a number of new elements appear. 'Hillforts' proliferate, with new forms of defences based on the palisade or the horizontally laced rampart, while the box style of enclosure continues to be widely used. The appearance of continental metal types belonging to the late Hallstatt B and Hallstatt C period, together with a vigorous Atlantic coastal trade, seem to initiate a wide ranging series of innovations in the native bronze industry. It is at this time, partly as a response to imported metal vessels, that a new range of local ceramics appears which, in the south, lies at the beginning of a series of well defined regional styles.

Many of the settlements established during this period continue to be inhabited for many centuries. It is a time of change and innovation which appears to have affected the whole country.

*The phase of development (c. 500-A D 43-84+)*

The latter half of the 1st millennium saw the intensification of the cultural split between the north-west and the south-east. In the north-west there was very little apparent change. With a few exceptions the surviving material culture was poor and social development gives the impression of remaining largely static. This may well result in part at least from the geographical isolation of the area, situated as it was far distant from contacts with continental Europe.

The south-east, on the other hand, shows clear evidence of both continental influence and local development. During the latter part of the 5th century European contact seems to have been at an optimum. It was at this time that the Arras culture of Yorkshire was founded, with its evident La Tène origins; the east of England, and in particular the Thames estuary, experienced the arrival of a group of continental daggers, as well as showing a development in its pottery styles which owes much to continental La Tène I types; and at the same time Cornwall was receiving a few imported metal types probably from along the Atlantic seaways. No doubt these contacts varied in intensity and significance, ranging from casual trading to folk movement, but together they define a brief horizon of maximum contact.

After this, from about the middle of the 4th century until

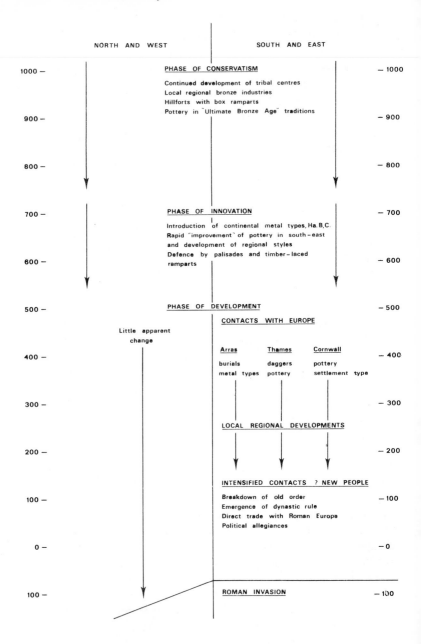

Figure 42. Developmental phases in the British iron age.

the end of the 2nd century, there appears to have been relatively little contact with continental Europe. This period sees the development of strong localised traditions.

In the second half of the 2nd century, the old order shows signs of breakdown, with the intensification of warlike activities and the emergence of dynastic rule. There was undoubtedly immigration, giving rise to the 'Aylesford-Swarling culture', and after the middle of the 1st century BC brisk trading patterns develop between the east of England and Roman Gaul.

In the south-east, the phase of development ends, and with it the pre-Roman iron age, in AD 43, with the arrival of the Roman army. The conquest was over for most of the country by AD 84: only the extreme north-west maintained its independence.

*DATE LIST: Radiocarbon dates for the iron age*

This list was prepared for my *Iron Age Communities in Britain*. I have added a few dates which have become available during the last year.

| Site | Feature | Lab. No. | Radiocarbon date bc (5568 half-life) | Calibrated date BC (approx.) |
|---|---|---|---|---|
| | *1. SOUTHERN BRITAIN* | | | |
| Chalton, Hampshire | Charcoal from a mid-bronze age hut circle | BM | 1243 ± 69 | 1500 |
| Itford Hill, Sussex | Charred grain | GrN 6167 | 1000 ± 35 | 1330-1220 |
| Longbridge Deverill, Cow Down, Wiltshire | Wood charcoal from post-hole of house 2 in enclosure 2 | NPL 105 | 630 ± 155 | 850-800 |
| | Wood charcoal from post-hole of house 2 in enclosure 2 | NPL 106 | 500 ± 90 | 780-550 |
| | Wood charcoal from loom post-hole of house 2 in enclosure 2 | NPL 107 | 420 ± 95 | 760-500 |
| | Wood charcoal from pit 7 | NPL 108 | 460 ± 140 | 780-520 |
| | Wood charcoal from pit 37 | NPL 109 | 490 ± 90 | 780-540 |
| Shearplace Hill, Dorset | Miscellaneous charcoal and animal bone from mid-bronze age hut | NPL 19 | 1180 ± 180 | 1470 |
| Weston Wood, Surrey | Carbonised cereal from a pit | Q 760 | 510 ± 110 | 790-550 |

## 2. THE MIDLANDS AND WALES

| | | | | |
|---|---|---|---|---|
| Bromfield, Shropshire | Bronze age cremation cemetery charcoal, from three separate cremations | Birm 64 | 1560 ± 180 | 2050-1750 |
| | | Birm 63 | 850 ± 71 | 1080-1000 |
| | | Birm 62 | 762 ± 75 | 880 |
| Midsummer Camp, Herefordshire | Charcoal from quarry ditch associated with first gate | Birm 142 | 420 ± 190 | 760-500 |
| | Carbonised grain associated with destruction of eighth gate | Birm 143 | 50 ± 100 | 120 BC-50 AD |
| Dinorben, Denbighshire | Charcoal from occupation layer below period I rampart | V 123 | 945 ± 95 | 1220-1120 |
| | Charcoal from collapsed beam, north-east of period I rampart | V 122 | 895 ± 95 | 1100 |
| | Charcoal (?) derived from period I rampart | V 125 | 765 ± 85 | 880 |
| | Charcoal (?) destruction of period 2 rampart | V 124 | 535 ± 85 | 790-550 |
| | Charcoal from timber lacing of period 2 rampart | V 176 | 420 ± 70 | 760-500 |
| Ryton-on-Dunsmoor, Warwickshire | Charcoal from a cremation | Birm 26 | 751 ± 41 | 880 |

## 3. NORTH-EAST BRITAIN

| | | | | |
|---|---|---|---|---|
| Ampleforth Moor, Yorkshire | Charcoal from ground surface beneath barrow 3 | BM 369 | 582 ± 90 | 790 |
| | Charcoal from ground surface beneath barrow 7 | BM 368 | 537 ± 90 | 790-550 |

## 3. NORTH-EAST BRITAIN (continued)

| Site | Feature | Lab. No. | Radiocarbon date bc (5568 half-life) | Calibrated date BC (approx.) |
|---|---|---|---|---|
| Burnswark | Charcoal from palisade | GaK 22036 | 500 ± 100 | 780-550 |
|  | Charcoal from gateway timber of hillfort | I 5314 | 525 ± 90 | 790-550 |
| Brough Law | Charcoal from beneath rampart | I 5315 | 245 ± 90 | 400-200 |
| Castle Hill, Almondbury, Yorkshire | Oak beams from uppermost ramparts | I 4542 | 555 ± 100 | 790-550 |
| Craig Phadrig, Inverness | Carbonised beam beneath fall of rampart | N 1122 | 330 ± 100 | 420 |
|  | Charcoal beneath rampart | N 1123 | 270 ± 100 | 400-230 |
|  | Charcoal beneath rampart | GX 2441 | 180 ± 110 | 180 |
| Craigmarlock Wood, Renfrewshire | Charcoal from palisaded enclosure | GaK 995 | 590 ± 40 | 790 |
|  | Core of vitrified wall | GaK 996 | 35 ± 40 | 100 BC-50 AD |
| Finavon, Angus | Charcoal from low in fallen rubble | GaK 1222 | 410 ± 80 | 410 |
|  | Occupation layer of fort | GaK 1223 1 | 320 ± 90 | 470 |
|  | Beams and planks along inner wall face | GaK 1224 | 590 ± 70 | 790 |
| Grimthorpe, Yorkshire | Bones from ditch | NPL 136 | 690 ± 130 | 870 |
|  | Bones from ditch | NPL 137 | 970 ± 130 | 1220 |

| Site | Description | Lab no. | Date | Range |
|---|---|---|---|---|
| Huckhoe, Northumberland | Charcoal from palisade trench | GaK 1388 | 510 ± 40 | 790-550 |
| Ingram Hill, Northumberland | Charcoal from settlement site with palisade: beneath bank | I 5316 | 220 ± 90 | 250-180 |
| McNaughton's Fort, Kirkcudbrightshire | Charcoal in palisade trench enclosing wooden round-house | GaK 808 | 280 ± 100 | 400-230 |
| Mam Tor, Derbyshire | Interior occupation | Birm 192 | 1130 ± 115 | 1450-1350 |
| | Interior occupation | Birm 202 | 1180 ± 132 | 1470 |
| Staple Howe, | Charred grain | BM 63 | 450 ± 150 | 770-520 |
| | *4. NORTH-WEST BRITAIN* | | | |
| Dun Ardtreck, Skye | Charcoal from rubble foundations of semibroch | GX 1120 | 55 ± 105 | 100 BC-50 AD |
| Dun Lagaidh, Wester Ross | Carbonised branch under vitrified fort wall | GX 1121 | 490 ± 90 | 780-540 |
| | Burnt grain associated with burning of timber fort | GaK 2492 | 460 ± 110 | 780-520 |
| Dun Mor Vaul, Tiree, Argyll | Roots from old ground surface below broch | GaK 1092 | 400 ± 110 | 470 |
| | Charred grain from pre-broch level | GaK 1098 | 445 ± 90 | 520 |

## 4. NORTH-WEST BRITAIN (continued)

| Site | Feature | Lab. No. | Radiocarbon date bc (5568 half-life) | Calibrated date BC (approx.) |
|---|---|---|---|---|
| | Bones from midden under outer wall | GaK 1225 | 280 ± 100 | 400-230 |
| | Primary floor in brock wall gallery | GaK 1097 | AD60 ± 90 | 60 AD |
| | Rubble in wall gallery | GaK 1099 | AD160 ± 90 | 130 AD |
| Kilphedir, Sutherland | Charcoal from hut 3 | GU 299 | 420 ± 40 | 760-500 |
| | Charcoal from hut 5 | L 1061 | 150 ± 80 | 150 |
| | Charcoal from hut 5 | GU 11 | 114 ± 55 | 130 |

# Bibliographies and notes

For each chapter, the short bibliography gives a reading list of the main works on the period, and the notes contain more detailed references. In the notes, a reference of the form 'Childe, 1940, 3' means that the book is given in the bibliography; otherwise the reader is referred thus [n. 23] to the note in which the book is first cited, for bibliographical information.

ABBREVIATIONS

The following abbreviations have been used:

| | |
|---|---|
| *Ant. J.* | *Antiquaries' Journal* |
| *Arch.* | *Archaeologia* |
| *Arch. J.* | *Archaeological Journal* |
| *C. Arch.* | *Current Archaeology* |
| *PPS* | *Proceedings of the Prehistoric Society* |
| *PRIA* | *Proceedings of the Royal Irish Academy* |
| *PSAS* | *Proceedings of the Society of Antiquaries of Scotland* |
| *Rev. Arch.* | *Revue Archéologique* |
| *WA* | *World Archaeology* |
| *WAM* | *Wiltshire Archaeological Magazine* |
| *YAJ* | *Yorkshire Archaeological Journal* |

# Bibliography for Chapter 1

COLIN RENFREW
*Changing configurations*

Childe, V.G., 1940, *Prehistoric Communities of the British Isles.* London.

Clark, G., 1966, The invasion hypothesis in British archaeology, *Antiquity* 40, 172-89.

Daniel, G.E., 1950, *A Hundred Years of Archaeology.* London.

Hawkes, C., 1959, 'The ABC of the British Iron Age', *Antiquity* 33, 170-182. (Reprinted in S.S. Frere (ed.), *Problems of the Iron Age in South Britain*, University of London Institute of Archaeology Occasional Paper 11, 1-16.)

Hodson, F.R., 1964, 'Cultural grouping within the British pre-Roman Iron Age', *PPS* 30, 99-110.

Montelius, O., 1909, 'The chronology of the British Bronze Age', *Arch.* 61, 97-162.

Piggott, S., 1954, *Neolithic Cultures of the British Isles.* London.

Renfrew, C., 1973, *Before Civilisation, the Radiocarbon Revolution and Prehistoric Europe.* London.

# Notes to Chapter 1

1. T. Wright, 1875, *The Celt, the Roman and the Saxon*, 3rd. ed., quoted Daniel, 1950, 83-4.
2. Lord Avebury, 1913, *Prehistoric Times, as Illustrated by Ancient Remains and the Manners and Customs of Modern Savages*, 7th edn. (London), 2-3.
3. Childe, 1940, 3.
4. Sir J. Evans, 1872, *Ancient Stone Implements, Weapons and Ornaments of Great Britain.*
5. O. Montelius, 1897, 'The Tyrrhenians in Greece and Italy', *Journal of the Anthropological Institute of Great Britain and Ireland* 26, 254-71.
6. Montelius, 1909, reported in brief in *Proceedings of the Society of Antiquaries of London* 22, 120-1.
7. V.G. Childe, 1925, *The Dawn of European Civilisation*, (London), 295.
8. A.J. Evans, 1909, 'Criticisms on the paper of Dr Montelius', *Proceedings of the Society of Antiquaries of London* 22, 121-8.
9. Daniel 1950, 151.

10. J. Abercromby, 1904, 'A proposed chronological arrangement of the Drinking Cup or Beaker Class of Fictilia in Britain', *PSAS* 37, 323-410.
11. O.G.S. Crawford, 1912, 'The distribution of Early Bronze Age settlements in Britain', *Geographical Journal* 40, 184-203.
12. V.G. Childe, 1929, *The Danube in Prehistory* (London), v-vi.
13. Childe, 1929 [n. 12], vi.
14. V.G. Childe, 1933, 'Is prehistory practical?' *Antiquity* 7, 417.
15. Childe, 1940, 2.
16. Childe, 1940, 3-4.
17. G. Clark, 1933, Review of C. Fox, *The Personality of Britain, Antiquity* 7, 232.
18. V.G. Childe, 1958, 'Retrospect', *Antiquity* 32, 70.
19. S. Piggott, 1931, 'The Neolithic pottery of the British Isles', *Arch. J.* 88, 67-158.
20. C. Hawkes, 1931, 'Hill-forts', *Antiquity* 5, 60-97.
21. Hawkes, 1959.
22. R.E.M. Wheeler, 1943, *Maiden Castle, Dorset* (London).
23. G. Bersu, 1940, Excavations at Little Woodbury, Wiltshire, *PPS* 6, 30-111.
24. Piggott, 1954, 381.
25. S. Piggott, 1938, 'The Early Bronze Age in Wessex', *PPS* 4, 52-106.
26. Piggott, 1938 [n. 25], 95.
27. V.G. Childe, 1948, 'The Final Bronze Age in the Near East and in Temperate Europe', *PPS* 14, 177-95; C.F.C. Hawkes, 1948, 'From Bronze Age to Iron Age: Middle Europe, Italy and the North and West', *PPS* 14, 196-218.
28. Clark, 1966, 172.
29. W.F. Libby, 1965, *Radiocarbon Dating* (Chicago).
30. Renfrew, 1973, 54-62.
31. Renfrew, 1973, 69-83.
32. H.E. Suess, 1970, 'Bristlecone pine calibration of the radiocarbon time scale 5200 BC to the present', in I.U. Olsson (ed.), *Radiocarbon Variations and Absolute Chronology* (London and New York), 303-12.
33. I.E.S. Edwards, 1970, 'Absolute dating from Egyptian records and comparison with carbon-14 dating', *Philosophical Transactions of the Royal Society London*, series A, 269, 11-18; R. Berger, 1970, 'Ancient Egyptian radiocarbon chronology', ibid., 23-36.
34. H. McKerrell, 1972, 'On the origins of the British faience beads and some aspects of the Wessex-Mycenae relationship', *PPS* 38, 286-301.
35. R.M. Clark and C. Renfrew, 1973, 'Tree-ring calibration of radiocarbon dates and the chronology of ancient Egypt', *Nature* 243, 266-270.
36. W.M. Wendland and D.L. Donley, 1971, 'Radiocarbon — calendar age relationship', *Earth and Planetary Science Letters* 11, 135-9; H.N. Michael and E.K. Ralph, 1972, 'Discussion of radiocarbon dates obtained from precisely dated Sequoia and bristlecone pine samples', *Proceedings of the 8th International Conference on*

*Radiocarbon Dating, Lower Hutt City* 1, 28-43; P.E. Damon, A Long and E.I. Wallick, 1972, 'Dendrochronological calibration of the Carbon-14 time scale', ibid., 45-49.

37. The arithmetic mean used in Fig. 1 is given by V.R. Switsur, 1973, 'The radiocarbon calendar recalibrated', *Antiquity* 47, 131-7.
38. Clark and Renfrew, 1973 [n. 35].
39. McKerrell, 1972 [n. 34].
40. Clark and Renfrew, 1973 [n. 35].
41. G.E. Daniel, 1959, Editorial, *Antiquity* 33, 79-80.
42. H.L. Movius, 1960, 'Radiocarbon dates and Upper Palaeolithic Archaeology in Central and Western Europe', *Current Anthropology* 1, 355-92.
43. H. Godwin, 1960, 'Radiocarbon dating and Quaternary history in Britain: the Croonian lecture', *Proceedings of the Royal Society*, Series B, 153, 287-320.
44. H.T. Waterbolk, 1960, 'The 1969 Carbon-14 Symposium at Groningen', *Antiquity* 34, 14-18.
45. G.E. Daniel, 1960, Editorial, *Antiquity* 34, 161-2.
46. J.G.D. Clark and H. Godwin, 1962, 'The Neolithic in the Cambridgeshire Fens', *Antiquity* 36, 10.
47. C. Renfrew, 1965, *The Neolithic and Bronze Age Cultures of the Cyclades and their External Relations*. Unpublished Ph D thesis, Cambridge University Library, 183-8.
48. C. Renfrew, 1967, 'Colonialism and Megalithismus', *Antiquity* 41, 287.
49. G.E. Daniel, 1967, 'Northmen and Southmen', *Antiquity* 41, 316-7.
50. C. Renfrew, 1968, 'Wessex without Mycenae', *Annual of the British School of Archaeology at Athens* 63, 277-85.
51. R.G. Newton and C. Renfrew, 1970, 'British faience beads reconsidered', *Antiquity* 44, 199-206.
52. McKerrell, 1972 [n. 34].
53. A. Harding and S.E. Warren, 1973, 'Early Bronze Age faience beads from Central Europe', *Antiquity* 47, 64-66.
54. F.R. Hodson, 1960, 'Reflections on the "ABC of the British Iron Age" ', *Antiquity* 34, 138-40.
55. F.R. Hodson, 1962, 'Some pottery from Eastbourne, the 'Marnians' and the pre-Roman Iron Age in Britain', *PPS* 28, 140-55; and Hodson, 1964.
56. E. MacKie, 1969, 'Radiocarbon dates and the Scottish Iron Age', *Antiquity* 43, 15-26.
57. Clark, 1966.
58. C. Renfrew, 1970a, 'New configurations in Old World archaeology', *World Archaeology* 2, 199-211; 1970b, 'The tree-ring calibration of radiocarbon, an archaeological evaluation', *PPS* 36, 280-311; 1971, 'Carbon 14 and the prehistory of Europe', *Scientific American* 225, 63-72; Renfrew, 1973.
59. L.R. Binford, 1965, 'Archaeological systematics and the study of culture process', *American Antiquity* 31, 203.

60. C. Renfrew, 1972, *The Emergence of Civilisation, the Cyclades and the Aegean in the Third Millennium* BC. (London).
61. D. Britton, 1963, 'Traditions of metal-working in the Later Neolithic and Early Bronze Age of Britain', *PPS* 29, 258-325.
62. D.D. Simpson (ed.), 1971, *Economy and Settlement in Neolithic and Early Bronze Age Britain and Europe* (Leicester).
63. A. Keiller, S. Piggott and F.S. Wallis, 1941, 'First report of the Sub-Committee of the Southwestern Group of Museums and Art Galleries on the petrological identification of stone axes', *PPS* 7, 50-72, and subsequent papers.
64. D.P.S. Peacock, 1969, 'Neolithic pottery production in Cornwall', *Antiquity* 43, 145-9, and other papers.
65. M. Jesson and D..Hill (eds.), 1971, *The Iron Age and its Hill-Forts* (Southampton). C. Renfrew (ed.), 1973, *The Explanation of Culture Change: Models in Prehistory* (London).
66. D.L. Clarke, 1973, 'The loss of innocence', *Antiquity* 47, 6-18.

# Bibliography for Chapter 2

PAUL A. MELLARS
*The palaeolithic and mesolithic*

Clark, J.G.D., 1932, *The Mesolithic Age in Britain*. London.
Clark, J.G.D., 1954, *Excavations at Star Carr*. London.
Clark, J.G.D., 1955, 'A microlithic industry from the Cambridgeshire fenland and other industries of Sauveterrian affinities from Britain', *PPS* 21, 3-20.
Clark, J.G.D., 1972, *Star Carr: a Case Study in Bioarchaeology*. Reading (Massachusetts).
Garrod, D.A., 1926, *The Upper Palaeolithic Age in Britain*. London.
Howell, F.C., 1966, 'Observations on the earlier phases of the European Lower Palaeolithic', in J.D. Clark and F.C. Howell (eds.), *Recent Studies in Palaeoanthropology* (*American Anthropologist* 68, no. 2, pt. 2, special publication), 88-201.
Lacaille, A.D., 1954, *The Stone Age in Scotland*. London.
Pennington, W.A., 1969, *The History of the British Vegetation*. London.
Roe, D.A., 1968a, 'British Lower and Middle Palaeolithic handaxe groups', *PPS*, 35, 1-82.
Roe, D.A., 1968b, *A Gazetteer of British Lower and Middle Palaeolithic Sites*. London.
Wainwright, G.J., 1963, 'A reinterpretation of the microlithic industries of Wales', *PPS*, 29, 99-132.
West, R.G., 1968, *Pleistocene Geology and Biology*. London.
Wymer, J.J., 1968, *Lower Palaeolithic Archaeology in Britain*. London.

# Notes to Chapter 2

1. An excellent summary of the whole of the British Pleistocene is provided in West, 1968, 235-355. A shorter account concentrating on the vegetational aspects of the Pleistocene will be found in Pennington (1969) Chapter 2.
2. West, 1968, 241-51.
3. West, 1968, 302-8; Pennington 1969, 13-21.
4. West, 1968, 240-1.
5. West, 1968, 339-43.
6. A.J. Sutcliffe, 1964, 'The mammalian fauna', in C.D. Ovey (ed.), *The Swanscombe Skull: a Survey of Research on a Pleistocene Site* (London, Royal Anthropological Institute), 102-5.

7. West, 1968, 276-278.
8. K.W. Butzer, 1972, *Environment and Archaeology*, 2nd ed., (London), 217. K.W. Butzer, 1968, 'Comments on paper by C. Emiliani ("The Pleistocene epoch and the evolution of Man")', *Current Anthropology* 9, 31-2.
9. No general survey of the British lower palaeolithic has been attempted this century, but a number of extremely useful summaries dealing with selected aspects of the period have appeared in recent years. J. Wymer's *Lower Palaeolithic Archaeology in Britain with special reference to the Thames Valley* (1968) provides an excellent account of the abundant and important sites in the Thames River drainage, and D.A. Roe (1968*b*) has produced what amounts to a comprehensive catalogue of the extant archaeological material from all parts of Britain. Detailed accounts of the major British sites are provided in F.C. Howell's paper 'Observations on the earlier phases of the European Lower Palaeolithic' (Howell, 1966) which attempts to relate the British evidence to that from continental sites.
10. e.g. Howell, 1966, 104; Wymer, 1968, 42, 372.
11. Roe, 1968*a*, 14-15, 71.
12. Roe, 1968*a*, 14; see also R.A. Smith, 1933, 'Implements from high level gravel near Canterbury', *Proceedings of the Prehistoric Society of East Anglia* 7, 165-70.
13. J.B. Campbell and C.G. Sampson, 1971, 'A new analysis of Kent's Cavern, Devonshire, England', *University of Oregon Anthropological Papers* 3, 17-23.
14. Roe, 1968*a*, 14, 18, 71; Wymer, 1968, 125-6.
15. Howell, 1966, 93-9, 111-40; H. de Lumley, 1969, 'A Palaeolithic camp at Nice', *Scientific American* 220(5), 42-50.
16. Howell, 1966, 91.
17. J. Frere, 1800, 'Account of flint weapons discovered at Hoxne in Suffolk', *Archaeologia* 13, 204-5; see also G. Daniel, 1967, *The Origins and Growth of Archaeology* (Harmondsworth), 57-9.
18. R.G. West, 1956, 'The Quaternary deposits at Hoxne, Suffolk', *Philosophical Transactions of the Royal Society*, Series B, 239, 265-356; R.G. West and C.B.M. McBurney, 1955, 'The Quaternary deposits at Hoxne, Suffolk, and their archaeology', *PPS* 20, 131-54.
19. J.J. Wymer, unpublished information.
20. Details of the hand-axes found prior to the present excavations are given in West and McBurney, 1955 [n. 18] and Roe, 1968*b*; further details are given in J.R. Moir, 1926, 'The silted-up lake of Hoxne and its contained implements', *Proceedings of the Prehistoric Society of East Anglia* 5, 156-60.
21. Controlled excavations in the Middle Gravels at Swanscombe were carried out in 1937 following the original discovery of the occipital and left parietal bones of the human skull; further excavations were undertaken by J.J. Wymer in 1955-60, leading to the discovery (in July 1955) of the right parietal of the same skull. For full accounts of both these excavations see Ovey, 1964, 11-61 [n. 6]. For more general accounts of the site (with full references to earlier

publications) see Wymer, 1968, 334-43, and Howell, 1966, 102-3, 140-4.

22. M.P. Kerney, 1971, 'Interglacial deposits in Barnfield Pit, Swanscombe, and their molluscan fauna', *Journal of the Geological Society* 127, 79-81.

23. Roe, 1968a, 36-7; Wymer, 1968, 338-43.

24. A full discussion of the taxonomic status of the Swanscombe skull appears in Ovey, 1964, 175-209 [n. 6].

25. Roe, 1968a, 49, 55; Wymer, 1968, 343-5;

26. Kerney, 1971, 80 [n. 22].

27. e.g. Wymer, 1968, 360, 373; D. Collins, 1969, 'Culture traditions and environment of early Man', *Current Anthropology* 10, 274. Wymer regards the pointed hand-axes from the Middle Gravels at Swanscombe as characteristic of his 'Middle Acheulian' stage, while the ovate hand-axes from the Upper Loam horizon are typical of his 'Late-Middle Acheulian'; unfortunately, Swanscombe appears to be the only site in southern Britain where this succession can be clearly observed.

28. Other important sites which appear to relate to the '100-foot' terrace of the Thames include Toot's Farm and Tilehurst near Reading, Furze Platt and Lent Rise near Maidenhead, and Bowman's Lodge near Dartford: c.f. Wymer, 1968, 137-42, 148-50, 221-5, 233-6, 328-9.

29. J.B. Calkin, 1934, 'Implements from higher raised beaches of Sussex', *Proceedings of the Prehistoric Society of East Anglia*, 7, 335-46.

30. See Howell, 1966, 99-102, with full references to earlier literature. Recent excavations by J.J. Wymer in the Clacton channel deposits have been reported briefly in *World Archaeology* 2, 12-16 (1970).

31. K. Pike and H. Godwin, 1953, 'The interglacial at Clacton-on-Sea, Essex', *Quarterly Journal of the Geological Society* 108, 261-72; see also Kerney, 1971, 87-93 (appendix by M.P. Kerney and C. Turner) [n. 22].

32. Wymer, 1968, 334-7; Howell, 1966, 102-3. At Swanscombe Clactonian artefacts occur in the basal Lower Gravel deposit and in the upper portion of the overlying Lower Loam. Excavations at present being conducted by J. Waechter in the Lower Loam deposits appear to have revealed a series of undisturbed Clactonian occupation surfaces in association with bones of butchered animals; preliminary accounts of this new work are provided in *Proceedings of the Royal Anthropological Institute* 1968 (53-61), 1969 (83-93) and 1970 (43-64).

33. Kerney, 1971, 79-80 [n. 22].

34. T.T. Paterson, 1937, 'Studies on the Palaeolithic succession in England': No. 1, The Barnham sequence', *PPS* 3, 87-135.

35. A further Clactonian assemblage was excavated by J. Wymer from a gravel deposit located approximately 18 metres above the present level of the Thames at Little Thurrock in Essex (Wymer, 1968, 314-17); unfortunately the age of this deposit is very uncertain.

36. S.H. Warren, 1951, 'The Clacton flint industry: a new interpretation', *Proceedings of the Geologists Association* 62, 107-35; Howell, 1966, 100-5.

37. Howell, 1966, 105-9; the site is believed to date from the time of the 'Elster' ('Mindel') glaciation.

38. Collins, 1969, 278-93 [n. 27].

39. e.g. Wymer, 1968, 343; Calkin, 1934, 343-5 [n.29].

40. Wymer, 1968, 354-6; R.A. Smith, 1911, 'A Palaeolithic industry at Northfleet, Kent', *Archaeologia* 62, 515-32.

41. F. Bordes, 1968, *The Old Stone Age* (London), 56-63.

42. Wymer, 1968, 356-9; new excavations in the Ebbsfleet deposits have been undertaken recently by G. de G. Sieveking.

43. See Roe, 1968*a*, 17; the results of the recent excavations have not yet been published.

44. Roe, 1968*a*, 50.

45. J.E. Marr, J.R. Moir, and R.A. Smith, 1921, 'Excavations at High Lodge, Mildenhall, in 1920 A.D.', *Proceedings of the Prehistoric Society of East Anglia* 3, 353-79. For details of continental industries see H. de Lumley-Woodyear, 1969, *Le Paléolithique inférieur et moyen du Midi méditerranéen dans son cadre géologique* (Paris, Centre National de la Recherche Scientifique), 242-68..

46. Wymer, 1968, 322-6, with references.

47. Wymer, 1968, 325.

48. R.G. West, C.A. Lambert and B.W. Sparks, 1964, 'Interglacial deposits at Ilford, Essex', *Philosophical Transactions of the Royal Society*, Series B, 247, 206-7;.West, 1968, 342.

49. Unpublished information supplied by R.G. West; see R.G. West and B.W. Sparks, 1960, 'Coastal interglacial deposits of the English Channel', *Philosophical Transactions of the Royal Society*, Series B, 243, 95-133.

50. J.R. Moir and A.T. Hopwood, 1939, 'Excavations at Brundon, Suffolk (1935-37)', *PPS* 5, 1-32; B.W. Sparks and R.G. West, 1963, 'The interglacial deposits at Stutton, Suffolk', *Proceedings of the Geologists' Association* 74, 430.

51. Roe, 1968*b*, vii.

52. W.G. Smith, 1894, *Man the Primeval Savage* (London). The Stoke Newington site is believed to date from the Hoxnian interglacial (Kerney, 1971, 81 [n. 22]), but the age of Caddington is unknown. New excavations at both sites have recently been undertaken by D.A. Roe, C.G. Sampson and J.B. Campbell.

53. See Wymer, 1968.

54. Wymer, 1968, 322-6, with references.

55. See chapter by A.J. Sutcliffe in Ovey, 1964, 85-111 [n. 6], especially 101-2; also Wymer, 1968, 336.

56. J. D'A. Waechter, 1969, 'Swanscombe 1969', *Proceedings of the Royal Anthropological Institute* (1969), 83-4.

57. J.J. Wymer, unpublished information.

58. Ovey, 1964, 88-9 [n. 6]; Wymer, 1968, 337-8.

59. West, 1956 [n.18]; C. Turner, 1970, 'The Middle Pleistocene

deposits at Marks Tey, Essex', *Philosphical Transactions of the Royal Society*, Series B, 257, 373-40; West, 1968, 306-7.

60. Smith, 1911, 519-20 [n. 40]; Wymer, 1968, 324; Moir and Hopwood, 1939, 13-15 [n. 50].

61. Wymer 1968, 261.

62. R.B. Lee and I. DeVore, 1968, *Man the Hunter* (Chicago), 40-3.

63. For general reviews of this period see West, 1968, Chapters 12 and 13, and Pennington, 1969, Chapters 3 and 4.

64. I.M. Simpson and R.G. West, 1958, 'On the stratigraphy and palaeobotany of a Late Pleistocene organic deposit at Chelford, Cheshire', *New Phytologist* 57, 239-50; also G.R. Coope, A. Morgan and P.J. Osborne, 1971, 'Fossil Coleoptera as indicators of climatic fluctuations during the last glaciation in Britain', *Palaeogeography, Palaeoclimatology, Palaeoecology* 10, 89-90.

65. G.R. Coope, F.W. Shotton and I. Stratchan, 1961, 'A Late Pleistocene fauna and flora from Upton Warren, Worcestershire', *Philosophical Transactions of the Royal Society*, Series B, 244, 379-421; Coope et al., 1971, 91 [n. 64].

66. T. Van Der Hammen, G.C. Maarleveld, J.C. Vogel and W.H. Zagwijn, 1967, 'Stratigraphy, climatic succession and radiocarbon dating of the Last Glacial in the Netherlands', *Geologie en Mijnbouw* 46 (3), 79-95.

67. Coope et al., 1971, 95-9 [n. 64].

68. See L.F. Penny, G.R. Coope and J.A. Catt, 1969, 'The age and insect fauna of the Dimlington silts, East Yorkshire', *Nature* 224, 65-7.

69. A major lobe of ice is also thought to have occupied the greater part of the North Sea basin and to have reached to the East Anglian coast in the neighbourhood of Hunstanton; see West, 1968, 240.

70. Pennington, 1969, 31-40.

71. Coope et al., 1971, 93-8 [n. 64].

72. M. Degerbøl, 1964, 'Some remarks on Late- and Post-glacial vertebrate fauna and its ecological relations in northern Europe', *Journal of Animal Ecology* 33 (supplement), 71-85.

73. Butzer, 1972, 217 [n. 8]; the maximum fall in sea level probably occurred during the later stages of the last glaciation between *circa* 18,000 and 14,000 bc; the positions of sea levels during the earlier stages of the glaciation are at present very poorly documented.

74. See Roe, 1968a, 18.

75. T.T. Paterson and C.F. Tebbutt, 1947, 'Studies in the Palaeolithic succession in England, no. 3: Palaeoliths from St. Neots, Huntingdonshire', *PPS* 13, 37-46.

76. J.B. Calkin and J.F.N. Green, 1949, 'Palaeoliths and terraces near Bournemouth', *PPS* 15, 29-37.

77. Unpublished excavations of C.B.M. McBurney.

78. Campbell and Sampson, 1971, 23-5 [n. 13].

79. The closest parallels for *bout coupé* hand-axes on the continent appear to derive from sites at the base of the Younger Loess deposits in northern France; see F. Bordes, 1954, 'Les limons

Quarternaires du bassin de la Seine', *Archives de l'Institut de Paléontologie Humaine* 26, 371-83, 441.

80. Wymer, 1968, 263-8, with references to earlier literature.

81. Wymer, 1968, 268.

82. D. Collins and A. Collins, 1970, 'Excavations at Oldbury in Kent: cultural evidence for Last Glacial occupation in Britain', *Bulletin of the Institute of Archaeology* 8-9, 151-76.

83. E.K. Tratman, D.T. Donovan and J.B. Campbell, 1971, 'The Hyaena Den (Wookey Hole) Mendip Hills, Somerset', *Proceedings of the University of Bristol Spelaeological Society* 12, 245-79.

84. J.M. Mello, 1876, 'The bone caves of Creswell Crags: 2nd paper', *Quarterly Journal of the Geological Society* 32, 240-58; A. L. Armstrong, 1929-31, 'Excavations in the Pin Hole Cave, Creswell Crags, Derbyshire', *Proceedings of the Prehistoric Society of East Anglia* 6, 330-4.

85. P.A. Mellars, 1969, 'The chronology of Mousterian industries in the Périgord region of south-west France', *PPS* 35, 140-50, 162.

86. Collins and Collins, 1970, 158-69 [n. 82].

87. Mello, 1876, 250-5 [n. 84]. The collections from Creswell are housed in the British Museum and the Manchester University Museum.

88. Tratman et al., 1971, 257-67 [n. 83].

89. J.B. Campbell, 1971, *The Upper Palaeolithic of Britain: a Study of British Upper Palaeolithic Material and its relation to Environmental and Chronological Evidence*, Ph D dissertation, University of Oxford.

90. Detailed accounts of most of these sites, together with full references to the earlier literature, are provided in Garrod, 1926. For accounts of more recent work see R.F. Parry, 1930, 'Excavations at Cheddar', *Proceedings of the Somerset Archaeological and Natural History Society* 76, 49-53; J.B. Campbell, 1969, 'Excavations at Creswell Crags: preliminary report', *Derbyshire Archaeological Journal* 89, 47-52; J.B. Campbell, D. Elkington, P. Fowler and L. Grinsell, 1970, *The Mendip Hills in Prehistoric and Roman Times* (Bristol, Bristol Archaeological Research Group), 5-8; Campbell and Sampson, 1971, 24-9 [n. 13].

91. Other sites which have yielded evidence of early upper palaeolithic occupation include the Bench Fissure (Devon), Wookey Hole Hyaena Den and Uphill Cave (Somerset) and King Arthur's Cave (Herefordshire).

92. S.H. Warren, 1938, 'The correlation of the Lea Valley arctic beds', *PPS* 4, 328-9.

93. Cambell, 1971 [n. 89].

94. Campbell and Sampson, 1971, 24-9 [n. 13].

95. Garrod 1926, 105-9.

96. H.T. Waterbolk, 1971, 'Working with radiocarbon dates', *PPS* 37, 2, 28-9. Further examples of buskate burins are known from the Paviland Cave (Glamorganshire) but the stratigraphic position of these finds is uncertain; see W.J. Sollas, 1913, 'Paviland Cave, an

Aurignacian station in Wales', *Journal of the Royal Anthropological Institute* 43, 325-74.

97. Campbell and Sampson, 1971, 34 [n. 13].
98. Campbell et al., 1970, 8 [n. 90].
99. For example Mello, 1876, 253, 255 [n. 84].
100. Garrod, 1926, 38, 192.
101. C.B.M. McBurney, 1965, 'The Old Stone Age in Wales', in I. Ll. Foster and G. Daniel (eds.), *Prehistoric and Early Wales* (London), 27-30. The possibility that certain finds of bifacial leaf-points in Britain could be appreciably earlier than the dates suggested here should perhaps be kept in mind. In central and eastern Europe implements of this type are known to have a long ancestry extending back into at least the later stages of the middle palaeolithic (see A. Bohmers, 1951, 'Die Höhlen von Mauern', *Palaeohistoria* 1, 1-107). Hence the possibility arises that groups manufacturing *Blattspitzen* industries could have entered southern England well before the beginning of the upper palaeolithic — for example, at the time of the Upton Warren interstadial, around 40,000 bc. Some of the implements recovered from river gravel deposits in East Anglia might conceivably belong to this period (see J.R. Moir, 1922, 'A series of Solutré blades from Suffolk and Cambridgeshire', *Proceedings of the Prehistoric Society of East Anglia* 4, 71-81).
102. Garrod, 1926, 49-64; Sollas, 1913 [n. 96].
103. Garrod, 1926, pl. II.
104. K.P. Oakley, 1968, 'The date of the 'Red Lady' of Paviland', *Antiquity* 42, 306-7.
105. Garrod, 1926, provides detailed summaries and references for most of these sites; in addition, see Campbell, 1969, 47-58 [n. 90]; Campbell and Sampson, 1971, 1-40 [n. 13]; R.F. Parry, 1928, 'Excavations at the Caves, Cheddar', *Proceedings of the Somerset Archaeological and Natural History Society* 74, 102-21.
106. Campbell, 1971, 352-3, 365-6, Figs. 129, 147 [n. 89].
107. S. Palmer, 1970, 'The stone age industries of the Isle of Portland, Dorset, and the utilization of Portland chert as artefact material in southern England', *PPS* 36, 89.
108. A. Mace, 1959, 'An Upper Palaeolithic open-site at Hengistbury Head, Christchurch, Hants.,' *PPS* 25, 233-59.
109. J.G.D. Clark, 1938, 'Reindeer hunters' summer camps in Britain?', *PPS* 4, 229.
110. J.J. Wymer, 1971, 'A possible late Upper Palaeolithic site at Cranwich, Norfolk', *Norfolk Archaeology* 35, 259-63. Possible traces of later upper palaeolithic occupation have also been detected at a number of open-air sites in south Yorkshire; see J. Radley, 1964, 'Late Upper Palaeolithic and Mesolithic surface sites in south Yorkshire', *Transactions of the Hunter Archaeological Society*, 9, 38-50.
111. A. Bohmers, 1957, 'Statistics and graphs in the study of flint assemblages II: A preliminary report on the statistical analysis of the Younger Palaeolithic in northwestern Europe', *Palaeohistoria* 5, 11,

Fig. 3. Both Creswell and Cheddar points are thought by Bohmers to have functioned as missile heads.

112. Bohmers, 1957, 23-4 [n. 111].

113. Garrod, 1926, 194 (footnote).

114. Garrod, 1926, 191-4.

115. H. Schwabedissen, 1954, 'Die Federmesser-Gruppen des Nordwesteuropäischen Flachlandes', *Offa-Bucher* 9 (Neumünster); Bohmers, 1957, 17-24 [n. 111]; K. Paddaya, 1972, 'The Late Palaeolithic of the Netherlands — a review', *Helinium* 11, 257-70.

116. A. Bohmers, 1961, 'Statistiques et graphiques dans l'étude des industries lithiques préhistoriques, V: Considérations générales au sujet du Hambourgien, du Tjongerien, du Magdalénien et de l'Azilien', *Palaeohistoria* 8, 15; Paddaya, 1972, 261-4, 267 [n. 115].

117. Garrod, 1926, 86-7; for Magdalenian parallels see D. de Sonneville-Bordes, 1960, · *Le Paléolithique supérieur en Périgord* (Bordeaux), 329-484.

118. Garrod, 1926, 40-1.

119. Garrod, 1926, 96, 41, 134, 171.

120. D. de Sonneville-Bordes, 1963, 'Upper Palaeolithic cultures in Western Europe', *Science* 142, 347-55. McBurney, 1965, 30-4 [n. 101].

121. Reference should also be made to the fragment of rib bone bearing a clear engraving of a horse's head recovered during the 19th century excavations in Robin Hood's Cave at Creswell. Unfortunately the stratigraphic position of this discovery is uncertain, and doubts have sometimes been raised as to its authenticity: see Garrod, 1926, 129, Fig. 31.

122. Campbell and Sampson, 1971, 34 [n. 13].

123. Campbell et al., 1970, 10-11 [n. 90]; *Radiocarbon* 13 (1971), 168.

124. J.B. Campbell, unpublished.

125. P.A. Mellars, 1969, 'Radiocarbon dates for a new Creswellian site', *Antiquity* 43, 308-10.

126. Deposits *overlying* Creswellian horizons at both these sites were found to contain very low proportions of tree pollen, characteristic of late-glacial pollen spectra (unpublished information, J.B. Campbell).

127. Three further radiocarbon dates of 6,850, 5,652 and 4,965 bc have been obtained for the site of Mother Grundy's Parlour in Creswell Crags. The recent excavations of Campbell suggest that these dates relate to the Mesolithic horizons on the site rather than to the underlying Creswellian levels: Campbell, 1969, 56 [n. 90].

128. Garrod, 1926, 83-83; J.A. Davies, 1920-21, 'Aveline's Hole, Burrington Coombe — an Upper Palaeolithic station', *Proceedings of the University of Bristol Spelaeological Society* 1(2), 64-8.

129. Parry, 1928, 104-5 [n. 105].

130. According to Mello (1876, 249 [n. 84]) hare appears to have formed 'the principal food of the inhabitants' during the occupation of the upper palaeolithic levels at Robin Hood's Cave.

131. Scales belonging to pike and, apparently, lemon sole (*Microstonus microcephalus*) are said to have been found in the Creswellian levels at the Pin Hole Cave, Creswell: A.L. Armstrong, 1929-31, 'Pin Hole Cave excavations, Creswell Crags, Derbyshire', *Proceedings of the Prehistoric Society of East Anglia* 6, 27.

132. Mace, 1959, 236-54 [n. 108].

133. Wymer, 1971, 260-1 [n. 110].

134. Bohmers, 1957, 7-25 [n. 111].

135. T. Mathiassen, 1946, 'En senglacial boplads ved Bromme', *Aarbøger* (1946), 121-97.

136. Typical Creswellian material appears to have been recovered so far from only two open-air sites in Britain — Oare in Kent (Clark 1938, 229 [n. 109]) and a recently discovered site excavated by Campbell on Hengistbury Head (J.B. Campbell, personal communication).

137. Clark 1954, 192-194 (appendix by J.W. Moore).

138. B. Barnes, B.J.N. Edwards, J.S. Hallam and A.J. Stuart, 1971, 'The skeleton of a late-glacial elk associated with barbed points from Poulton-le-Fylde, Lancashire', *Nature* 232, 488-9.

139. For a very full summary of post-glacial climatic and vegetational changes see Pennington (1969) chapters 5-8.

140. Pennington 1969, 41-77.

141. c.f. A.G. Smith, 1970, 'The influence of Mesolithic and Neolithic Man on British vegetation: a discussion', in D. Walker and R.G. West (eds.), *Studies in the Vegetational History of the British Isles* (London), 81-96; with references.

142. Pennington, 1969, 62-70.

143. c.f. Degerbøl, 1964 [n. 72]; Clark, 1954, 91-5.

144. West, 1968, 279-80; H. Godwin, R.P. Suggate and E.H. Willis, 1958, Radiocarbon dating of the eustatic rise in ocean level', *Nature* 181, 1518-19.

145. J.B. Sissons, 1965, 'Quaternary', in G.Y. Craig, *(ed.)*, *The Geology of Scotland* (Edinburgh), 467-503; also West, 1968, 278-9.

146. The only general review of the British mesolithic is Clark's *Mesolithic Age in Britain* published in 1932. A systematic attempt to record the large amount of material which has accumulated over the past 40 years has been inaugurated recently by the Council for British Archaeology with a view to publishing a comprehensive gazetteer of mesolithic sites similar to that already compiled for the lower palaeolithic period (Roe 1968*b*). In addition, detailed research on regional aspects of the mesolithic is currently in progress at the Universities of Birmingham, Cambridge and Sheffield. As a result of these new studies the current picture of the British mesolithic is likely to change radically within the next few years.

147. Clark, 1954.

148. J.W. Moore, 1950, 'Mesolithic sites in the neighbourhood of Flixton, north-east Yorkshire', *PPS* 16, 87-100.

149. S.H. Warren, J.G.D. Clark, H. Godwin, M.E. Godwin and W.A. MacFadyen, 1934, 'An early Mesolithic site at Broxbourne sealed under Boreal peat', *Journal of the Royal Anthropological Institute* 64, 101-28.

150. A.D. Lacaille, 1964, 'Mesolithic industries beside Colne waters in Iver and Denham, Buckinghamshire', *Records of Buckinghamshire* 17, 148-64.

151. J.J. Wymer, 1962, 'Excavations at the Maglemosian sites at Thatcham, Berkshire, England', *PPS* 28, 329-61.

152. R. Sheridan, P. Sheridan and P. Hassen, 1967, 'Rescue excavation of a Mesolithic site at Greenham Dairy Farm, Newbury, 1963', *Transactions of the Newbury and District Field Club* 11, 4, 66-73.

153. P.A.M. Keef, J.J. Wymer and G.W. Dimbleby, 1965, 'A Mesolithic site on Iping Common, Sussex, England', *PPS* 31, 85-92.

154. Microliths mounted in this fashion have been found at Lilla Loshult in southern Sweden; see Clark, 1954, 103.

155. Trunks of birch trees encountered in the cultural horizon at Star Carr appeared to have been felled with the aid of flint axes: Clark, 1954, 2, 177.

156. H.J.E. Peake and O.G.S. Crawford, 1922, 'A flint factory at Thatcham, Berkshire', *Proceedings of the Prehistoric Society of East Anglia* 3, 499-514.

157. Clark, 1955, Fig. 5.

158. G.J. Wainwright, 1960, 'Three microlithic industries from south-west England and their affinities', *PPS* 26, 193-201.

159. J. Radley and P. Mellars, 1964, 'A Mesolithic structure at Deepcar, Yorkshire, England, and the affinities of its associated flint industry', *PPS* 30, 1-24.

160. A possible tranchet flint axe was found at Deepcar, and a typical axe sharpening flake was found in association with a 'broad blade' microlithic industry at Pike Low in the southern Pennines (Radley and Mellars 1964, 20 [n. 159]). Isolated discoveries of mesolithic axes have been recorded from Ringstone Edge near Huddersgield (J. Davies and W.F. Rankine, 1960, 'Mesolithic flint axes from the West Riding of Yorkshire', *Yorkshire Archaeological Journal* 40, 209-14) and from the neighbourhood of Arbor Low in north Derbyshire (Sheffield City Museum, Bateman Collection).

161. Clark, 1972, 31-9.

162. Wainwright, 1963, 108-12, 120-2.

163. J.M. Coles, 1971, 'The early settlement of Scotland: excavations at Morton, Fife', *PPS* 37, 284-366.

164. J. Mercer, 1970, 'The microlithic succession in N. Jura, Argyll, W. Scotland', *Quaternaria* 13, 177-85.

165. Clark, 1954, 115-75.

166. Wymer, 1962, 351-3 [n. 152].

167. H. and M.E. Godwin, 1933, 'British Maglemosian harpoon sites', *Antiquity* 7, 36-48; J.G.D. Clark and H. Godwin, 1956, 'A Maglemosian site at Brandesburton, Holderness, Yorkshire', *PPS* 22, 6-22; J. Radley, 1969, 'A note on four Maglemosian bone points from Brandesburton, and a flint site at Brigham, Yorkshire', *Antiquaries Journal* 49, 377-8.

168. Clark and Godwin, 1956, 13 [n. 167].

169. Clark, 1954, 166-7, 177-8. A lump of resin was found still

adhering to one of the microliths at Star Carr; traces of resin were also detected on the tangs of two of the antler points from the site: Clark 1954, 102, 127.

170. *Radiocarbon* 6 (1964), 125; J. Radley, J.H. Tallis and V.R. Switsur, 1974, 'The excavation of three 'Narrow Blade' Mesolithic sites in the southern Pennines', *PPS* (forthcoming).

171. Clark, 1955, 14-19.

172. Clark, 1955, 3-11; J.G.D. Clark and H. Goodwin, 1962, 'The Neolithic in the Cambridgeshire fens', *Antiquity* 36, 10-21.

173. *Radiocarbon* 13 (1971), 168-9.

174. Palmer, 1970, 88-89 [n. 107]. The industry from Culver Well is said to include a large number of roughly-pointed pick-like objects (known as 'Portland picks') as well as several characteristic sharpening flakes from tranchet-type flint axes.

175. The radiocarbon date from Westward Ho! relates to the base of a peat deposit which immediately overlay the mesolithic 'kitchen midden' horizon: D.M. Churchill, 1965, 'The kitchen-midden site at Westward Ho!, Devon, England: ecology, age, and relation to changes in land and sea level', *PPS* 31, 74-84.

176. Site currently being excavated by P. Mellars.

177. W.F. Cormack, 1970, 'A Mesolithic site at Barsalloch, Wigtownshire', *Transactions of the Dumfriesshire and Galloway Natural History and Antiquarian Society* 47, 63-80.

178. J.H. Money, 1968, 'Excavations at High Rocks, Tunbridge Wells', *Sussex Archaeological Collections* 106, 158-207. The mesolithic artefacts from site C at High Rocks are claimed to have been found in association with sherds of neolithic pottery; for comments on this discovery see the next chapter.

179. Radley et al., 1974 [n. 170].

180. *Radiocarbon* 13 (1971), 173.

181. J. Radley, 1968, 'The Mesolithic period in north-east Yorkshire', *Yorkshire Archaeological Journal* 42, 314-27 (with appendix on pollen analyses by I.G. Simmons and P.R. Cundill); Clark, 1972, 34, footnote 22; G.A.L. Johnson and K.C. Dunham, 1963, *The Geology of Moorhouse*, London (Stationery Office), 149-57; J. Mercer, 1968, 'Stone tools from a washing-limit deposit of the highest postglacial transgression, Lealt Bay, Isle of Jura', *Proceedings of the Society of Antiquaries of Scotland* 100, 1-46.

182. Mercer, 1970, 177-85 [n. 164].

183. Clark, 1932, Fig. 27; H. Mulholland, 1970, The microlithic industries of the Tweed valley', *Transactions of the Dumfriesshire and Galloway Natural History and Antiquarian Society* 47, 81-110, Fig. 9. Since all of these discoveries represent surface finds their associations with the mesolithic artefacts cannot, of course, be demonstrated.

184. Radley and Mellars, 1964, 19 [n. 159]; Radley, 1968, 318-24 [n. 180].

185. For example, the industry from Crimdon Dene near Hartlepool: A. Raistrick, G. Coupland and F. Coupland, 1936, 'A Mesolithic site on the south-east Durham coast', *Transactions of the Northern Naturalists Union* 1, 207-16.

186. Mercer, 1968, 25-6, 40 [n. 181].

187. W.F. Rankine and G.W. Dimbleby, 1961, 'Further excavations at Oakhanger, Selborne, Hants.: Site VIII', *Wealden Mesolithic Research Bulletin*, 1-8.

188. Palmer, 1970, 88-9 [n. 107].

189. Considerable variations are apparent in the composition of the 'pure' geometric industries of northern England. In some of the industries the majority of the microliths consist of scalene triangles, whereas in other assemblages rod-like forms or trapezoids may form the dominant type. How far these variations reflect 'functional' as opposed to 'cultural' factors is impossible at present to assess.

190. A later mesolithic industry from which small geometric forms of microliths appear to be entirely lacking has been reported from site VII at Oakhanger in Surrey: see W.F. Rankine, W.M. Rankine and G.W. Dimbleby, 1960, 'Further excavations at a mesolithic site at Oakhanger, Selborne, Hants.', *PPS* 26, 246-62. The site is dated by two radiocarbon determinations of 4,350 and 4,430 bc.

191. J.G.D. Clark and W.F. Rankine, 1939, 'Excavations at Farnham, Surrey (1937-8', *PPS* 5, 61-118.

192. J.G.D. Clark, 1934, 'A late Mesolithic settlement at Selmeston, Sussex', *Ant. J.* 14, 134-58.

193. E. Higgs, 1959, 'Excavations at a Mesolithic site at Downton, near Salisbury, Wiltshire', *PPS* 25, 209-32.

194. Clark, 1955, 6-11.

195. A.L. Armstrong, 1929-31, 'A late Upper Aurignacian station in north Lincolnshire', *Proceedings of the Prehistoric Society of East Anglia* 6, 335-9.

196. Clark, 1932, 38-9, Fig. 18.

197. J.G.D. Clark, 1938, 'Microlithic industries from the tufa deposits at Prestatyn, Flintshire, and Blashenwell, Dorset', *PPS* 4, 330-4.

198. J.G.D. Clark, 1935, 'The Prehistory of the Isle of Man', *PPS* 1, 71-4. Other outlying occurrences of hollow-based points are recorded from Enstone in north Oxfordshire, Yelland in Cornwall and Wangford in Suffolk; see Clark, 1932, Figs. 15, 20.

199. Clark and Rankine, 1939, 91-8 [n. 191].

200. Clark, 1935, 71-4 [n. 198].

201. Lacaille, 1954, 196-245; P. Mellars and S. Payne, 1971, 'Excavation of two Mesolithic shell middens on the island of Oronsay (Inner Hebrides)', *Nature* 231, 397-8.

202. E.W. MacKie, 1972, 'Radiocarbon dates for two Mesolithic shell heaps and a Neolithic axe factory in Scotland', *PPS* 38, 412-6; *Radiocarbon* 15 (1973), 455-6.

203. J.G.D. Clark, 1995-6, 'Notes on the Obanian with special reference to antler- and bone-work', *PSAS* 89, 91-106.

204. Lacaille, 1954, 156-7, 287-8.

205. P.A. Mellars, 1970, 'An antler harpoon-head of 'Obanian' affinities from Whitburn, County Durham', *Archaeologia Aeliana* 48, 337-46.

206. Lacaille, 1954, 169-75; the Carse clay deposits appear to relate to the same episode of marine transgression as that represented by the 'main postglacial strandline' in western Scotland.

207. Coles, 1971, Fig. 15. [n. 163].

# Bibliography for Chapter 3

I.F. SMITH
*The neolithic*

Ashbee, P., 1970, *The Earthen Long Barrow in Britain*. London.

Burl, H.A.W., 1969, 'Henges: internal features and regional groups', *Arch. J.* 126, 1-28.

Case, H., 1961, 'Irish neolithic pottery: distribution and sequence', *PPS* 27, 174-233.

Case, H., 1969a, 'Settlement-patterns in the north Irish neolithic', *Ulster Journal of Archaeology* 32, 3-27.

De Valéra, R., 1960, 'The court cairns of Ireland', *PRIA* 60 C, 9-140.

De Valéra, R., 1965, 'Transeptal court cairns', *Journal of the Royal Society of Antiquaries of Ireland* 95, 5-37.

Henshall, A.S., 1972, *The Chambered Tombs of Scotland*, vol. 2. Edinburgh.

Manby, T.G., 1970, 'Long barrows of northern England: structural and dating evidence', *Scottish Archaeological Forum: Glasgow 1970*, 1-27.

Piggott, S., 1954, *The Neolithic Cultures of the British Isles*. London.

Piggott, S., 1962, *The West Kennet Long Barrow: Excavations 1955-56*. Ministry of Works Archaeological Reports, no. 4., London.

Powell, T.G.E., J.X.W.P. Corcoran, F. Lynch and J.G. Scott, 1969, *Megalithic Enquiries in the West of Britain: a Liverpool Symposium*. Liverpool.

Simpson, D.D.A. (ed.), 1971, *Economy and Settlement in Neolithic and Early Bronze Age Britain and Europe*. Leicester.

Smith, I.F., 1965, *Windmill Hill and Avebury: Excavations by Alexander Keiller, 1925-1939*. Oxford.

Wainwright, G.J., 1969, 'A review of henge monuments in the light of recent research', *PPS* 35, 112-33.

Wainwright, G.J. and I.H. Longworth, 1971, *Durrington Walls: Excavations 1966-1968*. Reports of the Research Committee of the Society of Antiquaries of London, no. XXIX.

# Notes to Chapter 3

1. For permission to quote unpublished dates the writer is grateful to T.H. McK. Clough (Langdale chipping-floor, BM-676), C.H. Houlder (Llandegai henge), Professor Stuart Piggott (Dalladies long barrow) and Dr G.J. Wainwright (Broome Heath).

2. As set forth by Piggott, 1954, 374, and by J.G.D. Clark and H. Godwin, 1962, 'The Neolithic in the Cambridgeshire fens', *Antiquity* 36, 22.

3. It is assumed here that neolithic culture represents the implantation in the British Isles of an integrated economic, social and technological system, alien to the mesolithic inhabitants. This may prove to be an over-simplification, but as Case has pointed out (1969*a*, 5) the introduction of domesticated sheep and goats and of wheat and barley, all lacking wild progenitors in these islands, seems to demand explanation in terms of settlement by people knowledgeable in the management of these animals and with a tradition of cereal cultivation.

4. A.G. Smith, J.R. Pilcher and G.W. Pearson, 1971, 'New radiocarbon dates from Ireland', *Antiquity* 45, 97.

5. Pending confirmation from better stratified sites, it seems unwise to accept at face value the determinations of 3710 bc ± 150 (BM-40) and 3780 bc ± 150 (BM-91) obtained from a deposit in which pottery, a leaf-shaped arrowhead and a mesolithic flint industry were 'associated' (J.H. Money, 1960, 'Excavations at High Rocks, Tunbridge Wells, 1954-1956', *Sussex Archaeological Collections* 98, 188-92; 1962, 'Supplementary note', *Sussex Archaeological Collections* 100, 149-51). The deposit was much disturbed and the pottery is not a homogeneous assemblage.

6. Smith, Pilcher and Pearson, 1971, 97 [n. 4].

7. A.M. ApSimon, 1969, 'An early Neolithic house in Co. Tyrone', *Journal of the Royal Society of Antiquaries of Ireland* 99, 165-8.

8. Summary discussions of the evidence from the British Isles as a whole will be found in J. Murray, 1970, *The First European Agriculture: a Study of the Osteological and Botanical Evidence until 2000 BC* (Edinburgh), 81, and in Powell et al., 1969, 247-8. See also D. Walker and R.G. West (eds.), 1970, *Studies in the Vegetational History of the British Isles: Essays in Honour of Harry Godwin* (London), 41-80; T.G.E. Powell, F. Oldfield and J.X.W.P. Corcoran, 1971, 'Excavations in zone VII peat at Storrs Moss, Lancashire, England, 1965-67', *PPS* 37, pt. 1, 112-37; and A.G. Smith and A.E.P. Collins, 1971, 'The stratigraphy, palynology and archaeology of diatomite deposits at Newferry, Co. Antrim, Northern Ireland', *Ulster Journal of Archaeology* 34, 15-18.

9. Simpson (ed.), 1971, 49-68.

10. J.J. Wymer, 1966, 'Excavations of the Lambourn long barrow, 1964', *Berkshire Archaeological Journal* 62, 4.

11. As suggested in Powell et al., 1969, 262.

12. Murray, 1970, 72-4, tables 137-40 [n. 8]. Hembury should be deleted from table 137; no bone survived there. Additional information in Simpson (ed.), 1971, 101-2.

13. Smith, 1965, 41, 142-4.

14. Simpson (ed.), 1971, 101-2.

15. Simpson (ed.), 1971, 46-8.

16. Piggott, 1954, 33-4 (Haldon and Clegyr Boia, but not the

Dartmoor sites and probably not the round huts on Carn Brea). Details of Lough Gur houses in S.P. O'Riordain, 1954, 'Lough Gur excavations: Neolithic and Bronze Age houses on Knockadoon', *PRIA* 56 C, 297-459.

17. Unpublished information from Francis Pryor.

18. C.H. Houlder, 1963, 'A Neolithic settlement on Hazard Hill, Totnes', *Transactions of the Devon Archaeological Exploration Society* 21, 2-31; J.G.D. Clark, E.S. Higgs and I.H. Longworth, 1960, 'Excavations at the Neolithic site at Hurst Fen, Mildenhall, Suffolk (1954, 1957 and 1958)', *PPS* 26, 202-45.

19. Clark, Higgs and Longworth, 1960, 214-26 [n. 18]; Smith, 1965, 85-103; Houlder, 1963, 23-5 [n. 18]; Case, 1969*a*, 10.

20. Early exploitation of Cornish rocks: E.D. Evens, I.F. Smith and F.S. Wallis, 1972.'The petrological identification of stone implements from south-western England',*PPS* 38, 235-275.

21. Walker and West (eds.), 1970, 71 [n. 8].

22. Case, 1969*a*, 11.

23. Pottery from Ballynagilly and Broome Heath unpublished at time of writing. Other sites: G.J. Wainwright, 1967, *Coygan Camp: a Prehistoric, Romano-British and Dark Age Settlement in Carmarthenshire* (Cambrian Archaeological Association), Fig. 31; T.G. Manby, 1963, 'The excavation of the Willerby Wold long barrow, East Riding of Yorkshire', *PPS* 29, 187-9; N. Newbigin, 1937, 'The Neolithic pottery of Yorkshire', *PPS* 3, 211, Pl. 17, no. 2 (bowl from Kilham) and see T.G. Manby, 1971, 'The Kilham long barrow excavations, 1965 to 1969', *Antiquity* 45, 50-3; J.M. Coles and D.D.A. Simpson, 1965, 'The excavation of a Neolithic round barrow at Pitnacree, Perthshire, Scotland', *PPS* 31, 41-3; D. Reaney, 1968, 'Beaker burials in South Derbyshire', *Derbyshire Archaeological Journal* 88, 80-1 (bowls from Aston-on-Trent). Approximate terminal dates for Ireland are those from Townleyhall II and Goodland (see p. 120); each assemblage included only one sherd. Associations with beakers: Henshall, 1972, 171, and Newbigin, 1937, 205 [this note].

24. Piggott, 1954, 114-7 (Grimston and Heslerton ware), 167-70 (Lyles Hill ware). Grimston and Heslerton are now seen to constitute a single style (Manby, 1970, 17), comprising both carinated and S-profiled bowls. S-profiles are common in East Anglia and Kent (S.H. Warren and I.F. Smith, 1954, 'Neolithic pottery from the submerged land-surface of the Essex coast', *Tenth Annual Report* (Institute of Archaeology, University of London), 28-31 (plain pottery from the 'lower floor'); E. Greenfield, 1960, 'A Neolithic pit and other finds from Wingham, East Kent', *Archaeologia Cantiana* 74, 62-5. The Irish bowls seem invariably to be carinated; Case's typological subdivisions of the original 'Lyles Hill ware' may not represent a chronological sequence (1961, 175-80; 1969*a*, 10). Salient characteristics of series as a whole: 1. Extremely limited range of forms, consisting mainly of undecorated carinated and S-profiled bowls, with a few hemispherical cups or small bowls. 2.

Carinated bowls most frequently of open form with greatest diameter at rim and with concave necks; closed forms, with greatest diameter at shoulder infrequent (but subsequently selected for elaboration as Beacharra, Ballyalton bowls, etc.). 3. Treatment of the surface, usually rim and inner side of neck, by shallow fluting or rippling. 4. Absence of lugs or handles.

25. Manby, 1970, 16-17, 21-2; Case, 1961, 223-4 ('Western Neolithic ware'); Henshall, 1972, 170-3; Powell et al., 1969, 149-53; S. Piggott and D.D.A. Simpson, 1971, 'Excavation of a stone circle at Croft Moraig, Perthshire, Scotland', *PPS* 37, pt. 1, 10-13.

26. P. Ashbee, 1966, 'The Fussell's Lodge long barrow excavations, 1957', *Arch.* 100, 18-21. The carinated bowl (Fig. 5, W1) is especially significant as a form derived from the Grimston/Lyles Hill series (see n.24), with added features of decoration and lugs, and for the implied links with the Mildenhall style at Hurst Fen in Suffolk and with the Beacharra/Ballyalton bowls of Scotland/Ireland.

27. In addition to flint industry, note antler combs associated with Grimston style pottery in Yorkshire (Piggott, 1954, 118) and in Kent (Greenfield, 1960 [n. 24]); with Hembury style at Maiden Castle, and with decorated styles at Abingdon, Maiden Bower, Whitehawk and Windmill Hill (Piggott, 1954, 83).

28. D.P.S. Peacock, 1969, 'Neolithic pottery production in Cornwall', *Antiquity* 43, 145-9. It is difficult to identify any ceramic style in Cornwall, Devon and western Wessex other than that represented by the gabbroic ware and imitations or possible adaptations. The range of forms is wider than in the Grimston/Lyles Hill series and comprises mainly deep storage (?) pots and simple bowls, both frequently provided with lugs, and cups. Carinated bowls are relatively uncommon and usually have straight necks; a girth-cordon sometimes replaces a carination. Lugs are quite varied (Smith, 1965, Figs. 12, 20-3). Fluting or rippling of the type specific to the Grimston/Lyles Hill series does not occur.

29. The pottery from Abingdon itself contains fragments of fresh-water bivalves (H. Case, 1956, 'The Neolithic causewayed camp at Abingdon, Berks.,' *Ant. J.* 36, 19).

30. Smith, 1965, 60-74.

31. At Whitehawk the Hembury style is represented by, *inter alia*, a deep bag-shaped pot with lugs (E.C. Curwen, 1936, 'Excavations in Whitehawk camp, Brighton: Third season, 1935', *Sussex Archaeological Collections* 77, 76 (Fig. 3), and probably by a wide shallow bowl: ibid., 79 (Fig. 25). Decoration applied to Hembury forms: ibid., 79 (Fig. 26); R.P. Ross Williamson, 1930, 'Excavations in Whitehawk Neolithic camp, near Brighton', *Sussex Archaeological Collections* 71, Pl. 9, no. 25. Decoration applied to Grimston/Lyles Hill forms: ibid., Pl. 9, no. 26, Pl. 10, no. 30, and many other examples. Ebbsfleet bowls: Curwen, 1936, 78 (Figs. 20-2) [this note].

32. R. Bradley, 1971, 'Trade competition and artefact distribution', *WA* 2, 347-52.

33. Case has discussed the role of seasonal movements in the diffusion

of ceramic traits (1969a, 16; 1969b, 'Neolithic explanations', *Antiquity* 43, 185).

34. J.W. Moore, 1964, 'Excavations at Beacon Hill, Flamborough Head, East Yorkshire', *YAJ* 41, 200-2 ('Towthorpe ware'); Powell et al., 1969, 169; S. Piggott (ed.), 1962, *The Prehistoric Peoples of Scotland* (London), 8-10; Henshall, 1972, 166.

35. Retention of the term 'Peterborough ware' has been deprecated on the grounds that, as formerly employed, it connoted an intrusive ceramic tradition (G. Clark, 1966, 'The invasion hypothesis in British archaeology', *Antiquity* 40, 176). It is retained here because a general term is needed for a series of styles embodying a coherent developmental sequence.

36. Bowls of this stage: R. Musson, 1950, 'An excavation at Combe Hill camp near Eastbourne', *Sussex Archaeological Collections* 89, 105-16, Fig. 3; J.P.T. Burchell and S. Piggott, 1939, 'Decorated prehistoric pottery from the bed of the Ebbsfleet, Northfleet, Kent', *Ant. J.* 19, 405-20, Figs. 3-8. Derivation from the Grimston/Lyles Hill series is indicated by morphology, absence of lugs or handles, and by the geographical situation of the nuclear area.

37. Smith, 1965, 11, 14, 73-4, Figs. 31-2.

38. Piggott, 1954, Pl. 10, 1, 3-5; 1962, Fig. 11, P10 and Fig. 12, P16-P17. A somewhat over-stated case for beaker influence has been made by D.L. Clarke, *Beaker Pottery of Great Britain and Ireland* (London), 267-8.

39. Piggott, 1954, Pl. 10, 2; 1962, Fig. 12, P12-P14 and Figs. 11-12, P6, P18 (possible round-based bowls with collars).

40. I.H. Longworth, 1961, 'The origins and development of the primary series in the collared urn tradition in England and Wales', *PPS* 27, 264-7, 273-80.

41. Longworth, 1961, 264 [n. 40].

42. Case, 1961, 189-96; 1969a, 17 — Carrowkeel bowls here included as a type of Sandhills ware.

43. Classed as Beacharra B and C by Piggott, 1954, 171-2.

44. Sandhills Western may have appeared several centuries earlier if sherds from Newferry (Case, 1961, Fig. 14: 10, Fig. 15: 2) can be correlated with the occupation layer dated 3330 bc (Smith and Collins, 1971, 22 [n. 8]).

45. G. Eogan, 1963, 'A Neolithic habitation-site and megalithic tomb in Townleyhall townland, Co. Louth', *Journal of the Royal Society of Antiquaries of Ireland* 93, 51-61.

46. Case, 1961, 205; 1969a, 16.

47. Case, 1969a, 16; 1963, 'Foreign connections in the Irish Neolithic', *Ulster Journal of Archaeology* 26, 8.

48. Henshall, 1972, 172-6.

49. J.G. Scott, 1964, 'The chambered cairn at Beacharra, Kintyre, Argyll, Scotland', *PPS* 30, 150-8, pottery from Rothesay, Fig. 11; Powell et al., 1969, 198-206, 217-22.

50. Henshall, 1972, 308-09; W.L. Scott, 1951, 'Eilean an Tighe: a pottery workshop of the second millennium BC', *PSAS* 85,

1-37 — but interpretation as a workshop open to doubt.

51. Report unpublished; for some of the pottery, see I.J. McInnes, 1969, 'A Scottish Neolithic pottery sequence', *Scottish Archaeological Forum: Edinburgh 1969*, 24, Figs. 11-13.

52. It is interesting that these sherds were incorporated in the blocking of a chambered tomb (Henshall, 1972, 180, 307, 441) in view of similar occurrences of Peterborough ware in tombs of the Cotswold-Severn group (Powell et al., 1969, 69-72).

53. McInnes, 1969, 22-3 [n. 51]. See also I.J. McInnes, 1964, 'The Neolithic and Early Bronze Age pottery from Luce Sands, Wigtownshire', *PSAS* 97, 49-54, 68-75.

54. Clarke, 1970, 268-70 [n. 38].

55. Wainwright and Longworth, 1971, 235-48.

56. G.D. Liversage, 1968, 'Excavations at Dalkey Island, Co. Dublin, 1956-1959', *PRIA* 66 C, 154.

57. Wainwright and Longworth, 1971, 246-7.

58. Henshall, 1972, 285-6.

59. G.J. Wainwright, 1971*a*, 'The excavation of prehistoric and Romano-British settlements near Durrington Walls, Wiltshire, 1970', *WAM* 66, 81.

60. G.J. Wainwright, 1971*b*, 'The excavation of a late Neolithic enclosure at Marden, Wiltshire', *Ant. J.* 51, 201.

61. T. Bateman, 1861, *Ten Years' Diggings in Celtic and Saxon Grave Hills . . .* (London), 254-5.

62. Wainwright and Longworth, 1971, 248; Wainwright, 1971*b*, 202 [n. 60].

63. Smith, 1965, 57, 69. Other examples: Piggott and Simpson, 1971, 10-11 [n. 25]; Eogan, 1963, 56 [n. 45].

64. Eogan, 1963, 48 [n. 45].

65. Case, 1969*a*, 17.

66. A supposed transverse arrowhead from the Larnian midden at Sutton is now discounted (G.F. Mitchell, 1971, 'The Larnian culture: a minimal view', *PPS* 37, pt. 2, 274-5).

67. Liversage, 1968, 172-3 [n. 56]; N. Stephens and A.E.P. Collins, 1961, 'The quaternary deposits at Ringneill Quay and Ardmillan, Co. Down', *PRIA* 61 C, 66-9.

68. Mitchell, 1971, 274, [n. 66]; Smith and Collins, 1971, 10 [n. 8].

69. Piggott, 1954, 302, 369-70.

70. Case, 1969*a*, 3.

71. Mitchell, 1971, 282 [n. 66]. See also Smith and Collins, 1971, 23 [n. 8].

72. Wainwright and Longworth, 1971, 257. Another specimen comes from Broome Heath (information from G.J. Wainwright).

73. Wainwright and Longworth, 1971, 255.

74. G.J. Wainwright, 1962, 'The excavation of an earthwork at Castell Bryn-Gwyn, Llanidan parish, Anglesey', *Archaeologia Cambrensis* 111, 50-1.

75. J. Alexander, P.C. Ozanne and A. Ozanne, 1960, 'Report on the investigation of a round barrow on Arreton Down, Isle of Wight',

*PPS* 26, 276-96. The homogeneity of the pottery and flint assemblages seems doubtful, however.

76. Wainwright and Longworth, 1971, 162.

77. Wainwright and Longworth, 1971, 168.

78. The alternative proposed by Clark, ceremonial gift-exchanges, offers a less convincing explanation for the distribution patterns (J.G.D. Clark, 1965, 'Traffic in stone axe and adze blades', *Economic History Review* 18, 1-28).

79. L. Keen and J. Radley, 1971, 'Report on the petrological identification of stone axes from Yorkshire', *PPS* 37, Pt. 1, 16-37; T.H. McK. Clough and B. Green, 1972, 'The petrological identification of stone implements from East Anglia', *PPS* 38, 108-155; Evens, Smith and Wallis, 1972, 235-75 [n. 20]; E. Rynne, 1965, 'Two stone axe-heads from Killamoat Upper, co. Wicklow', *Journal of the County Kildare Archaeological Society* 14, 50-3; R.G. Livens, 1959, 'Petrology of Scottish stone implements', *PSAS* 92, 56-69; J.M. Coles and D.D.A. Simpson (eds.), 1968, *Studies in Ancient Europe: Essays presented to Stuart Piggott* (Leicester), 117-36.

80. Coles and Simpson (eds.), 1968, 145-72 [n. 79].

81. I.F. Smith, 1968, 'Report on late Neolithic pits from Cam, Gloucestershire', *Transactions of the Bristol and Gloucestershire Archaeological Society* 87, 14-28.

82. Wainwright and Longworth, 1971, 264.

83. Wainwright and Longworth, 1971, 188-91, 264-5; Wainwright, 1971*a*, 81 [n. 59]; N.H. Field, C.L. Matthews and I.F. Smith, 1964, 'New Neolithic sites in Dorset and Bedfordshire . . .', *PPS* 30, 364-5.

84. Simpson (ed.), 1971, 113-30.

85. D. Webley, 1960, 'A 'cairn cemetery' and secondary Neolithic dwelling on Cefn Cilsanws, Vaynor (Brecknockshire), *Bulletin of the Board of Celtic Studies* 18, 79-88.

86. A. Oswald (ed.), 1969, 'Excavations for the Avon/Severn Research Committee at Barford, Warwickshire', *Transactions of the Birmingham Archaeological Society* 83, 19-27.

87. Oswald (ed.), 1969, 27-33 [n. 86].

88. G.D. Liversage, 1960, 'A Neolithic site at Townleyhall, Co. Louth', *Journal of the Royal Society of Antiquaries of Ireland* 90, 49-60.

89. Eogan, 1963, 40-2 [n. 45].

90. J.M. Coles, F.A. Hibbert and C.F. Clements, 1970, 'Prehistoric roads and tracks in Somerset, 2: Neolithic', *PPS* 36, 125-51; reference to earlier discoveries, lists of finds and radiocarbon dates.

91. Earthen long barrows: general survey, Ashbee, 1970; northern England, Manby, 1970. Cotswold-Severn: Powell et al., 1969, Chapters 2, 3, Appendix A.

92. Powell et al., 1969, Chapters 4, 5, Appendix B.

93. Court cairns: De Valéra, 1960, 1965. Passage-graves: S. O'Nuallain, 1968, 'A ruined megalithic cemetery in Co. Donegal and its context in the Irish passage grave series', *Journal of the Royal Society of Antiquaries of Ireland* 98, 1-29 (gazetteer and map).

94. Details of most of the dated barrows will be found in Ashbee, 1970, and Manby, 1970. For Dalladies, see: Department of the Environment, *Archaeological Excavations, 1970*, 39; *Archaeological Excavations, 1971*, 39; T.G. Manby, 1971, 'The Kilham long barrow excavations, 1965 to 1969', *Antiquity* 45, 50-3.
95. Wymer, 1966, 9 [n. 10].
96. Four sites (Horslip, South Street, Normanton and Beckhampton Road) produced no evidence of funerary use.
97. Clyde: Monamore: Henshall, 1972, 378-81. Cotswold-Severn: R.J.C. Atkinson, 1965, 'Wayland's Smithy', *Antiquity* 39, 126-33; anon, 1971, 'Ascott-under-Wychwood', *CA* 24, 7-10. Court cairns: D.M. Waterman, 1965, 'The court cairn at Annaghmare, Co. Armagh', *Ulster Journal of Archaeology* 28, 3-46; other references in De Valéra, 1960, 118, 124.
98. Discussion of implications and origins: Case, 1969*a*, 19-20.
99. G. Eogan, 1967, 'The Knowth (Co. Meath) excavations', *Antiquity* 41, 302-4; 1968, 'Excavations at Knowth, Co. Meath, 1962-1965', *PRIA* 66 C, 302-82; 1969, 'Excavations at Knowth, Co. Meath, 1968', *Antiquity* 43, 8-14. Anon, 1970, 'Knowth', *CA* 22, 292-6.
100. M.J. O'Kelly, 1964, 'Newgrange, Co. Meath', *Antiquity* 38, 288-90; 1968, 'Excavations at Newgrange, Co. Meath', *Antiquity* 42, 40-2; 1969, 'Radiocarbon dates for the Newgrange passage-grave, Co. Meath', *Antiquity* 43, 140-1; 1972, 'Further radiocarbon dates from Newgrange, Co. Meath, Ireland', *Antiquity* 46, 226-7. Anon, 1970, 'New Grange', *CA* 22, 297-300.
101. P.J. Hartnett, 1971, 'The excavation of two tumuli at Fourknocks (sites II and III), Co. Meath', *PRIA* 71 C, 35-75.
102. Simpson (ed.), 1971, 89-112. New multi-phase enclosure in Gloucestershire: P. Dixon, 1972, 'Crickley Hill 1969-1971', *Antiquity* 46, 50-2.
103. Burl, 1969; Wainwright, 1969.
104. Particularly when it is evident that the contents of the ditches had been distributed repeatedly, as discussed in Simpson (ed.), 1971, 98-100.
105. C. Houlder, 1968, 'The henge monuments at Llandegai', *Antiquity* 42, 216-21.
106. The disparity between this date, derived from a post-hole of the internal setting, and the presumably much later date of the rusticated pottery from the ditch remains to be explained.
107. Oswald (ed.), 1969, 5-15 [n. 86].
108. Wainwright and Longworth, 1971.
109. Wainwright, 1971*b* [n. 60].
110. R.J.C. Atkinson, 1967, 'Silbury Hill', *Antiquity* 41, 259-62; 1968, 'Silbury Hill, 1968', *Antiquity* 42, 299; 1969, 'The date of Silbury Hill', *Antiquity* 43, 216; 1970, 'Silbury Hill, 1969-70', *Antiquity* 44, 313-4.

# Bibliography for Chapter 4

AUDREY S. HENSHALL
*Scottish tombs*

Childe, V.G., 1935, *The Prehistory of Scotland*. London.
Corcoran, J.X.W.P., 1967, 'Excavation of three chambered cairns at Loch Calder, Caithness', *PSAS* 98, 1-75.
Corcoran, J.X.W.P., 1969a, 'Excavation of two chambered cairns at Mid Gleniron Farm, Glenluce, Wigtownshire', *Transactions of the Dumfriesshire and Galloway Natural History and Antiquarian Society* 46, 29-99.
Corcoran, J.X.W.P.,, 1969b, 'Multiperiod chambered cairns', *Scottish Archaeological Forum*, 9-17.
Henshall, A.S., 1963, 1972, *Chambered Tombs of Scotland*, 2 vols. Edinburgh.
Henshall, A.S., 1970, 'The long cairns of eastern Scotland', *Scottish Archaeological Forum*, 28-46.
Piggott, S., 1954, *The Neolithic Cultures of the British Isles*. London.
Scott, J.G., 1969, 'The Clyde Cairns of Scotland', in T.G.E. Powell et al., *Megalithic Enquiries in the West of Britain*. Liverpool.

# Notes to Chapter 4

1. Childe, 1935, 22-61; G.E. Daniel, 1941, 'The dual nature of the megalithic colonisation of prehistoric Europe', *PPS* 7, 1-49; 1962, 'The megalithic builders', in S. Piggott (ed.), *The Prehistoric Peoples of Scotland*, 39-72.
2. Formerly the Scottish part of the Clyde-Carlingford culture, briefly known as the Clyde-Solway group. Childe, 1935, 25-32; V.G. Childe, 1934, 'Neolithic settlement in the West of Scotland', *Scottish Geographical Magazine* 50, 18-25; Piggott, 1954, 152-89.
3. Piggott, 1954, 186-7.
4. General discussion in Corcoran, 1969b; see also his analysis of the Cotswold-Severn Group, in J.X.W.P. Corcoran, 1969 'The Cotswold-Severn Group', in T.G.E. Powell et al., *Megalithic Enquiries in the West of Britain* (Liverpool), 73-104 and J.X.W.P. Corcoran, 1972, 'Multiperiod construction and the origins of the chambered long cairn', in F. Lynch and C. Burgess (eds.), *Prehistoric Man in Wales and the West*, published since this chapter was written.
5. Corcoran, 1969a. A sequence of small chambers in round cairns later enclosed in a long cairn has been shown at Glenvoidean (BUT 1), preliminary note of excavation, *Discovery and Excavation: Scotland*, 1971, 14.

6. A code system for British chambered tombs was introduced in Powell et al., 1969 [n. 4], xix-xxi, and is also explained Henshall, 1972, 313. The code is used in this chapter. The following counties or islands code letters are used: ABN Aberdeenshire, ARG Argyll, ARN Arran, BUT Bute, CAT Caithness, KNC Kincardine-shire, KRK Kirkcudbrightshire, ORK Orkney, ROS Ross-shire, SKY Skye, SUT Sutherland, UST North Uist, Benbecula, South Uist, WIG Wigtownshire.

References to Scottish sites, unless given in the text, will be found in Henshall 1963, 1972. Note that the appendix to vol. 2 gives additional information on sites already catalogued in vol. 1.

7. The area of the entrance to the lateral chamber had been destroyed, so evidence was lacking whether the chamber was earlier than or contemporary with the long cairn, but the excavator favoured the latter interpretation.

8. Discussed more fully in Henshall, 1972, 222-3. The site is under excavation by Corcoran; preliminary note in *Discovery and Excavation: Scotland*, 1971, 52-3.

9. Corcoran, 1967, 5-22, 48-75.

10. Scott, 1969.

11. Henshall, 1972, 47-57, 66-70, 249-50.

12. V.G. Childe, 1935, 32-50; Piggott, 1954, 223-56, 262-3; G.E. Daniel and T.G.E. Powell, 1949, 'The distribution and date of the passage-graves of the British Isles', *PPS* 15, 176-8. The Orcadian tombs were discussed in V.G. Childe, 1964, 'The earliest inhabitants', in F.T. Wainwright, *The Northern Isles* (Edinburgh). The Shetland tombs were first published as late as 1940 in T.H. Bryce, 1940, 'The so-called heel-shaped cairns of Shetland', *PSAS* 74, 23-36.

13. The development of the chambers of the O-C-H passage-graves is discussed more fully in Henshall, 1972, 257-64, Figs. 39-40.

14. G. Eogan, 1968, 'Excavations at Knowth, Co. Meath', 1962-1965, *PRIA* 66 C 4, 299-336.

15. The excavation reports and discussion: S. Piggott, 1956, 'Excavations in passage-graves and ring-cairns of the Clava group', 1952-53, *PSAS* 88, 173-207. My own views in more detail: Henshall, 1972, 270-6. The problem has been approached through a study of stone circles and ring-cairns by H.A.W. Burl, who would derive Clava ring-cairns from Clava passage-graves: 1972, 'Stone circles and ring-cairns', *Scottish Archaeological Forum* 4, 31-47.

16. S.P. O'Riordain and G.E. Daniel, 1964, *New Grange* (London); H.C. O'Kelly, 1967, *Guide to New Grange*, Wexford.

17. Results of a field survey of Scottish long cairns summarised in Henshall, 1970; see also Henshall, 1972, 207-40.

18. Preliminary notes on both excavations in *C. Arch* 1972, 295-9; L. Masters, 1973, 'The Lockhill long cairn', and S. Piggott, 1973, 'The Dalladies long barrow', *Antiquity* 47, 32-36 and 96-100.

19. J.M. Coles and D.D.A. Simpson, 1965, 'The excavation of a Neolithic round barrow at Pitnacree, Perthshire', *PPS* 31, 34-48.

20. I.F. Smith and J.G. Evans, 1968, 'Excavation of two long barrows in north Wiltshire', *Antiquity* 42, 138-42.
21. Heel-shaped and square cairns discussed in more detail in Henshall, 1970, 43-5; Henshall, 1972, 240-5, 282-3.
22. Achategan, Cowal, Argyll. Preliminary note of the excavation only, *Discovery and Excavation: Scotland*, 1969, 7-8, 1970, 10.
23. V.G. Childe, 1931, *Skara Brae* (London); V.G. Childe and W.G. Grant, 1939, 1948, 'A Stone Age settlement at the Braes of Rinyo, Rousay, Orkney', *PSAS* 73, 6-31; 81, 16-42.
24. e.g. Ilesburgh: C.S.T. Calder, 1963, 'Cairns, Neolithic houses and burnt mounds in Shetland', *PSAS* 96, 45-7, 71-3; or Pettigarth's Field: C.S.T. Calder, 1961, 'Excavations in Whalsay, Shetland', *PSAS* 94, 28-39. Also the heel-shaped "temple" at Stanydale: C.S.T. Calder, 1950, 'Report on the excavation of a Neolithic temple', *PSAS* 84, 185-205; and 1956, 'Report on the discovery of numerous Stone Age house-sites in Shetland', *PSAS* 89, 340-362, especially 372.
25. The structure interpreted thus in Henshall, 1972, 61, 294.

# Bibliography for Chapter 5

COLIN BURGESS
*The bronze age*

Britton, D., 1963, 'Traditions of metal-working in the later Neolithic and Early Bronze Age of Britain: Part I', *PPS* 29, 258-325.

Burgess, C.B. 1968*a*, *Bronze Age Metalwork in Northern England, c.1000-700* BC. Newcastle upon Tyne.

Burgess, C.B., 1968*b*, 'The later Bronze Age in the British Isles and north-western France', *Arch. J.* 125, 1-45.

Burgess, C.B., 1969, 'Chronology and terminology in the British Bronze Age', *Ant. J.* 49, 22-9.

Burgess, C.B., 1970, 'The Bronze Age', *Current Archaeology* 2, no. 8, 208-15.

Burgess, C.B., D. Coombs and D.G. Davies, 1972, 'The Broadward Complex and barbed spearheads', in F. Lynch and C. Burgess (eds.), *Prehistoric Man in Wales and the West: Essays in Honour of Lily F. Chitty*, Bath, 211-83.

Butler, J.J., 1963, 'Bronze Age connections across the North Sea', *Palaeohistoria* 9 (entire volume).

Butler, J.J. and I.F. Smith, 1956, 'Razors, urns, and the British Middle Bronze Age', *University of London Institute of Archaeology Annual Report* 12, 20-52.

Case, H.J., 1966, 'Were Beaker-people the first metallurgists in Ireland?', *Palaeohistoria* 12, 141-77.

Clarke, D.L., 1970, *Beaker Pottery of Great Britain and Ireland.* London, 2 vols.

Coles, J.M., 1959-60, 'Scottish Late Bronze Age Metalwork . . .', *PSAS* 93, 16-134.

Coles, J.M., 1963-64, 'Scottish Middle Bronze Metalwork', *PSAS* 97, 82-156.

Coles, J.M., 1968-69, 'Scottish Early Bronze Age Metalwork', *PSAS* 101, 1-110.

Eogan, G., 1964, 'The later Bronze Age in Ireland in the light of recent research', *PPS* 30, 268-351.

Hawkes, C.F.C., 1960, 'A scheme for the British Bronze Age' (address to the Council for British Archaeology Bronze Age Conference, London, December 1960).

Hawkes, C.F.C. and M.A. Smith, 1957, 'On some buckets and cauldrons of the Bronze and Early Iron Ages', *Ant. J.* 37, 131-98.

Piggott, S., 1963, 'Abercromby and after: the Beaker cultures of Britain re-examined', in I.Ll. Foster and L. Alcock (eds.), 1963, *Culture and Environment: Essays in Honour of Sir Cyril Fox*, London, 53-91.

Savory, H.N., 1958, 'The Late Bronze Age in Wales: some new discoveries and new interpretations', *Archaeologia Cambrensis* 107, 3-63.

Smith, M.A., 1959, 'Some Somerset hoards and their place in the Bronze Age of southern Britain', *PPS* 25, 144-87.

# Notes to Chapter 5

1. A number of the objects illustrated in Figs. 27 to 31 are taken from published sources. These are as follows:

   Fig. 27 after Evans and Paterson, *Ulster Journal of Archaeology* 2, 1939.

   Fig. 28: 1-3, 8 and 10 after Simpson, *Transactions of the Dumfriesshire and Galloway Natural History and Antiquarian Society* 42, 1965.

   Fig. 28: 4 after Forde-Johnston, *Proceeding of the Dorset Natural History and Archaeological Society* 87, 1965.

   Fig. 28: 5-7 after Simpson in Coles and Simpson (eds.), *Studies in Ancient Europe*, 1968.

   Fig. 29: 1, 4 and 5 after Simpson in Coles and Simpson (eds.), *Studies in Ancient Europe*, 1968.

   Fig. 29: 2 and 3 after Manby, *Derbyshire Archaeol. J.* 78, 1958.

   Fig. 29: 6 after Forde-Johnston, *Proceedings of the Dorset Natural History and Archaeological Society* 87, 1965.

   Fig. 29: 7-9 after Simpson, *Transactions of the Dumfriesshire and Galloway Natural History and Antiquarian Society* 42, 1965.

   Fig. 30: 1 and 3 after Simpson in Coles and Simpson (eds.), *Studies in Ancient Europe*, 1968

   Fig. 30: 2 after *Archaeological Survey of Northern Ireland; Co. Down*, 1966.

   Fig. 30: 4 after Raftery, *PRIA* 61c, 1960.

   Fig. 30: 5, 6 and 8 after Simpson, *Transactions of the Dumfriesshire and Galloway Natural History and Antiquarian Society* 42, 1965.

   Fig. 30: 7 after Manby, *Derbyshire Archaeological Journal* 78, 1958.

   The palstaves illustrated in Fig. 31 are located as follows:

   Fig. 31: 1 and 3, National Museum of Wales, Cardiff.

   Fig. 31: 2, Welshpool Museum.

   Fig. 31: 4, private collection, after Bronze Implements Catalogue, British Museum.

   Fig. 31: 5, London Museum.

   Fig. 31: 6, British Museum.

   The palstaves illustrated in Fig. 32 are in the National Museum, Dublin, except nos 1, 2 and 5 which are in the Museum of Antiquities, Newcastle upon Tyne.

2. Hawkes, J. and C. Hawkes, 1958, *Prehistoric Britain*, 2nd ed. (Harmondsworth), 14.

3. See for Mediaeval figures: A.H.A. Hogg, 1971, 'Some applications of

surface fieldwork', in D. Hill and M. Jesson (eds.), 1971, *The Iron Age and its Hill-forts* (Southampton), 116, Fig. 27. A density of 1-2 per square km. over much of northern England in Domesday times compares with 9-18 over the lowland zone generally.

4. S.C. Stanford, 1972, 'The function and population of hill-forts in the central Marches', in F. Lynch and C. Burgess (eds.), 1972, *Prehistoric Man in Wales and the West: Essays in Honour of Lily F. Chitty* (Bath), 317.

5. Many of the observations on climatic change made here are based on W. Pennington, 1969, *The History of British Vegetation* (London, English Universities Library); and H. Godwin, 1956, *The History of the British Flora* (London). I am most grateful to Dr J. Turner and Dr B. Roberts of the University of Durham for their comments on the problem of climatic change and its effects.

   For climatic change in the bronze age, see H. Godwin, 1956, 62-3, 339-40 [n. 5]; and H. Godwin, 1960, 'Prehistoric wooden trackways of the Somerset Levels: their construction, age and relation to climatic change', *PPS* 26, 28-31. Recent work has emphasised caution in interpreting vegetational change, which may result as much from human factors as from climatic change: cf. Pennington, 1969 [n. 5]; and J. Turner, 1964, 'The anthropogenic factor in vegetational history', *New Phytologist* 63, 73-89.

6. H.H. Lamb, 1966, *The Changing Climate* (London); M.L. Parry, 1971, *Secular Climatic Change and Marginal Land*, paper to Institute of British Geographers Aberdeen Conference, January 1971.

7. e.g. Meare Heath track, 900 ± 110 bc (Q52): Westhay track, 850 ± 110 bc (Q308), both in Somerset; Godwin, 1960 [n. 5], at Tregaron, Cardiganshire, 1004 ± 70 bc (mean, Q389) for level below the *Grenzhorizont*, and 696 ± 70 bc (Q388) for level above it: Turner, 1964, 75 [n. 5].

8. Llan Llwych, Carmarthenshire: 1270 ± 110 bc (Q458), for fresh sphagnum peat above a major recurrence surface: B. Seddon, 1967, 'Prehistoric climate and agriculture: a review of recent palaeo-ecological investigations', in J.A. Taylor (ed.), 1967, *Weather and Agriculture* (Oxford), 173-85.

9. Hawkes, 1960.

10. e.g. Britton, 1963; Burgess, 1968*a*, 1968*b*; Coles, 1959-60, 1963-4, 1968-9; Eogan, 1964.

11. Burgess, 1969.

12. It is hard to understand why some recent writers, particularly in Ireland, have found it difficult to divide middle from early bronze age, and have stressed their continuity; see G. Eogan, 1962, 'Some observations on the Middle Bronze Age in Ireland', *Journal of the Royal Society of Antiquaries of Ireland* 92, 46; and Eogan, 1964, 268; A.M. ApSimon, 1969, 'The Earlier Bronze Age in the north of Ireland', *Ulster Journal of Archaeology* 32, 28-72; J. Raftery, 1972, 'Iron Age and Irish Sea: problems for research', in C. Thomas (ed.), 1972, *The Iron Age in the Irish Sea Province* (London, C.B.A. Research Report 9, 2). Doubts have been cast on the whole concept

of a middle bronze age, and ApSimon, for example (1969, 31), has sought to suppress it completely, distinguishing only between an earlier and later bronze age. Such doubts made sense in the days when bronze age pottery and burial monuments were divided into neat typological packets which were scattered in a continuum through the whole period, but this hardly applies today. cf. Burgess, 1969.

13. All three had been introduced from the Continent some time previously, socketed axes in the Taunton phase, and the leaf-shaped swords and pegged spearheads in the Penard phase. But there was a long period of sporadic and experimental manufacture before they were widely accepted. cf. C.B. Burgess, 1962, 'A socketed axe from central Monmouthshire and its significance for the Bronze Age in Wales and the Marches', *Monmouthshire Antiquary* 1, 17-27; 1968*b*, 34-5.

14. cf. S. Piggott, 1949, *British Prehistory* (London), 130-4; and V.G. Childe, 1940, *Prehistoric Communities of the British Isles* (London), 145-56, for the traditional view of urns which has prevailed until the last year or so.

15. H. McKerrell, 1972, 'On the origins of British faience beads and some aspects of the Wessex-Mycenae relationship', *PPS* 38, 286-301, Fig. 4.

16. The arguments have been summarised by Clarke (1970, 45-51), who favours an origin in the Golfe du Lion area. But see also H.N. Savory, 1971, Review of Clarke, 1970, *Archaeologia Cambrensis* 120, 112-16, reiterating Iberian origins; also J.N. Lanting and J.D. van der Waals, 1972, 'British Beakers as seen from the Continent', *Helinium* 12, 20-46, especially p. 45; and S. Piggott, 1971, Review of Clarke, 1970, *Antiquity* 45, 148-50.

17. e.g. Piggott, 1963, 61-4; Clarke, 1970; Lanting and van der Waals, 1972 [n. 16].

18. Clarke, 1970.

19. Lanting and van der Waals, 1972 [n. 16].

20. While admitting that such contacts must have occurred, Lanting and van der Waals (1972, 44-5 [n. 16]) offer no opinion on their nature.

21. In both the Clarke and the Lanting and van der Waals schemes, echoes of the traditional three-fold division of beakers remain. Vessels of steps 1-3, Clarke's intrusive and East Anglian beakers, are bell beakers, those of step 4, broadly Clarke's Northern tradition, are short-necked, and those of steps 5-7, mostly Clarke's Southern tradition, are long-necked.

22. I.F. Smith and D.D.A. Simpson, 1966, 'Excavation of a round barrow on Overton Hill, north Wiltshire', *PPS* 32, 132-4; Clarke, 1970, 279.

23. D.D.A. Simpson, 1971, 'Beaker houses and settlements in Britain', in D.D.A. Simpson (ed.), 1971, *Economy and Settlement in Neolithic and Early Bronze Age Britain and Europe* (Leicester), 131-52.

24. There is some evidence that flat-based pottery was already used in the neolithic, e.g. at Windmill Hill: I.F. Smith, 1965, *Windmill Hill and Avebury: Excavations by Alexander Keiller, 1925-1939* (London), 57, 69, with reference to other examples. But flat bases appear to have been very rare until the arrival of the beaker folk.

25. There seems to be no evidence for textiles in Britain until the beaker period, when cloth is recorded from graves: A.S. Henshall, 1950, 'Textiles and weaving appliances in prehistoric Britain', *PPS* 16, 131-5. A most notable beaker burial with cloth is that from Driffield C38: J.R. Mortimer, 1905, *Forty Years' Researches in Britain and Saxon Burial Mounds of East Yorkshire* (London), 274-5.

26. Simpson, 1971 [n. 23].

27. Unpublished, but see ApSimon, 1969, 34-5 [n. 12].

28. G. Briscoe, 1949, 'Combined Beaker and Iron Age sites at Lakenheath, Suffolk', *Proceedings of the Cambridge Antiquarian Society* 42, 92-111. For general comments on these East Anglian sites, R.R. Clarke, 1960, *East Anglian* (London), 65. Note D. Clarke's impassioned statement on the abundant evidence for beaker houses (timber, wattle and daub, but apparently no plans) and cultivation in East Anglia, in *PPS* 32, 1966, 366, reviewing J. Tait, 1965, *Beakers from Northumberland* (Newcastle upon Tyne).

29. Simpson, 1971, 132 [n. 23].

30. Simpson, 1971 [n. 23]. But rectilinear structures also occur, as at Belle Tout, Sussex: R. Bradley, 1970, 'The excavation of a Beaker settlement at Belle Tout, East Sussex, England', *PPS* 36, 312-79.

31. Evidence summarised in Simpson, 1971 [n. 23]; and Bradley, 1970, 359-3 [n. 30].

32. e.g. Haldon, Devon, and Clegyr Boia, Pembrokeshire, most conveniently in S. Piggott, 1954, *The Neolithic Cultures of the British Isles* (London), 33-4; Llandegai, Caernarvonshire, in C. Houlder, 1968, 'The henge monuments at Llandegai', *Antiquity* 42, 219; Lough Gur, Co. Limerick, in S.P. O'Riordain, 1954, 'Lough Gur excavations: Neolithic and Bronze Age houses at Knockadoon', *PRIA* 56C, 443-7; 'Ballynagilly, Co. Tyrone', in A.M. ApSimon, 1969, 'Early Neolithic house in Co. Tyrone', *Journal of the Royal Society of Antiquaries of Ireland* 99, 165-8. But note that circular buildings also existed in the neolithic, as at Clegyr Boia again, A. Williams, 1953, 'Clegyr Boia, St. David's (Pemb.): excavation in 1943', *Archaeologia Cambrensis* 102, 20-47; and frequently in henges: G.J. Wainwright and I.H. Longworth, 1971, *Durrington Walls: Excavations 1966-1968* (London, Society of Antiquaries Research Report no. 29), 204-34, 363-77. Circularity in building clearly already existed in neolithic Britain.

33. P.J. Fowler, 1971, 'Early prehistoric agriculture in western Europe: some archaeological evidence', in Simpson, 1971, 163 [n. 23].

34. Fowler 1971 [n. 33]; N.H. Field, C.L. Matthews and I.F. Smith, 1964, 'New Neolithic sites in Dorset and Bedfordshire, with a note on the distribution of Neolithic storage-pits in Britain', *PPS* 30,

352-81. Field systems, ploughing methods and storage-pits may just be among the more readily observable aspects of indigenous agriculture assimilated by beaker settlers.

35.  H. Helbaek, 1952, 'Early crops in southern England', *PPS* 18, 204-7.
36.  Clarke (1970, 438-47) lists many double burials. Examples of multiple burials include that from Kelloe Law, Co. Durham, with five individuals represented, T. Wake and R.P. Wright, 1951, 'An Early Bronze Age cist at Kelloe Law, Co. Durham', *Archaeologia Aeliana*, 4 ser., 29, 213-20; and Painsthorpe Wold 4, Yorkshire, with four individuals: Mortimer, 1905, 113-17 [n. 25].
37.  T.G. Manby, 1969, 'Rudston Barrow LII; Beaker-cremation associations', *YAJ* 42, 254-8; list of beaker cremations in Clarke, 1970, 453.
38.  Piggott, 1963, 76.
39.  For example beaker burials in graves, one a pit grave, under a cairn at Chatton Sandyford, Northumberland, 75 miles north of the Tees; G. Jobey, 1968, 'Excavations of cairns at Chatton Sandyford, Northumberland', *Archaeologia Aeliana*, 4 ser., 46, 5-50.
40.  Beaker folk are thought to have been responsible for the development of double entrance Class II henges: R.J.C. Atkinson, 1951, 'The henge monuments of Great Britain', in R.J.C. Atkinson, C.M. Piggott and N.K. Sanders, 1951, *Excavations at Dorchester, Oxon.* (Oxford, Ashmolean Museum), 81-96; also G.J. Wainwright, 1969, 'A review of henge monuments in the light of recent research', *PPS* 25, 112-33.
41.  As at Rudston, Yorkshire, with beaker pottery on the ditch bottom: D.P. Dymond, 1966, 'Ritual monuments at Rudston, E. Yorkshire, England', *PPS* 32, 86-95.
42.  Notably various works by Professor Alexander Thom, especially 1967, *Megalithic Sites in Britain* (London); 1971, *Megalithic Lunar Observatories* (London). See also D.C. Heggie, 1972, 'Megalithic lunar observatories: an astronomer's view', *Antiquity* 46, 43-8.
43.  Wainwright and Longworth, 1971, 235-68 [n. 32]; Clarke, 1970, 268-70.
44.  I.F. Smith, 1956, *The Decorative Art of Neolithic Ceramics in South-Eastern England and its Relations* (Unpublished PhD thesis, London University); see also Clarke, 1970, 132-4.
45.  Clarke, 1970, 271.
46.  D.D.A. Simpson, 1968, 'Food vessels: associations and chronology', in D.D.A. Simpson and J.M. Coles (eds.), 1968, *Studies in Ancient Europe: Essays presented to Stuart Piggott* (Leicester), 197-211, maps, Figs. 47-8.
47.  i.e. in the Peak District, east Yorkshire, Northumberland and eastern Scotland. For the distribution of food vessel inhumations, Simpson, 1968 [n. 46]; for beaker distributions, Clarke, 1970, 557-66.
48.  e.g. under long barrows, as at Giants' Hills, Skendleby, Lincolnshire: C.W. Phillips, 1936, 'The excavation of the Giants' Hills long barrow, Skendleby, Lincs.', *Arch.* 85, 37-106; under round

barrows, e.g. Duggleby Howe, Yorkshire, Mortimer, 1905, 23-42 [n. 25] ; and in caves, as at Church Dale, Derbyshire, T.A. Harris, 1938, 'Church Dale, Derbyshire', *PPS* 4, 317.

49. C14 dates for southern long barrows are all in the early and middle neolithic, as listed in P. Ashbee, 1970, *The Earthen Long Barrow in Britain* (London), 86-7. Known late neolithic burials are usually cremations, often in henges, though all authorities seem to agree that henges were not primarily sepulchral monuments: cf. Wainwright, 1969, 116-18 [n. 40].

50. Piggott (1954, 64-5, 111-12, 354-3 [n. 32]), discusses neolithic round mound burials. See also J.M. Coles and D.D.A. Simpson, 1965, 'The excavation of a neolithic round barrow at Pitnacree, Perthshire, Scotland', *PPS* 31, 34-57.

51. Burgess, 1969, 24-7.

52. Burgess, 1969; also Burgess, 1970, 209; J.D. Bu'Lock, 1961, 'The Bronze Age in the North-West', *Transactions of the Lancashire and Cheshire Antiquarian Society* 71, 37.

53. E.E. Evans and T.G.F. Paterson, 1939, 'A Bronze Age burial group from Kilskeery, County Tyrone', *Ulster Journal of Archaeology* 2, 65-71.

54. As at Fargo Plantation, Wiltshire: J.F.S. Stone, 1938, 'An Early Bronze Age grave in Fargo Plantation', *WAM* 48, 357-70; and Gortcorbies, Co. Derry: P. Harbison, 1969, 'The relative chronology of Irish Early Bronze Age pottery', *Journal of the Royal Society of Antiquaries of Ireland* 99, 67, 72, Fig. 2.

55. Note especially some of the Yorkshire pit graves, with beaker burials on the bottom of the grave and food vessels higher up in the fill, as at Garton Slack 75, and Painsthorpe 21. In the latter case sherds of one beaker occurred throughout the fill from top to bottom, suggesting its contents, including lower beaker and upper food vessel burials, were broadly contemporary: Mortimer, 1905, 222-4 (Garton Slack), 11-12 (Painsthorpe) [n. 25].

56. Note those Yorkshire pit graves which resemble the famous beaker examples, but which have food vessel primary burials, e.g. Garton Slack C53, Mortimer, 1905, 218 [n. 25].

57. e.g. beads, toggles and buttons of various substances, miscellaneous flint implements, barbed and tanged arrowheads, stone axes and battle axes, and, rarely, metal implements and ornaments, usually simple forms such as awls, blades, tanged and riveted knives, armlets and ear-rings. For convenient summaries see Simpson, 1968 [n. 46] (food vessels), and Bu'Lock, 1961, 20-34 [n. 52].

58. Note the variety of wooden articles, especially wooden vessels, recovered from the bottom of the Wilsford shaft, Wiltshire: P. Ashbee, 'The Wilsford Shaft', *Antiquity* 37, 118-19.

59. The term 'collared urn' is used in a much broader sense than formally, and takes in all those vessels formerly described as overhanging rim urns, a term now abandoned. See I.H. Longworth, 1961, 'The origins and development of the primary series in the collared urn tradition in England and Wales', *PPS* 27, 263.

60. ApSimon, 1969, 39, 66, note 8 [n. 12]; and ApSimon, 1972, 'Biconical Urns outside Wessex', in Lynch and Burgess (eds.), 1972, 143-6 [n. 4].

61. Cornish urns, falling within ApSimon's Trevisker series of south-western bronze age pottery, occur widely in settlements in the south west: A.M. ApSimon and E. Greenfield, 1972, 'The excavation of Bronze Age and Iron Age settlements at Trevisker, St. Eval, Cornwall', *PPS* 38, 326-41. Biconical urns in the settlement at Mildenhall Fen, Suffolk: J.G.D. Clark, 1936, 'Report on a Late Bronze Age site in Mildenhall Fen, west Suffolk', *Ant. J.* 16, 29-50.

62. As at Mildenhall Fen, Clark, 1936 [n. 61].

63. e.g. Trevisker, Cornwall: ApSimon, 1972 [n. 61]; Downpatrick, Co. Down: A.J. Pollock and D.M. Waterman, 1964, 'A Bronze Age habitation site at Downpatrick', *Ulster Journal of Archaeology* 27, 31-58.

64. S. Piggott and C.M. Piggott, 1940, 'Excavations on Ram's Hill, Berks.', *Ant. J.* 20, 465-80. Information on the more recent (1972) excavations kindly supplied by the co-excavator, Mr Richard Bradley.

65. N. Langmaid, 1971, 'Norton Fitzwarren', *C. Arch.* 28, 116-20.

66. Helbaek, 1952, 204-7, 226-7 [n. 35].

67. S. Piggott, 1947-8, 'The excavations at Cairnpapple Hill, West Lothian, 1947-8', *PSAS* 82, 68-123.

68. H.E. Kilbride-Jones, 1935-6, 'Late Bronze Age cemetery: being an account of the excavations of 1935 at Loanhead of Daviot, Aberdeenshire, on behalf of H.M. Office of Works', *PSAS* 70, 278-310.

69. There is no comprehensive survey of such cemeteries, but see Childe, 1940, 151-2 [n. 14]; Bu'Lock, 1961, 15-20 [n. 52]. Also V.G. Childe, 1935, *The Prehistory of Scotland* (London), 129-30.

70. C.B. Burgess, 1972, 'Goatscrag: a Bronze Age rock shelter cemetery in north Northumberland. With notes on other rock shelters and crag lines in the region', *Archaeologia Aeliana*, 4 ser., 50, 15-69.

71. Especially in southern Britain. There are no convenient lists of such sites, but Fox excavated several such barrows in south Wales: C. Fox., 1959, *Life and Death in the Bronze Age* (London), 105-77, with full references.

72. Especially in northern Britain, e.g. the Anglesey examples conveniently treated together by F. Lynch, 1970, *Prehistoric Anglesey* (Llangefni, Anglesey Antiquarian Society), 123-59.

73. Clearly illustrated by Grimes' reconstruction drawing of the multiple secondaries inserted into the Rhoscrowther barrow, Pembrokeshire: W.F. Grimes, 1951, *The Prehistory of Wales*, 2nd ed. (Cardiff, National Museum of Wales), 101, Fig. 32; C. Fox, 1926, 'A Bronze Age barrow on Kilpaison Burrows, Rhoscrowther, Pembrokeshire', *Archaeologia Cambrensis*, 7 ser., 6, 1-32. At Rhoscrowther the mound had been raised over an unaccompanied cremation, but the original ownership of the mound was immaterial;

compare urns inserted into megalithic tombs, as at Harristown, Co. Waterford: J. Hawkes, 1941, 'Excavation of a megalithic tomb at Harristown, Co. Waterford', *Journal of the Royal Society of Antiquaries of Ireland* 71, 130-47; and into beaker mounds, as at Chatton Sandyford, Northumberland, Jobey, 1968, 18 [n. 39]. Such additions frequently involved enlarging the existing mound, as at Sutton 268, Glamorganshire: C. Fox, 1943, 'A Bronze Age barrow (Sutton 268) in Llandow parish, Glamorgan', *Arch.* 89, 89-126; and Witton, Norfolk, Clarke, 1960, 80-1 [n. 28].

74. Urn burials without covering mound have frequently been recorded in the south, but it is generally not clear whether these represent flat graves, or have had their mounds removed by ploughing. Note also ring ditch urn cemeteries on southern river gravels, especially in the upper Thames valley, as at Hanborough 3, Oxfordshire: H. Case, N. Bayne, S. Steel, G. Avery and H. Sutermeister, 1964-5, 'Excavations at City Farm, Hanborough, Oxon', *Oxoniensia* 29-30, 6-21, 66-71.

75. F. Lynch, 1971, 'Report on the re-excavation of two Bronze Age cairns in Anglesey: Bedd Branwen and Treiorwerth', *Archaeologia Cambrensis* 120, 11-83.

76. Lynch, 1971, 52-63 [n. 75].

77. This might be implied by cemeteries such as Loanhead of Daviot, where the burials with urns are divided roughly half and half enlarged food vessels and collared urns; and Llanddyfnan, Anglesey, where the surviving urns from an arc of burials in the northern part of the mound are all cordoned, contrasting with an isolated burial to the south associated with two enlarged food vessels and bronzes: Lynch, 1970, 136-43 [n. 72].

78. It seems likely that Wessex culture, beaker, food vessel, enlarged food vessel, collared and biconical urn burials were all being interred in this period. The answers to these complex problems of social and political relationships no doubt lies in the elusive settlements, as so often in the bronze age.

79. ApSimon, 1972, 143-52 [n. 60].

80. A Morrison, 1968, 'Cinerary urns and pygmy vessels in south-west Scotland', *Transactions of the Dumfriesshire and Galloway Natural History and Antiquarian Society*, 3 ser., 45, 33-5, 122, 124, Figs. 2, 4.

81. e.g. Enlarged food vessels with relief crosses or wheels on the inside base, and finger tipped cordons: ApSimon, 1969, 41-2, Fig. 6:3 [n. 12] (Ballytresna, Co. Antrim); E. Prendergast, 1962, 'Urn burial at Maganey Lower, Co. Kildare', *Journal of the Royal Society of Antiquaries of Ireland* 92, 169-73.

82. Certainly in the absence of relevant corpora.

83. Quoting Miss Lynch rather out of context: Lynch, 1971, 56 [n. 75].

84. I.H. Longworth, 1961, 'The origins and development of the Primary Series in the Collared Urn tradition in England and Wales', *PPS* 27, 263-306, for discussion of origins and the primary series; also Clarke, 1970, 271. For the secondary series, I.H. Longworth,

1970, 'The Secondary Series in the Collared Urn tradition in England and Wales', in J. Filip (ed.), 1970, *Actes du VII<sup>e</sup> congrès international des sciences préhistoriques et protohistoriques: Prague, 1966* (Prague, Academia-Institut d'Archéologie de l'Académie Tchecoslovaque des Sciences), 662-5.

85. Longworth's original chronological arguments were hardly convincing, 1961, 288-90 [n. 84]. Note particularly the situation at Bedd Branwen, Anglesey, where urns were deposited in two successive phases. In both phases both primary and secondary series vessels were deposited roughly contemporaneously, exhibiting startling trait variation: Lynch, 1971 [n. 75]. C14 dates for primary and secondary series vessels are equally instructive, e.g. 1274 ± 81 bc (BM-453) for a 3-trait primary series urn at Bedd Branwen, and 1490 ± 60 bc (GrN-1686) for a 0-trait secondary series urn at Hanborough 3, Oxon; Case, et al., 1964-5, 14, 68, Fig. 26: 3/3 [n. 74].

86. e.g. Lough Gur Class II ware: O'Riordain, 1954 [n. 32]; H. Case, 1961, 'Irish Neolithic pottery: distribution and sequence', *PPS* 27, 196-8, 206-8, 227. Similar wares occur on the eastern side of the Irish Sea, e.g. at Dyffryn, Ardudwy, Merion: F. Lynch, 1969, 'The contents of excavated tombs in north Wales', in T.G.E. Powell et al., 1969, *Megalithic Enquiries in the West of Britain* (Liverpool), 149-55, Figs. 55-6.

87. S. Piggott, 1962, *The Prehistoric Peoples of Scotland* (London), 94-5.

88. I.H. Longworth, in W.F. Cormack, 1963-64, 'Burial site at Kirkburn, Lockerbie', *PSAS* 96, 129-31.

89. Whether this represents the conversion of food vessel communities to in-urned cremation, or the adoption of yet another cinerary urn form by cremating groups, is uncertain.

90. cf. ApSimon, 1969, 38-40 [n. 12]; and 1972, 143-9 [n. 60], preferring the term 'food vessel urn'. But 'enlarged food vessel' has at least the advantage of being descriptive, and less contradictory: Burgess, 1972, 39-40 [n. 70].

91. The similarity has often been noted, e.g. by Piggott, 1962, 96 [n. 87], but has been vigorously disputed, by ApSimon amongst others, 1972, 146 [n. 60].

92. The considerably overlap between grooved and beaker wares is confirmed by C14 dates (Wainwright and Longworth, 1971, 265-6 [n. 32]). While there are no C14 dates for 'encrusted urns', associations place them firmly in the early bronze age alongside other urns and food vessels (Burgess, 1969, 26; 1970, 209), so that overlap with late beakers is almost certain, and with late grooved wares possible.

93. Listed and discussed in Wainwright and Longworth, 1971, 235-54, 268-306.

94. For general discussions, Butler and Smith, 1956, 26-48; I.F. Smith, 1961, 'An essay towards the reformation of the British Bronze Age', *Helinium* 1, 97-118; J.B. Calkin, 1962, 'The Bournemouth area in the Middle and Late Bronze Age, with the 'Deverel-Rimbury'

problem reconsidered', *Arch. J.* 119, 1-65.

95. Examples from the Midlands and eastern counties are common in local museums, but are often poorly published or unpublished. Museums with notable collections include Lincoln, Nottingham University, Grantham, Norwich and Ipswich.

96. e.g. Ringwould, Kent (Smith, 1961, 102, Fig. 1: 1 [n. 94]), compared by ApSimon (1972, 143-5, Fig. 1: 1, 2 [n. 60]) with highland zone bipartite enlarged food vessels such as that from Uddingston, Lanarkshire.

97. e.g. the rather rounded biconical urns like that from Winterbourne Monkton, Wiltshire (Smith, 1961, 103-4, Fig. 2:5 [n. 94]) can be compared with such cordoned urns as that from Garrowby Wold 169, Yorkshire (ApSimon, 1972, 147, Fig. 3:5 [n. 60]).

98. Calkin (1962, 35-40 [n. 94]) and ApSimon (1962, in P. Rahtz, 1962, 'Excavations at Shearplace Hill, Sydling St. Nicholas, Dorset, England', *PPS* 28, 319-21; 1972, 142-3 [n. 60]) have been the leading proponents of the Trevisker-biconical relationship.

99. Proposed originally by Butler and Smith, 1956, 44-6, and subsequently retracted by Smith, 1961, 100 [n. 94]. The idea revived more recently by Wainwright and Longworth, 1971, 248 [n. 32].

100. e.g. some of the vessels from Mildenhall Fen; Clark, 1936, Figs. 5-8 [n. 61].

101. e.g. Calkin's 'sub-biconical' vessels (1962, 29-32 [n. 94]).

102. e.g. Butler and Smith, 1956; Smith, 1961 [n. 94].

103. Associations are listed by Butler and Smith, 1956, and Smith, 1961 [n. 94], and discussed by Burgess, 1969, 27.

104. Smith has argued (1961, 108 [n. 94]) that because the mass of biconical urn burials lack other grave-goods they must be middle bronze age. But this argument is misleading and irrelevant, since most early bronze age burials similarly lacked grave-goods.

105. W. Glasbergen, 1954, 'Barrow excavations in the Eight Beatitudes', *Palaeohistoria* 3, 1-204; W. Glasbergen, 1957, 'De Urn van Toterfout en de Reformatie van de Britse Bronstijd', *Dijdragen tot de Studie van het Brabantse Heem* 8; Butler and Smith, 1956; Smith, 1961 [n. 94].

106. Attempts made to link this movement with the appearance of British-style bronzes in the Low Countries at the beginning of the middle bronze age (e.g. Smith, 1961, 110 [n. 94]; Calkin, 1962, 47, note 1 [n. 94]) clearly will not do on two counts. First there is the obvious geographical discrepancy between the south English source of the Hilversum urns and the north Welsh source of at least some of the bronzes. And second is the chronological difficulty, C14 dating placing the Hilversum settlement well back in the early bronze age.

107. See Clarke, 1970, 270.

108. J. Abercromby, 1912, *A Study of the Bronze Age Pottery of Great Britain and Ireland*, 2 vols. (Oxford).

109. e.g. T.G. Manby, 1958, 'Food Vessels of the Peak District', *Derbyshire Archaeological Journal* 78, 1-5.

110. e.g. Simpson, 1968, 197 [n. 46], though Simpson here and in 1965 ('Food Vessels in south-west Scotland', *Transactions of the Dumfriesshire and Galloway Natural History and Antiquarian Society*, 3 ser., 42, 25-50) makes no attempt to propose a new classification, merely treating his material within a simplified version of the Abercromby scheme.
111. It is difficult to account for the emphasis on bowl forms in Ireland and vase forms in England. The strong beaker presence – a tall ceramic form – in England, and the repeated Irish fondness for squat shapes (cf. middle bronze age Irish palstaves and late bronze age bag-shaped socketed axes) may have contributed to the contrast.
112. e.g. four inhumed bodies, one with a food vessel, in a grave in Garton Slack C71; Mortimer, 1905, 225-6 [n. 25].
113. This must be the explanation of the groups of graves found under so many Yorkshire barrows.
114. e.g. Garton Slack 75, Yorkshire, central grave pit. Burial 2, an inhumation with food vessel, had a cremation at its feet: Mortimer, 1905, 222-3, Fig. 569a [n. 25].
115. J. Waddell, 1970, 'Irish Bronze Age cists: a survey', *Journal of the Royal Society of Antiquaries of Ireland* 100, 99-102; H.N. Savory, 1972, 'Copper Age cists and cist-cairns in Wales: with special reference to Newton, Swansea, and other 'multiple-cist' cairns', in Lynch and Burgess, 1972, 117-39 [n. 4].
116. Note food vessel burials in henges at Fargo Plantation, Wiltshire, (Stone, 1938 [n. 54]), and Cairnpapple, West Lothian (Piggott, 1947-8 [n. 67]), though in both cases the henge was probably built by beaker folk. Food vessels have been associated with stone circles, at Meini Gwyr, Pembrokeshire, for example: W.F. Grimes, 1963, 'The stone circles and related monuments of Wales', in I. Ll. Foster and L. Alcock, 1963, *Culture and Environment: Essays in Honour of Sir Cyril Fox* (London), 95, 101, 107, 141-3; and at several Scottish sites: Childe, 1935, 112 [n. 69].
117. The most spectacular of these markings are on rock outcrops, in circumstances where there is little chance of identifying the carver. But many are on slabs and boulders which have been used as cist covers or side slabs, or have otherwise been incorporated in graves or cairns. For the most part such contexts have food vessel associations, though beaker examples are known. Childe (1940, 126 [n. 14]) provides a convenient summary with references. Thus it is that cup-and-ring markings have generally been linked with food vessel users. But it should be noted that the cup-and-ring rocks incorporated in graves are often fragments broken from larger rocks. Such sepulchral associations need not reflect either their original use or context. It must be stressed that the function of cup-and-ring markings is unknown, their ancestry uncertain. Neolithic beginnings seem definite. A simple cup-marked stone was included in the long barrow at Dalladies, Kincardineshire (S. Piggott, 1972, 'Dalladies', *C. Arch.* 34, 295-6), and all the elements of cup-and-ring markings are to be found in Boyne art: G. Eogan, 1968, 'Excavations at Knowth,

Co. Meath, 1962-1965', *PRIA* 66c, 335-52.
118. S. Piggott, 1938, 'The Early Bronze Age in Wessex', *PPS* 4, 52-106.
119. Piggott, 1938, 61 [n. 118].
120. In Wessex graves such as those from Collingbourne Kingston G8, Wiltshire: F.K. Annable and D.D.A. Simpson, 1964, *Guide Catalogue of the Neolithic and Bronze Age Collections in Devizes Museum* (Devizes, Wiltshire Archaeological and Natural History Society), 64, 119, Figs. 515-18; and Stockbridge Down, Hampshire: J.F.S. Stone and N.G. Hill, 1940, 'A round barrow on Stockbridge Down, Hampshire', *Ant. J.* 20, 39-51. Further afield, from Oxteddle Bottom, Sussex: E.C. Curwen, 1954, *The Archaeology of Sussex*, 2nd ed. (London), 157-9, Fig. 42; many of the food vessel burials illustrated by Simpson (1968 [n. 46], e.g. Goodmanham CXV, Garton Slack 153, Folkton LXXI and Wharram Percy 7, all Yorkshire, Fig. 45, p. 99); Bedd Emlyn 3, Denbighshire: H.N. Savory, 1961, 'Bronze Age burials near Bedd Emlyn, Clocaenog', *Transactions of the Denbighshire Historical Society* 10, 7-22, Figs. 5-6; Bedd Branwen H, Anglesey: Lynch, 1971, 30-2, Fig. 10 [n. 75]; Embo, Sutherland: A.S. Henshall and J.C. Wallace, 1962-3, 'The excavation of a chambered cairn at Embo, Sutherland', *PSAS* 96, 23-4, Fig. 6: 1, 4, 6, 7; and Corrandrum, Cò. Galway: L.F. Chitty, 1934-5, 'Notes on Iberian affinities of a bone object found in County Galway', *Journal of the Galway Archaeological and Historical Society* 16, 125-33. This is merely a random selection of first category graves to illustrate their great geographical range.
121. e.g. G. Wilsford 7 and Upton Lovell G2(*e*), Wiltshire: Annable and Simpson, 1964, 44, 48, 98, 103, Figs. 147-158, 225-233 [n. 120].
122. C.F.C. Hawkes, 1972, 'Europe and England: fact and fog', *Helinium* 12, 113.
123. e.g. J.F.S. Stone, 1958, *Wessex* (London), 105-110; R.J.C. Atkinson, 1960, *Stonehenge*, 2nd ed. (Harmondsworth), 160-3; J.G.D. Clark, 1966, 'The invasion hypothesis in British Archaeology', *Antiquity* 40, 182-4; Lynch, 1970, 110 [n. 72]; J.M. Coles and J. Taylor, 1971, 'The Wessex culture: a minimal view', *Antiquity* 45, 13. But note some persistence of the immigration view, e.g. Annable and Simpson, 1964, 21 [n. 120]; Clarke, 1970, 279.
124. Undoubted Irish material of this period is practically unknown in Wessex, and influence from the continent (Brittany excepted) and the Mediterranean more often than not suggests the receipt of ideas rather than actual imports. The amount of exotic material in Wessex is no more than would be attracted naturally to an area rich in agriculture and manpower, dominated by an aristocracy with a liking for exotic trappings. The imported material need represent no more than a few shipments.
125. e.g. from Dorchester, Oxfordshire; Winterslow, Wiltshire; and Roundway, Wiltshire, conveniently illustrated together by H. Case, 1965, 'A tin-bronze in bell-beaker association', *Antiquity* 39, 219-22, Fig. 1.

126. e.g. craftsmen's graves of West Overton G6*b* type, Smith and Simpson, 1966, 129-41 [n. 22].
127. Notably in parts of Yorkshire and East Anglia. One might have added parts of Ireland, especially Co. Meath, except that this area apparently had no comparable beaker single grave tradition.
128. Piggott, 1938, 64-9 [n. 118]. Breton connections alone demand more than a commercial explanation. Alternative sources for an intrusive element in the Wessex culture have focussed on Germany and Poland, especially the Elbe-Saale-Warta area (e.g. V.G. Childe, 1957, *The Dawn of European Civilisation* (London), 320, 335; P. Ashbee, 1960, *The Bronze Age Round Barrow in Britain* (London), 140; Annable and Simpson, 1964, 21 [n. 120]; Clark, 1970, 279), but these seem less satisfactory, at least from the point of view of immediate origins, than Brittany.
129. Dagger graves, with Armorico-British daggers, on both sides of the Channel are strikingly similar, differences no more than 'sea change' and the strange geology and environment of Wessex would force on intruders from a stony land. The connections include the daggers, gold pin decoration, barbed and tanged arrowheads of Breton form, bone replica grooved daggers (cf. Lescongar, Finistère: J. Briard, 1969, 'Un tumulus du Bronze ancien à Lescongar en Plouhinec (Finistère)', *Gallia préhistoire* 11, 254-5; and Crug-yr-Afan, Glamorganshire: C.B. Burgess, 1962, 'Two grooved ogival daggers of the Early Bronze Age from South Wales', *Bulletin of the Board of Celtic Studies* 20, 78-82, Pl. II); and handled and carinated vessels, and dentated 'mounts' (bone at Bush Barrow, Wiltshire, gold at Kerlagat, Carnac: Z. Le Rouzic, 1930, 'Bijoux en or découverts dans les dolmens du Morbihan', *Revue des musées, fouilles et découvertes archéologiques* 30, Figs. 2-4). Movement in the reverse direction is perhaps suggested by the jet spacer bead in the grave from Kerguevarec, Finistère: S. Piggott, 1939, 'Further Bronze Age "dagger-graves" in Brittany', *PPS* 5, 193; and by the collared vessel from Tourony, C.-du-N.: J. Briard, 1965, *Les dépôts Bretons et l'age du bronze atlantique* (Rennes, Travaux du Laboratoire d'Anthropologie Préhistorique de la Faculté des Sciences), 290-1, Fig. 110.
130. A. Fleming, 1971, 'Territorial patterns in Bronze Age Wessex', *PPS* 37, 164. But something of this idea was already foreshadowed by Childe, 1940, 135 [n. 14]; and Childe, 1957, 334-6 [n. 128].
131. cf. A.M. ApSimon, 1954, 'Dagger graves in the "Wessex" Bronze Age', *University of London Institute of Archaeology Annual Report*, 51 (1550-1370); Hawkes, 1960 (1650/1600-1400); R.J.C. Atkinson, 1960, *A statistical consideration of the Wessex Culture*, unpublished lecture delivered to CBA Bronze Age Conference, London, December 1960 (1600-1400).
132. C. Renfrew, 1968, 'Wessex without Mycenae', *Annual of the British School of Archaeology at Athens* 63, 277-85.
133. For a summary of these supposed Mycenaean elements, Atkinson, 1960, 92-3, 163-6 [n. 123]; Annable and Simpson, 1964, 22-6 [n. 120].

134. R.G. Newton and C. Renfrew, 1970, 'British faience beads reconsidered', *Antiquity* 44, 199-206.
135. Coles and Taylor, 1971 [n. 123].
136. McKerrell, 1972, 293-7, Fig. 4. [n. 15].
137. McKerrell, 1972, 298-9 [n. 15].
138. McKerrell, 1972, 286-95 [n. 15]. Note also his claim that the gold wire pin technique must have been derived from the eastern Mediterranean, ibid., 300.
139. K. Branigan, 1970, 'Wessex and Mycenae: some evidence reviewed', *WAM* 65, 89-107.
140. P.R. Giot, 1971, 'The impact of radiocarbon dating on the establishment of the prehistoric chronology of Brittany', *PPS* 37, 212, 214, Fig. 3. The considerable number of dates available fails to indicate any chronological separation of the two series of Breton graves, confirming the impression that the difference involved, whatever their nature, were not chronological. The original elucidation of the two series (J. Cogne and P.-R. Giot, 1951, 'L'Age du Bronze ancien en Bretagne', *L'Anthropologie* 55, 425-44) made no claims that they were chronologically successive, but this idea has subsequently crept in: see P.-R. Giot, 1960, *Brittany* (London), 142-5. Simultaneously the tendency has developed to describe the first series as 'early bronze age', and the second series as 'middle bronze age' for reasons which have always seemed obscure on this side of the Channel, and which now seem at variance with the evidence both of C14 dates and associations: cf. J. Briard and P.-R. Giot, 1956, 'Typologie et chronologie du bronze ancien et du premier bronze moyen en Bretagne', *Bulletin de la société préhistorique française* 53, 370-3; also Giot, 1971, 214 [n. 140].
141. Coles and Taylor (1971, 10 [n. 123]) claim that at Ridgeway 7, Dorset, a dagger 'apparently related to the ogival type' was earlier than a Bush Barrow dagger, and that this provides stratigraphic evidence against the divisions usually postulated. But the earlier Ridgeway 7 dagger, while ogival in outline, is certainly not related to the Camerton-Snowshill type, and can have no bearing on the problem.
142. The chronological complexities, and longevity, of Únětice are now widely accepted, and in the present state of knowledge it seems risky to draw too many chronological conclusions from Únětice connections. Coles and Taylor themselves recognise the dangers of transplanting the Reinecke system to Britain (1971, 8 [n. 123]). C14 dates for Unetice are at present so few that it seems rash to regard those available as necessarily relevant to the whole span of the culture.
143. D. Britton, 1961, 'A study of the composition of Wessex Culture bronzes', *Archaeometry* 4, 41-4.
144. ApSimon, 1954 [n. 131]. Piggott in his pioneer survey of the material (1938 [n. 118]) made no formal attempt to sub-divide the material, but clearly thought that some of it represented an earlier, and some a later, phase.

145. Atkinson, 1960 [n. 131].

146. Unpublished PhD thesis, University of Oxford. But Dr Gerloff's classification of grooved daggers has been published in C.N. Moore and M. Rowlands, 1972, *Bronze Age Metalwork in Salisbury Museum* (Salisbury, Salisbury and South Wiltshire Museum Occasional Publication).

147. Aldbourne: W. Greenwell, 1890, 'Recent researches in barrows in Yorkshire, Wiltshire, Berkshire etc.', *Arch.* 52, 50-3; Piggott, 1938, 74, Fig. 12 [n. 118]. Edmondsham: E.V.W. Proudfoot, 1963, 'Report on the excavation of a bell barrow in the parish of Edmondsham, Dorset, England', 1959, *PPS* 29, 395-425.

148. e.g. Ashbee's Hove-Snowshill and Stourton-Loose Howe types (1960, 107-9, Fig. 33 [n. 128]). For a fuller and more recent survey of battle-axes, F.E.S. Roe, 'The battle-axe series in Britain', *PPS* 32, 199-245.

149. From Avebury, Wiltshire: Annable and Simpson, 1964, 69, 129, no.591 [n. 120]; and Beacon Hill, near Amesbury, Wiltshire: Moore and Rowlands, 1972, 52, Pl.VI, no.11 [n. 146].

150. e.g. Wilsford G23, Wiltshire, with Bush-Barrow and Bush-Barrow-related daggers appropriate to the Bush Barrow group; and perforated whetstone and crutch-headed pin more characteristic of the Aldbourne-Edmondsham group: most conveniently in Annable and Simpson, 1964, 44-5, 98, nos. 163-7 [n. 120].

151. Britton, 1963, 284-97. Distribution patterns of Arreton bronzes suggest that it was largely an extra-Wessex phenomenon, centred in eastern and south-eastern England. Camerton-Snowshill daggers alone amongst its products were acquired in quantity by Wessex warriors: Burgess in C.B. Burgess and J.D. Cowen, 1972, 'The Ebnal hoard and Early Bronze Age metalworking traditions', in Lynch and Burgess, 1972, 175-8, Figs. 6, 7 [n. 4].

152. Compare Hawkes, 1960; Case, 1966.

153. Iberia and central Europe have been the most favoured sources. Iberian origins have been linked with movements of megalith builders, especially with passage graves: cf. Childe, 1940, 116 [n. 14]. Links with wedge-shaped gallery-graves, and thus with Brittany, have also been sought. For a summary of these possibilities, Case, 1966, 166-8. A further possibility for Atlantic origins is provided by the spread of maritime beaker folk, which touched parts of Ireland and western Britain: Piggott, 1963, 62-4.

154. Notably Case, 1966.

155. But the beaker situation in Ireland differed generally from that in Britain. The beaker single-grave tradition is largely unknown in Ireland, and a majority of beaker finds there have settlement associations. This contrasts directly with the British state of affairs, and at present its significance is difficult to interpret.

156. With another possible tanged knife in the hoard from Whitespots, Co. Down. The Knocknague and Whitespots hoards are figured together by Case, 1966, 162-3, Fig. 13; and P. Harbison, 1969a, *The Daggers and the Halberds of the Early Bronze Age in Ireland*

(Prähistorische Bronzefunde, VI/I, Munich), Fig. 1,A,B. See also P. Harbison, 1968, 'Catalogue of Irish Early Bronze Age associated finds containing copper or bronze', *PRIA* 67C, 53, 58, 85, Fig. 26, 91, Fig. 32.

157. Case, 1966, 149, 166.

158. Case, 1966, 160-1, Fig. 12.

159. Case, 1966, 166-8.

160. e.g. in Wales this is suggested by vagaries in the analyses of local copper implements, which tend not to conform with what would be expected of Irish copper-work (author's unpublished work). Further, some Welsh halberds exhibit distinctive local 'tricks' not matched in Ireland, notably a splaying upper midrib: S.P. O'Riordain, 1937, 'The halberd in Bronze Age Europe', *Arch.* 86, 276.

161. Case, 1966, 142-52; Coles, 1968-9, 2-29.

162. AB axes are indistinguishable from ordinary A thick-butt axes in general character and form, except that they substitute the thin butt. For AB axes, Coles, 1968-9, 2. Note that Case describes such axes as 'of type A shape in plan but with thin butts', and uses 'AB' in quite a different way to denote thick butt axes with a type B plan shape: Case, 1966, 150. The present writer prefers to follow Coles in this as in other aspects of flat axe development.

163. For detailed discussion of copper flat axe types, Case, 1966, 142-9; Coles, 1968-9, 2-10.

164. The basic form broadly equates with Coles' Ba axes, the embellished versions with his Bb and Bc implements: Coles, 1968-9, 7-26, Figs. 5-21.

165. For a discussion of the features which supposedly betray the 'impact' of B axes on A, Case, 1966, 150.

166. Coles, 1968-9, 10.

167. Some of these features, e.g. the distinctive splayed shape, could have developed gradually from post-casting hammering of straight forms. It may be significant that associations of A and AB axes are fairly common, but seldom have either been found with B axes: Harbison, 1968 [n. 156].

168. Case, 1966, 147, Fig. 4: 1, 2; Harbison, 1968, 45, 70, Fig. 11: 64-5 [n. 156], for full references.

169. P. Harbison, 1969*b*, *The Axes of the Early Bronze Age in Ireland* (Prähistorische Bronzefunde IX/I. Munich), 70-83; 1969*a*, 20-26 [n. 156]; 1969*c*, 'The relative chronology of Irish Early Bronze Age pottery', *Journal of the Royal Society of Antiquaries of Ireland* 99, 63-6.

170. Case, 1966, 155-66, 168; 1965 [n. 125].

171. No corpus exists, but the writer has records of 16 copper axes from Wales and the Marches and 9 for northern England, while Coles lists 15 for Scotland. The total for the whole of Britain is hardly likely to be more than 70-80, which compares with over 500 for Ireland: Harbison, 1969*b*, 10-24 [n. 169].

172. See n.160.

173. Available C14 dates suggest that Reinecke A2 metalworking was

already under way by c.19th century BC (after calibration), and the background of Migdale metalworking pre-dates this in A1. Note the C14 date from Mount Pleasant, Dorset, of 1778 ± 59 bc (BM-646) for a sample immediately below an embellished type B flat axe appropriate to Stage IV: R. Burleigh, I.H. Longworth and G.J. Wainwright, 1972, 'Relative and absolute dating of four late Neolithic enclosures: an exercise in the interpretation of radiocarbon determinations', *PPS* 38, 398; G.J. Wainwright, 1970, 'Mount Pleasant', *C. Arch.* 12, 320-4.

174. 'Narrow-butt' seems a safer blanket label for Group B than 'thin-butt' in view of the Group A axes with thin butts.

175. Group B axes surely represent a logical development from Group A, via AB, and the present writer, like Coles (1968-9, 10) can see no need to envisage an over-riding central European influence. Exotic contribution there may have been, but it was surely incidental to the basic development.

176. Coles, 1968-9, 70-1.

177. Or possibly late A1; but the dangers of transposing a central European scheme to Britain have already been noted (n. 142).

178. Since no moulds are known for many Migdale types, notably halberds, the use of less durable moulds, probably of clay, also seems likely.

179. e.g. riveted knives of Piggott's Group 1, and smaller examples of Group II: Piggott, 1963, 82-4, Fig. 18; and tanged blades of Kirkcaldy type (S. Piggott and M. Stewart, 1958, 'Early and Middle Bronze Age grave-groups and hoards from Scotland', *Inventaria Archaeologica* GB 5, 32), which compare well with A1 blades such as those from the Vyčapy-Opatovce and Abraham cemeteries, Slovakia: most conveniently in M. Gimbutas, 1965, *Bronze Age Cultures in Central and Eastern Europe* (The Hague), 40, Fig. 10: 21-2, Pl. 3: 3-4. Such blades must surely have contributed to the development of our early bronze age tanged razors.

180. e.g. sheet metal button covers, tubular sheet beads, basket ear-rings, incised armlets, and repousséed sheet metal, especially armlets. Most of these types are represented in the Migdale hoard: Piggott and Stewart, 1958, GB 26 [n. 179]; Coles, 1968-9, 50-3, Fig. 39. For the central European background, Gimbutas, 1965, 40, Fig. 10, 41, Fig. 11, 252-5, Figs. 162-164, Pls. 3, 39 [n. 179].

181. J.J. Taylor, 1970, 'Lunulae reconsidered', *PPS* 36, 38-81.

182. Coles, 1968-9, 51.

183. e.g. tubular sheet beads were included in a grave with segmented faience beads at the Mound of the Hostages, Tara, Co. Meath, suggesting a date contemporary with Aldbourne-Edmondsham burials in Wessex, when Stage V was under way: S.P. O'Riordain, 1955, 'A burial with faience beads at Tara', *PPS* 21, 163-73. Note too the occasional association of simple B axes, nominally of Stage III, with embellished versions of Stage IV, as at Brithdir, Glamorganshire: R.E.M. Wheeler, 1925, *Prehistoric and Roman Wales* (Oxford), 140.

184. Harbison, 1969*a*, 1969*b* [n. 169]. Note that the crucial hoard from Killaha East, Co. Kerry, combines Stage III flat axes with a Stage IV grooved dagger: S.P. O'Riordain, 1946, 'Prehistory in Ireland, 1937-46', *PPS* 12, 155, Pl. 12.

185. Britton, 1963, 284-97; Burgess and Cowen, 1972 [n. 151].

186. It is difficult to estimate the extent of the Sögel contribution to such major Arreton types as flanged axes and Camerton-Snowshill daggers, but tangible evidence of Sögel influence is provided by Arreton flanged axes with 'nicked' sides, e.g. in the Westbury-on-Trym hoard, Gloucestershire (B.R.S. Megaw and E.M. Hardy, 1938, 'British decorated axes and their diffusion during the earlier part of the Bronze Age', *PPS* 4, 284, Fig. 11*d*), and the Postlingford Hall hoard, Suffolk (in the British Museum: full refs. in Britton, 1963, 317).

187. Almost invariably with solid-cast blade of complex form, but once with plain leaf-shaped blade with midrib: Britton, 1963, 288-9, Fig. 19, Pl.XXVII.

188. Other Arreton products included chisel-like tools of bar and lugged forms, collared tanged spearheads, heavy ribbed daggers, possibly dress pins based on central European patterns, and, no doubt, less distinctive types such as awls, riveted knives and tanged razors, which turn up in the graves of this period. See Britton, 1963, 286-9, though some of the supposedly Arreton products listed there, notably end-looped spearheads, are now seen to be appropriate to other industries: Burgess and Cowen, 1972, 172-9 [n. 151].

189. Burgess, in Burgess and Cowen, 1972, 178-9 [n. 151].

190. ibid., 174-5, 178-9; for 'end-looped' spearheads, Burgess, 1962, 85 [n. 129].

191. Piggott and Stewart, 1958, GB 28 [n. 179]; Coles, 1968-9, 74, Pl. 3.

192. Burgess, 1962, 87-94 [n. 129]; Burgess and Cowen, 1972 [n. 151]; for the Menai Bridge hoard, Lynch, 1970, 182-4, Fig. 60 [n. 72].

193. Burgess in G. Jobey et al., 1965, 'An Early Bronze Age burial on Reaverhill Farm, Barrasford, Northumberland', *Archaeologia Aeliana*, 4 ser. 43, 74-5; also in Burgess and Cowen, 1972, 179 [n. 151]. Compare Coles, 1968-9, 73-6.

194. Witness stone sources where production seems only to have started in the early bronze age, as indicated by grouped rocks whose products are all perforated battle-axes or axe-hammers. The notable example is Group XII, Hyssington/Cwm Mawr picrite: F.W. Shotton, L.F. Chitty and W.A. Seaby, 1951, 'A new centre of stone axe dispersal on the Welsh border', *PPS* 17, 159-67; E.D. Evens, I.F. Smith and F.S. Wallis, 1972, 'The petrological identification of stone implements from south-western England', *PPS* 38, 257.

195. Flat and flanged axes were replaced by palstaves and short-flanged axes, tanged and solid-blade socketed spearheads by fully-socketed (hollow midrib) spearheads, riveted knives and daggers by dirks and rapiers. Only basic types such as chisels, lugged tools and tanged razors survived.

196. Bivalve and core casting were already known in the early bronze age, but socketed spearheads with hollow midribs perhaps imply a better grasp of core-casting techniques. Further, the first bronze moulds appear after the hiatus (e.g. mould for Group I Anglo-Welsh palstaves from 'Ireland': Gough's ed. of Camden's *Britannia* (1789), 477, Pl. 38: 10. In the National Museum of Antiquities, Dublin), implying at least new technical refinements: R.F. Tylecote, 1962, *Metallurgy in Archaeology* (London), 123-8.

197. Notably Thom, 1967, 1971 [n. 42]. The literature on this subject is now considerable, and a list of relevant sources would be most desirable.

198. Godwin (1960, 31 [n. 5]) interpolated a date of *c.* 1350 BC for the beginning on the basis of C14 dates from the Somerset levels. As this chapter goes to press, a note by Professor Piggott has been published which is in broad agreement with the arguments presented here for an earlier start to the deterioration: S. Piggott, 1972, 'A note on climatic deterioration in the first millennium BC in Britain', *Scottish Archaeological Forum* 4, 109-13. Note too the percipient remarks of Curwen (1954, 155 [n. 120]), placing the onset of wetter conditions at the early middle bronze age transition, thereby anticipating one of the essential conclusions of the present contribution.

199. Ashbee, 1963 [n. 58]; 1966, 'The dating of the Wilsford shaft', *Antiquity* 40, 227-8; S. Piggott, 1965, *Ancient Europe* (Edinburgh), 232; A. Ross, 1968, 'Shafts, pits, wells — sanctuaries of the Belgic Britons?', in Coles and Simpson, 1968, 256-7 [n. 46].

200. I am grateful to Frances Lynch (Mrs Llewellyn) for the suggestion that this interest in water may already have been anticipated in the early bronze age, on the strength of the siting of certain cairns in Wales close to springs and rising streams.

201. C. Fox, 1946, *A Find of the Early Iron Age from Llyn Cerrig Bach, Anglesey* (Cardiff, National Museum of Wales), 69-70; Piggott, 1965, 230-1, with note 36 [n. 199]; A. Ross, 1967, *Pagan Celtic Britain* (London), 19-33. The proportion of certain categories of middle and late bronze age metalwork with 'wet' provenances is striking, e.g. up to 80% of the 1100 dirks and rapiers from the British Isles (C.B. Burgess, 1971, 'The Bronze Age dirks and rapiers of Britain and Ireland', lecture to Prehistoric Society, London, 13 March, 1971). It is instructive to compare the find places of early bronze age hoards in Scotland and Ireland, usually in cairns, barrows, under stones or in rock clefts or caves, with the wet find spots of so many middle and late bronze age hoards: Harbison, 1968 [n. 156]; Eogan, 1964; Coles, 1959-60, 1963-4, 1968-9. Compare, too, the find spots of early bronze age riveted knives and daggers, so often in graves, with the 'wet' provenances of the dirks which replaced them.

202. c.f. R.J.C. Atkinson, 1972, 'Burial and population in the British Bronze Age', in Lynch and Burgess, 1972, 112 [n. 4]; citing G.W. Dimbleby, 1962, *The Development of British Heathlands and their*

*Soils* (Oxford). See also I.G. Simmons, 1969, 'Environment and early man on Dartmoor, Devon, England', *PPS* 35, 203-19.

203. See Thom, 1971, *passim* [n. 42]; also 1954, 'The solar observatories of megalithic man', *Journal of the British Astronomical Association* 64, 397; 1958, 'An empirical investigation of atmospheric refraction', *Empirical Survey Review* 14, 248. I am indebted to Dr G. Hulme, Department of Environmental Sciences, Lancaster University, for his comments on these problems.

204. Mam Tor: D. Coombs, 1971, 'Mam Tor: a Bronze Age hill-fort?', *C. Arch.* 27, 100-2; Kaimes: D.D.A. Simpson, 1969, 'Excavations at Kaimes hillfort, Midlothian, 1964-68', *Glasgow Archaeological Journal* 1, 7-28.

205. The vast majority of the enormous quantities of metal finds from these regions, including much of the finest material ever found in Britain, has come from the rivers, streams, pools and marshes of these regions. B.A.V. Trump, 1968, 'Fenland rapiers', in Coles and Simpson, 1968, 222 [n. 46].

206. Rich grave groups, e.g. Bedd Branwen H, Anglesey (Lynch, 1971, 32, Fig. 10 [n. 75]), Llanddyfnan, Anglesey (Lynch, 1970, 140-4, Fig. 48 [n. 72]), and Bryn Crug, Caernarvonshire (Wheeler, 1925, 146, Fig. 48 [n. 183]). Evidence for lowland English contacts includes the Menai Bridge hoard, Anglesey: Lynch, 1970, 182-4, Fig. 60 [n. 72]; Irish contact represented by the Bodwrdin stone mould for end-looped spearheads, Anglesey: Burgess and Cowen, 1972, 179 [n. 151]; Lynch 1970, 185-9, Fig. 62 [n. 72].

207. T.G.E. Powell, 1953, 'The gold ornament from Mold, Flintshire, north Wales', *PPS* 19, 161-79. The mere fact that this was a rich burial with gold and amber suggests that it belonged to the early bronze age, and technical and stylistic comparisons can be made with such early bronze age repoussé sheet metal ornaments as the Melfort armlet, the Migdale strip (Piggott and Stewart, 1958, GB 25-6 [n. 179]) and the Masterton armlets (A.S. Henshall and J.C. Wallace, 1962-3, 'A Bronze Age cist burial at Masterton, Pitreavie, Fife', *PSAS* 96, 149-50, Fig. 3). But Powell, 1953, noted that the best continental parallels were middle bronze age. As long as the piece is unique, no certain answer is possible.

208. Apart from ornament hoards, middle bronze age hoards are practically unknown in Ireland: Eogan, 1962 [n. 12]; 1964, 268-88. In Britain the majority of middle bronze age hoards belongs to the central Taunton phase. There is a scattering of important associations belonging to the subsequent Penard phase, but hoards of the opening Acton Park phase are almost unknown outside north Wales.

209. For the chronology of the various looped spearhead forms, Burgess, 1968*a*, 3, 19-22; 1968*b*, 38; Their later history is very much better documented than their beginnings. Side-looped, socket-looped, and leaf basal-looped spearheads are likely to have had a life of 600-700 years.

210. Anglo-Welsh palstaves can be divided into five main groups: cf.

C.B. Burgess, 1964, 'A palstave from Chepstow: with some observations on the earliest palstaves of the British Isles', *Monmouthsire Antiquary* 1, 123,n.7. This considers the Group I (shield-pattern) and II (early midribbed) palstaves of the Acton Park phase. For later developments, Group III (low-flanged and south-western), IV ('transitional') and V ('late'), see Smith, 1959. An important work on Anglo-Welsh palstaves is Butler, 1963, 48-73. The Irish series parallels the Anglo-Welsh series in general stylistic and chronological terms, but shows distinctive local treatment, notably the preponderance of small, squat forms, undercut stops and massive casting seams. Group A corresponds with Anglo-Welsh Group I, Group B with Group II, Group C has low-flanged and high-flanged variants, like Anglo-Welsh Group III, and Group D matches Group IV. Irish palstave development ceased with Group D implements, local smiths producing no equivalent to Anglo-Welsh Group V.

211. C.B. Burgess, 1968, 'Bronze Age dirks and rapiers as illustrated by examples from Durham and Northumberland', *Transactions of the Architectural and Archaeological Society of Durham and Northumberland*, new ser. 1, 3-26.

212. e.g. the Acton Park phase in Wales probably lasted longer than its equivalent in southern England (Author, unpublished research: see n. 239).

213. E. Sprockhoff, 1941, 'Niedersachsens Bedeutung für die Bronzezeit Westeuropas', *Bericht der Römisch-Germanischen Kommission* 31, II Teil, 45-50, taf. 24-31; Butler, 1963, 59-62, 212-5, 267, map 3.

214. Briard, 1965, 79-108 [n. 129].

215. e.g. Group II rapier in the hoard from Cascina Ranza, Milan: Sprockhoff, 1941, 70-2, taf. 37:6 [n. 213]; Burgess, 1968, 11-12 [n. 211].

216. Sprockhoff, 1941 [n. 213]; Butler, 1963 [n. 213]. Whether these represent imports from Britain, local copies, or the presence of itinerant Anglo-Welsh smiths, is difficult to ascertain. A combination of these circumstances seems likely. For the best summary, Butler, ibid., 60-1. Some examples might even be north-west French and not Anglo-Welsh at all, the two series being generally identical.

217. E. Davies, 1929, *The Prehistoric and Roman Remains of Denbighshire* (Cardiff), 50.

218. Sprockhoff, 1941, taf. 26 [n. 213]; J.J. Butler, 1959, 'Vergeten schatvondsten uit de Bronstijd', in *Honderd Eeuwen Nederland (Antiquity and Survival II)*, 125-42; 1960, 'A Bronze Age concentration at Bargeroosterveld, with some notes on the axe trade across northern Europe', *Palaeohistoria* 8, 120: 1963, 51-3, 60-2, Fig. 11.

219. Butler, 1959, 1960, 1963 [n. 218].

220. The Acton Park hoard originally contained a dagger blade, but this no longer survives, and nothing is known of its form.

221. G. Jacob-Friesen, 1967, *Bronzezeitliche Lanzenspitzen Nord-*

*deutschlands und Skandinaviens* (Hildersheim), taf. 46: 9.

222. The hoard from Lessart, La Vicomté-sur-Rance, C. du-N., has both a Group II dirk and a Wohlde dirk, the type directly ancestral to Group II weapons: Briard, 1965, 89, 91, 104-5, Fig. 26: 1, 6, 8, 9 [n. 129]. See also Burgess, 1968, 11-12 [n. 211]. The Tréboul hoard itself also has fragments of Group II dirks or rapiers: Briard, 1965, 93, Fig. 29: 1, 3, 4 [n. 129].

223. See n. 215.

224. Briard, 1965, 86-94, Figs. 26-28 [n. 129]. Burgess, 1968, 7-8 [n. 211].

225. e.g. the hoards from Tréboul (Group I palstaves of heavy north Welsh form: Briard, 1965; 85, Fig. 24 [n. 129]; but not showing the true character of these pieces); Kergadiou, Fin. (Group II palstave, Penmarc'h Museum: Briard, 1965, 311, no. 244 [n. 129]; Mangouro, Morbihan (Group I palstave, Vannes Museum: Briard, 1965, 318, no. 425 [n. 129]): and Plouguerneau, Fin. (Group I palstaves, thin-bladed flanged axe: Briard, 1965, 85, Fig. 24: 6, 7; 311, no. 235 [n. 129]. For bar-stop axes and another thin-bladed flanged axe, Briard, 1965, 83, Fig. 23 [n. 129].

226. Except where a specific regional form is concerned, such as the heavy Acton Park Group I palstaves of north Wales. But future work on French palstaves may make it necessary to qualify even this conclusion. For north French palstaves, other than Breton examples, see H. Breuil, 1905, 'L'Age du Bronze dans le Bassin de Paris: V.-Haches du Bassin de la Somme', *L'Anthropologie* 16, 149-71; and J-P. Mohen, 1972, 'Que savons-nous de l'Age du Bronze dans le Nord de la France?', *Bulletin de la société préhistorique francaise* 69, 444-64.

227. As there are no other spearhead types which could have been current in this period, the alternative would be to envisage a period without spearheads. Neither side-looped nor leaf basal-looped spearheads are attested in the British hoard record until the succeeding Taunton phase, but in view of the scarcity of hoards of the Acton Park phase, this need not be significant.

228. A Group I palstave of the heavy Acton Park form from Waterford (Ulster Museum, Belfast, 239-1937) is from the same mould as one from 'North Wales' (British Museum, Sloane Coll. 315). A specimen from Broughshane, Co. Antrim, may also come from this mould (Ulster Museum, Belfast, Grainger Collection 1507). The bronze mould for Group I palstaves from Ireland (n. 196 above) suggests the possibility of itinerant Welsh smiths in Ireland.

229. Comparative little work has been carried out on the developed or short-flanged axes which were an alternative axe form in middle bronze age Ireland, and the main form in northern England and Scotland. The pioneer work is Smith, 1959. 168-75, who distinguished haft-flanged and wing-flanged versions. Knowledge of their development, particularly the early stages, is hampered by an extreme shortage of associated finds. Typology suggests that features such as a broad, splaying form, nicked or shouldered sides,

comparatively long, low flanges (generally, but not always, convex), and shield-pattern ornament, should be early, and this is confirmed by the only example in an Acton Park Context, in the Battlefield hoard, Shropshire (Shrewsbury Museum: L.F. Chitty, 1943, 'Two bronze palstaves from Llandrinio, Montgomeryshire', *Transactions of the Shropshire Archaeological Society* 51, 150). Conversely, examples with a narrow, straight form, with short, high, angular flanges, should be late, and this is confirmed by the form of the short-flanged axes in several hoards of the Taunton phase, e.g. Hotham Carr, Yorkshire (Burgess, 1968a 3-6, Fig. 3), 'Tredarvah, Cornwall' (H.L. Douch, 1964, 'Tredarvah, Penzance', *Cornish Archaeology* 3, 85); Glentrool, Kircudbrightshire; Balcarry, Wigtown; and Caldonshill, Wigtown (the last three conveniently accessible together in Coles, 1963-4, 121, Fig. 16, 123, Fig. 17, 153, 155-6. Smith's 'Haft-flanged' and 'wing-flanged' terms may be conveniently retained for these respective groups.

230. Since the great majority of the enormous numbers of Irish middle bronze age axes are unprovenanced, it is impossible to plot more than token distribution maps. This is a problem which affects Irish bronze age metalwork of all types and phases.

231. H.H. Coghlan and J. Raftery, 1961, 'Irish Prehistoric casting moulds', *Sibrium* 6, 232-3, 239-41, tav. 8, 9, 16, 17, 19, 20.

232. There is, however, no relevant hoard evidence.

233. Burgess, 1968, 3-5, Fig. 2: 3-4. In northern England this was the Pickering phase, Burgess, ibid., in Scotland Coles' Caverton phase: Coles, 1963-4, 83-94, 126-8; Group I Anglo-Welsh palstaves, Fig. 3: 4, 6 (not Class II flanged axes of the Haddington group as claimed by Coles).

234. e.g. from Branthwaite and Penrith, Cumberland, and 'Scotland', Burgess, 1968a, 4, Fig. 2: 1, 2; Coles, 1963-4, 91, Fig. 3:5.

235. J. Evans, 1881, *The Ancient Bronze Implements, Weapons, and Ornaments, of Great Britain and Ireland* (London), 434-5, Figs. 520-1.

236. Burgess, 1964 [n. 210]. There is an interesting concentration of Group II palstaves in the southern part of Wales, however, especially the south-east, providing an interesting contrast with north Wales and its mass of Group I implements: Burgess, ibid., 121-2, Fig. 2.

237. Weapons, especially dirks, rapiers and spearheads, are particularly common, but Group I and II palstaves, bar-stop axes and even short-flanged axes are plentiful (see Smith, 1959, 174, map 4 for distribution of last). In quantity and fineness of workmanship of dirks, rapiers and spearheads, these areas alone in Britain can rival Ireland.

238. Butler, 1963, 62-5, Fig. 16, 215-18. This is the usually accepted position and chronology of the Frøjk-Ostenfeld group, but one has to admit some worry at the sophisticated form of some of the 'British' palstaves in the Frøjk-Ostenfeld hoards if they are indeed as early as this; witness an example in the Ostenfeld hoard, Butler, 1963, 64, Fig. 16: 6.

239. This observation is based partly on the greater proportion of Acton Park phase to Taunton phase material, especially palstaves, in Wales and the Marches, compared with southern England; and also on a detailed study of Welsh low-flanged palstaves, whose sophistication, compared with southern examples, suggests a late introduction, fully developed, from the south (author's unpublished research).

240. For northern contacts, E. Sprockhoff, 1937, *Jungbronzezeitliche Hortfunde Norddeutschlands: Periode IV* (Kataloge des Römisch-Germanischen Zentral-Museums, Mainz), 12, 57-8. For summaries of the north German connections of this period, Smith, 1959, 144-64: Butler, 1963, 75-81, 136-50, 155-8, 218-23. But France can also provide parallels for much of the material involved, and French links, which were two-way, have perhaps been seriously underestimated. Briard (1965, 116-35 [n. 129]), and M.J. Rowlands, 1971, 'A group of incised decorated armrings and their significance for the Middle Bronze Age of southern Britain', in G. de G. Sieveking (ed.), 1971, *Prehistoric and Roman Studies (British Museum Quarterly* 35), 183-99, have dealt with the decorated armlets that form one aspect of this problem. But as well as these Bignan-type armlets, twisted torcs and armlets, ribbed bracelets, plain penannular armlets, ribbon torcs, cones, knobbed sickles and slender socketed axes/chisels, hammers and punches can all be found in France, some of them in considerably quantities: see hoard from Malassis, Cher (J. Briard, G. Cordier and G. Gaucher, 1969, 'Un dépôt de la fin du Bronze Moyen à Malassis, Commune de Chéry (Cher)', *Gallia préhistoire* 12, 37-73) which has decorated, twisted and plain armlets, ribbed bracelets and sickles in quantity, and also bronze cones. Much new work is needed to determine the nature of this triangular north German-French-south British connection. The scarcity of British/French material in north Germany should be significant.

241. Smith, 1959.

242. Twisted torcs and armlets, ribbed bracelets and rings, plain penannular armlets, especially of lozenge section, incised-decorated armlets, coiled finger-rings and bronze cones: Smith, 1959,.

243. e.g. Ribbon torcs and armlets, Sussex loops, and quoit pins: Smith, 1959.

244. Slender socketed axes/chisels of Hademarschen type: Sprockhoff, 1941, 112 [n. 213]; Butler, 1963, 75-81; Burgess, 1962 [n. 13]; socketed hammers and punches, saws and knobbed sickles: Smith, 1959.

245. e.g. hoards of low-flanged palstaves from Sucy-en-Brie, S.-et-O. (J.P. Mohen, 1968, 'Les bronzes protohistoriques de Paris et de sa région au Musée de l'Armée (Invalides)', *Bulletin de la société préhistorique française* 65, 783-8, Pl. 3-5) and Pointhoile, Somme (Breuil, 1905, 151-6, Fig. 3 [n. 226]. This is the local Baux-Saint-Croix — Mont-Saint-Aignan phase (Burgess, 1968, 13 [n. 211]), both these type hoards having low-flanged palstaves.

246. For Portrieux palstaves, Briard's *haches à talon à tranchant étroit* (1965, 109-22 [n. 129]), and their distribution in Britain, C.B. Burgess, 1970, 'Breton Palstaves from the British Isles', *Arch. J.* 126, 149-53.

247. As reflected not only in palstaves and ornaments (n. 240, 245, 246), but also rapiers. Here too the north-west French product was indistinguishable from the British: compare the Malassis hoard again, with large numbers of rapiers identical with Irish/British Group III, as well as the ornaments and sickles noted above (n. 240). This hoard also contains a fragment of an Irish/British basal-looped spearhead, considerable numbers of Portrieux palstaves, and a few low-flanged palstaves: Briard, Cordier and Gaucher, 1969 [n. 240]. Whereas low-flanged palstaves and rapiers may have been in parallel production on both sides of the Channel, other products may have been traded, e.g. Portrieux palstaves from Brittany to Britain and looped spearheads from Britain to France: J. Briard, 1963, 'Pointes de lance de type Britannique découvertes en Bretagne. Leur répartition en France', *L'Anthropologie* 67, 571-8.

248. Burgess, 1968, 12-15 [n. 211].

249. For lists of relevant moulds, Tylecote, 1962, 114-15, 124 [n. 196]. These of course are the surviving moulds, and the possibility of more fragile moulds being used, notably of clay, remains as uncertain in this, as in earlier phases.

250. Comprising low-flanged palstave, Group II, III and IV rapiers, slender-looped socketed chisel or axe, and pegged leaf spearhead. I am indebted to D.G. Davies for drawing my attention to this find, to Mr and Mrs Morgan of Orsett Hall for their kindness in allowing me to draw the hoard when it was in their possession, and to W. Rodwell for all his help in this matter. The hoard is now in Thurrock Museum, and I am grateful to the curator, D.A. Wickham, for further information about the find.

251. This is the local Cemmaes-Deansfield phase: C.B. Burgess, 1962, 'The Bronze Age in Radnorshire: a re-appraisal', *Transactions of the Radnorshire Society* 32, 19. See also Lynch, 1970, 195-6 [n. 72]. The enormous rapier hoard from Beddgelert, Caernarvonshire, shows that the region was still metallurgically important, its brilliance dimmed only relatively by the rise of vigorous new metalworking centres: Royal Commisson on the Ancient and Historical Monuments in Wales and Monmouthshire, 1960, *Caernarvonshire: Volume II: Central* (London), liv, Fig. 13: 3-8.

252. Savory, 1958, 6-14.

253. Eogan, 1962, 47-58 [n. 12]; 1964, 277-88.

254. O'Riordain, 1946, 161 [n. 184]; Eogan, 1964, 273-7, Fig. 5.

255. G. Coffey and E.C.R. Armstrong, 1914, 'Find of bronze objects at Annesborough, Co. Armagh', *PRIA* 32c, 171-5; Eogan, 1964, 273-4, Fig. 4.

256. i.e. Group C palstaves and wing-flanged axes were developed from Group A and B and haft-flanged axes respectively, Group III then IV dirks and rapiers appeared, and socket-looped and leaf basal-looped

spearheads remained in production: Eogan, 1964, 268-72.
257. As in such magnificent Group III rapiers as that from Lissane, Co. Derry; Evans, 1881, 252, Fig. 318 [n.235].
258. Coles, 1963-4, 117-18, 122-6: Auchterhouse and Glentrool phases. Burgess, 1968a, 3, 5.
259. Burgess, 1968a, 3-5, Fig. 3. The hoard combines a local wing-flanged axe, local versions of Anglo-Welsh low-flanged palstaves, an Irish Group C palstave, and three unusual axes hybrid between Group C palstaves, and wing-flanged axes. Two of these were cast in a bronze mould found in the hoard, which represents south English-Welsh influence.
260. cf. Gimbutas, 1965, 113-31, 296-339 [n. 179] Piggott, 1965, 146-60 [n. 199] Powell, T.G.E., 1963, 'The inception of the Final Bronze Age in Middle Europe', *PPS* 29, 214-34. The earliest urnfields, of Reinecke D, have usually been dated from the 13th century, but Sandars has recently argued for beginnings not earlier than the 12th century: N.K. Sanders, 1971, 'From Bronze Age to Iron Age: a sequel to a sequel', in J. Boardman, M.A. Brown and T.G.E. Powell (eds.), 1971, *The European Community in Later Prehistory* (London), 3-18, 24-5, chronological tables.
261. Burgess, 1968a, 5, 7; 1968b, 3-9, 34-6, Figs. 1-7.
262. C. Fox, 1939, 'The socketed bronze sickles of the British Isles', *PPS* 5, 223-36, 243-7; see also Burgess, 1968b, 3, note 12. And even more outlandish experiments were produced, such as the socketed palstaves of north Wales; Burgess, 1968b, 3; Lynch, 1970, 197-8, Fig. 64 [n. 72].
263. Burgess, 1968b, 34, with note 6.
264. Burgess, 1968b, 3, 44, with further refs. For rod-tanged swords, V.B. Peroni, 1970, *Die Schwerter in Italien* (Prähistorische Bronzefunde IV/I, Munich, 26-39, taf. 8-12). For general problems of Rixheim and rod-tanged swords, N.K. Sandars, 1957, *Bronze Age Cultures in France* (London), 61, 85-7, 98, 100, 112-13, 120, 125-9, 149-50, 173-4; Figs. 19, 20, Pl. 5 (Rixheim swords), Pl.7 (rod-ranged swords).
265. J.D. Cowen, 1951, 'The earliest bronze swords in Britain and their origins on the Continent of Europe', *PPS* 17, 195-213.
266. Ferrules: Sprockhoff, 1937, 30-1 [n. 240]; Coles, 1959-60, 24; Butler, 1963, 133-4. Curved knives, notably in the Ffynhonnau hoard, Breconshire: Savory, 1958, 27-8, Fig. 3; Burgess, 1968b, 5, Fig. 2. Compare knives from Aulnay-aux-Planches, Marne (Sandars, 1957, 166-7, Fig. 39: 8 [n. 264]), and Cannes-Ecluse dépôt 1, S.-et-M. (G. Gaucher and Y. Robert, 1967, 'Les dépôts de bronze de Cannes-Ecluse (Seine-et-Marne)', *Gallia préhistoire* 10, Fig. 23: 1). This hoard also contains rod-tanged and Rosnöen swords (Fig. 24), and broken objects suspiciously like cylinder-socket sickles (Fig. 41: 3, 12).
267. Burgess, 1962, 22 [n. 13]; 1968b, 5, 34, Fig. 2: 2 (Penard hoard); R.J. Mercer, 1970, 'Metal arrow-heads in the European Bronze and Early Iron Ages', *PPS* 36, 190-4.

268. The traditional view has favoured an early beginning for shields, in Ha A/M IV, and an early urnfield background, e.g. Butler, 1963, 127-31. But Coles in his survey (J.M. Coles, 1962, 'European Bronze Age shields', *PPS* 28, 156-90) can find no evidence for their beginning before late urnfields, the Ewart Park phase, Ha/B3/M/V. However, a recent early urnfield shield find, in a Reinecke D hoard from Nyírtura, Hungary, confirms the traditional early beginnings: P. Patay, 1968, 'Urnenfelderzeitliche Bronzeschilde im Karpeten-beken', *Germania* 46, 241-8. I am grateful to David Coombs for drawing this find to my attention.

269. Sandars, 1971, 24-5, chronological tables [n. 260].

270. Burgess, 1968*b*, 5-6, Fig. 3, 35-6. The tendency in the past has been to stress the native rapier and Rixheim contribution, and to invoke local incompetence in copying the novel flanged-hilt, leaf-shaped swords, e.g. H.W.M. Hodges, 1956, 'Studies in the Late-Bronze in Ireland: 2. The typology and distribution of bronze implements', *Ulster Journal of Archaeology* 19, 37; G. Eogan, 1965, *Catalogue of Irish Bronze Swords* (Dublin), 7-8; Burgess, 1968*b*, 35. This view gives primacy to the Lambeth/Rosnöen form as a Rixheim derivative, and makes Ballintober swords a later development under leaf-shaped sword influence. But the much greater knowledge of rod-tanged swords now available (Peroni, 1970 [n. 264]) makes it clear that Ballintober swords are merely rod-tanged swords without the rod, and with different rivet arrangement, as anticipated by Burgess, 1968*b*, 44. In this case those Ballintober swords with tonged tang ends assume added significance. As rod-tanged swords are at least as early as Rixheim swords, Ballintober swords are likely to have been developed as early as Lambeth/Rosnöen swords. It is the latter which mix Rixheim and rapier influence.

271. Burgess Group IIC, 1968*b*, 35, with note 12. To judge from the blade proportions of the early native products, both Erbenheim (slender, graceful blades) and Hemigkofen (broader, clumsier blades) influenced native sword-smiths.

272. Burgess Group III, 1968*b*, 2, 35, Fig. 1: 5.

273. No overall maps have been published, but for maps of the various sword types, Burgess, 1968*b*, 10-11, Figs. 6-7.

274. The Irish tanged swords comprise mostly Ballintober weapons: Eogan, 1965, Figs. 3-6 [n. 270]. The only actual urnfield sword from Ireland seems to be a Hemigkofen sword from the Erne near Ballyshannon, Co. Donegal, Eogan's no. 51. I am grateful to Dr J.D. Cowen for confirming this identification. A number of Group IIC and III swords have been found in Ireland, but their character does not emerge from Eogan's illustrations, ibid., Figs. 8-11.

275. Various forms of notched butt Group IV dirks and rapiers are known, with differing distributions (Burgess, 1971 [n. 201]). Only the Cutts type is a clear entity (B.A.V. Trump, 1962, 'The origin and development of British Middle Bronze Age rapiers', *PPS* 28, 92-3), Mrs Trump's 'Lisburn' class being in effect a blanket label to cover all other notched butt rapiers (Trump, ibid., 91-2, Fig. 15). The area

of difference is the outline of the lower hilt plate, below the notches, on the basis of which Mildenhall, Imeroo and Portna variants can be distinguished (Fig. 34). The Mildenhall form is widespread, but the Imeroo and Portna forms are mostly Irish, though not as markedly so as the Cutts type.

276. Penard: O.G.S. Crawford and R.E.M. Wheeler, 1920-1, 'The Llynfawr and other hoards of the Bronze Age', *Arch.* 71, 138. Ffynhonnau: Savory, 1958, 27-8, 45, Fig. 3. Urnfield types comprise pointed ferrules, tanged knife (Ffynhonnau) and bronze arrowhead (Penard), south-eastern types a Lambeth sword (Penard), and Irish types a Cutts dirk (Ffynhonnau). Local elements consist of the Ffynhonnau transitional palstaves and the Penard socketed axe. The Penard Ballintober swords could have come from either England or Ireland, while the origin of the Penard pegged spearhead is uncertain: Burgess, 1962 [n. 13]; 1968*a*, 5, 7, Fig. 5; 1968*b*, 4-9, 34-5, Figs. 2, 4.

277. There is a possible hoard, containing Ballintober sword, gold fragments and 'ring money', from Strabane, Co. Tyrone: Eogan, 1965, 25 [n. 270]. The principal south English hoards include those from Eriswell, Suffolk (rod-tanged sword, Portna notched rapiers: Lady Briscoe and A. Furness, 1955, 'A hoard of Bronze Age weapons from Eriswell, near Mildenhall', *Ant. J.* .35, 218-19); Thorpe Hall, Essex (possible hoard, Ballintober sword, transitional palstave: Smith, 1959, 184); Downham Fen, Norfolk (Mildenhall notched-butt rapier, cylinder-socket sickle, transitional palstave : C. Fox, 1923, *The Archaeology of the Cambridge Region* (London), Pl. 8; Crowle, Isle of Axholme, Lincolnshire (lost: notched-butt rapiers, straight-based basal-looped spearheads, transitional palstaves: Trump, 1962, 91 [n. 275] : and Appleby, Lincolnshire (trapeze-butt and Mildenhall notched-butt Group IV rapiers, Lambeth/Rosnöen sword, cast-hilt sword, straight-based basal-looped spearheads, pegged spearhead: P.J. Davey and G.C. Knowles, 1972, 'The Appleby hoard', *Arch. J.* 28, 154-61).

278. Coles, 1959-60, 20-4, for the situation in Scotland; Burgess, 1968*a* 5, 7, for northern England.

279. C. Fell and J.M. Coles, 1965, 'Reconsideration of the Ambleside hoard and the burial at Butt's Beck Quarry, Dalton-in-Furness', *Transactions of the Cumberland and Westmorland Antiquarian and Archaeological Society*, new ser. 65, 38-47; Burgess, 1968*a*, 7-8, Fig. 4.

280. Burgess, 1968*b*, 5-9, 35-6, Figs. 3-5. For a detailed study of this the Rosnöen phase in Brittany, Briard, 1965, 151-73 [n. 129].

281. Compare the distribution of Rosnöen swords throughout north-west France: Briard, 165, 1968, Fig. 56 [n. 129] Note such typical Rosnöen associations outside Britanny as those from Tirancourt, Somme (rod-tanged sword, straight-based basal-looped spearhead: A. de Francqueville, 1905, 'Bronzes de Picardie', *L'Anthropologie* 16, 371) and Noireau, Calvados (Rosnöen swords, Mildenhall notched-butt rapier, slender socketed chisel etc.: Evreux

Museum; see Burgess, 1968*b*, 7, Fig. 4: 3 for the rapier).

282. Compare Hawkes, 1960, 5, hinting at an urnfield 'colony'.

283. Grimthorpe: I.M. Stead, 1968, 'An Iron Age hill-fort at Grim-thorpe, Yorkshire, England', *PPS* 34, 148-90; Dinorben: H.N. Savory, 1971, 'A Welsh Bronze Age hill-fort', *Antiquity* 45, 251-61. But note Alcock's attack on Savory's interpretation of the Dinorben evidence: L. Alcock, 1972, Review of H.N. Savory, 1971, *Excavations at Dinorben, 1965-9* (Cardiff, National Museum of Wales), in *Antiquity* 46, 330-1.

284. Crook-head pin from Dinorben: Savory, 1971, 257, Fig. 2:2 [n. 283]; Breiddin pin: C. Musson, 1970, 'The Breiddin, 1969', *C. Arch.* 19, 217, Fig., with swollen stem; vase-headed pin from Totternhoe: C.F.C. Hawkes, 1940, 'A site of the Late Bronze Age-Early Iron Age transition at Totternhoe, Beds.', *Ant. J.* 20, 487-91. For urnfield hill-forts, Gimbutas, 1965, 301 [n. 179]; Piggott, 1965, 202-3 [n. 199]; Savory, 1971, 259-60 [n. 283].

285. M.A. Brown and A.E. Blin-Stoyle, 1959, 'A sample analysis of British Middle and Late Bronze Age material, using optical spectrometry', *PPS* 25, 193-200; Burgess, 1962, 22 [n. 13]; 1968*b*, 9; I.M. Allen, D. Britton and H.H. Coghlan, 1970, *Metallurgical Reports on British and Irish Bronze Age Implements and Weapons in the Pitt Rivers Museum* (Pitt Rivers Museum Occasional Papers on Technology 10, London), 22-3; Tylecote, 1962, 43-5 [n. 196]. For the Wilburton Complex in Britain and the Saint-Brieuc-des-Iffs group in France, H.N. Savory, 1958, 28-34, and 1965, 'The Guilsfield hoard', *Bulletin of the Board of Celtic Studies* 21, 179-206; D. Britton, 1960, 'The Isleham hoard, Cambridgeshire', *Antiquity* 34, 278-82; Burgess, 1968*a*, 1-2, 29-34, 36-40; 1968*b*, 9-17, 36-7; Burgess, Coombs and Davies, 1972, 213-9, 222-6, 233-5; Eogan, 1964, 288-93; Briard, 1965, 175-98 [n. 129].

286. These had all been introduced previously, socketed axes as far back as the Taunton phase, but production had hitherto been slight, localised and usually experimental: Burgess, 1962, 22-3 [n. 13]. The situation was somewhat different in France, where pegged leaf-shaped spearheads had been standard through the middle bronze age. In north-west France as in England, leaf-shaped swords were put into quantity production now, but socketed axes continued to be rare. Hoards of the Saint Brieuc-des-Iffs group have neither the indented nor multiple moulding socketed axes of the Wilburton complex, though the former do occur as stray finds in north-west France, e.g. from Amiens and Abbeville: Breuil, 1905, 160-1; 163-4, Fig. 7: 71, 96 [n. 226].

287. Lunate opening, stepped-blade, fillet-defined and hollow lozenge-sectioned blade spearheads: Burgess, 1968*b*, 36; Burgess, Coombs and Davies, 1972, 213-4. There are a few stray lunate-opening spearheads from north-west France: Briard, 1963 [n. 247]. The differences between lowland England and north-west France amount to no more than the regional differences in emphasis that one would expect.

288. Burgess, 1968a.
289. Burgess, 1968a, 2, 38, Fig. 1, map; Savory, 1965 [n. 235].
290. Burgess, 1968a, 36-40; 1968b, 13-17; Burgess, Coombs and Davies, 1972, 226.
291. Burgess, 1968b, 17-26.
292. For the Ewart Park phase, Burgess, Coombs and Davies, 1972, 214. For the various exotic influences, Hawkes and Smith, 1957; Savory, 1958; Coles, 1959-60; Eogan, 1964; Burgess, 1968b.
293. G. Jacob-Friesen, 1968, 'Ein Depotfund des Formenkreises um die 'Karpfenzungenschwerter' aus der Normandie', *Germania* 46, 272-4; H.-J. Hundt, 1955, 'Versuch zur Deutung der Depotfunde der Nordischen jüngeren Bronzezeit unter besonderer Brücksichtigung Mecklenburgs', *Jahrbuch des Römisch-Germanischen Zentralmuseums Mainz* 2, 95-132; C.F.C. Hawkes and R.R. Clarke, 1963, 'Gahlstorf and Caister-on-Sea: two finds of late Bronze Age Irish gold', in Foster and Alcock, 1963, 240 [n. 116].
294. For this climatic deterioration, Godwin, 1960, 29-31 [n. 5]; Piggott, 1972, 111 [n. 198]. For the spread of Hallstatt power, T.G.E. Powell, 1958, *The Celts* (London), 45-56; Piggott, 1965, 174-207 [n. 199].
295. For Ireland, Eogan, 1964, 311-23, Fig. 18, map; Hawkes and Clarke, 1963 [n. 293]. For maps of English hoards and Hallstatt C swords, Burgess, 1968b, 23, Fig. 14; 26-33, Fig. 19.
296. It would perhaps be better to approach the matter from the other end, with those late Wilburton hoards – Blackmoor, Fulbourn Common, Isleham etc. – which contain a small element appropriate to the succeeding carp's tongue metalworking: Burgess, 1968b, 13, 36-7.
297. Note the number of South Welsh socketed axes in France, derived from the Llantwit-Stogursey industry of the Bristol Channel region: Savory 1965, 186-7, map, Fig. 9 [n. 285]; Burgess, 1968b, 21, with note 83. For Llantwit-Stogursey metalworking, Burgess, 1968b, 19, 21: Burgess, Coombs and Davies, 1972, 232-4.
298. Hawkes and Smith, 1957. Coles would bring shields in here as part of this sheet metalwork development, but the latest continental evidence restores their traditional early urnfield beginnings, so that their position in the Ewart Park phase becomes uncertain. See n. 268 above.
299. e.g. amber, rattle pendants, sunflower and disc-headed pins. Summarised Eogan, 1964, 302-7, Figs. 15-16.
300. No comprehensive survey of the continental background to these horse and vehicle fittings has been attempted, but see Hawkes and Smith, 1957, 153-6. Connections with northern Europe are likely to have been closer than has been realised, and need urgent study. Witness the socketed axe *mit profiliertem Tüllenmund* (Sprockhoff, 1941, 84-6, abb. 67 [n. 213]) and northern end-winged axes in the Minnis Bay hoard, Kent (F.H. Worsfold, 1943, 'A report on the Late Bronze Age site excavated at Minnis Bay, Birchington, Kent, 1938-40', *PPS* 9, 33-5, Pls. 11-12). See also Butler, 1963, 90-2, 94-5,

Fig. 25. Note too an urnfield razor with blade decorated with hatched triangles from the Thames-side pile dwellings at Old England, Brentford (C.M. Piggott, 1946, 'The Late Bronze Age razors of the British Isles', *PPS* 12, 121-41, Fig. 9), which has an exact parallel from Dotlingen, near Bremen (E. Sprockhoff, 1956, *Jungbronzezeitliche Hortfunde der Südzone des Nordischen Kreises (Periode V)* (Mainz), 1, 117.

301. Burgess, 1968*b*, 17-26, 38-42, for a general summary. For Scotland, Coles, 1959-60, 25-55; for Ireland, Eogan, 1964, 293-320; for Wales and the West, Savory, 1958, 34-42, and Burgess, Coombs and Davies, 1972, 228-35; for the Heathery Burn tradition, Burgess, 1968*a*, 29-30, Fig. 20. Note Coles' warnings on the problems of the Dowris find: J.M. Coles, 1971, 'Dowris and the Late Bronze Age of Ireland: a footnote', *Journal of the Royal Society of Antiquaries of Ireland* 101, 164-5.

302. For an account of some of these regional differences, Burgess, 1968*b*, 17-26, 38-42; Burgess, Coombs and Davies, 1972, 228-35.

303. Stone and clay moulds from Scotland and Ireland, stone and bronze moulds from south-west England, bronze moulds from the rest of England: see lists of moulds and discussion in Tylecote, 1962, 116-28 [n. 196]. It is uncertain to what extent this reflects regional variations in casting methods.

304. Hoards of socketed axes: e.g. Branston Hall, Lincolnshire (J. Evans, 1907-9, 'Notes on a hoard of bronze instruments found in Lincolnshire', *Proceedings of the Society of Antiquaries of London* 22, 3-5); Roxby, Lincolnshire (British Museum, Scunthorpe Museum); Haxey, Lincolnshire (Evans, 1881, 89, 129, 465 [n. 235]); Everthorpe, Yorkshire (Hull Museum: Burgess, 1968*b*, 29, Fig. 18: 1-2). For Irish hoards, Eogan, 1964, 331-50.

305. Burgess, Coombs and Davies, 1972, 220-35, maps, Fig. 1.

306. Burgess, Coombs and Davies, 1972, 221, 229-30, map, Fig. 1*d*. For Scottish sword hoards, Coles, 1959-60, 94-134; for the Northumberland finds, J.D. Cowen, 1935, 1940, Prehistoric sections, *History of Northumberland* (Newcastle upon Tyne), vol. 14, 26, 28-9, Pl. 1; vol. 15, 22, 24, 55.

307. Hawkes, 1972, 113-114 [n. 122].

308. Compare Cowen's maps of Hallstatt C bronze swords: J.D. Cowen, 1967, 'The Hallstatt sword of bronze: on the Continent and in Britain', *PPS* 33, 401-9, maps C–E. The earliest swords, of Class A, are common in southern and eastern France, but it is only with Class B finds that we see a spread westwards and northwards to Scandinavia, and through the Low Countries to Britain. For Hallstatt penetration of the Low Countries, see M.-E. Marien, 1958, *Trouvailles du champ d'urnes et des tombelles hallstattiennes de Court-Saint-Etienne* (Monographies d'Archéologie Nationale, 1, Brussels).

309. Cowen, 1967, 402, 405, map D [n. 308].

310. Hawkes, 1960, 7; Hawkes and Smith, 1957, 190; Hawkes and Clarke, 1963, 239 [n. 293].

311. For raiding, see for example C.F.C. Hawkes, 1959, 'The ABC of

the British Iron Age', *Antiquity* 33, 177-8; Hawkes and Clarke, 1963, 293-40 [n. 293]; Coles, 1959-60, 47; Eogan, 1964, 320-1. For more peaceable movements, Cowen, 1967, 422 [n. 308]. General discussion of these problems, Burgess, 1968*b*, 26.

312. Compare the Scandinavian distribution: Cowen, 1967, 392, Map B. [n. 308].

313. Cowen, 1967, 402, 406-9, map E [n. 308].

314. Burgess, 1968*b*, 28, 43. Pommel finial, 'swept-back' ricasso notches, and broad, blunt tip are the features most commonly borrowed from the Hallstatt swords, but a fat hilt, wide-splayed shoulders, and rounded blade section with beaded edge bevel are other features which ought to be searched for. The number of such swords is much greater than most authorities have implied (e.g. Cowen, 1967, 412-6 [n. 308]; Eogan, 1965, 12-16 [n. 270]), but no detailed study has been carried out.

315. L. Alcock, 1972*a*, 'Excavations at Cadbury-Camelot', 1966-70, *Antiquity* 46, 31. But must the ceramic break at Cadbury necessarily imply continental intruders? Alcock notes a possible indigenous background for the pottery, and the quantity of undoubted continental material there is tiny. In such troubled times newcomers could come from within Britain as well as without. See L. Alcock, 1972*b*, '*By South Cadbury is that Camelot . . .*' *Excavations at Cadbury Castle 1966-70* (London), 118-21.

316. Burgess, 1968*b*, 42-3; Alcock, 1972*b* 120-1, Pl. 23.

317. Hawkes, 1959, 177 [n. 311].

318. Hawkes, 1959, 177 [n. 311]; Powell, 1958, 25-7, with map [n. 294].

319. Hawkes, 1959, 177 [n. 311].

320. Compare Cowen's map of Gundlingen swords (1967, 392, map B [n. 308]) with maps of Armorican socketed axes (G.C. Dunning, 1959, 'The distribution of socketed axes of Breton type', *Ulster Journal of Archaeology* 22, 53) and carp's tongue swords (Briard, 1965, 231, Fig. 85 [n. 129]). There is only one Hallstatt sword from Normandy and Brittany, which were the main centres both of the carp's tongue phenomenon and Armorican axes.

321. C.B. Burgess, 1969, 'Some decorated socketed axes in Canon Greenwell's collection', in 'Studies in commemoration of William Greenwell, 1820-1918', *YAJ* 42, 267-72.

322. e.g. E.M. Jope, 1961, 'Daggers of the Early Iron Age in Britain', *PPS* 27, 307, 324-5.

323. ApSimon, 1962, 319-21 [n. 98].

324. e.g. S.C.Hawkes, 1969, 'Finds from two Middle Bronze Age pits at Winnall, Winchester, Hampshire', *Proceedings ·of the Hampshire Field Club* 26, 14-15.

325. Re-dating to the middle bronze age mainly through the work of M.A. Smith (1959, 155-9). Ideas of an indigenous background stemmed from the revolutionary work of Butler and Smith, 1956, 33-48, the accompanying disillusionment with exotic origins being part of the general demise of the 'invasion hypothesis': Clark, 1966, 184-5 [n. 123].

326. Calkin, 1962, 22-4, Fig. 9 [n. 94].

327. Calkin, 1962, 22-9 [n. 94]; ApSimon, 1962, 319-21 [n. 98].

328. Very well summarised in Curwen, 1954, 164-94 [n. 120].

329. See Case et al., 1964-5, 70, 73-5, Fig. 28 [n. 74].

330. F.H. Erith and I.H. Longworth, 1960, 'A Bronze Age urnfield on Vinces Farm, Ardleigh, Essex', *PPS* 26, 178-92.

331. Bromfield: S.C. Stanford, 1972, 'Welsh Border hill-forts', in C. Thomas (ed.), 1972, *The Iron Age in the Irish Sea Province* (C.B.A. Research Report 9, London, Council for British Archaeology), 32-3, 36, note 37, Fig. 13. Ryton-on-Dunsmore: unpublished, but see *Radiocarbon* 10, 1968, 204.

332. Cemetery at Rhuddlan, Flints: H. Miles, 1972, 'Rhuddlan', *C. Arch.* 32, 248.

333. e.g. flat cemetery at Hoveringham, Nottinghamshire; bucket/ biconical urns from Stathern, Leicestershire and Burton Latimer, Nottinghamshire, in Nottingham University Museum.

334. Cemetery at Catfoss, Yorkshire: I.J. McInnes, 1968, 'The excavation of a Bronze Age cemetery at Catfoss, east Yorkshire', *East Riding Archaeologist* 1, 1-10.

335. Curwen, 1954, 171-93 [n. 120]. But this type of settlement extended much more widely over southern England, as the site at Shearplace Hill, Dorset, shows: Rahtz, 1962 [n. 98].

336. G.P. Burstow and G.A. Holleyman, 1957, 'Late Bronze Age settlement on Itford Hill, Sussex', pps 23, 167-212; E.C. Curwen and G.A. Holleyman, 1935, 'Late Bronze Age lynchet settlements on Plumpton Plain, Sussex', *PPS* 1, 16-38.

337. Note a pit containing carbonised barley at Itford Hill: Burstow and Holleyman, 1957, 177-8, Fig. 10 [n. 336]. For a summary of pit functions, Hawkes, 1969, 5-6, 8 [n. 324].

338. C.M. Piggott, 1942, 'Five Late Bronze Age enclosures in north Wiltshire', *PPS* 8, 48-61.

339. South Lodge, Handley Down Angle Ditch, Martin's Down: A. Pitt-Rivers, 1898, *Excavations in Cranborne Chase: Volume IV*, privately printed, 16-57, 102-13, 185-215.

340. J.F.S. Stone, 1941, 'The Deverel-Rimbury settlement on Thorny Down, Winterbourne Gunner, south Wilts.,' *PPS* 7, 114-33. But compare Stone's interpretation of the post-hole patterns with those of C.R. Musson, 1970, 'House-plans and prehistory', *C. Arch.* 21, 267-77. The wide gaps in the perimeters of some of these sites are difficult to reconcile with use as stock enclosures.

341. Flat cemetery with collared urn burials, Pokesdown, Hants: R.C.C. Clay, 1927, 'A Late Bronze Age urn-field at Pokesdown, Hants.,' *Ant. J.* 7, 465-84; barrow with collared urn burials, Latch Farm, Hants.: C.M. Piggott, 1938, 'A Middle Bronze Age barrow and Deverel-Rimbury urnfield, at Latch Farm, Christchurch, Hampshire', *PPS* 4, 169-87.

342. cf. L.V. Grinsell, 1959, *Dorset Barrows* (Dorchester, Dorset Natural History and Archaeological Society), 13-14.

343. E. Holden, 1972, 'Itford Hill', *C. Arch.* 32, 232-5.

344. e.g. ApSimon, 1962, 319-21 [n. 98]; 1968, 'The Bronze Age pottery from Ash Hole, Brixham Devon', *Proceedings of the Devon Archaeological Society* 26, 26-8; Calkin, 1962, 19-47 [n. 94].

345. As a result particularly of Wainwright's recent excavations of large late neolithic enclosures, notably Durrington Walls: Wainwright, 1971 [n. 32].

346. Clark, 1936 [n. 61].

347. Bucket Urn burial at Worgret Hill, Dorset: 1740 ± 90 bc (NPL-199): G.J. Wainwright, 1966, 'The excavation of a round barrow on Worgret Hill, Arne, Dorset', *Proceedings of the Dorset Natural History and Archaeological Society* 87, 119-25; *Radiocarbon* 12 (1970), 185. Note, too, the date from near the bottom of the Wilsford shaft: 1380 ± 90 bc (NPL-74). Sherds of globular urn came from a rather higher level: 1966: Ashbee, 1963 [n. 58]; Ashbee, 1966 [n. 199]. See also the comments on the Shearplace Hill evidence, n. 348 below.

348. The C14 date from the Shearplace Hill settlement Dorset, of 1180 ± 180 bc (NPL-19), came from a mixture of samples appropriate to phases 1 and 2. Re-interpretation (M. Avery and J. Close-Brooks, 1969, 'Shearplace Hill, Sydling St. Nicholas, Dorset, House A: a suggested re-interpretation', *PPS* 35, 345-51) of the excavation report (Rahtz, 1962 [n. 98]) suggests that Deverel-Rimbury pottery was certainly associated with phase 2 collared urn, and possibly biconical urn. It was already known to be associated with these early phases: ApSimon, in Rahtz, 1962, 309-10, Fig. 16 [n. 98].

349. In a flat cemetery such as Pokesdown, with collared urn burials amongst a mass of Deverel-Rimbury burials, there is usually no way of telling which was the primary burial. Further, at Latch Farm, while a collared urn burial was primary, the secondary Deverel-Rimbury cemetery had a collared urn burial mixed in with it. See n. 341 above.

350. i.e. different types seldom occur in associations with each other, and it is mutual associations with other material, and C14 dates, which best demonstrate contemporaneity. The ceramic isolation of biconical urns is especially marked.

351. e.g. Saint-Jude, Côtes-du-Nord, and Kervellerin, Morbihan: J. Briard and P.-R. Giot, 1963, 'Fouille d'un tumulus de l'âge du bronze à Saint-Jude en Bourbriac (Côtes-du-Nord)', *Annales de Bretagne* 70, 17-20, Figs. 9-10; P.-R. Giot and J.L'Helgouach, 1961, 'Fouille d'un deuxième tumulus de l'âge du bronze à Kervellerin en Cléguer (Morbihan)', *Annales de Bretagne* 68, 16-20, Fig. 6.

352. M. Tessier, 1965, 'Sites cotiers de l'âge du bronze du pays de Retz (Loire-Atlantique)', *Annales de Bretagne* 72, 76, Fig. 1.

353. J. Philippe, 1936, 1937, 'Le Fort-Harrouard', *L'Anthropologie* 46, 257-301, 541-612; 47, 253-308.

354. H. Mariette, 1961, 'Une urne de l'âge du bronze à Hardelot (Pas-de-Calais)', *Helinium* 1, 229-32; ApSimon, 1972, 365 [n. 61].

355. See Wainwright and Longworth, 1971, 249-54, 266 [n. 32].

356. 1000 ± 35 bc (GrN-6167): Holden, 1972, 232 [n. 343].

357. Smith, 1959, 155-9.
358. Bromfield and Ryton-on-Dunsmore: see n. 331.
359. The well-known exotic vessels from Plumpton Plain B are completely out of place in any British context, and must surely have been brought direct from France: C.F.C. Hawkes, 1935, 'The pottery from the sites on Plumpton Plain', *PPS* 1, 39-59.
360. B. Cunliffe and D.W. Phillipson, 1968, 'Excavations at Eldon's Seat, Encombe, Dorset', *PPS* 34, 191-237; see Fig. 10.
361. The position of the apparently Deverel-Rimbury example from Shearplace Hill (Rahtz, 1962, 323-4, Fig. 23. 5 [n. 98]) has been shown to be uncertain (Avery and Close-Brooks, 1969, 347 [n. 348]). But that it certainly could belong to the Deverel-Rimbury settlement is shown by another middle bronze age example, from the Ogof-yr-esgyrn cave, Breconshire: H.N. Savory, 1968, 'The prehistoric material', in E.J. Mason, 1968, 'Ogof-yr-esgyrn, Dan-yr-ogof caves, Brecknock: excavations, 1938-50', *Archaeologia Cambrensis* 117, 36-7, Fig. 6:7.
362. The few Deverel-Rimbury burials with datable associations all appear to belong to the middle bronze age: Smith, 1959, 156.
363. Most notably through the works of Lady Fox, summarised in her *South West England* (London, 1964), 84-96. See also I.G. Simmons, 1969, 'Environment and early man on Dartmoor, Devon, England', *PPS* 35, 203-19.
364. ApSimon and Greenfield, 1972 [n. 61].
365. There are two C14 dates relevant to developed Trevisker pottery, which ought to relate to the latest of the south-western upland settlements: at Trevisker itself, 1110 ± 95 bc (NPL-134); and at Gwithian, 1120 ± 105 bc (NPL-21), both calibrating to c.1300 BC: ApSimon and Greenfield, 1972, 356 [n. 61]. This agrees well with the likely date of the Bohemian palstave from the field system of the Horridge Common settlement on Dartmoor: A. Fox and D. Britton, 1969, 'A Continental palstave from the ancient field system on Horridge Common, Dartmoor, England', *PPS* 35, 223-5.
366. Simmons, 1969, 208-11, 212-16 [n. 363].
367. Gimbutas, 1965, 270 [n. 179].
368. Basic bank and ditch works were already delimiting causewayed camps in the early neolithic, and became commonplace, and often of enormous size, in the henges and enclosures of the late neolithic: Wainwright and Longworth, 1971, 198-203 [n. 32]; G.J. Wainwright, 1969, 'A review of henge monuments in the light of recent research', *PPS* 35, 112-33. To these can now be added a stone-faced wall round a neolithic settlement at Carn Brea, and timber-revetted ramparts and palisades around the Broome Heath settlement, Norfolk: G.J. Wainwright, 1972, 'The excavation of a Neolithic settlement on Broome Heath, Ditchingham, Norfolk', *PPS* 38, 76-7.
369. e.g. Ffridd Faldwyn, Montgomeryshire (B.H. St. J. O'Neil, 1942, 'Excavations at Ffridd Faldwyn camp, Montgomery, 1937-9', *Archaeologia Cambrensis* 97, 1-57); Cadbury Castle, Somerset (Alcock, 1972*b*, 108-13 [n. 315]); and Feltrim Hill, Co. Dublin (P.J.

Hartnett and G. Eogan, 1964, 'Feltrim Hill,.Co. Dublin; a Neolithic and Early Christian site', *Journal of the Royal Society of Antiquaries of Ireland* 94, 1-37.

370. Norton Fitzwarren: Langmaid, 1971 [n. 65]; Rams Hill: original excavations by Piggott, 1942 [n. 64]. In recent (1972) excavations, the ditch and bank enclosure, associated with collared urn sherds in the original excavation, was found to follow on from a palisade enclosure (unpublished: information kindly supplied by the excavators, Richard Bradley and Ann Ellison).

371. Wainwright, 1970 [n. 173]; Burleigh, Longworth and Wainwright, 1972, 399 [n. 173].

372. G.J. Wainwright, 1963, 'The excavation of an earthwork at Castell Bryn-Gwyn, Llanidan Parish, Anglesey', *Archaeologia Cambrensis* 111, 25-58. Convincingly interpreted as a henge by Lynch (1970, 64-7, Fig. 26 [n. 72], though admitting herself that the identification can be far from certain given the available evidence.

373. Rahtz, 1962 [n. 98], modified by Avery and Close-Brooks, 1969 [n. 347].

374. E.C. Curwen, 1933, 'Excavations on Thundersbarrow Hill, Sussex', *Ant. J.* 13, 109-33; M.E. Cunnington, 1933, 'Excavations in Yarnbury Castle, 1932', *WAM* 46, 198-213.

375. B. Cunliffe, 1971, 'Some aspects of hill-forts and their cultural environments'; and R. Bradley, 1971, 'Economic change in the growth of early hill-forts', both in Hill and Jesson, 1971, 53-64, 71-83 [n. 3].

376. Though the fact that one house produced a socketed axe of the Ewart Park phase shows just how long occupation of this site lasted.

377. See S.C. Stanford, 1971, 'Invention, adoption and imposition: the evidence of the hill-forts', in Hill and Jesson, 1971, 41-3 [n. 3]. By analogy one could place sites such as Ffridd Faldwyn, Montgomeryshire, and Caynham Camp, Shropshire, alongside Dinorben and Grimthorpe (Stanford, ibid), and recent excavations suggest that the beginnings of the Breiddin defences should also belong here: Musson, 1970 [n. 284]; and 1972, 'Two winters at the Breiddin', *C. Arch.* 33, 263-7.

378. Ivinghoe Beacon, though a timber-framed rampart site like Grimthorpe, is littered with metalwork of the Ewart Park phase, and should thus be later: M.A. Cotton and S.S. Frere, 1968, 'Ivinghoe Beacon: excavations, 1963-5', *Records of Buckinghamshire* 18, 187-260.

379. The extensive collection of bronzes from Ham Hill is in Somerset County Museum, Taunton. For Portfield Camp and its bronze hoard, J.D. Blundell and I.H. Longworth, 1968, 'A Bronze Age hoard from Portfield Farm, Whalley, Lancashire', *British Museum Quarterly* 32, 8-14.

380. Evidence summarised by A. Ritchie, 1970, 'Palisaded sites in north Britain: their context and affinities', *Scottish Archaeological Forum* 2, 54-5. At Fenton Hill, Northumberland, the present writer is currently excavating a rare example of a palisade enclosure

overlaid by an enclosure with timber-revetted ramparts.

381. The difficulty of determining at some sites whether one is dealing with a timber framed rampart or palisades perhaps illustrates this comparison. Ffridd Faldwyn is a well-known example of this difficulty (O'Neil, 1942 [n. 369]), and one can now add Burnswark, Dumfries (information from the excavator, Mr G. Jobey).

382. cf. Huckhoe, Northumberland, where the excavator considered the stone enclosure wall followed hard on the burning down of a comparatively short-lived palisade with a C14 date of 510 ± 40 bc (GaK-1388): G. Jobey, 1968, 'A radiocarbon date for the palisaded settlement at Huckhoe', *Archaeologia Aeliana*, 4 ser., 46, 293-5.

383. E. MacKie, 1969, 'Radiocarbon dates and the Scottish Iron Age', *Antiquity* 43, 15-26; 1970, 'The Scottish "Iron Age"', *Scottish Historical Review* 49, 17-19. See also Stanford, 1971 [n. 377].

384. cf. Childe, 1940, 210-11 [n. 14], and Coles, 1959-60, 44. But MacKie is more cautious (1970, 10-11, 18-19 [n. 383]), and the evidence hardly supports the arrival of more than traders or a few scattered bands of newcomers.

385. i.e. some of the bipartite examples, which are frequently undecorated, e.g. vessels from High Banks Farm, Kirkcudbrightshire (with row of circular impressions on shoulder, and simple rim: Simpson, 1965, 39, 45, no. 27, Fig. 4 [n. 110]), and Stanton Park, Derbyshire (with impressed decoration running round shoulder: Manby, 1958, 25, Fig. 6, no. A35 [n. 109]).

386. e.g. Kilellan Farm, Ardnave, Isle of Islay: large plain and cord-decorated situate vessels with simple rims, from an occupation site producing a wide range of late neolithic/early bronze age wares: author's unpublished excavations. Also common among Deverel-Rimbury settlement wares, although many such instances will be later than the early bronze age.

387. e.g. with bronze hoards at Isleham (Britton, 1960 [n. 285]), and Forty Acre Brickfield, Worthing, Sussex (M.A. Smith, 1958, 'Late Bronze hoards in the British Museum', *Inventaria Archaeologica* GB, 6th set, GB 37 (1)), and with a vase-headed pin in an enclosure ditch at Totternhoe, Bedfordshire (Hawkes, 1940 [n. 284]).

388. B. Cunliffe, 1968, 'Early pre-Roman Iron Age communities in eastern England', *Ant. J.* 48, 175-7.

389. e.g. at Eldon's Seat, Dorset, shouldered forms appear alongside Deverel-Rimbury bucket urns in phase Ia (the 'Eldon's Seat I assemblage'), but after a break in occupation, the pottery of phase II is completely different, having a high proportion of bowl forms ('Eldon's Seat II assemblage'): Cunliffe and Phillipson, 1963 [n. 360].

390. It will be obvious just how much this chapter owes to all those museum curators throughout Britain, Ireland and France who have willingly allowed me to examine material in their charge. I am grateful to Miss Sandra Coates for typing the text, to the staff of the General Office, Dept. of Adult Education, University of Newcastle upon Tyne, and Mrs V. Conneely for their patient help in innumer-

able ways, and to Mrs Maureen Fadian for most of the drawings. Professor Christopher Hawkes, directly and through his writings, has been a constant source of inspiration. I am grateful to Professor Renfrew for inviting me to write this contribution, and waiting so patiently for it, and above all I am indebted to Miss Frances Lynch (Mrs Llewellyn) for much stimulating discussion and constructive criticism.

# Bibliography for Chapter 6

BARRY CUNLIFFE
*The iron age*

Birchall, A., 1965, 'The Aylesford-Swarling culture: the problem of the Belgae reconsidered', *PPS* 31, 241-367.

Cunliffe, B.W. 1974, *Iron Age Communities in Britain*. London.

Evans, A.J., 1890, 'On a late Celtic urnfield at Aylesford, Kent', *Archaeologia* 52, 369-74.

Frere, S.S. (ed.), 1961, *Problems of the Iron Age in Southern Britain*. London.

Frere, S.S., 1967, *Britannia*. London.

Jesson, M. and D. Hill, (eds.), 1971, *The Iron Age and its Hillforts*. Southampton.

MacKie, E., 1969, 'Radiocarbon dates and the Scottish Iron Age', *Antiquity* 43, 15-26.

Rivet, A.L.F. (ed.), 1966, *The Iron Age in Northern Britain*. Edinburgh.

Smith, R.A., 1925, *British Museum Guide to Early Iron Age Antiquities*. London.

Stead, I.M., 1965, *The La Tène Cultures of Eastern Yorkshire*. York.

Wheeler, R.E.M., 1943, *Maiden Castle, Dorset*. Oxford.

# Notes to Chapter 6

1. The author has given a somewhat fuller treatment of the basic data in his *Iron Age Communities of Britain*. The chapter offered here is but a brief summary of a few of the points made there.

2. The most up to date assessment of the invasions of Caesar and Claudius is given in Frere, 1967. For an assessment of the coin evidence seen in terms of invasions, see C.F.C. Hawkes, 1968, 'New thoughts on the Belgae', *Antiquity* 42, 6-16.

3. Evans, 1890.

4. No attempt will be made here to give references to individual sites. A comprehensive list of sites with full bibliographical details will be found in Cunliffe, 1974.

5. Smith, 1925.

6. E.T. Leeds, 1927, 'Excavations at Chun Castle in Penwith, Cornwall', *Archaeologia* 76, 205-240.

7. C.F.C. Hawkes, 1931, 'Hillforts', *Antiquity* 5, 60-111.

8. C.F.C. Hawkes, 1939, 'The Caburn pottery and its implications',

*Sussex Archaeological Collections* 80, 238-9.

9. The papers of the CBA Conference were published three years later: Frere (ed.), 1961. Hodson's comments on the re-stated ABC system and his subsequent thoughts are contained in three papers: F.R. Hodson, 1960, 'Reflections on the ABC of the British Iron Age', *Antiquity* 34, 318-9; 1962, 'Some pottery from Eastbourne, the "Marnians" and the pre-Roman Iron Age in Southern England',*PPS* 28, 140-155; 1964, 'Cultural groupings within the British pre-Roman Iron Age', *PPS* 30, 99-110. For the Arras culture see Stead, 1965, and for the Aylesford-Swarling Culture see Birchall, 1965.

10. MacKie, 1969.

11. D.P.S. Peacock, 1968, 'A petrological study of certain Iron Age pottery from Western England', *PPS* 34, 414-27; 1969, 'A contribution to the study of Glastonbury ware from south-western Britain', *Antiquity* 49, 41-61.

12. The original work was presented as a Cambridge PhD dissertation in 1966 under the title *Regional groupings within the Iron Age of Southern Britain.* A modified and simplified account with be found in Cunliffe, 1974.

13. The only general account of radiocarbon dates in the British iron age is given by MacKie, 1969.

14. It should be stressed that horizontal timber lacing must have been used in box ramparts to tie the front and rear timbers together as at Blewburton, Berkshire. (D.W. Harding, 1972, *The Iron Age in the Upper Thames Basin* (Oxford) 45-8) and Ranscombe Camp, Sussex (G.P. Burstow and G.A. Holleyman, 1964, 'Excavations at Ranscombe Camp, 1959-1960', *Sussex Archaeological Collections* 102, 55-67). Thus it could be argued that the timber-laced stonefaced type of rampart was a natural development from the early box type in areas where stone was common.

15. Brief discussions have been given by R.J. Bradley, 'Economic change in the growth of early hillforts', in Jesson and Hill (eds.), 1971, 71-84; and B.W. Cunliffe, 'Some aspects of hillforts and their cultural environments', in Jesson and Hill (eds.), 1971, 53-70.

16. Considerations of population and function in hillforts and the problems thereof are well exposed in A.H.A. Hogg, 1962, 'Garn Boduan and Trer Ceiri, excavations at two Caernarvonshire Hillforts', *Arch. J.* 127, 1-39; L. Alcock, 1965, 'Hillforts in Wales and the Marches', *Antiquity* 39, 184-95.

17. S.C. Stanford, 1971, 'Credenhill Camp, Herefordshire; an Iron Age hillfort capital', *Arch. J.* 127, 82-129.

18. For South Cadbury: L. Alcock, 1970, 'Excavations at South Cadbury Castle, 1969', *Antiquity* 50, 14-25. For Heathrow: W.F. Grimes, note in Frere (ed.) 1961, 25-6. For Maiden Castle, the possible pre-Roman religious focus lies beneath the later Roman temple complex: see Wheeler, 1943.

19. G.J. Wainwright, 1968, 'The excavation of a Durotrigian farmstead near Tolland Royal in Cranbourne Chase, southern England', *PPS* 34, 102-47.

20. For example, in northern England the work of G. Jobey, 1959, 'Excavations at a native settlement at Huckhoe, Northumberland', *Archaeologia Aeliana* 37, 217-78; 1962, 'An Iron Age homestead at West Brandon, Durham', *Archaeologia Aeliana* 40, 1-34; 1970, 'An Iron Age settlement and homestead at Burradon, Northumberland', *Archaeologia Aeliana* 48, 51-95.

   For the two extensively excavated Shetland sites: J.R.C. Hamilton, 1956, *Excavations at Jarlshof, Shetland*, (Edinburgh); 1968, *Excavations at Clickhimin, Shetland* (London).

21. A recent assessment of Durotrigian coinage is given by D.F. Allen, in his discussion on 'The Celtic coins' in I.A. Richmond, 1968, *Hod Hill*, vol. 2 (London), 43-57.

# Index